The Elusive Empire

The Elusive Empire

Kazan and the Creation of Russia
1552–1671

Matthew P. Romaniello

The University of Wisconsin Press

Publication of this volume has been made possible, in part, through support from the Andrew W. Mellon Foundation.

The University of Wisconsin Press
1930 Monroe Street, 3rd Floor
Madison, Wisconsin 53711-2059
uwpress.wisc.edu

3 Henrietta Street
London WC2E 8LU, England
eurospanbookstore.com

Library of Congress Cataloging-in-Publication Data
Romaniello, Matthew P.
The elusive empire: Kazan and the creation of Russia, 1552–1671 /
Matthew P. Romaniello.
p.   cm.
Includes bibliographical references and index.
ISBN 978-0-299-28514-2 (pbk.: alk. paper)
ISBN 978-0-299-28513-5 (e-book)
  1. Soviet Union—Foreign relations—Kazanskoe Khanstvo.
  2. Kazanskoe khanstvo—Foreign relations—Soviet Union.
  3. Russia—History—Period of Consolidation, 1462–1605
    4. Russia—History—Time of Troubles, 1598–1613.
    5. Orthodox Eastern Church—Russia—History
  6. Religion and politics—Russia—History.   I. Title.
      DK100.R66   2012
      947′.04—dc22
      2011011573

To my grandparents

Contents

Illustrations

Figures

Maps

Tables

Acknowledgments

In the spring of 2005 I was teaching a seminar on the Muscovite Empire at Hamilton College. On the last day of class, my students discussed the various problems and challenges Muscovy's tsars faced in managing their empire. After we covered a broad span of issues, I asked them a final question—considering all the problems, why did the empire work? No one, including me, had an answer. This book is my answer to that question, a few years too late, but I suspect other parts of the empire will inspire other ideas.

The project began more than a decade ago at Ohio State University. The advice and guidance of Eve Levin has been essential at every stage of the process. David Hoffman, Nick Breyfogle, and Geoffrey Parker pushed me to expand my ideas into a comparative framework that has continued to influence my ideas about empires. Beyond the faculty, my fellow students provided inspiration and support throughout the process. This included my original writing group with Aaron Retish, Matt Masur, and Jenn Walton; and my fellow Russian and East European graduate students—Jen Anderson, Lorraine Abraham, Kate Heilman, Sean Martin, Basia Nowak, Bill Risch, and Tricia Starks.

My colleagues at various stages of my career since Ohio State have provided both insight and guidance. This includes Shoshanna Keller; the *kruzhok* of Steve Barnes, Steve Harris, Chuck Lipp, Claudia Verhoeven, and Rex Wade; and Mills Kelly, Kelly Schrum, and the Center for History and New Media. Since arriving here at Hawaiʻi, I am grateful for the rich academic community in the history department. Without the "faculty-housing writing group," I am not sure there would have been an "elusive" empire. This began with our original group of Njoroge Njoroge, Suzanna Reiss, and Becky Puljos in 2008; and expanded to include Ned Bertz, Shana Brown, Marcus Daniel, Matt Lauzon, Vina Lanzona, Kieko Matteson, Saundra Schwartz, and Wensheng Wang. In addition, I have benefited along the way from fruitful discussions at conferences and on research trips with my colleagues in Muscovite history, including Val Kivelson, Ann Kleimola, Don Ostrowski, Kira Stevens, the late Ben Uroff, Brian Boeck, Alexandra Haugh, and Erika Monahan.

Along the way, research for this book was made possible by grants and fellowships from the Hilandar Research Library; the Department of History, the Graduate School, and the Center for Medieval and Renaissance Studies at Ohio State University; the Russian, East European, and Eurasian Center of the University of Illinois; George Mason University; the Kennan Institute of the Woodrow Wilson International Center for Scholars; and the Ella Wiswell Fund for the Promotion of Russian Studies at the University of Hawai'i.

No part of this project would have been possible without the support of the staffs at numerous libraries and archives. I have benefited greatly from the assistance of Predrag Matejic and the staff of the Hilandar Research Library at Ohio State University, and Pat Polansky, here at UH. In addition, I must thank the staffs at the Russian State Archive of Ancient Acts, the Russian State Library, and the State Public Historical Library, all in Moscow; the National Archives in Kew, Great Britain; the European Reading Room and the Law Library of the Library of Congress; and the Slavic and East European Library at the University of Illinois at Urbana-Champaign.

Material from the following articles has been included with permission from the publishers: "The Profit Motive: Regional Economic Development in Muscovy after the Conquest of Kazan'," *Journal of European Economic History* 33, no. 3 (2004): 663–85 in chapter 3; and "Grant, Settle, Negotiate: Military Service in the Middle Volga Region," in *Peopling the Russian Periphery: Borderland Colonization in Eurasian History*, edited by Nicholas Breyfogle, Abby Schrader, and Willard Sunderland (Routledge, 2007), 61–77 in chapter 4. Most of the images in the book are courtesy of Lynn Davis and the Preservation Department of Hamilton Library, here at the University of Hawai'i. All of the maps were produced by Ev Wingert of the Department of Geography. Having such generous colleagues has made the process far more enjoyable. Finally, I would like to thank David Goldfrank and the anonymous reviewer for the University of Wisconsin Press, as well as my exceptional editors, Gwen Walker and Sheila McMahon, for their advice and guidance throughout the project. The final version of this monograph is much stronger for their recommendations. If problems remain, they are my fault alone.

None of this would have been possible without the support of my family throughout the entire process. I owe the greatest debt to Paul Hibbeln, who made all of this possible.

Glossary of Terms

boiar	nobleman
chetvert' (pl. *cheti*)	land measurement (1 *chetvert'* = 1.35 acres); dry measure for grain (approx. 216 lbs. of rye)
syn boiarskii (pl. *deti boiarskii*)	nobleman (lit., boiar's son)
d'iak (pl. *d'iaki*)	official, secretary
dvorianin (pl. *dvoriane*)	lesser nobleman, gentry
gramota (pl. *gramoty*)	official document, deed, charter
iasachnye liudi	tribute payer, non-Russian subject of the tsar
inozemets (pl. *inozemtsy*)	foreigner
krest'ianin (pl. *krest'iane*)	peasant
mestnichestvo	system of social precedence
mirza (Russian *murzii*)	elite Muslim
nakaz (pl. *nakazy*)	official document, instruction
novokreshchanin (pl. *novokreshchane*)	convert (lit., newly baptized)
pomeshchik (pl. *pomeshchiki*)	elite military servitor
pomest'e (pl. *pomest'ia*)	estate, land grant
Posol'skii Prikaz	Foreign Chancellery
prikaz (pl. *prikazy*)	chancellery, office, bureau
Prikaz Kazanskogo dvortsa	Chancellery of the Kazan Palace
pud	unit of weight (1 pud = 36.11 lbs.)
strelets (pl. *strel'tsy*)	musketman
sudebnik	law code
Ulozhenie	law code
voevoda (pl. *voevody*)	governor

The Elusive Empire

Introduction

> From that incident I could deduce where the colonel's magnificent Russian clothes came from: they were all borrowed goods which, like everything else in the whole of Russia, belonged to the tsar alone.
>
> Johann Jakob Christoffel von Grimmelshausen,
> Simplicissimus, 1668

> Here I am in Asia; I wanted to see it for myself. There are in this city [Kazan] twenty different peoples, who bear absolutely no resemblance to each other. However, I have to make them a suit which will fit them all.
>
> Catherine the Great,
> in a letter to Voltaire, 29 May 1767

In 1552 Muscovy conquered the city of Kazan, the center of a once powerful khanate.[1] Both were successor states of the Qipchaq Khanate (itself a successor of the Mongol Empire), though Muscovy had the advantage over Kazan of size, population, and resources. This was the first Orthodox victory against an Islamic state since the fall of Constantinople, and the Russian Orthodox Church proclaimed Moscow's tsar as the emergent leader of the Christian community. At the same time, military success created a number of enormous challenges for both tsar and church: no precedent existed for assimilating a non-Slavic, non-Orthodox state. When the Khanate of Astrakhan fell four years later, it was evident that Muscovy successfully had seized the entire Volga River basin, cutting off the Central Asian Turkic nomads from direct access to Ukraine and Poland-Lithuania beyond. By any standard the tsar's defeat of Kazan did not simply improve Muscovy's strategic fortunes, it dramatically reshaped the future of the Eurasian steppe.[2]

Map 1 Moscow and Kazan in the sixteenth century (Courtesy of Ev Wingert, University of Hawai'i at Mānoa)

In 1670, the lands and peoples of the former khanate and the Middle Volga Region were embroiled in another military conflict, sparked by the arrival of Stepan Razin and his Cossacks, who laid siege to the new Muscovite fortress of Simbirsk.[3] Within two months, a large number of Muscovite outposts and towns rebelled. It took the combined efforts of the tsarist garrisons and the army to suppress the rebellion. The local garrisons were comprised of the tsar's non-Russian subjects, Turkic Tatars and Chuvashes, and Finno-Ugric Maris, Mordvins, and Udmurts.[4] By the winter of 1671, the region was under Muscovite control again. However, the upheaval revealed the limits of Moscow's control over its extended frontier, forcing a retrenchment but, significantly, no reconsideration of the imperial policies implemented between 1552 and 1670 and the methods employed to align the region with the economic and legal system of the empire. The Cossacks were repelled, limiting Razin's damage to the far south, territory well outside of the state's defined border. Kazan and the Volga were firmly within the tsar's demesne.

If the conquest and the Razin revolt are viewed as the bookends of the story of Muscovy's absorption of the Middle Volga Region, Russian expansion appears as a rather linear process. The state established its "right by conquest" over new land, enlisted new subjects, and then defended its new border.[5] Viewed closely, however, a more complex narrative emerges. The conquest was swift in 1552, but the construction of the most rudimentary structures of control over the new territory took a century. Kazan was indeed the gateway to a new empire, but Muscovite Russia succeeded in empire building in the Volga Region not because of any advantages of strength, leadership, or wealth—it succeeded despite its markedly limited resources. Swift successes imposing firm control over the region were few. They were also unnecessary, if the state could convince the populace and outsiders that its authority was real. Muscovy lacked the ability to establish an expansive administration, infrastructure, and large garrisons designed to deter the interference of a strong external enemy. But its meager resources could suffice if no such opponent existed, and the threat of sustained revolt was remote. In the absence of a power capable of contesting Moscow's assertion of its strength, the lack of real control could be made good over time, incrementally, without admitting to setbacks. Even defeat could be redressed eventually, if no further exertions of force proved necessary for survival. From a historical perspective, the empire was "elusive"—the projection of a powerful state created by a successful conquest, disguising an extremely slow, contingent, and heavily negotiated process by which the state built its authority and knit together existing economic, political, and social networks. Faced with resistance and with few resources in the region, Muscovy's greatest advantage was the remoteness of its new land, and its most useful tool was the portion of the local population that would be easily integrated into existing Muscovite structures. These were more practical instruments of empire than overt power, and enabled eventual dominance in a vast region where expensive political and military failures were frequent and could not be admitted.[6] In essence, the manipulation of a religious and political language of conquest and victory provided the time necessary to control the vast spaces of the Middle Volga Region. What began as the military defeat of one city in 1552 slowly grew into the management of an ever-enlarging frontier, a true empire worthy of the name—but more than a century after the state claimed it.

This study focuses primarily on the slow growth and evolution of state control rather than Moscow's grandiose imperial claims. Its officials and those of the Russian Orthodox Church established outposts along the length of the Volga River over the course of the sixteenth century, and in southern Siberia during the seventeenth. Its goal was that the Middle Volga would develop into a part of the Muscovite heartland after a period of integration. The state could not afford many officials nor build endless outposts, and so Muscovite expansion was halting and episodic, limited by the state's inability to assimilate culturally and religiously alien peoples across thousands of miles. Such problems were, as current Russian history demonstrates, exceedingly difficult for the colonizing state to solve permanently. Trying to control the land and people within its new borders demanded an unforeseen evolution in Moscow's governing institutions, followed by slow work toward administrative control and popular acceptance through engagement with the local population, taking generations.

Claiming victory in 1552 was the easier accomplishment. Tsar Ivan IV Vasil'evich (the Terrible) ordered a new church built upon the spot where he had defeated Kazan's armies. In a moment, Russian Orthodoxy had displaced Islam at the heart of a Muslim state. The Russian Orthodox Church established Kazan as the center of a new archbishopric in 1555; notably, the election of the new bishop was held in Moscow's Kremlin to demonstrate to the court the tsar's Orthodox victory. Outside of the Kremlin, Ivan ordered the construction of a new cathedral, the Church of the Intercession on the Moat (popularly St. Basil's), demonstrating his great victory to residents of Moscow. Most of the public presentations of the tsar's glorious Orthodox victory occurred in Moscow, not in Kazan. The victory was not only important because of the territorial expansion or the defeat of an entrenched enemy but also because it developed into the justification for the tsar's growing "charismatic authority," the representation of his power to his subjects, which was as much an idea as it was actual power.[7]

Figure 1   St. Basil's Cathedral (Reproduced from Saint-Julien, *Voyage pittoresque en Russie*)

Making the incremental steps that brought the regional administration closer to Moscow's goal of control over the population and its resources in a secured territory remained the greater challenge. But the local difficulties in implementing policies that worked, after casting failures aside or modifying approaches to policies on trade, the legal status of the population, and defense, could be easily hidden from the streets of distant Moscow. The lands of the former khanate were overwhelmingly populated by non-Russian "peasants"—Turkic and Finno-Ugric peoples still residing in town and throughout the countryside. Islam remained, as did the animistic faiths of many of the rural peasants. It was not until the 1571 construction of the first major Muscovite defenses in the region—a strategic line of outposts, watchtowers, and earthen ramparts running parallel to the Volga River from a new outpost south of Nizhnii Novgorod to a new outpost south of Kazan—that the tsar demonstrated his ability to command in his new land to any degree resembling what he had presented in Moscow as an accomplished fact. Nor was the defensive line an immediate success, as it only inspired a new rebellion against the tsar. It was, after all, the first exposure of most of the residents of the region to the tsar's presence. However, the construction of the line, followed by the suppression of the revolt, was still a victory for the tsar, and it set the parameters for Moscow's future attempts to rule the region.

After the conquest of Kazan in 1552, the process of creating an empire was not what the tsarist government expected. To accomplish it, the conscious manipulation of victorious rhetoric was slowly replaced by bureaucratic experience, the establishment of infrastructure, and a new society built on the carcass of Kazan's own system of trade and agriculture. Muscovy relied upon a type of "institutional bricolage," combining the preexisting administrative, military, economic, and social structures in Kazan with its own in order to find an assemblage that could effectively govern its growing frontier.[8] All of this was completed in the face of setbacks and losses. One was growth in the face of unrealized ambitions and nominal influence over the tsar's land and people. The second was a marvelous vision of victory followed by endless success. The Russian Empire was a case of the tsar's "new clothes"—a magnificent display of charismatic authority that disguised the glacial pace of material accomplishment.

Composite Sovereignty

The emergent empire relied upon a system of "layered sovereignty." The central government accommodated local conditions, establishing autonomous networks connecting the periphery with the metropole, governed by different administrative regimes.[9] No early-modern empire possessed a workable method of constructing a single, unified sovereignty over its territories. However, few, if any, strove for uniformity. Movement toward greater centralization of political authority or standardization of legal practices might be accomplished over time, but early-modern states could often not afford to make such centralization an immediate goal. Recent historiography suggests instead that in Europe, early-modern states were "composite monarchies," loosely affiliated and administered territories unified by a single head of state, where political, military, economic, religious, and social structures could vary widely.[10] This is not to argue that all states had the same political system (or the lack of one), as different systems existed throughout Europe, but that the existence of regional differences inside the borders of early-modern states was the standard rather than the exception. Though "layered sovereignty" has generally been applied only to empires and "composite monarchy" to European states, these are complementary ideas. Early-modern empires faced enormous difficulties managing time and distance, able to conquer lands they could not rule effectively. They lacked the technological, industrial, and educational solutions later created to elide pernicious diversity and unify regimes (if not the population). Ruling houses developed many methods that attempted to control the empires they established, but there were only a finite number of techniques available. As a result, several imperial systems functioned contemporaneously in the early-modern world, but they shared this common element of "composite sovereignty."

Any study of the Muscovite empire must consider the importance of its nature as a conglomeration of land and peoples, where distinct and separate networks built links with the metropole in unplanned and novel ways, creating a system fitting well into the model of composite sovereignty. There was a common image of empire projected from Moscow, with the tsar at its center, supported by the Russian Orthodox Church. But beyond the walls of the Kremlin, administrators developed a large number of variations in regional governance adapted to local conditions. These frequently neglected the image Moscow attempted to impose. Therefore, the most successful method for understanding the empire was to break it down into a series of separate regions. The land of the former Khanate of Kazan formed one of these regions and was distinct from Muscovy's territory to the north, claimed centuries earlier, and the open steppe lands to the south where Muscovy would continue to struggle for another two centuries.[11]

The historiography addressing the region around Kazan has neglected its distinctive place within the early-modern Russian state. Previous scholars have delved into the preconquest relationship between Kazan and Moscow, but all have stopped with 1552, often considered a decisive break in the region's history.[12]

Scholars studying the post-1552 period have tended to reinforce this break by using the conquest as their starting point. The territory of the khanate now comprises multiple autonomous regions and republics in the Russian Federation. Most observers even have projected these present political relationships into the past, but modern political geography is an untrustworthy guide to earlier eras. As a result, several studies have produced a rather disjointed narrative of the region's integration into the Muscovite empire.[13] Modern national groups are also illegible signposts to the early-modern past. In the sixteenth and seventeenth centuries, multiple Turkic and Finno-Ugric groups composed the population. The Muscovite state generally considered Tatars part of the same group as the Mordvins or Maris, and set policy accordingly, yet there is no study that examines these peoples within one common legal or social space.[14] However, these earlier studies still contribute tremendous information about individual sites, peoples, and places.[15] While they do not provide an answer for how the region was integrated into Muscovy, they contribute toward its pursuit.[16]

Beyond the territory of the former khanate, recent studies have made great progress examining different regions and imperial networks within Muscovy. When the tsar constructed the first defensive line in south of Kazan in 1571, he clearly demarcated his border, but it is the region beyond the defensive line that has received more focus than the lands "inside" the line's boundary. On the steppe, the tsar had only very informal mechanisms on which to rely for influence, as the steppe's nomadic population (including Bashkirs, Nogais, and Kalmyks) resisted Muscovy's presence well into the eighteenth century.[17] Similarly, great attention has been drawn to the imperial networks at work across Siberia, but once again it was a diverse region with its own ethnolinguistic groups, economic challenges, and, at best, limited tsarist legal authority. Not until the nineteenth century, for instance, was there an attempt to achieve any large-scale settlement of Russians in Siberia.[18] These other regions demonstrate the composite sovereignty of the Muscovite Empire. Regional variations could be great, and Moscow's administrators produced drastically different mechanisms of rule, adjusted to meet local conditions.

As much as the state relied on a variable set of practices to manage its diverse territories and peoples, the Kremlin's chancelleries still built on collective historical experience to make more informed decisions to manage the state. Seizing the Khanate of Kazan brought an agrarian population within the borders, and who were ethnolinguistically and religiously diverse. Learning to manage this region created blueprints for the assimilation of future populations by adapting to local circumstances in areas possessing what Moscow considered to be similar back-grounds. In Kazan, politically the state would establish a new type of provincial governor with different authority than officials in the interior of equivalent rank, develop a new method for instructing the local government to delimit their discretionary authority, and adjust enlistment to allow numerous non-Russian and non-Orthodox men to serve in the region's militia. Economically and legally, it would learn to manage international trade along the Volga River, develop domestic agricultural production, and expand the social categories of tsarist subjects to incorporate its new peoples. These were all lessons that could be adopted elsewhere. They would never work for the nomads on the steppe, barely under tsarist control at the best of times, but could operate for other settled, agrarian peasants. As such, the methods of imperial rule developed for Kazan and its hinterland became a model, adapted eventually for the Caucasus, the Baltic region, and Poland, other places with ethnolinguistically and religiously diverse populations.[19]

But the varied networks employed by the tsarist state, and their weaknesses, were disguised by the far more impressive performance of universal tsarist power and authority. The Russian Orthodox Church endorsed an image of the tsar as the lord of the world's last great empire, and as long as it did so the state could permit many accommodations to local conditions assuming that they did not threaten the dominant ideology or the enhanced authority resting on it. This enabled Peter the Great, early in the eighteenth century, to name and claim a Russian Empire, but it was always ethnolinguistically diverse and multiconfessional, and it encompassed a broad range of environments and ways of life.[20] Its scale was expansive; the time it took to travel from border to border paralleled that of any overseas empire, at least of the early-modern era. It was also never governed in a completely uniform fashion, any more than it comprised only Russian Orthodox subjects. The tsar's authority never lay equally across his whole territory, even in the twentieth century, although it remained a goal of nearly every ruler after 1552.[21]

The Elusive Empire

The Russian Empire was a joint project of the tsar, the Russian Orthodox Church, and the state's administration. It was an ongoing quest for hegemonic control under well-defined political, economic, and military structures; "elusive" because it was continually conditioned by compromises and accommodations with local interests. Following the conquest of Kazan, Moscow developed a colonial system resulting from a process of "cooperative competition" within the Kremlin. There were at least four separate poles of authority with an ability to influence events on the ground. In Moscow, the center of the empire, the state and church were separate actors. The tsars managed the state with a growing bureaucracy, as they continued to pursue a long-term goal of creating a centralized and responsive administrative, legal, and military system. The metropolitans (later patriarchs) of Moscow managed the Church with their own bureaucracy, positioning themselves as the "tsars" of religious matters. This division of political and religious authority, with each possessing executive power in their respective sphere, was repeated by a parallel system at the local level. A new form of local governors (*voevody*) and their secretaries (*d'iaki*) had day-to-day authority over judicial, taxation, and military matters, worked within a system partially defined by Moscow's chancelleries. Moscow could set the parameters of their actions, but implementation of policy was largely left to the voevoda's individual discretion. Their push-pull would have been familiar to any early-modern state's ruler, where tensions between center and periphery always shaped local policy. Similarly, the new Orthodox bishopric in Kazan was independent from Moscow but expected to cooperate with the goals of its metropolitan. These four poles (church and state, center and periphery) operated asynchronously, and often independently of each other, creating friction and providing spaces to pursue competing individual agendas. Generally, the best results occurred when they cooperated toward a single goal, but any particular short-term interest could outweigh the state's long-term goals of control and further expansion.

In this framework, any assumption that the khanate joined Muscovy in 1552 as an integrated component of the metropolitan core is highly optimistic. The conquest was an absorption of territory, but its nature was equivocal and in many ways tentative. Specifically, Muscovy, as a state with an embryonic religious and political ideology, and an untested administrative and military capacity to rule a large territory, had to address many challenges, not the least of which was whether the Muslim and animist populations of Kazan would accept an Orthodox tsar. They did, with a surprising small amount of active resentment, but it appeared a problematic issue in 1552. The success of this development depended on the inability of Moscow to impose uniformity immediately after its victory. The friction between the four poles facilitated the transfer of loyalty to the tsar and his new empire, with the confused lines of authority allowing non-Russians to negotiate with the authorities in order to accomplish their own agendas within the empire. This, rather than the outright exertion of state power in the form of laws or troops, brought new subjects to participate in the system and to claim the tsar as their sovereign. The Tatars, Chuvashes, Maris, Mordvins, and Udmurts could benefit, but so could new Russian colonists who discovered opportunities on the frontier. In fact, because the state and church believed Russians to be desirable inhabitants on the frontier, the colonists found negotiation with the authorities advantageous. This operated, at times, to the government's disadvantage; differences in social rank, responsibilities to religious and secular authorities, languages, religion, and occupation led to resentment, disorder, competition, and, eventually, revolt. The state, in turn, often could manipulate these unsettled situations to its own advantage.

In this way, the imperial system that was developed in the aftermath of the battle in 1552 eventually came to work smoothly. Hegemony, that is to say, control over the Volga Region, remained elusive; however, it is impossible to argue that the tsar's administrators implemented a single strategy or plan for the governance of this emergent empire. It is also difficult to claim that Moscow directed the management of the population in any particular direction. There was, for instance, no sustained state goal of converting the local population to Orthodoxy during this period. It is clear, though, that the evolving colonial system maintained Russian influence over this non-Russian region for centuries. The empire succeeded in constructing a governing apparatus even if its parts never operated in harmony. These parts were often replaced, but the system itself provided the tsar with men, revenue, and resources—haltingly at first, but in a more reliable and sophisticated fashion after 1670. This is not to suggest that building an administration was haphazard or random. Instead, the cooperative competition among all of the forces involved created a process that, at its inception, was crude and followed the path of least resistance. It coalesced, however, into an effective system.

Yet the realization of the Muscovite state's long-term project—in short, the creation of hegemony—remained far beyond the reach of its sixteenth-century political authorities. For more than a century it was elusive, an empire in name only, contributing to the tsar's authority only symbolically. Without the participation of all actors at all levels of Muscovite society—church and state, Russian and non-Russian, free and not—it could not build effective institutions and certainly was not able to channel the resources into new territories necessary to impose well-organized structures of governance. The region possessed several well-formed networks, but those did not, and could not, self-organize into a cohesive framework Moscow could quickly exploit. It took enormous effort and many compromises to enable it to function at all. At the same time, the institutions in the Middle Volga Region created by the various levels in Muscovite society were able to operate indifferently for decades without harming state interests because any cooperation showed that the empire was real. The hallmark of the Muscovite system in this period was a combination of attempted centralization coupled uneasily with a resilient decentralization, subject to the continual problems of distance, heterogeneous culture, and precarious geopolitical security. Its mere existence, however, inspired the idea of a new Muscovite empire. What solidified it was the willingness to bend to necessity and accommodate local interests in the short-term, in order to enable possible long-term control. Providentially, Muscovy lacked a strong eastern enemy to complicate its administration, and the evolution of tsar's experiment in state building proceeded without molestation beyond occasional nomadic incursions until after 1670.

The Muscovite state needed to discover mechanisms to allow the growing empire to meet the challenge of distance coupled with the diversity of frontier society. Kazan was militarily defeated in 1552, but the "conquest" of the region was a long-term process. Chapter 1 presents the many conquests of Kazan. The state experimented with mechanisms for controlling its new lands and peoples. As its military might and the Russian Orthodox Church's establishment in the region failed to produce effective administration or a pacified population, further innovations allowed for the solution of the strategic dilemma with the utilization of Tatar troops and the development of the defensive line. The long set of embankments, outposts, and forts took at least a decade to construct but became a visible sign of possession marking the frontier. It did nothing to ensure a pacified populace, but it did mark the lands at the edge of the tsar's territory. By far the most valuable accomplishment of first decades of Muscovite "control" was the lesson learned constructing the line—even the most basic management of the border took decades to achieve.

This reshaping of the land into Muscovite territory proved more immediately fruitful than the project of establishing effective political, military, and religious control, which was well outside the state's capabilities. After the settlement of the war with Poland in 1618, the new Romanov dynasty set itself on a path of centralization, bureaucratization, and, to the best of its ability, "modernization."[22] The compromises developed and exploited by Ivan IV continued to serve as the standard of Muscovite planning; in other words, Moscow projected a demand for state authority into the countryside, and hoped that local accommodations would limit resistance and make the demand appear successful, even if the particular policy's impact was attenuated. The costs of a greater commitment to enforcing central directives in the region were simply too high, and this remained the long-term pattern for Russian colonial rule.

Chapter 2 examines the new administrative structure developed for the tsar's possessions during the seventeenth century, as the expanding bureaucracy experimented with the implementation of cameralism, focusing on the management of population rather than the land itself. The tsar's administrators relied on both secular and religious personnel, as the challenges to supervising the frontier population were many, and officials were thin on the ground. Though following a pattern typical of bureaucratizing states throughout Europe, the chancelleries' increased monitoring of, and involvement in, the frontier's governance produced even more limited success than in Spain, France, or Holland. The tsar's officials in the country-side wielded considerable independence and could buttress their authority by exploiting purely personal connections with local communities. The bureaucratizing process, such as it was, evolved as more of a response to the continuing independence of local officials than because of any systematic attempt to increase their effectiveness. At the same time, the combination of cooperative competition among the central chancelleries and the Orthodox Church, and the local competition among regional administrators, still produced a working administration. If all "four poles" of authority coordinated their efforts, they could, and did, establish and extend tsarist control.

Chapter 3 explores the growth of local and international economic development strategies. Visions of Russia as the newest trade route between Europe and Asia (for West Europeans, at least) were never fully realized. Moscow's attempt to manage the region's resources closely ran in parallel with other European attempts to use the state to channel trade revenues. It produced only sporadic successes. The tsar also completely failed to coax trade from South or East Asia, a scheme seeking to capitalize on the supposed promise of the Volga River as a new silk road. The greatest economic benefit from the new territory appeared in the form of local commodities produced in the region and exported to Muscovy proper. Yet even with the final implementation of a mercantile system adopted in the New Commercial Code in 1667, the state's actual control over the economy remained quite nominal, although the tsar proclaimed great benefits for the government. While the development of the local economic sphere on the Volga appeared to fall far short of the ambitions of controlling a global trade route, its growth was sufficient to support further tsarist expansion in the region. The elusive target was not reached, but the outcome, however unlooked-for, was very valuable.

Constructing a new political and economic system, imperfectly monitored by the four poles of authority, created a liminal space on the frontier, which allowed the tsar's new non-Russian and non-Orthodox populations to prosper. Chapter 4 follows the emergence of the tsars' provincial elites, both Russian and non-Russian, as distinct social groups of military servitors. These included Muslim and Orthodox men, some former Tatar enemies, and some Russian political exiles from the interior. They were certainly suspect in central Muscovy, but this group was a suitable new gentry in Kazan. Not surprisingly, both the state and the Russian Orthodox Church upheld loyalty as the ideal virtue for this group, compromising other state interests in order to maintain reliability of these local servitors. The center constructed a narrative of the tsar's "loyal enemies," men who had fought against

Moscow but now dedicated themselves to its defense. Their lives on the frontier were above reproach, reflecting both Orthodox piety and military virtue. In reality, however, these paragons of loyal service remained primarily Muslim and non-Russian. Although the Church declared Islam vanquished in 1552, it spent the next hundred years welcoming its Muslim defenders. As long as the center's need for able military troops to secure the frontier overrode religious or political concerns, this did not change, and the gentry found opportunities within the tsar's borders. It was in the creation of a system defined by opportunity—not ethnolinguistic or religious discrimination—that the frontier was secured. As a result, the Tatars and Russian exiles emerged as a social group distinct from their equivalents elsewhere in Muscovy.

Chapter 5 reveals the parallel experiences of the non-Russian peasants, who also found opportunities created by the cooperative competition among the four poles of the church and state. In the aftermath of the conquest of 1552, the khanate's former population was placed into one of three new legal categories. The *iasachnye liudi* (lit., people who pay tribute) experienced the least change, as their new tribute payments to the tsar were similar to their previous tribute payments to the khan. A large group of non-Russians became peasants living on monastic and other church estates, and the third group became military servitor peasants, often gaining new Russian landlords. Each of these groups had a more complex relationship with the state than did the gentry, although the pattern displayed parallels to the way the elite interacted with local officials. As with non-Russian elites, the state's need for garrison troops to defend the territory against internal and external threats, provided peasants with opportunities. However, the enserfment of military servitor peasants in 1649, the state's runaway peasant commissions, which systematically investigated every village in the region in the 1650s and '60s, and the forced relocation of the Mordvins to the southern steppe to become new frontier troops, undeniably created large shifts and inspired unrest. All levels in society protested in policy changes as they occurred, but particularly notable were petitions from local churchmen, who defended their non-Russian (and non-Orthodox) peasants against the increasingly aggressive state policies. It was at this level that the innate tensions among the four poles of authority became most clear. No common church-state goal of integrating the non-Russian peasantry within the state existed, nor did any plan for transforming non-Russian peasants into Russian-speaking, Orthodox men and women. When the state attempted to erase local differences or alter the status quo, it harmed church interests. And when state officials attempted to exploit the Orthodox Church, the Church protested. It defended the right of Chuvashes, Maris, Mordvins, and Udmurts to remain distinct peoples within the tsar's kingdom, often to protect itself.

Chapter 6 examines the outcome of the century of evolving frontier policies and cooperative competition among the four poles. It begins with the arrival of Stepan Razin and his Cossacks in the fall of 1670. As Razin laid siege to the new fortress of Simbirsk, at the southern edge of the region, a large revolt exploded across the entire territory. The new southern defensive line, running from Tambov to Simbirsk revolted, and peasants attacked both Arzamas and Alatyr' in the north. The damage was extensive, and the local administration was clearly targeted by the rebels. While the combined garrisons of Simbirsk and Kazan easily repelled Razin, the revolt itself took months to contain.

The swift elimination of Razin's threat demonstrated that the region's military security system had performed as it had been designed, and thus turned back a steppe invasion. Non-Russian troops formed the majority of the defenders, even if they were neither Russian-speaking nor Orthodox, proving that local accommodation still created loyal men for the tsar. The revolt also illuminated political conditions in the region. The Russian Orthodox Church, which had proclaimed 1552 as a victory against Islam, but then defended its non-Orthodox peasants, was almost completely untouched by the rebels. They also ignored military servitors, demonstrating that they were motivated to revolt by reasons other than the gentry's supervision of serfdom. Rebel rage fell upon the heads of the *voevody* and other officials. The populace displayed great anger toward the state, but it was the local administration that had perpetrated the most invasive policies and, since 1649, removed many privileges erected after 1552. The runaway peasant investigations that upended individual villages in the interests of landlords in the central provinces and the massively disruptive forced relocation of the Mordvins were the two most significant causes of the violence against officials. Where the region most closely resembled the status quo of 1552, the populace did not revolt but fought to defend the tsar. The lesson of the revolt of 1670–71 was clear—long-standing accommodations created loyal subjects. In the end, the revolt confirmed the success of that aspect of Moscow's 120-year persistence and slow evolution. It also confirmed that some of the risky policies chosen had failed, even if stability had been restored quickly.

The state's long experience governing the populace of Kazan and the Volga shaped the emergence of the Russian Empire. An energetic assertion of hegemonic control over the region never proved possible, or necessary. A combination of projected and symbolic authority, implicitly supported by the population, created a colonial system that was capable of accommodating local communities when necessary and suppressing them when the state was stronger. It also proved adaptable enough to govern the region by accepting and manipulating the diverse populace, as other early-modern states did elsewhere, creating a composite sovereignty. The lack of uniform governance within the empire was not a weakness but rather an opportunity to develop the structures of the state that would eventually appear workable in the long-term. To succeed, the necessary condition, and the greatest weapon in the state's arsenal, was time. The colonial administration produced region able to support trade and defend itself because it was able to spend decades in lieu of Moscow's focus, wealth, or a dense labor supply. Together, these were the components that turned an elusive empire that existed more as a rhetorical device than as an administrative, economic, or military apparatus into a viable imperial system. Accommodation and local adaptability, beyond the immediate supervision of the Kremlin, created the Russian Empire.

I

Imperial Ideas

It is perfectly natural and normal to want to acquire new territory; and whenever men do what will succeed towards this end, they will be praised, or at least not condemned.

Niccoló Machiavelli,
The Prince, 1532

All happy families are alike; every unhappy family is unhappy in its own way.

Leo Tolstoy,
Anna Karenina, 1878

There is no mystery about the imperial aspirations of early-modern monarchs. All desired territorial aggrandizement; all planned for increasingly large armies to enforce their wills. Machiavelli's observations of the Italian city-states inspired *The Prince*, but its lessons were applied as truths across Europe. The policies suggested by Machiavelli's precepts reflected an ongoing political transformation across the continent, beginning with the corrosion of medieval state structures. The new monarchs centralized their authority, increased taxation and economic regulation, and chipped away at elite privileges, largely in order to achieve military success.[1]

Histories of Muscovy's conquest of Kazan emphasized 1552 as the decisive year. In reality, the expansion started decades earlier and included a series of military losses, and the fighting between Muscovy and the local population would not end until the 1570s. The military triumph in 1552 corrected the shortcomings of the past but without any progress in terms of the political, religious, economic, or social transformation of the khanate into a Russian land. What the sixteenth century witnessed instead was a series of "conquests," as Muscovite authority expanded into different niches very gradually. Until the former khanate proved its loyalty to the monarchy during the Muscovite civil war (known as the "Time of Troubles") in the early seventeenth century, there was no sign the local community accepted Muscovite rule.

Nevertheless, the monarchy celebrated the victory and memorialized 1552 as a glorious year. Indeed, it had some significant immediate benefits. It was the first substantial improvement in Muscovy's geopolitical position on the steppe. It increased pressure on the Khanate of Astrakhan, which was confirmed with the seizure of that city in 1556, and eliminated the threat that the Tatars of Kazan would form a military alliance with the Khanate of Crimea, which removed at least one strut of Crimea's dominance over Moscow.[2] With the seizure of Kazan, Moscow extended its control over the Volga trade route, which immediately offered new tariff revenue and improved security against nomadic raiders. In addition, it had been an established agricultural region since the twelfth century, and would now produce solely for Muscovy, although controlling Kazan's hinterland would take decades.[3] Undoubtedly, even with only nominal control over the city's population, Muscovy's "conquest" of a foreign state was a tremendous boost to the tsar's authority. Kazan was the historical seat of a khan (tsar, in Russian). While the Russian Orthodox Church gave the tsar the right to claim the Byzantine title of caesar (tsar, in Russian), the conquest gave a new status, increasing his political prestige among the steppe nomads as a legitimate successor to the Mongols.[4] By the seventeenth century, Muscovite scholars would claim that the conquest of Kazan was the event that made Ivan IV Vasil'evich a tsar and Muscovy an empire, even though he had claimed the title well before 1552.[5]

The disadvantages of the occupation of Kazan were harder for the tsar to acknowledge, much less for his Russian subjects to understand. The region's tremendous ethnolinguistic diversity had been a challenge for the previous regimes; local revolts against the Tatars assisted Muscovy's advance in the region. Russian Orthodoxy's failure to produce immediate conversions among its new animist and Muslim populations portended a serious and long-term limiting factor on Muscovy's military and economic ambitions. Specifically, the court possessed the reasonable fear that Islam fostered a natural and dangerous connection between the tsar's new subjects and the Crimean and Ottoman threat. Furthermore, too many of the tsar's new subjects made their livelihood through hunting, fishing, trapping, and beekeeping to satisfy Muscovite authorities. Itinerants were apt to evade service obligations, and, as such, difficult to tax.[6] In order to obtain some control over this chaotic new frontier, the tsars garrisoned the territory. Maintaining these forces during the ongoing Livonian War being fought on the far western border must have been a considerable expense for the tsar's coffers.[7]

With genuine political, military, or religious control seemingly out of the grasp of the tsar, the appearance of control became the practical fallback position. Demonstrating authority for an illiterate, largely rural, and "foreign" population residing with the tsar's claimed territory replaced any attempt to resolve the various regional conflicts.[8] A well-organized façade comprised of symbols of authority would disguise the real (and weak) supports of Muscovite power until they could be strengthened. Initial moves to absorb Kazan reflected this scheme. After the physical military victory, Moscow followed with a religious one, which served as a symbolic demonstration of tsarist authority. In Kazan, the conquest's demonstrable signs of success were in the form of Muscovite administrators, soldiers, and Russian Orthodox officials who settled in Kazan's kremlin, even though they exercised no authority outside of the city's walls. Far more grand was the symbol of victory in Moscow. The tsar publicly commemorated his triumph with the construction of the Cathedral of the Intercession on the Moat (commonly called St. Basil's) on Red Square. Each idea emerged with the intention of creating an image of the tsar's "charismatic authority," which preceded military, economic, or political control.[9]

The proclamation of success, however, did little to check the continuing military resistance to Muscovite occupation of Kazan. Almost two decades later, the tsar announced a new phase of conquest—the construction of a defensive line that would physically delineate the border. It protected the tsar's subjects from physical threats from the open steppe, but it also defined his area of control over his own subjects.[10] While none of these three attempts to assert authority over the former khanate was entirely successful, each added to the impression of control. The construction of the Muscovite Empire, therefore, began as much as a visible presentation of the tsar's authority than as an achievement of the more elusive goals of military, political, or religious domination. In fact, the ease of building a façade of success, compared to exerting effort to achieve outright control, became the key to the tsar's new "right of conquest," in which the limits of his power were less and less an impediment to sweeping imperial claims.[11]

Imperial Legacies

Muscovite Russia's position and interaction with its neighbors fostered an idea of empire. As Muscovy was surrounded by imperial states, it was only natural for its leadership to presume an empire was the sole model of governance capable of controlling the Eurasian steppe. Its most significant ideological relationship was both historic and religious, forged with Byzantine Orthodox culture. As the Eastern Roman Empire, both the political and religious leadership in Constantinople considered "empire" a necessity to the functioning of the state.[12] However,

Moscow's political separation from the Byzantine Empire was only reinforced by Constantinople's fall in 1453, suggesting that the Byzantine model might not provide the best path to success, at least in the face of Islamic expansion. At the same time, Orthodox Christianity, the religious legacy of the Byzantine Empire, still presented a potential model of imperial trappings that the Muscovites could draw upon. With its roots in Roman imperial ideology, the Byzantine Empire had a rich historical legacy, a tradition of controlling a multiethnic and multiconfessional population, and it had endured for centuries. Since the conversion of Grand Prince Vladimir of Kiev to Orthodoxy in 988, Byzantine imperial ideology was imprinted on his Rurikid dynastic successors.[13]

As Moscow was the inheritor of the Rurikid legacy, the Byzantine trappings and symbols always appealed to its princes. By 1325 the leading hierarch of the Orthodox Church in Russian lands, the metropolitan of Kiev, had taken up residency in Moscow's Kremlin, transforming this small city into a center of Orthodoxy for the East Slavs.[14] As a result, it was logical that Moscow's new grand princes would rely upon Orthodox (and traditionally Byzantine) imagery and symbolism to forge their own public identity.[15] By the fifteenth century, the grand princes of Moscow had claimed the right to use the Byzantine imperial title of "tsar" (caesar), the double-headed eagle as a crest of the new empire, and a set of associated rituals, including marriages, coronations, and public religious festivals.[16]

The Qipchaq Khanate (the western Mongol Empire) presented another model worthy of admiration. The Mongol Empire bestrode two continents, created one of the world's longest trade networks, utilized the most successful war machine of its era, and dominated the earlier medieval empires of South and East Asia. Its division and slow collapse, however, made it vulnerable and tarnished its legacy of imperial governance as much as did the fall of Constantinople. Yet, Muscovy's own princes had been raised and trained in the Qipchaq system.[17] The possibility that Moscow could succeed in unifying the steppe, where the Mongols had recently failed, inspired visions of imperial opportunities. As much as the Orthodox tradition justified a southward push through Ukrainian territory to reclaim "all Rus'" from the open steppe, the Mongol legacy was more than enough reason to plan the annexation of the Khanates of Kazan, Astrakhan, and Sibir', reunifying the western Mongol Empire.

The legacy of the Mongols was one of centralization of political authority and efficient military forces. Early in the Mongol rise, solutions for managing the empire including the postal roads, tax structures, economic development, and flexible management to accommodate both sedentary and nomadic subjects had been implemented. As the empire grew, the East Slavs experienced population registrations and military recruitment.[18] Furthermore, even as the Mongol elites adopted Islam as their primary faith, the Mongol Empire did not institute exclusionary practices based on faith.[19] As Muscovy's princely families had been trained (and served) within these Mongol structures, it was a logical evolution that this flexible, adaptable, and effective system would be the basis for their own imperial administration.

While Moscow's right to claim the legacy of its imperial predecessors might be contested, there can be no doubt that each suggested the same model of governance for Muscovite ruling dynasts: an empire, complete with a multiethnic and multi-confessional population. An empire in this sense was both a symbolic framework of political authority and a physical space of interactive cultures. In Muscovy, the idea of empire combined with a symbolic language built upon Orthodox Byzantine traditions coupled with Mongol administrative, military, and economic practices. As a result, Muscovy could have an Orthodox tsar as the charismatic symbol of the state, leading a territory filled with diverse peoples, languages, cultures, and religions.

Muscovy's conception of empire was neither an innovation of the sixteenth century nor a personal aspiration of Tsar Ivan Vasil'evich. More or less since Moscow was first mentioned in the Orthodox Church chronicles of the medieval era, its princes had sought ways to increase their personal authority and claims over land and people. This was not a "Muscovite" trait either, having been considered "politics as usual" among all of the ruling princes among the East Slavs. Without the Mongol intervention in the internal politics of the East Slavic principalities, however, the Rurikid princes of Moscow would probably have followed a dramatically different course.

Personal relationships with the Mongols, coupled with good (if not the best) family claims toward the title of Grand Prince had pushed Moscow onto the center stage of "Russian" political development by the fourteenth century. When Iurii of Moscow received the title of Grand Prince in 1317, he had already been elevated above his status, chosen over the so-called legitimate ruler of the northern Slavs. This would remain perhaps the most significant aspect of Muscovite expansion for centuries to come. For Moscow's assertions of authority, the benefit of the support of the Mongol state and the institution of the Russian Orthodox Church would be invaluable for its future success.

Successive generations of Moscow princes continued, with some notable failures, to increase Muscovite control in northern Russia. The culmination of the process was achieved during the reign of Ivan III (the Great), who acquired in turn Iaroslavl' (1463) and Rostov (1474), conquered Novgorod (twice!), and removed the last formal resistance in the north with the annexation of Tver' in 1485.[20] Russian historians of the nineteenth century described these "victories" as the "Gathering of the Russian lands," which added an ahistorical element of manifest destiny to their success. It was anything but inevitable. Legitimacy did not lie with Moscow's princes, and the idea of a united "Russian" homeland was also innovative, as there had yet to be a period in the history of the East Slavs when one prince ruled a unitary state.

Much like the other "new monarchs" of Europe in the sixteenth century, certain trends favored the tentative unification of a set of loosely related principalities, comprised of a mostly common ethnolinguistic community with a shared religion. The state assembled by Ivan III could best be described as a "composite monarchy," a group of political entities unified only by a common ruler—in this case, the Grand Prince of Moscow.[21] Ivan III arrived at the same conclusion as did rulers in Paris and Vienna, and enacted a series of legal and administrative reforms designed to dissolve the differences among his territories. The long-term goal was to create a centralized monarchy, or, at the very least, a centralized bureaucracy, even if regional differences continued to persist well into the modern era.[22]

While records from Ivan III's reign are scarce, two noteworthy developments mark his steps in striving to create a unitary kingdom from a composite monarchy. First arose the practice of a formalized system of social precedence, *mestnichestvo*, which evaluated social rank on the basis of ancestry and a record of military service. Position in the *mestnichestvo* system determined all aspects of elite life, from rank in government service to a seat at a dining table. *Mestnichestvo* accorded high status to some of Ivan's most recent victims, including the former appanage princes of Tver', reconciling them to Moscow's rule. Though among the last to his table, they enjoyed a seat near the center of power among the highest elites.[23] At the same time, the first attempt to standardize the new Muscovite legal system, the *Sudebnik* of 1497, began the essential process of creating one legal system for the entire network of former independent principalities, undermining the previous divisions within Ivan's new kingdom.[24] As John Elliott has noted for Europe at this time, unifying the legal system and co-opting foreign elites into a centralized political system were the key steps in forging one kingdom from a composite state.[25]

It was this composite state that Ivan IV Vasil'evich inherited in 1533 at the age of three. Centralizing authority by eliminating the social and political differences among the numerous principalities had made some progress before his succession, but Ivan's youth undid much of this progress. In fact, Moscow's Kremlin was divided among various factions, including members of Ivan's family, vying for influence and control.[26] The Byzantine legacy exploited in the court to provide a ceremonial culture could not make young Ivan a "caesar" (or tsar), as no one dominated the court sufficiently to make that claim, least of all the titular head of state. With confusion among the political elites, the influence of Makarii, the metropolitan of

Moscow and the leader of the Russian Orthodox Church after 1542, was necessary to bolster the child's authority and prevent a palace coup. This tight bond between church and state, formed while Ivan was an infant, prepared the way for Metropolitan Makarii to influence Ivan until his majority.

In 1547 Ivan Vasil'evich and Metropolitan Makarii commemorated Ivan's majority with two significant symbolic measures. First came the coronation of Ivan IV as tsar. According to later accounts, it appears that the coronation was intentionally based upon the Byzantine coronation ceremony, with the metropolitan assuming the role of the patriarch of Constantinople. It was a claim to power and prestige for both participants in the ceremony.[27] Second, Ivan married Anastasiia Romanova, a member of the Zakharin-Iurev clan, which was among the prominent families of the court. As with the coronation, the metropolitan planned the wedding as an elaborate court ritual to reinforce the divine presence of Ivan's rule as God's chosen emperor.[28]

With these plans accomplished, the new tsar, like his grandfather Ivan III, worked to centralize his government, while the metropolitan moved to do the same to the Church. Ivan Vasil'evich summoned a group of advisors to "assist" his writing of a new law code for his kingdom, which became the *Sudebnik* of 1550.[29] As with the original *sudebnik*, the 1550 code focused on weakening the power of the elites by making them more dependent upon the throne, in order prevent the conflicts that had marked Ivan's youth. The tsar provided a combination of concessions to landed elites, such as limiting peasant movement to a two-week period beginning on St. George's Day in the fall, confirming an earlier principle of Muscovite law, and freeing the elite from petitioning the throne through local governors by allowing each man to petition the tsar directly. This only reinforced the importance of the *mestnichestvo* system as it positioned the tsar as the sole authority capable of resolving elite disputes.[30] At the same time, a new church council held in Moscow was challenged to answer the tsar's one hundred questions about the faith, its practices, and its material rights, which would produce a comprehensive set of answers the following year. The decisions of the "*Stoglav*" (100 Chapters) council acted as a parallel to the *Sudebnik*. The Russian Orthodox Church moved toward a centralized structure of authority, with an increase of bishops' authority. Monastic independence and wealth, and differences in liturgy, among other issues, were addressed. As there was a tsar above the elite, there were bishops (including the metropolitan) above the clergy and the laity.[31]

Ivan IV's reforms were a success in terms of institutionalizing the state at the expense of elite initiative and local prerogatives, resulting in a shift toward centralized authority. At the same time, Ivan IV started a process that would end more successfully than in his wildest dreams—conquering territory beyond the original Eastern Slav lands. In 1552 Ivan's army conquered the city of Kazan, seizing a Muslim khanate's lands for Moscow. He managed to acquire the Khanate of Astrakhan in 1556 and, with it, a claim to the entirety of Volga River. By the end of his reign, a mercenary army under the leadership of the Cossack Ermak defeated the Khanate of Sibir', potentially opening up all of Siberia to Muscovite influence.[32] In nearly all aspects, the beginning of Ivan IV's reign ran parallel to that of Ivan III—more centralized authority at the expense of local independence coupled with territorial expansion. These victories justified Ivan IV's title "the Terrible" (or Awe-Inspiring), much as his grandfather's had done.

Ivan Vasil'evich was able to exercise great authority, directly and without delicate maneuverings or significant delays, based on his public position as tsar. Supported by the Church, his power was based on the ritualized and formalized position he had inherited, not his own military success. Even before accomplishing his conquests, Ivan existed above the rest of the court and his rivals largely because of the influence of the Orthodox Church and his grandfather's legacy. Metropolitan Makarii's influence in the process was a necessity. Ivan's "charismatic authority"— his ceremonial presentation of power, authority, and influence—was based now in a set of Orthodox religious imagery borrowed from the Byzantine Empire. Ivan's public displays of piety throughout his reign, such as his constant pilgrimages to holy sites and the construction of new churches and monasteries, were later reminders of his fundamental role in promoting Muscovy as an Orthodox space.[33] Both he and Makarii were consciously promoting this Orthodox symbolic language. It served to present Ivan as the ruler and defender of Orthodoxy against its religious enemies, both east and west. The tsar had to hold political and judicial authority in order to dispense justice and create a heavenly space on earth.[34] It reinforced the unique authority of the metropolitan as well, as the emergent head of the last, true Orthodox kingdom on earth. Both church and state actively promoted a symbolic space in which Ivan's role as tsar was celebrated.

There was a far more practical side to this symbolic construction as well. It was, to a great extent, congruent with the underpinnings of Mongol rule. The mechanics of the state—the diplomatic and military structures, the tax and postal systems, just to name a few—remained largely Mongol.[35] All Muscovite princes were raised in, and ruled with, these methods. The Mongol system was also imperial and fully capable of managing a multiethnic and multiconfessional population. It was a practical solution for governing the centralizing state of Muscovy and already extant—there was no need to alter it to adapt to a new tsarist iconography, however based on Byzantine imagery. There was no attempt, for instance, to resurrect Byzantine administrative practice in Moscow. Thus, what first might appear as a contradiction, this combination of an Orthodox symbolic space with a political culture built upon a Mongol governing system, was not. Both traditions assumed the existence of an empire. The church and the Orthodox public understood the ritual culture of Christianity, while the tsar and his army understood the political-military strategies of the Mongol state. The fact that Orthodoxy presented itself as the only true faith, while the Muslim Mongols were the enemy, only helped construct an aura of charismatic authority. Orthodoxy remained the public face of an empire built upon Mongol roots.

This Orthodox-Mongol construct was the base of the "elusive" empire. The Orthodox imperial symbolism that defined the status of the tsar and his elites was largely separate from the Mongol-derived state administration. The tsar willingly borrowed from either system when need arose. The Orthodox charisma of the tsar as displayed in Moscow was not intended, nor necessary, for his new Muslim and animist subjects. Instead, the tsar reframed himself as the "white khan," privileging the Mongol legacy as his primary identity, positioning himself as the true inheritor of the open steppe.[36] Therefore, the Muscovite state was neither Byzantine nor Mongol but rather a combination of both that became its own unique construct. The Muscovite empire was its elusive goal—the quest to achieve centralized authority in the heartland and hegemonic political, military, and economic control over the frontier, which would take more than a century. As this new imperial system was evolving, however, it was not only the inherited structures but also the population that had opportunities to further influence its development, attempting to shape the state as much for their own purposes as for the tsars'.

The Conquests of Kazan

With Muscovy's empire firmly founded as a concept, Tsar Ivan IV faced innumerable challenges to establishing its authority to the edges of its borders. The problems began with the challenging geopolitical position of Moscow.[37] To the west, two developing military powers threatened the integrity of his border. Both Sweden and Poland were growing into "great power" status. The mineral wealth of Sweden guaranteed its army would be among the best equipped throughout all of continental Europe. After the Union of Lublin in 1569, the expansive Commonwealth of Poland-Lithuania produced the most numerous cavalry in Europe. Poland-Lithuania claimed most the former territory of medieval Kievan Rus', directly competing with Muscovy's claims to the tsar's Orthodox patrimony. The Qipchaq Khanate had long since devolved, but control over its former possessions remained unresolved.

Farther south, away from competition with the aggressively expanding commonwealth, the situation was not much better.[38] The Khanate of Crimea, another political successor of the Qipchaq Khanate, was a constant threat. By the sixteenth century, Crimea had converted to Islam and was closely allied to the Ottoman Empire.[39] The Muscovites were well aware of Ottoman military prowess. Crimean raids for Slavic slaves along the southern border, in combination with occasional invasions of the interior, continuously demonstrated the threat from the south. Rather than competing against the combined power of these two Muslim states, Moscow's ambition was only to defend itself against their harassment.

To Muscovy's east, however, the situation was a bit different. By the reign of Ivan IV, Moscow's immediate neighbor was the new Khanate of Kazan. Kazan, along with its neighbors the Khanates of Astrakhan and Sibir', emerged from the devolution of the Qipchaq Khanate as a small, independent state. Unlike the Khanate of Crimea, Kazan was comparatively weak and had difficulty maintaining its political independence from Crimea or Moscow. For the bulk of its years of "independence" (the fifteenth and first half of the sixteenth century), Kazan served mainly as a pawn in the strategic competition between Moscow and Crimea. On occasion, Muscovy and Crimea cooperated in order to maintain some independence in Kazan, but each continued to seek greater influence in Kazan in order to pressure the other for potential concessions. Moscow's grand princes entertained hopes that an eventual alliance with Kazan could decisively end their subservience to Crimea as well as create opportunities for dominating other steppe peoples farther to the east.[40]

One of Moscow's first major steps toward this hoped-for alliance was the establishment of a nominally independent territory, called the Khanate of Kasimov, which created a buffer state between Kazan and Moscow in the mid-fifteenth century.[41] This decision freed Moscow from the direct threat of invasion by Crimea through Kazan. With increased frontier security, Moscow began to support further Russian settlement and military incursions into Kazan's territory to permanently neutralize its eastern border. However, this move toward the east had the potential to unleash a cascading set of disasters: securing Kazan would only bring Muscovy into closer contact with the steppe nomads, including the Nogais, Bashkirs, and Kalmyks. In addition, and potentially more dangerous for Muscovite plans, the Crimeans, Ottomans, and Safavids each protested Muscovy's interference in the lives of the Muslims of Kazan.

To some extent, the organization and composition of the Khanate of Kazan worked to Moscow's benefit. Kazan lacked a homogenous population but gathered its cohesion through shared Mongol subjecthood. One ethnolinguistic group did dominate Kazan politically—the Tatars. By the sixteenth century, the Tatars were primarily a sedentary, agricultural population. Their numbers also included urban merchants in the city. At the top of the Tatar social hierarchy was the political and military elite, composed of cavalrymen serving in Kazan's army. Its most elite families were the *mirza*s (known to the Russians as *murzii*). In this, the Tatars were similar to Muscovite Russians in terms of their social hierarchy, but also possessed a long history of political independence in Kazan.[42] While the Tatars dominated, they also were not the only Turks within the khanate. The Chuvashes were almost entirely sedentary agriculturalists, split religiously between animism and Islam.[43] Many Chuvashes were peasants tied to Tatar estates, which may have fueled resentment against Tatar political authority and a pronounced pro-Muscovite sentiment, but there is no evidence to suggest that this was a universal attitude.[44]

Groups of Finno-Ugric descent formed a significant non-Turkish population. As speakers of languages that were entirely different than those of the Turks, they held to a long-standing separatism. They also shared a common cultural background with the Finno-Ugric peoples of Muscovy's north, many of whom had been under East Slavic control for centuries. They were agriculturists, and generally sedentary, though many relied upon forest crafts, for instance beekeeping or trapping, rather than taking up farming as their livelihood. Moscow's rulers could presume familiarity with their culture, even if reality did not quite support an assumption of loyalty.

The largest of these Finno-Ugric groups were labeled "Mordvins" by Muscovy, and the Russians had regular contact with them as early as the thirteenth century, after the establishment of the new outpost of Nizhnii Novgorod along the Volga River. As a result, the Mordvins were also the first people who opted (albeit under the direct threat of military force) for Moscow's political control rather than Kazan's. Deeper within the territory of the khanate, along the Volga River, were other Finno-Ugric tribes identified as Cheremisses (now Maris) and Votiaks (now Udmurts).[45] One of the greatest advantages for Moscow in its relations with the khanate, therefore, was that the path between Moscow and Kazan was lined with subject peoples who were exploited, to varying degrees, by the Muslim Tatars. Muscovy's forces faced only uneven opposition along the Volga during Ivan's minority, suggesting that discontent with the Tatars could inspire an easy victory. Moscow absorbed the Mordvins by the 1530s. Their territory was quite near to Nizhnii Novgorod on Muscovy's easternmost frontier, and the expansion was the necessary first step on the path toward Kazan.[46]

Spurred on by this success, Ivan pursued the absorption of the entire khanate. It was not an unqualified success. He personally led a failed campaign in the winter of 1547/48, followed by a second one year later.[47] Muscovite forces made insufficient preparations for a sustained campaign against Kazan. They succeeded in defeating the khanate's subject levies, but the main army of the khanate, comprised largely of Tatar cavalry, proved a far greater challenge. Despite Moscow's ability to exert constant pressure on the border of the khanate, Ivan's supply lines still stretched two hundred miles from Nizhnii Novgorod to the city of Kazan. These failures necessitated a change in military strategy, initiated in 1550.[48]

Moscow's failure against Kazan was easy to explain. Both Muscovy and the Khanate of Kazan employed the same tactics and troops. Both exploited horse archers in preference to gunpowder weapons.[49] Thus, in the field neither side enjoyed a technological nor a tactical advantage. Moscow's fortunes turned on its ability to out-supply its otherwise equal opponent.[50] Only after perfecting its logistics did Ivan's army succeed in erasing Kazan's defensive advantages.

The key to Muscovy's victory was a new outpost at the confluence of the Volga and Sviiaga Rivers, proximate to Kazan itself. The new fortress, named Sviiazhsk, was built in 1551 in anticipation of a climactic campaign. Of course, the construction of Sviiazhsk already presaged a Muscovite strategic victory, as the khanate could not prevent its establishment, nor contest the territory between the fortress and Nizhnii Novgorod, comprising the majority of the khanate's arable land. Furthermore, the fortress was erected with the tacit support of the khanate's subject peoples. By 1551 the Finno-Ugric Mordvins, Maris, Udmurts, and Turkic Chuvashes had accepted at least a nominal allegiance to the Muscovite tsar. The khanate was not beaten, however, without the city itself.

This was accomplished in the summer of 1552.[51] The tsar reputedly gathered as many as 150,000 men to begin the siege. The city of Kazan was defended with massive wooden walls, which included several large cannons. The Muscovite army took the field with numerous cannon as well. With both sides equally prepared, a long siege of attrition began.

Given the technological equivalence, it was the combined advantage of the nearby Sviiazhsk fortress and the cooperation of the subject peoples of the khanate that allowed the Muscovite army to besiege Kazan successfully. With a logistical advantage, the tsar pressed the city from all sides.[52] As the Muscovite forces were well supplied, the final stage was less difficult than the previous decades of slow progress. After several weeks of costly fighting, Kazan's walls were successfully undermined. It is unclear whether undermining the walls was intended to cut off the city's water supply or prepare the way for destroying the walls themselves. In any case, it achieved both. In the tunnels dug under the walls, several barrels of gunpowder were placed on 4 September, and Kazan's main tower was destroyed by the blast.[53] Though the siege lasted several more weeks, after this point the outcome was not in doubt. Sapping continued throughout September, and the final demolition of the fortifications occurred just before dawn on 2 October, which marked the signal for a simultaneous assault on all seven of Kazan's gates.

Although there are no extant eyewitness accounts from that day, certainly flight was difficult for the Tatar garrison. Unquestionably, the conquest of the city was bloody. The records depicted it as quite violent, which European travelers enjoyed recounting back at home. For example:

> [Kazan] was plundered and its inhabitants were murdered, stripped naked, and placed in a heap. Then the ankles or feet of the corpses were tied together, and afterward a long log was taken and stuck between their legs. They were then thrown into the Volga, twenty, thirty, forty, or fifty on a log. The logs with the bodies floated downstream. The bodies hung from the logs in the water, only the feet showing above, where they were bound.[54]

In Moscow, however, the celebration was joyous. The Russians had conquered one of their great enemies and proclaimed the first Orthodox victory against Islam since the fall of Constantinople in 1453.[55]

Muscovy was captivated by the religious dimension of the victory. The Russian Orthodox Church presented its believers with a singular interpretation. It was not the tsar or his logistical advances, but the work of God:

> And with God's grace, and because of the great faith of the Orthodox Tsar Ivan Vasil'evich, and on account of his heartfelt desire, God turned over to him the godless Tatars of Kazan, and on account of his faith, desiring the love of God, our pious sovereign destroyed their Muslim faith, and he ruined and demolished their mosques.[56]

In this account, tsarist expansion developed from religious motives, not political, military, or economic imperatives, much less to Moscow's slow, steady progress in claiming the banks of Volga River over the previous thirty years. In fact, the victory over Kazan has traditionally been presented foremost as a religious victory, and as a military victory second, if at all.[57] However, the religious conquest was merely a gloss on a well-executed conquest of an independent state for the tsar's personal benefit.

The reality of Muscovite success against the khanate diverged from the symbolic victory of Orthodoxy over Islam. While the religious presentation was clearly an idealized construction, it quickly became the dominant view of tsarist success. The Russian Orthodox Church zealously pursued the promotion of the religious victory. This was not novel. Throughout the long history of conflict between Moscow and Kazan, the metropolitan of Moscow encouraged the idea that Moscow and Kazan were not in conflict over resources, trade routes, or geopolitical security, but over religion. This narrative had proven inconvenient during the years of Muscovite failures, especially given the obvious power of the Ottomans and Crimeans. Victory, however, confirmed and validated it, providing the Orthodox Church with a stirring symbol of a rejuvenated Orthodox realm.

The influential Metropolitan Makarii of Moscow developed this triumphant narrative over many years.[58] Aside from adding to Ivan's early reign the imprinteur of religious authority, Makarii was a staunch advocate of converting Muscovy's non-Orthodox populations; as the archbishop of Novgorod and Pskov earlier in his career, he had dedicated himself to this task in Novgorod's extensive northern territories.[59] Makarii presented the conquest and conversion of the Khanate of Kazan as an extension of his earlier campaign. According to contemporary religious chronicles, Makarii blessed Ivan IV's decision to attack the khanate for "the holy churches and for Orthodox Christianity."[60] Thus, Makarii framed the war against the khanate as a religious struggle of the Church Militant. Muscovy would conquer the khanate, and the Orthodox Church would convert its populace to the true faith.

Once military maneuvers began, he exhorted more virtuous behavior from the troops stationed at the Sviiazhsk fortress. He promised the army God's blessing for their holy work; Ivan's victory would confirm them as the renewed and holy defenders of Orthodoxy. He condemned the Tatars to the "furious wrath of God," for their impiety "shamed the word of God" and "desecrated" the faith.[61] Makarii's self-conscious decision to record (and preserve) his words to the troops on the frontlines explicitly and intentionally exerted the authority of the Church over a righteous crusade.

To further connect the military conquest to religious imperatives, Makarii blessed the tsar before his departure in a public ceremony in Moscow, employing Russian Orthodox rituals to support Ivan IV's person. For his part, Ivan IV highlighted the connection between Orthodox ritual and conquest by stopping in Vladimir and Murom for blessings at their cathedrals. Upon arriving at Sviiazhsk, he proceeded immediately to its new church for a local blessing. This ritual connection between the Church Militant and victory culminated after Ivan took Kazan. He commanded that a church be built on the spot where his banner stood during battle.[62] This was followed almost immediately by the establishment of the Zilantov

Uspenskii Monastery, the region's first, marking the permanence of Orthodoxy's conquest with a stone structure outside of Kazan's walls.

As if Orthodoxy had not already "triumphed" in its conflict with Islam, a religious procession repeated the tsar's actions along the Volga and in Kazan itself. Preparations for the religious conquest of the city took three years to organize, as the Church required its own logistical revolution to muster the resources to man and supply the city. The first archbishop of Kazan arrived in the city on 28 July 1555, following a series of ceremonies designed to raise public awareness and connect the city of Kazan symbolically with Moscow. The most complete account of these events is the combined *vitae* of Kazan's first archbishop, Gurii, and one of the elite churchmen who accompanied him, Archimandrite Varsonofii.[63] The Church records, including the *vitae*, emphasized that a request from the new Muscovite governor in Kazan inspired the decision to create an archbishopric for the city. This presentation of the events stresses that the institutional Church did not arrive during an invasion, but in response to the desires of the local community.

According to Gurii and Varsonofii's *vitae*, following the governor's request, a church council convened in Moscow to decide the best way to found a new archbishopric in Kazan. The council included Metropolitan Makarii, the bishops of Novgorod-Pskov, Rostov, Suzdal, Smolensk, Riazan', Tver', and Kolomna, and important abbots from several local monasteries. In addition, Ivan and several prominent elites attended, including his brother Prince Iur'ii Vasil'evich and the boiars of the Muscovite court.[64] Given Makarii's rhetoric about the importance of the conquest, and the prestige of the council that created it, it seems unlikely that the governor independently sought a new bishopric for the local Orthodox community. As before, Makarii, in conjunction with the tsar, guided the selection process. The council selected distinguished churchmen to fill the new archbishopric's positions. It would oversee Kazan, Sviiazhsk, and their environs, and soon gained authority over the lower Volga, including Astrakhan. The new archbishopric ranked third in the Orthodox Church's hierarchy, after the metropolitanate of Moscow and the archbishopric of Novgorod-Pskov, and ahead of the archbishopric of Rostov.[65] Despite its very recent acquisition, Kazan was clearly of signal importance to the Church. As Muscovite bishops were able to enact policies at their own discretion, the new archbishop of Kazan would be largely responsible for executing whatever policies the Russian Orthodox Church advocated for the region.[66] This strongly suggests that the archbishopric of Kazan was methodically planned as a prominent component of the Church's future in Muscovy.

The choice of the men who filled the posts in the bishopric also indicates this intent. Each was a prominent member of one of Muscovy's most prestigious monasteries. Gurii was a former hegumen of the Iosifo-Volokolamskii Monastery, one of the most important institutions in Muscovy, and one with a long association with Moscow's grand princes. Having selected a former leader of this Iosifo-Volokolamskii Monastery for the position was one method for assuring that the policies of the new archbishop would be those that were planned in Moscow. Furthermore, the two other new hierarchs selected for the region were also men with long careers of dedicated service to the Church. German was another monk of the Iosifo-Volokolamskii Monastery, who was assigned to found the new Bogoroditskii Monastery in Sviiazhsk, and the other was Varsonofii, a former archimandrite of the Pesnoshskii Monastery, who would establish an urban monastery in Kazan, the Spaso-Preobrazhenskii.[67] As German became the second archbishop of Kazan following Gurii's death, the decisions made early in 1555 continued to shape the region for some time.

Gurii's arrival in Kazan was the final stop on an official procession that ultimately included all of the territory between Moscow and Kazan, identifying the whole country as Orthodox space. Appropriately, Gurii's procession began inside the Kremlin in Moscow, both the religious and political center of Muscovite authority. Following a church service in the Uspenskii Cathedral, Metropolitan Makarii and the entire assembled church council gathered together to bless Gurii. Before the liturgy, Makarii blessed some holy water for Gurii to take with him on his procession, and which was needed for blessings in the new see. This entire group proceeded to the Frolovskii gates, carrying church banners and holy icons, while all the bells of the Kremlin were rung. Ivan IV received a blessing from Gurii, and then departed. Makarii blessed the entire procession and returned to the Kremlin as well. The rest of the assembled church council proceeded with Gurii for a distance outside the city to help him prepare for his journey.[68] This pageant closely resembled Ivan IV's departure from Moscow on his way to conquer Kazan, thus associating the ideas of military and religious conquest in the minds of the viewing public. The utilization of the Uspenskii Cathedral, followed by the Frolovskii gates, visibly demonstrated this connection to the public. To expand the influence of this procession, a version of his blessing ritual was reenacted at every town and outpost between Moscow and Kazan, causing Gurii's procession to last four months.

When the new archbishop finally arrived at Kazan on 28 July 1555, he repeated the ritual blessings, fulfilling the symbolism of the procession by claiming the local kremlin as sacred Orthodox space. As it had been the seat of Muslim power in the khanate, Gurii completed a ritual blessing of the space, sprinkling the walls with holy water. In order to extend his blessing, he read a prayer for the preservation of the Orthodox tsar, his Christian army, and the entire Orthodox community in front of each gate, to symbolically cover the four corners of the tsar's new kingdom.[69]

In order to promote further the image of the conquest as a religious victory, the Church organized a series of public demonstrations in Moscow. For the elite living inside the Kremlin walls, a new icon, "Blessed Is the Host of the King of Heaven," was painted in commemoration of the victory and prominently displayed in the Kremlin's Dormition Cathedral. The image reinforced the earlier rhetoric: Archangel Michael led Ivan IV and the Muscovite army back from Kazan, while numerous angels brought martyrs' crowns to those fallen in battle.[70] Those left outside of the Kremlin's hallowed grounds were not forgotten. In one of the greatest public exhibitions ever undertaken in Russian history, the tsar ordered the construction of a new church to commemorate the day of the glorious victory against Islam. The Church of the Intercession on the Moat dominated one side of Red Square, physically trapping Muscovite residents between this religious symbol of the tsar's victory and the walls of the Kremlin itself.[71]

The Church's triumphant narrative dominated public commemorations of Kazan, and this also served the tsar's interests. It began with the production of the *History of the Kazan Khanate*, completed by the end of the sixteenth century. It was an "official" history of the khanate, and its authors depicted Kazan's (and Islam's) inevitable fate was to fall to an Orthodox emperor.[72] This text fit neatly into a recurring theme of church texts in the sixteenth century, which portrayed the tsar as a divinely appointed Orthodox emperor. For example, the *Stepennaia kniga*, written during Ivan IV's life, traced a succession of emperors from Alexander the Great through the Romans and Byzantines until at last arriving at Ivan and his empire, Muscovy.[73] Ivan's military success fulfilled this role of defender of the faith. The conqueror tsar was also a holy defender of true Christianity, as Rome had been until the Great Schism of 1054 and afterward the Byzantines until the fall of Constantinople. The conquests reinforced the concept of Muscovy as a holy kingdom, and the tsar's resulting charismatic authority became an enduring feature of Muscovite political culture.

This was the reason Kazan was conquered twice—once by Ivan, and then by his Church. These victories did not equal genuine administrative control over the territory. Neither guaranteed loyalty or productivity from the tsar's new subjects, who were, after all, neither Russian nor Orthodox. At the same time, the view from Moscow was one only of success. For its residents in the Kremlin or in the streets, knowledge of any continuing resistance in and around Kazan might have been difficult to understand. Once the tsar and the metropolitan proclaimed victory, there was little contrary evidence available to dispute their versions of events.

Indeed, on the surface the conquest was complete. In 1560, the Englishman Anthony Jenkinson wrote an account of his travels through Muscovy to Bukhara, which had begun two years earlier. His route passed through Kazan, providing him an opportunity to view the tsar's recent acquisition:

> Cazan is a fair town after the Russe or Tartar fashion, with a strong castle, situated upon a high hill, and was walled round about with timber and earth, but now the Emperor of Russia hath given order to pluck down the old walls, and to build them again of free stone. It hath been a city of great wealth and riches, and being in the hands of the Tartars it was a kingdom of itself, and did more vex the Russes in their wars, then any other nation: but nine years past, this Emperor of Russia conquered it, and took the king captive, who being but young is now baptized, and brought up in his court with two other princes, which were also kings of the said Cazan, and being each of them in time of their reigns in danger of their subjects through civil discord, came and rendered themselves at several times unto the said Emperor, so that at this present there are three princes in the court of Russia, which had been Emperors of the said Cazan, whom the Emperor useth with great honor.[74]

Jenkinson reiterated the Kremlin's established narrative of victory: the tremendous military victory, the importance of the religious victory seen in the baptism of the Tatar elite, and also the gain in political prestige with the tsar's association with these Chingissid princes. Russians presented with foreigners like Jenkinson a convincing material and spiritual victory for Christianity. As in Jenkinson's narrative, Muscovites could present the military and religious victories as integrated achievements. This was essential for the tsar's imperial strategies and ideology. The pageant of the conquest presented this process as already complete. The effort and expense of conquest, however, demanded a real and secure integration of Kazan into Muscovy. This had not yet taken place.

The tsar and his allies, therefore, were far more pragmatic than many scholars have acknowledged.[75] The empire could allow the tsar's subjects to retain the freedom to pursue their own agendas and maintain their own cultures, as long as the narrative of victory remained unchallenged.[76] Conquest had been difficult; assimilation was even more so. As long as the state could plausibly keep a veneer of successful administration in place, padded with a few profits and guarded by complicit participants, Moscow could present its conquest as an important precedent for, and an integral part of, Muscovite expansion. In fact, the absorption of Kazan suggested how little the tsar could expend to create another support for his charismatic authority and to prepare for future expansion.

The Incremental Conquest

While the proclamation of a religious victory against Islam portended a glorious future for Orthodoxy and its tsar, the reality of the conquest was that it increased the complexity of Moscow's already insecure political relationships with its neighbors. Hand in hand with the conquest went announcements to the Ottoman sultan of the tsar's good intentions for his new Muslim subjects.[77] Whatever faith the sultan put in this attempt at conciliation was quickly tested, as Muscovy's forces soon continued down the Volga to capture the Khanate of Astrakhan. This gave Muscovy direct access to the Caspian Sea and brought the tsar into direct conflict over boundaries with both the Ottomans and Safavids.[78] In terms of his relations with the Muslim Empires, the tsar's actions in Kazan had not improved the situation notably.[79]

At the same time, while the tsar's administrators, military officers, and religious authorities resided in Kazan's kremlin, the situation outside of the city walls was still unsettled in the 1550s. The Tatars in particular continued to resist Muscovite rule, with periods of assistance from the local Chuvashes, Maris, and Udmurts. Part of Moscow's approach appeared to be to ignore the resistance, as if failing to record the events would avoid the difficulty of quelling opposition. This decision suited the tsar's government, which already glossed over the confounding complexity of his diverse empire. For its part, the Church declined to pursue the conversion of the restive populace.[80]

While records are spotty for the remainder of the sixteenth century, it appears that the fighting over Kazan, regardless of the Tatar "defeat," continued at least until 1557.[81] The motives, extent, and success or failure of the resistance is harder to assess. Prince Kurbskii, the region's military leader, reported that the local Mari population continued to rebel with the support of the nearby (and unconquered) Nogai Tatars.[82] It was possible that the Nogai Tatars encouraged the Mari revolt from afar, but by blaming them rather than the "conquered" population within the borders, Kurbskii also justified his continuing failure to pacify the region. A Russian Orthodox chronicle from the era recorded a contradictory set of motivations for the unrest, suggesting the widespread involvement of all of the region's populations— Tatars, Maris, Mordvins, and Chuvashes. The chronicle depicts a frontier in revolt, but that the trustworthy local governor, his musketeers (*strel'tsy*), troops, and newly converted (*novokreshchane*) Tatars supported Muscovite efforts to pacify the region.[83] Notably missing from the Church's account was the sizeable group of Muslims who had recently joined the tsar's forces. As the rebels were largely animist and the tsar's army was partially Muslim, the chronicle's depiction of this conflict as a continuing Orthodox-Muslim struggle seems highly questionable, certainly no more trustworthy than Kurbskii's account.

Even in areas without open revolt, and despite a proclamation that Islam be rejected within the tsar's lands, Islam and Tatar culture persisted.[84] After 1552, Tatar residents had been relocated to a new district outside of the newly rebuilt city walls, and the new archbishop resided in the kremlin following his public blessing of the tsar's new territory as an Orthodox space in 1555.[85] Functionally, the new "Tatar district" and its new mosque created opportunities for the continuation of Tatar and Muslim culture within the tsar's claims. Without question, the proclamation of a religious victory against Islam, culminating in Gurii's triumphant procession, seemed premature.

In other words, Muscovy's position in Kazan remained undeveloped, and its control had to be strengthened while the unrest was managed and ameliorated. The solution to the administrative problem was the construction of new fortresses at key locations throughout the region, which both reinforced the Muscovite military presence in the region and garrisoned its main artery of trade, the Volga River itself. These garrison forts were the first sign of a Muscovite imperial strategic vision. First came the wooden palisade forts of Alatyr' and Cheboksary, followed by Laishev, Temnikov, and Tetiushii. By the early 1560s, Muscovite structures were at least physically implanted in the countryside, and with the slackening of revolt in the 1560s, the first stage seemed a success.[86]

The second stage was the planning and construction of a defensive line to defend the tsar's new land and peoples. It began as a reactive policy, sporadically implemented, and then was formalized on 1 January 1571. Ivan IV issued an order to Prince Mikhail Ivanovich Vorotynskii to construct a set of small settlements (*stanitsy*) and guard towers to protect his new territory.[87] This would be the first military defensive line in Muscovite history. This radical (and expensive) proposition developed out of the security fears created by both external forces (in the form of continuing nomadic raids) and internal pressures (from local revolts). By 1578, the final portion of the new "Arzamas Line" had been constructed, extending from the new town of Arzamas south of Nizhnii Novgorod east to the new town of Tetiushii on the Volga River south of Kazan. While the line itself was a motley mix of earthen barriers, watch towers, and some new settlements, it was a visible sign of the tsar's claim over his new territory. In other words, the tsar had drawn a border between Muscovy and the untamed steppe in the most literal fashion possible.

The expense of construction was considerable and involved a wide range of projects from the establishment of new military outposts to construction of the

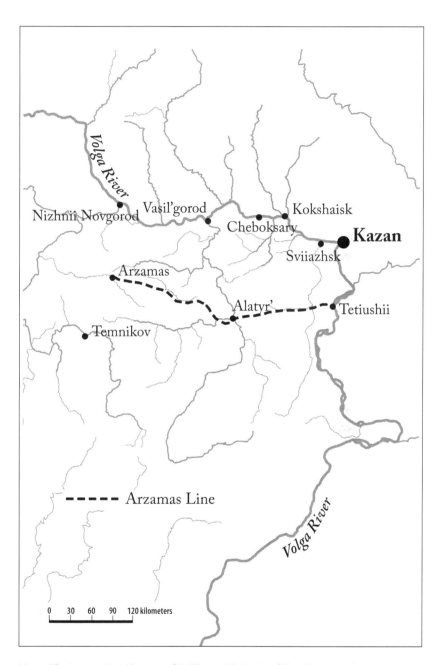

Map 2 The Arzamas Line (Courtesy of Ev Wingert, University of Hawai'i at Mānoa)

Table 1 Outposts and fortifications on the Arzamas Line

Outposts and towns	Year est.	Monasteries and convents	Year est.
Sviiazhsk	1551	Kazan's Zilantov Uspenskii Mon.	1552
Alatyr'	1552	Sviiazhsk's Uspenskii Bogoroditskii Mon.	1555
Cheboksary	1552	Spasskii-Arzamasskii Mon.	1555
Laishev	1557	Kazan's Spaso-Preobrazhenskii Mon.	1555
Temnikov	1557	Cheboksary's Spaso-Gerontieva Mon.	before 1563
Tetiushii	1558	Cheboksary's Sviiato-Troitskii Mon.	1566
Kokshaisk	1574	Kazan's Bogoroditskii Convent	1579
Arsk	1576	Arzamas's Nikolaevskii Convent	1580
Arzamas	1578	Kazan's Ioanno-Predtechenskii Mon.	1595
		Sviiazhsk's Ioanno-Predtechenskii Convent	before 1600
Line complete	1578	Cheboksary's Nikolaevskii Convent	1601
		Kazan's Troitskii Feodorovskii Convent	before 1607
		Alatyr's Sviiato-Troitskii Mon.	1612
		Kazan's Sedmiozernyi Bogoroditskii Mon.	1613
		Arzamas's Spaso-Preobrazhenskii Convent	1626
		Arzamas's Troitse-Sergeevskii Mon.	before 1628
		Tetiushii's Pokrovskii Mon.	before 1631

Source: Data drawn from Romaniello, "Absolutism and Empire," 22, 30, 33.

physical barriers.[88] Moscow's intent was to place an outpost on each of the routes most likely to be used by migrating nomads, particularly the Nogais, in order to prevent their entrance to, or exit from, Muscovite territory. Moscow designated certain of the outposts to become "towns." It then instructed regional governors and secretaries to develop an urban settlement to support the defense, while also creating a protected trade route along the border.[89]

To share the burden of financing the new constructions, the tsar and his government ordered the Russian Orthodox Church to construct religious institutions to anchor the towns culturally and economically. Traditionally, the state had relied on fortified monasteries to defend border towns, and this new region was no exception.[90] Each was strongly built with watchtowers, in keeping with the Muscovite tendency to place much of the expense of frontier defense on the Church.[91] As seen in table 1, new monasteries followed quite closely on the establishment of the new outposts. In this way, the Muscovite tsars linked their political and economic goals for the conquered territory with the symbolic force of the Orthodox religion. Whereas the earlier military and religious conquests made for momentary displays of state power, reshaping the frontier with physical structure was a far more permanent state of affairs.

Monasteries were the dominant feature of the new defenses. The pattern for establishing monasteries was similar to that of founding new cities; these institutions generally accompanied the creation of new outposts, though certain important towns, especially Kazan, continued to have new monasteries established both inside and outside of its city walls. Monasteries founded outside city walls could create an important connection between city and countryside, extending Muscovite influence, governance practices, and religious traditions farther into the territory.[92] Urban monasteries also received land and villages in the hinterland, as well as economic rights over certain fields or rivers, as part of their foundation, further connecting these new cities to the countryside. Many of these monasteries possessed extensive lands in largely non-Russian territory, bringing the Russian Orthodox Church into close contact with non-Orthodox populations.[93] Thus, the Church became a most important institution of the Muscovite state.

Monasteries were well suited to bolster the defensive line and could effectively maintain themselves without state financial investment. These physical defenses were integral parts of the region's defenses. For example, in 1585, the state ordered the construction of a new Spaso-Preobrazhenskii Monastery in Samara, to defend the outpost against the nearby Nogais.[94] Monasteries in the Middle Volga Region tended to supervise the construction and repair of their own stone walls, as was the case for the Troitse-Sergeevskii Monastery of Arzamas, which hired local peasants for the masonry work.[95] However, if the monastery possessed additional defensive structures, such as turrets, then Muscovite authorities provided both the impetus and the financial support for the structure. Kazan's two oldest monasteries, the Zilantov Uspenskii and the Spaso-Preobrazhenskii, both had several turrets, constructed over two decades in the 1570s and 1580s. Moscow instructed successive metropolitans of Kazan to maintain these defenses for the protection of the city.[96]

Additionally, monasteries served Muscovite settlement on the frontier as "spiritual defenses," bolstering the strength of Russian Orthodoxy in a territory largely settled with Muslim and pagan populations. To grant these monasteries an immediate holy aura, the Church associated them with religious objects, important Church officials, or sacred locations. The first monastic foundation in the region, the Zilantov Uspenskii Monastery received a copy of Smolensk's miraculous Mother of God Icon as a gift from Ivan IV in 1552. The icon had survived the Moscow fire of 1547, and Ivan IV placed it in the All Saints' Cathedral within the monastery to sanctify the space.[97] Similarly, he ordered the foundation of Kazan's Bogoroditskii Devichii convent in 1579 to house Kazan's Mother of God Icon as well as an abbess and forty nuns.[98]

Thus, Ivan modified existing church-state cooperative traditions to utilize religious structures in building up Russian authority in his new territories. In this, the policy met with success. The constructed line served as an administrative and defensive bulwark. The beginning of construction likely caused another revolt in 1572 along the Volga. Records from this uprising are remarkably scarce, leading to continuing debates about the participants, responses, and even its success or failure.[99] All that is known for certain is that the revolt was pacified by 1574, and construction continued apace on the new defenses.

The Arzamas Line itself affected established towns in the region adversely, as the tsar encouraged the relocation of resources toward more strategically important sites. Kurmysh, for instance, established in 1372, suffered from Muscovy's encroachment into the lands of the khanate. When the tsar founded Alatyr' in 1552, following the conquest, the city and its monasteries received extensive rights over the Sura River, which previously served Kurmysh. Without access to these resources, no new villages were established in Kurmysh's administrative district from 1552 until the late seventeenth century despite the influx of population into the region.[100]

By 1578 the Arzamas Line was complete. The government had established six monasteries, joined by two convents in 1580. The border was now well defined—a physical barrier across the land. In territory that previously had only small settlements distributed among forests, slow streams, and swampland, there was now a continuous (albeit surmountable) divide between the tsar's dominions and the outside world. Nomads could no longer travel freely in and out of the tsar's space; the defensive line succeeded in constraining and monitoring their migrations at certain key crossings. There were no local forces sufficient to repel the nomads, but their arrivals and potential threat were now known and could be countered. Vigilance did not equate with safety, though it was unquestionably progress.

The tsar's plan ultimately encroached most forcefully on the freedom of his own subjects. Where an "open" frontier with the steppe allowed migration, a "closed" border kept the tsar's subjects inside his dominions, at least in theory. Military forces eventually spread all along the border in order to demonstrate the tsar's control. The postconstruction physical domination of the countryside was a more powerful statement of tsarist intrusion into their lives than the conquest of Kazan, which may not have affected small villages in any practical way. With the completion of the Arzamas Line, local resistance against tsarist rule rapidly diminished, after nearly three decades of steady, if minor, revolts. One last rebellion appeared in the records from 1582 to 1584, ascribed to the Tatars, Maris, Chuvashes, Mordvins, and Udmurts, but it was unclear whether the Church exaggerated its

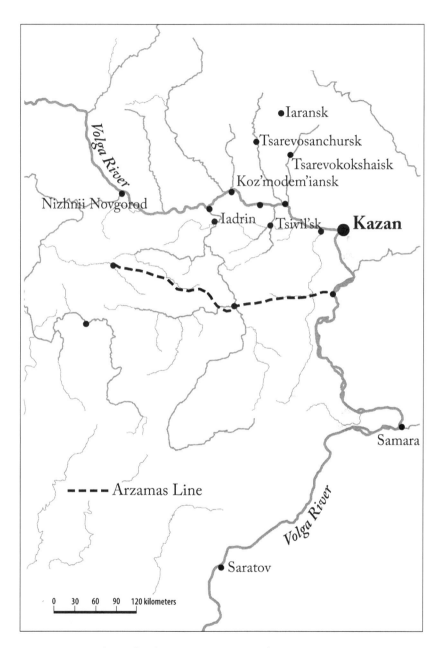

Map 3 Outposts and town foundations in 1613 (Courtesy of Ev Wingert, University of Hawai'i at Mānoa)

Table 2 Foundations north of the Arzamas Line

Outposts and towns	Year est.	First monasteries	Year est.
Koz'modem'iansk	1583	Koz'modem'iansk's Spaso-Iunginskii Mon.	1625
Urzhum	1584	Tsarevokokshaishk's Mironositskii Mon.	1647
Malmyzh	1584	Tsivil'sk's Tikhvinskii Bogoroditskii Mon.	1671
Tsarevokokshaisk	1584		
Tsivil'sk	1584		
Tsarevosansursk	1586		
Iadrin	1590		
Iaransk	1591		

Source: Data drawn from Romaniello, "Absolutism and Empire," 22, 30, 33.

significance as an argument that more conversions among the non-Orthodox would improve frontier security.[101]

The line was not part of a developed administrative solution for the new frontier, but it was nonetheless effective in claiming space. While there were repeated incidents before 1571, afterward the region was largely peaceful. Of course, with the tsar's attentions most closely on his western border, the defensive line remained the only intrusion into the daily lives of these people. A massive intrusion, undoubtedly, but perhaps the sole state attempt to exert direct influence over the territory. Active resistance to the construction was limited, which produced a passive acceptance of the new regime. The subjects of the former khanate appeared resolved to presence of the Muscovite military and religious incursions into their lives, if not necessarily their authority.

This is not to say the government ignored the region but, after constructing the defensive line, its interests moved toward the north and aimed at controlling the Volga River and its northern tributaries. While many of the new outposts began as military sites along the river, compared with the Arzamas outposts, these were fundamentally different. Table 2 demonstrates the difference; these eight outposts lacked a Church presence.[102] As the frontier had technically been "secured" by the Arzamas Line, the region north of that was safe from nomadic incursions. Therefore the defenses of the southern settlements did not need to be replicated, and limiting the cost of construction was an added benefit. As a result, the state took no active role in directing the establishment of monasteries in these sites. While monasteries were eventually established in these outposts, they followed the outpost foundations by decades. The local church was likely happy to delay the expense, as its commitment to the south remained considerable.

The construction of the defensive line was the decisive event in Muscovy's attempt to "conquer" Kazan. Moreover, it was a complex process by which the state defined its border and its possession of land and people. It fundamentally reshaped the landscape, imprinting permanent sites of administrative, economic, military, and religious authority. While the influence this new authority would have with the local population had not been settled, it was a far greater accomplishment than the military defeat of the khanate in 1552 had been. The instruction to Prince Vorotynskii to construct the Arzamas Line was more or less an outline of a principle—the region should be defended—but examining the physical infrastructure indicates this was a serious process involving considerable time, money, and effort. This was an early-modern state exerting its ability to muster resources: the Arzamas Line was another symbol of the state's control as well as a guarantee of eventual profit and security.

The tsar and his state existed in two worlds—one world of narrative and symbolism, and another of pragmatism and limitations. By the time the archbishop had claimed Kazan as Orthodox space in 1555, the world of ideology had created its narrative of success. There was no question in Moscow that the tsar had conquered Kazan through God's grace, but the experience on the frontier reveals the true limits of the tsar's authority, which only achieved a modicum of success in creating new mechanisms of control. It took another twenty years before the tsar and his officials could find a solution for demonstrating control in a recognizable manner to the residents of the frontier. Where Orthodox ritual might have failed to impress the local population in 1555, the massive construction project of the 1570s left few doubts that the tsar had claimed much of the lands and peoples of the former khanate. The defensive line, in fact, became the tsar's favorite ceremony of possession on the frontier for the next century.[103] In Muscovy, building the empire was, at its heart, the long and incremental process of mustering human and material resources in order to physically claim space. Whereas short-term conquest failed to quell resistance, long-term construction succeeded.

The Unlikely Success

The evidence suggests the conquest of the Khanate of Kazan lasted more than forty years. Thus, in essence, the construction of the Arzamas Line was the physical delineation of Muscovy's border with the open steppe. The line was designed to watch for potential incursions and local revolts, not begin Muscovy's expansion onto the steppe. Indeed, the state's development interest focused on the new "interior" spaces behind the Arzamas Line, land considered safe enough for potential settlement, as indicated by the lack of concern for the strength of the fortifications along the river. While the historiography has frequently depicted the independent steppe nomads beyond the border as "rebels," the state considered them potentially hostile warriors outside of Muscovite territory.[104] The goal for the defensive line was much more to contain Moscow's subjects than worry about forces well beyond the state's control.

After the last revolt in the early 1580s, the frontier relaxed. The government focused on dominating the Volga River route, and on maintaining its new defensive line to the south, but the region in between was largely left unsupervised. With the state so publicly demonstrating its commitment to key centers, opportunities were created for the population in the periphery. For the state itself, the last years of the Livonian War, followed by the succession crises in the wake of Ivan Vasil'evich's death in 1584, distracted the court. Resolving the massive debts acquired because of the war, and attempting to alleviate widely spread food shortfalls in the early 1600s, created more problems in the center that signally failed to inspire unrest on the borders of the state. Though it is impossible to know if the defensive line's existence was enough to dissuade potential revolts, certainly once it was constructed the affairs of the former khanate appeared more settled than those in the rest of the kingdom.

As the chaos of a civil war in Muscovy spread, coupled with a foreign invasion from Poland early in the seventeenth century, this frontier region proved its worth to the central heartlands. During this "Time of Troubles" (*Smutnoe vremia*) when the frontier finally became involved, it was not to fight for emancipation from the tsar but rather to restore a legitimate ruler back on the throne. Within sixty years of Muscovite conquest of Kazan, its lands and peoples emerged as a Muscovite stronghold rather than a disloyal and unproductive liability.

During the Time of Troubles, the allegiance of the region was challenged, but it never wavered. This is not to say that the loyalty was apparent to anyone in authority during the chaos. From 1584 to 1613, the throne was contested continuously. Although Fëdor Ivanovich, Ivan's second son, succeeded him, he was at best a titular figure. His death in 1598 magnified the extent of the vacuum at the top. No successors existed within the dynasty. Fëdor was succeeded by his brother-in-law, Boris Godunov, who was in turn succeeded by an imposter claiming to be Ivan's long-deceased son Dmitrii. The "false" Dmitrii's reign was short, as his Polish ties and political and religious connections exposed him as a usurper. The elites of the Kremlin then turned toward a "true" Russian, Vasilii Shuiskii, in 1606. Shuiskii's reign was short and unsuccessful, as the removal of the Polish-backed pretender only inspired the king of Poland-Lithuania to invade. He claimed the throne, even if he did not immediately assume the title of tsar. An emerging resistance move-ment in the countryside against the Poles ultimately resulted in another political shift, leading to the election of Mikhail Fedorovich Romanov to the throne in 1613. Though the war with Poland-Lithuania did not end until 1618, the Romanov dynasty endured until 1917.[105]

Throughout the Time of Troubles, the population of the former khanate pledged its loyalty to each new tsar in turn until the ascension of Vasilii Shuiskii. This was not a rejection of Shuiskii's authority so much as the region continuing to demonstrate loyalty to the false Dmitrii. For Kremlin insiders, and even residents of Moscow, Dmitrii's connection to Catholic Poland-Lithuania, and rumors of his witchcraft, were accepted as proofs of his illegitimate claim to the throne. Dmitrii's illegitimacy only reified the legitimacy of a true Rurikid successor—Vasilii Shuiskii. Assuming that this information seeped beyond the Kremlin walls, its extension as far as Kazan was hardly assured. After all, the region had been pacified only in latter years of Ivan IV's rule. Loyalty to the Rurikids would not have been great, nor would local knowledge of clan politics in the Kremlin. However, the military outposts and new towns throughout the region were led by men appointed to their positions by Dmitrii; these men were among the first people officially expelled from their offices by Shuiskii's new government. When Dmitrii's appointees led a revolt against the "usurper" in Moscow—Vasilii Shuiskii, the tsarist subjects of the Middle Volga Region joined their protest. From the perspective of the frontier, this revolt was in support of the legitimate ruler of Moscow.

Thus, following the political shift in the Kremlin from Dmitrii to Shuiskii, the frontier rebelled in the fall of 1606. The revolt of 1606/7 was more complicated that most historiographical accounts have previously allowed. It was not a revolt against Muscovite conquerors, or angry peasants rejecting increasing restrictions on their freedoms.[106] Of course, individuals with those complaints could certainly have joined in the chaos. But when examined from a frontier perspective, it was far more a fight to support the Rurikid line against usurpers than an anti-tsarist or anti-colonial revolt.

The rebels coalesced behind the leadership of the two sons of a former governor (*voevoda*) of Arzamas, as well as the recently converted Tatar *mirza*, Andrei Kazakov, from Kurmysh. As each had been displaced by Shuiskii's rise to power, the new tsar was undoubtedly the target of their anger. Violence erupted throughout the new settlements in quick succession—in Kurmysh, Arzamas, Alatyr', Iadrin, Cheboksary, and Sviiazhsk. The protest was both along the Arzamas defensive line and the new "interior" outposts along the Volga River. While the historical evidence indicates that Dmitrii was a pretender to the throne, and some contemporary critics understood this, he did appoint new officials throughout his kingdom. Once he was ousted by an uprising in Moscow, and Vasilii Shuiskii claimed the throne, the countryside responded to the overthrow of a legitimate tsar by a usurper. Additionally, even if Dmitrii's loyalists knew the truth of his false origins, losing their offices and authority provided "legitimate" grounds for anger against the new tsar.

In Moscow, however, this disloyalty was simply treason. The "rebels" in the former khanate killed several of Shuiskii's officials, including the new governor of Cheboksary. The rebel army marched on Nizhnii Novgorod in 1607, but its siege failed. As Shuiskii's family had originated from Nizhnii Novgorod, this attack was an assault on his reputation as well as a move toward the center of Muscovy. In less than a year, the combined military forces of Kazan and Nizhnii Novgorod, led by their new *voevody*, suppressed the ragtag band of "rebels," ending the final support for Dmitrii along the Volga.[107] This conflict was a tale of two perspectives. From Moscow, it was another revolt against a legitimate tsar by a contentious group of non-Russians and non-Orthodox peoples, continuously straining the weak lines of authority and continuing the revolts of the 1550s and '70s. Only the strong military presence on the frontier succeeded in maintaining tsarist control; the population in the region had been fighting for the restoration of the tsar, a commendable goal under other circumstances.

As Shuiskii and his government won this conflict, the counternarrative from the local perspective was lost. As reports of the violence in the countryside arrived back in Moscow, foreign merchants attempted to make sense of the chaos in the Middle Volga Region. For example, the Dutch merchant Isaac Massa wrote:

> The Tatars of the kingdom of Kazan were still very quiet, maintaining their neutrality, but they were waiting for a chance to throw themselves into the struggle on one side or the other. On the Volga, these towns were still most devoted to the tsar's cause: Kostroma, Yaroslavl, Uglich, Nizhny Novgorod, Samara, and Saratov, and some others, except for Astrakhan, which was in full rebellion, and the banks of the river, that were made unsafe by the depredations of the Cossacks.[108]

In Massa's view, the Muscovite outposts remained loyal, while the region struggled against the tsar. While his report was based on hearsay and largely inaccurate, it does have a core of truth in the sense that the current tsar, Vasilii Shuiskii, was facing a rebellion. The fact that the "rebels" were fighting to restore another tsar failed to make the process any more palatable.

In contrast, foreigners traveling down the Volga recorded a different narrative, closer to the idea that the local towns attempted to serve the true tsar. Who that tsar might be remained the central question. A group of Carmelite monks traveling through Muscovy in order to reach Iran on a conversion mission experienced the entire sequence of events. Having been promised safe passage by the Tsar Dmitrii, the Carmelite monks reached Kazan on 2 April 1606, where they were notified of Dmitrii's death and the ascension of Shuiskii to the throne. Held in Kazan until permission arrived from Shuiskii to permit their continuing travel, the monks encountered more problems in September in Tsaritsyn, where they were held until the spring. In Tsaritsyn, local officials sought approval of both Shuiskii and another Cossack leader claiming to be Dmitrii, allowing the monks to depart for Astrakhan.[109] The region's authorities were not in a state of rebellion, but rather faced the dilemma of lacking a clear and stable authority. At each stage, locals sought the proper authorization to allow the transit of the Carmelites. They clearly did not strive to act independent of Moscow but rather sought approval from all possible sources. This was not a region seeking to reclaim its emancipation from Muscovy but one that functioned as part of a greater Muscovite state.

Therefore, in the wake of this revolt against Shuiskii, it should have not been a surprise to discover the local population at the forefront of the new "national" army that ultimately restored to the throne to a legitimate Russian ruler. After all, it had been fighting for the restoration of the throne for a few years at that point.[110] As important as the region was in finally expelling the Poles from control over Moscow, it did little to alter the perception in the center that the frontier loomed as a potential threat. Yet, the new army could hardly have appeared any more Muscovite, to the extent that they carried a copy of Kazan's Mother of God Icon as a symbol of their commitment to resisting all foreign invaders. Contemporary accounts of this final stage of the Time of Troubles acknowledged the widespread support of the frontier for the state, drawing recruits from all ranks—Russians and non-Russians, and urban and rural residents. By 1613 the Romanovs would be ensconced on the throne, and the military force that put them there had been drawn from the recently conquered frontier.[111] From Moscow's perspective, however, this was a one-time aberration in a region with a history of resistance, rather than the second military campaign to support the tsar in less than a decade. The idea of the frontier as rebellious instead of loyal was part of the legacy inherited by the Romanovs in 1613.

Success did not arrive in the form predicted for Muscovy's empire. There were few if any conversions to Orthodoxy. The profits from Volga trade failed to immediately fill the tsar's coffers, and control over the region took the form of much more immediate expenses and investments with the construction of the defensive line and new outposts along the Volga River. The loyalty of the region's populace, however diverse and unlike Russian peasants, proved to be an asset at a time of crisis for the state. In a power vacuum, their commitment to the tsardom proved essential to Muscovite success. Whether this loyalty and support would continue under an active tsar intent on control and power was an entirely separate question.

To an extent, the lesson should have been heeded—this frontier worked best when governed least from Moscow. Left to largely its own devices, it restored a Russian tsar to the throne and assisted in the expulsion of Polish troops from the heartland. The Romanov dynasty owed a portion of its rise to the very populations it continued to suspect and observe for signs of insurrection. The multiethnic population at the edge of the empire remained at an ideological distance from the tsar, where they could contribute in valuable ways but still be considered "rebellious." The tsars believed that to control the frontier fully, it would have to be transformed, but the process was slower than they could have predicted in 1552, or even in 1613.

2

Conflicted Authorities

And on 25 March Andrei Obrastsov and his friends from Kazan arrived [in the court of] the sovereign tsar and great prince Mikhail Fedorovich of all Russias, and on 5 April Ignatei Dichkov and his friends from Kazan arrived, and [they] said that Nikanor Shulgin of Kazan, who lived in Sviiazhsk, had returned from his bailiff duties. And Andrei Obrastsov and Ignatei Dichkov did not say, or said they did not know, what things he did. And it was not written to the tsar about this matter from Kazan or from Sviiazhsk. And the *voevoda* Prince Iurii Petrovich and his *d'iaki* should interrogate the residents of Kazan [to find out] about what thing Nikanor Shulgin did on duty.

Instruction (*Nakaz*) to the new governor (*voevoda*) of Kazan,
16 April 1613

And the instructions regarding criminals—brigands and thieves and other evildoers—are the same as in Moscow. But it is forbidden to put them to death for their crimes, no matter what they may be, without reporting to the tsar and without his instructions, and no one dares to do this except in Siberia and Astrakhan and Terek, because it takes too long for messages to reach the tsar in Moscow from those regions, or for the tsar's instructions regarding various matters to arrive in response to the messages; and in those distant regions it is permitted to put to death Russians of ordinary rank, and Tatars and Chuvash and Cheremis [Maris], even without the tsar's instructions; but it is forbidden to put to death *dvoriane* and *mirzas* and princes and important and eminent men except on the tsar's instructions; and when they do put someone to death the *voevody* must write to Moscow explaining why and how that person was put to death.

G. K. Kotoshikhin,
O Rossii v tsarstvovnanie Aleksei Mikhailovicha, 1660s,
trans. Benjamin Phillip Uroff

The successive conquests of Kazan had achieved what Ivan Vasil'evich had not in 1552—a long-term Muscovite stamp on the very landscape of the countryside.[1] The construction of the Arzamas Line was a triumph of land, people, and resource management. It is an even more surprising achievement in light of Ivan's nearly endless, and expensive, Livonian War, with its consequent erosion of economic, political, and military stability. Even as the state struggled, Muscovy's advance into the frontier progressed because of the attention of officials toward the consolidation of the new provinces. With the tsar's attention elsewhere, it was their responsibility to defend the frontier, and their positions, against local revolts, nomadic incursions, and the decay of the new decrees and laws demanding taxes, tariffs, and tribute. Furthermore, the Russian Orthodox Church continued to work in the region, reinforcing Muscovite encroachments on formerly independent spaces and peoples.

Given the stresses on Muscovy in the Livonian War, the outbreak of Russia's first civil war, its "Time of Troubles," appears today as a nearly inevitable event. The majority of the people living in the Muscovite heartland possessed serious grievances against the state. When the civil war began, the former Khanate of Kazan had been pacified for only three decades, so it is not surprising that the tsar's newest subjects participated. However, the former khanate's people appear to have lacked the impetus to revolt—they were among the tsardom's loyal subjects. It was their relative freedom that put them on the side of the central authority, eventually forming part of the army that fought for the restoration of tsarist rule against the Polish invasion.

The new Romanov dynasty's transition after 1613 was relatively smooth. It swiftly overhauled the regional system of government in Muscovy. The servicemen who led Muscovite colonial policy remained in charge, but their numbers and tasks would grow exponentially as the state expanded. The chaos of the Time of Troubles taught the Romanovs and their central chancellery offices in Moscow a prime (if incorrect) lesson: greater control was necessary for better governance. As a result, the administrative orders sent into the frontier after 1613 were qualitatively different from those prevailing before the civil war.[2] Whereas the earlier governors had relatively unrestrained authority in their communities, now specific directives from the center limited their independence in an effort to improve governing practices.

The new bureaucratic apparatus at work in Kazan and in Moscow would prove more efficient over the course of the seventeenth century, primarily because it gained fluidity and adaptability. While it generally expanded, it was also adjusted several times as the government responded to a series of challenges. Among these were the Smolensk War (1632–34), the countrywide revolts of 1648–49, and the Thirteen Years' War with the Commonwealth of Poland-Lithuania (1654–67). Responding to these events, Muscovy steadily centralized political authority, attempting to remove the danger of rebellions in the countryside, and increasingly professionalized its administration, putting greater reliance upon its experienced officials.

The administrative transformation of Muscovy was hardly a unique phenomenon in the early-modern world. In this period, many states evolved from local, small polities into larger composite monarchies, and by the middle of the seventeenth century many had transformed into more "modern" and centralized forms as "fiscal-military" states, driven by the goal of fielding new, large-scale, armies.[3] Muscovy fit this model well. With its frequent conflicts during and after the Livonian War, Muscovy strove to match or exceed the strength of its European neighbors. While not apparent to foreign observers at the time, it was impossible for the tsars to manage foreign conflicts without developing features of the cameralist governments of Europe. Notably, these governments used their bureaucracies to develop a secure tax base that supported increasingly large armies. "Centralization," in other words, was a process of bureaucratic expansion as much as it increased the efficiency of the central political authorities.

At the regional level, Kazan's local leadership adjusted and responded to the demands of the central bureaucracy. As government in Moscow squabbled, expanded, and centralized, local *voevody* and *d'iaki* (governors and secretaries) strained to manage expectations enough to preserve their prerogatives, while delivering results for a demanding center. The local Russian Orthodox Church had its role in the local administration as well, which added to the tension between centralized authority and provincial officials by creating an even more complex set of relationships. An administrative system evolved gradually as a reaction to the push and pull of chancellery goals and individual agendas. The centralization of authority and individual local victories were not incompatible, but rather another way in which the state defined its own limits and established its long-term goals.

The Chancellery System

The chaos of the early seventeenth century in Muscovy was on a nearly unprecedented scale. A domestic civil war, coupled with a simultaneous foreign invasion, led to an empire in disarray—depopulated, bankrupt, and near starvation. Few regions remained stable or prosperous during the Time of Troubles. This was perhaps the most significant legacy of the reign of Ivan Vasil'evich, who achieved some success but undid most of his beneficial centralization with constant and unsuccessful campaigning against foreign and internal opponents. The new Romanov dynasty (both the new tsar Mikhail Fedorovich after 1613 and his father, Patriarch Filaret) had a dizzying array of difficulties to overcome. The war with Poland-Lithuania ended only in 1618, and Patriarch Filaret was not released from Polish custody until 1619. Mikhail Fedorovich's reign began inauspiciously.

The victorious army that reclaimed Moscow contained thousands of troops from the former khanate. It was possible, therefore, for the region to rise in prominence in the newly reforming state. However, this was not to be the case. In 1615, in fact, a short revolt broke out in the Middle Volga Region, supported by the Tatars, Chuvashes, Maris, Udmurts, and Bashkirs. In 1614 the Muscovite army, on campaign against the Crimean Tatars, passed through the region and requisitioned large quantities of food, which probably led to the revolt. The rebels seem to have been objecting to the loss of their grain, but not to the Muscovite government per se, for which they recently had demonstrated support.[4] Although this small rebellion was suppressed in 1616, the damage to the region's reputation had greater consequences.

Achieving greater control was not an easy task in the seventeenth century, no matter how intensely it was pursued. Numerous factors worked against a centralized authority attempting to extend its reach to the frontier. Both the distance between Moscow and Kazan and the time communication required remained efficiency's "first enemy."[5] The inability of the tsar's government to coordinate the actions of its chancelleries became another, and the state's elites continued to resist most tsarist claims of supreme authority. While the public in Moscow might have been impressed by the tsar's charismatic aura, his closest associates remained less intimidated.[6] The recent civil war only reinforced the intensity and frequency of political challenges. On the frontier, the problems were even greater. The ability of local governors and their staffs to administer effectively amid a diverse polyglot population remained difficult. The tense relationship between local church officials and the tsar's officers only magnified the disputes at the local level. Managing to achieve any level of agreement and obedience among these forces was an enormous, and vital, first step.

The problem began in Moscow, and had its roots in the changes to the administrative system instituted by Ivan IV. Following the conquest of the city of Kazan, one office was assigned primary responsibility over this extended frontier. Understanding the difficulty of managing a distant, "foreign," population, the tsar designated the new Stol Kazanskogo dvortsa (Desk of the Kazan Palace) as a department within the Posol'skii Prikaz (Foreign Chancellery). Thus, the state recognized that Kazan and its hinterland could not be administered as part of

Muscovy. This was a practical choice considering the limited control the tsar had until after the construction of the Arzamas Line, even if the decision to do so indicated an obvious break from the idea of victory proclaimed by the Russian Orthodox Church. Following the construction of the Arzamas fortifications, the Stol was upgraded into a chancellery of its own, as the new Prikaz Kazanskogo dvortsa (Chancellery of the Kazan Palace).[7]

Both the creation of a new chancellery and its subsequent innovations were part of the broader bureaucratization process that developed during the sixteenth and seventeenth centuries. Most Muscovite chancelleries grew enormously.[8] Muscovy created institutions like the Prikaz Kazanskogo dvortsa to address the needs of the expanding frontier, and at the same time attempted to reform existing institutions in the name of efficiency. A mix of regional and functional ministries resulted from this effort. In the late sixteenth century, one observer noted only four chancelleries: three functional bureaus, Posol'skii (Foreign Office), Razriadnyi (Military), and Pomestnyi (Service Land), and the regional Kazanskii dvorets.[9] Later visitors to Moscow numbered the *prikazy* at thirty-three in 1647 and forty-two by 1667.[10] Historians of the chancellery system count between sixty to seventy *prikazy* during most of the seventeenth century.[11] Some *prikazy* were periodically eliminated and reactivated: the Monastyrskii Prikaz (Monastic Lands) came and went with successive administrations. One of the reasons for the periodic expansion and contraction of the number of chancelleries was that bureaucratic growth was reactive. Their responsibilities were frequently redefined or eliminated. Therefore, while the Prikaz Kazanskogo dvorsta had only a very few competitors for its limited, regional, jurisdiction in the sixteenth century, it shared responsibilities with several chancelleries throughout the seventeenth century. This was intentional—the bureaucratic growth corresponded to a "divide and conquer" principle in terms of the dynasty's relationship with the boiars and other elites. In the seventeenth century, with the chancelleries attempting to seize influence and authority from each other, the tsar's authority was maximized. In a frontier region at a distance from Moscow, however, the competition at the center left local officials with greater autonomy, as their links to the levers of political power at the center became increasingly ill defined.

The Muscovite system of chancelleries was by no means efficient, as functional and geographic responsibilities were not clearly divided. The Prikaz Kazanskogo dvorsta lacked the exclusive right to supervise all of the newly founded outposts and settlements in the former khanate. The westernmost portion of the territory remained under the control of the Novgorodskaia chetvert' (Novgorod Quarter), an office similar to the Prikaz with all-encompassing responsibilities over its district, including management of the *voevody*, tax collection, monitoring of military service, and trade regulation. Most of the territory of the Novgorodskaia chetvert' contained well-established cities and towns but spread widely across northern Muscovy, including Novgorod, Pskov, Arkhangel'sk, Perm, and Nizhnii Novgorod. To an already diffuse array of towns, Arzamas was added in 1578. As a result, the pivotal Arzamas Line, essential for control over the land and people of the khanate, was regulated by a pair of competing chancelleries. It is impossible to know whether this was an intentional decision by the tsar, designed to impede the bureaucratic momentum of his chancelleries, or an accidental result of geography, but the end result was the same. There would not be a single institution with the authority to manage the frontier, and thus, local interests had an opportunity to set the two against each other.

Money, and who would collect and spend it, was as great a source of administrative friction as the division of responsibility for the territory. This negatively affected the pace of economic development the region. The two central concerns of the Prikaz Kazanskogo dvortsa and its *voevody* were trade regulation and tax collection. The Prikaz instructed its governors to patrol and garrison trade routes, build a storage infrastructure, and monitor all traffic with customs officials to enforce tolls. Foreign merchants, however, traveling in and out of the region, lay outside its authority; the Posol'skii Prikaz held that power. As the seventeenth century progressed, and the state desired greater economic development in the region, more chancelleries, not fewer, became involved; sometimes unlikely agencies held significant authority. In 1645, for example, the Prikaz Kazanskogo dvortsa sent a reminder to the Aptekarskii Prikaz (Pharmaceutical Chancellery) concerning the recent activities of Elizarii Rolant, a non-Russian, who was selling medicine to the Kalmyks. He was under the jurisdiction of the Prikaz Kazanskogo dvortsa, so these two chancelleries were forced to coordinate their regulation of Rolant's activities.[12] Even a single individual's trade could require regulations by multiple chancelleries. The Prikaz Kazanskogo dvortsa was often the dominant voice but became one among a chorus as the bureaucratization of the state expanded.

It is difficult to imagine that anyone in the central government, from the tsar to his lowest scribe, was unaware of the conflicting lines of authority among the chancelleries. It was also difficult to assess the effect of any one change on the system's efficiency (measured in revenue, to take one example). Indeed, the continual attempts to rectify and improve centralization and impose more logical divisions of authority often proved counterproductive; frequent changes meant that the chancelleries lost track of their own responsibilities or shirked them. For example, in 1660, the Prikaz Kazanskogo dvortsa received a dispatch reminding it to adjudicate disputes between individuals in the region. It had apparently passed too many judicial cases to other central chancelleries.[13] It may seem a commonplace, therefore, to surmise that even simplifying the process of bureaucratization was often needlessly complex. It also could be simultaneously as detrimental to centralization as it could be beneficial.

While the Muscovite government at the end of the seventeenth century was dramatically larger than in the late sixteenth century, whether it had improved its ability to govern its frontier is debatable. State efforts to rectify deficiencies made slow progress. The Prikaz Kazanskogo dvortsa both gained and lost specific powers over time, modifying its position as the primary authority over the frontier, but it never secured sole authority over the administration of its territory. Specifically, it never lost its power to appoint the *voevody*, but it always needed to maneuver such that they enforced its decisions rather than those of other chancelleries. Local officials in the region, even if they saw contradictory instructions as problematic, and even if they wished to avoid politics, had to accept demands from multiple institutions, limiting the impact of any central decisions (or potential reforms) on the frontier.

Local communities throughout the empire replicated the confusion in Moscow. Though the *voevody* were appointed by the central chancelleries, they shared power de facto with a wide array of individuals in the towns and outposts. *D'iaki* were trained officials who filed reports on current events with the Prikaz and were also responsible for the *voevody*'s daily correspondence. Both the *voevody* and *d'iaki* resided in the individual towns, working from the *prikaznaia izba* (chancellery office) in larger towns, or a *prikaznyi stol* (chancellery desk) in smaller ones. Carrying out the directives of the *voevody* and *d'iaki*, or serving in local court systems were various ranks of bailiffs, with individual titles usually linked to terms of service, such as *nedelshik* (week-officer). In general, the numbers of bailiffs serving at any one time varied by need, from only two or three to as many as fifteen, as was the case in Kazan during 1622/23.[14] Bailiffs appear to have been vocal in their discontent with their length of service or the town in which they served, more so than other officials in the frontier. For example, the Prikaz granted the bailiff Nedai Salamykov's request to leave service in Kokshaisk on 22 May 1585, but instructed him to remain one full year before leaving.[15] In that same year, Fëdor Gurev and Istomka Khvostov, both residents of Kazan, received instructions to extend their service for another six months as they had in the previous year.[16]

The *voevody* played the essential role of coordinators in the Prikaz Kazanskogo dvortsa's efforts to manage the territory under its control. Though uncommon in Muscovy, the Prikaz instructed its *voevody* while in their post, at times in detail. It issued a *nakaz* (instruction) to a particular *voevoda*, defining his responsibilities.

The *nakaz* began as an agenda for embassies, defining their specific goals. However, the Prikaz Kazanskogo dvortsa, with its origins as a desk in the Posol'skii Prikaz, adopted this, an established tool. The *nakaz* revolutionized the supervision of local officials by offering detailed guidelines for their behavior and authority. It was very common for a *nakaz* to be supplemented later by a series of individual responses to specific issues, generally called *gramoty* (charters). Each *voevoda* was expected to compile all of the information arriving from Moscow as a body of legislation to guide future actions.

A *nakaz* could be exhaustive, depending on the size of a town or its strategic importance. The instructions to Kazan numbered some pages, but many of the smaller outposts warranted a mere paragraph or short page noting a general principle, rather than specific tasks in pursuit of a defined goal.[17] As detailed as they are, the *nakazy* issued to the *voevody* of Kazan were the most important set of instructions issued by the Prikaz Kazanskogo dvortsa during the seventeenth century. But like most other contemporary documentation for the region, they are rare, particularly before the end of the seventeenth century. Only four *nakazy* remain from the pre-Petrine era (from 16 April 1613, 16 May 1649, 22 March 1677, 21 July 1686), copied into a chancellery file early in the eighteenth century.[18] Even though the sample is small, an examination of these *nakazy* reveals the outline of governance and the responsibilities of the *voevody*, as well as demonstrating the standardization of the Muscovite bureaucracy. Extrapolating from these *nakazy*, it appears clear that bureaucratization was not limited to the growth of the chancellery system, but included detailed correspondence between Moscow and its periphery.

The extant *nakazy* addressed the common problems facing the *voevody* in his term in office: security issues, tax collection and trade regulation, and justice. Over the seventeenth century the complexity of each *nakaz* increased, attempting to regulate the authority of the *voevody* more closely. For example, the *nakaz* of 1613 to Kazan's *voevoda* comprised seven clauses, that of 1649 contained twenty-six, and both 1677 and 1686 had thirty-three.[19] This reflected an improved awareness of the difficulties of frontier governance; most of the new articles specifically addressed solutions to recent problems.

The opening clauses of each *nakaz* addressed specific problems of the Muscovite governance. The first directed the incoming *voevoda* and *d'iaki* to claim the keys to the city from the previous officials, and for all residents of all ranks in the region to respect the authority of the new officials. Usually this was followed by one reminding the *voevoda* that he owed his personal loyalty to the tsar first and then to the Prikaz Kazanskogo dvortsa.[20] These were necessary because it was not impossible for a *voevoda* to ignore the arrival of his replacement. This was the case on 28 May 1600, when the Prikaz instructed Kazan's *Voevoda* Merkur'e Aleksandrovich

Shcherbatov and *d'iak* Aleksei Shapilov to turn over the key to the city to the new *Voevoda* Toma Onuchin and his *d'iak* Ivashka Gliadkov. This was, in fact, the second notice. The Prikaz threatened Shcherbatov with imprisonment if he disobeyed the order, along with any resident of Kazan who listened to him.[21] The article reminding the *voevoda* of his loyalty to the Prikaz Kazanskogo dvortsa was a necessity considering the ongoing conflict and competing interests among the Muscovite chancelleries. After the promulgation of the *Ulozhenie* (Law Code) of 1649, subsequent *nakazy* instructed the *voevody* they were responsible for following its clauses, as well as all previous *nakazy* and *gramoty* sent to Kazan.[22]

The security clauses addressed two major issues: internal threats of rebellion and external threats from nomads. During the seventeenth century, the potential for domestic rebellion received greater attention. Two of the seven articles in the *nakaz* to the first *voevoda* of Kazan appointed by Tsar Mikhail Fedorovich in 1613 demanded careful control of the local community:

> And the *voevoda*, Prince Iurii Ushatii, and the *d'iaki*, Fëdor and Stepan, should observe intently the city and district of Kazan, that all Russians, princes, *mirzas*, Tatars, Votiaks [Udmurts], Bashkirs, Chuvashes, and Cheremisses [Maris] are not causing instability or trouble. And if there are Russians, Tatars, Votiaks, Bashkirs, Chuvashes, and Cheremisses who think about instability or trouble, the *voevoda*, Prince Iurii Petrovich Ushatii, and the *d'iaki* of those Russians and Tatars are ordered to investigate and bring them to court, and then severely interrogate and search them to find out who was causing the trouble. After the investigation, if they [*voevoda* and *d'iaki*] cannot control these events, they should write to the sovereign in Moscow.[23]

The *voevoda* was also to monitor all population movements in the region, in conjunction with the other *voevody* of the lower Volga towns, paying special attention to the Nogai and Crimean Tatars.[24] Despite the recent support of the region for the restoration of the tsar, the tsar approached the local population as if they were merely awaiting an opportunity to expel the government. Additionally, though much of the instruction was in the form of general principles for the future, it could contain remarkably narrow requests. In 1613, the final clause fits this description, as the Prikaz instructed the new *voevoda* to locate Nikanor Shulgin who had returned from police work in Sviiazhsk to Kazan on 25 March. Visitors returning to Moscow from Kazan had reported the presence of Shulgin; the Prikaz was concerned about what he was doing once he had abandoned his duty.[25]

Although the region enjoyed calm between 1617 and 1670, the tsar approached the local population as if they were merely awaiting an opportunity to expel the government. The emphasis on internal security, however, might have reflected

Muscovy's relative instability throughout most of the seventeenth century rather than problems on its frontier. The state attempted to prevent further unrest through detailed instructions followed by close supervision of the *voevody* by the Prikaz. The next extant *nakaz* to the *voevody* of Kazan, that of 1649, reflected a growing reliance on detailed administrative procedures to control the frontier populace. This increasingly complex and sophisticated approach may have been Moscow's practical response to the numerous rebellions in 1648, which engulfed Moscow, Kursk, and Tomsk as well as other cities.[26] The Prikaz Kazanskogo dvortsa was responsible for suppressing the rebellion in Astrakhan in 1648, and also maintained close connections with Sibirskii Prikaz, which administered Tomsk.[27] As a warning of the continuing danger of rebellions, the events of 1648 provided a forceful message to the Prikaz about potential unrest.

As a result, the number and length of security clauses increased in the *nakaz* for 1649. It repeated the earlier instructions to monitor the populace and provided instructions for responding to attacks from nomadic raiders. However, instructions now focused solely on Tatars, Chuvashes, Maris, and Udmurts, omitting Russians from the categories of the suspect.[28] The *voevoda* was now to take hostages from the families of Tatars, Chuvashes, Maris, and Udmurts to ensure their loyalty, investigate all of the local non-Russian villages, and forbid the sale of military commodities (such as muskets, swords, or helmets) in certain districts, especially those that contained Maris, Udmurts, or Chuvashes.[29] Also, the Prikaz instructed the *voevoda* to regulate the horse trade, monitoring all purchases as well as forbidding any sales to Nogai Tatars or Bashkirs.[30] It added a further check on the populace by requiring the *voevoda* to monitor Russians and all non-Russians arriving or leaving Kazan. If runaway peasants were discovered entering the region, they were to be returned to the estates of their proper landlords.[31]

The *nakaz* of 1649 also included several new articles on military preparedness. The earlier decree had mandated that the *voevoda* of Kazan remain in contact with the region's other *voevody* to protect against nomads. The 1649 instructions added a specific list of actions the *voevoda* should take to defend Kazan, focusing on keeping the Volga navigable, as it was the main communications artery for the region.[32] Three separate articles regulated the military service of the region's *pomeshchiki* (elite military servitors). All people arriving in the city owing military service were required to report to the *sotnik* (lieutenant) of Kazan's *strel'tsy* (musketmen). The Prikaz Kazanskogo dvortsa also delineated which servitors served the *voevoda* and which served the *sotnik*, suggesting that these regional officials had previous jurisdictional conflicts. An additional clause instructed the *voevoda* to examine all non-Russian *pomeshchiki*, verifying their origins and the location of their current *pomest'ia* (land grant). Anyone who claimed they had been recruited but whose origins could not be verified should be turned away.[33]

The Prikaz Kazanskogo dvortsa also instructed the *voevody* on the subject of disasters, particularly the danger of fire, an almost universal experience for Muscovite officialdom. Kazan's buildings, including most town walls, were constructed of wood. A massive fire in early 1649 in Kazan necessitated new, detailed instructions to prevent the destruction of documents, wealth, and religious artifacts. The *nakaz* from later that year instructed the *voevoda* to keep water at all of the city's churches, which remained centrally located in town.[34] Some problems were far more than the chancellery or the *voevody* could manage. Flooding remained a recurrent regional problem, but no one ever proposed a solution, other than suggesting the removal of buildings and residents from frequently flooded areas.[35]

Following security, economic regulation was the most pressing concern of the local *voevody*. By the end of the seventeenth century, the number of clauses concerning trade in the *nakazy* was vast, and their specificity indicates both the growing importance of the Volga trade route, and the state's increasing command over it.[36] In the *nakaz* of 1613, taxes comprised one clause, but by 1649 the number of articles concerned with financial matters had increased to nine. Tax instructions were broken down by rank, with separate articles on the *iasachnye liudi* (non-Russian tribute payers), Muslims, and all other military servitors. Trade regulation was divided into distinct types of activity, with one article regulating the movement of traders on the Volga, one for regulating horse trade, one about the *gosti* (highest rank of Russian merchant), and, in the longest article of the entire *nakaz*, one assessing the fish market, tabulating recent returns from taxes gathered from fish sales.[37] The *nakazy* also demanded controls on bootlegged liquor to eliminate smuggling and tax dodging, especially among the region's non-Russian populations.[38]

When compared to the specific instructions addressing security, tax collection, and trade regulation, the number of articles in the *nakazy* concerning judicial prerogatives is small. The *nakaz* of 1613 had only one clause, which informed the *voevoda* that he had the right to dispense justice to all people in Kazan region and to collect the appropriate fees from his judgments.[39] During the seventeenth century, this wide latitude decreased, as the central chancelleries progressively claimed greater legal authority in the countryside. Some of the powers claimed by the central chancellery were simply too important to rest in the provinces, such as the *voevody*'s pre-1649 power to settle boundary disputes.[40] Along with stripping the *voevody* of this power, in 1649 the Prikaz added specific details about the types of judicial matters that should be reported in Moscow, even if they were settled locally. For example, debt slavery, a local matter, need not be reported. If someone claimed the tsar's (fallow) land for his own, however, the *voevoda* was required to report the individual to the Prikaz, and collect the appropriate taxes and service due for that land.[41] As the *voevody*'s power to adjudicate was transferred to Moscow, longer delays for judgments became more common.

One reason why judicial powers may have received less attention in the *nakazy* was the nature of the Muscovite judicial system. Neither the central government nor the *voevody* regularly investigated and prosecuted crimes. Instead, individuals petitioned the government for justice. The expanding bureaucracy of the seventeenth century was dependent upon local participation in the legal system in order to extend its authority into the countryside, especially on the frontier. Residents of the countryside frequently contacted their local government officials for justice, but it took years to establish a consistent role for them, and longer for the state to centralize the process.[42]

It appears clear that the central chancelleries were increasingly inclined to regulate the parameters of the *voevody*'s activities in the countryside during the seventeenth century. While expansion of the bureaucracy may be seen as a halting reform process intended to address specific problems of inefficiency within the Muscovite government, directions from Moscow gradually intruded into the power of the local *voevody* and could not help but affect the efficiency of the government at the local level. At the same time, and despite the apparent loss of authority suffered on paper by the *voevody* between 1613 and 1649, a vastly increased set of instructions did not necessarily result in decreased independence for regional officials. Distance and poor communications continued to attenuate the state's central control, and the exercise of power continued to be a melding of regulations by the central chancelleries expressed locally by the *voevody*.

The increased specificity of the instructions suggests two possible interpretations. The first is that increased experience and information led to sophisticated directions about the most useful and important tasks for the *voevody*. Judging by the qualitative improvement in the presentation of the *nakazy*, this was the case. The second, however, is that the *nakazy* became more specific and detailed because of the failure of the *voevody* to implement desirable policies. The Prikaz, of course, lacked daily or even monthly reports on the activities of the *voevody*. The provincial administrators remained largely independent, and the *nakazy*'s increasing restrictions could even have been the result of a lack of initiative. This was as likely a cause of the numerical rise of individual instructions. Most likely a combination of both of these pressures occurred—governance did become both better informed with experience but remained highly dependent on individual *voevody* for enforcement. Local discretion was as large a factor in the actual implementation of policy as was the Prikaz in Moscow.

Furthermore, the *nakazy* marked a general turn toward a cameralist style of government that increasingly focused on control over population rather than the land itself.[43] The topics of concern in the *nakazy* all reflect this trend. Security issues arose from the danger of revolt; tax and tariff collection required monitoring the population. When the chancellery instructed the *voevody* to register all people entering the region, it enabled these policies and generally furthered the state's aspiration for hegemonic control over a diverse population.[44] The effectiveness of these policies could certainly be challenged. Cameralist governments aimed as high a quality of implementation as they could but, often to achieve any result, the quantity of interference in local affairs outweighed it.

The frontier's influence on cameralist development appears even more clear when comparing the policies implemented in Kazan to the other regions of the expanding empire. The number of security provisions in general, and surveillance policies in particular, implemented for Kazan increased over the course of the seventeenth century. At the same time, the region was far more placid than those Muscovite outposts beyond the security of the defensive line. The governor of Ufa continuously struggled with violence perpetuated by the Bashkirs on both the town and its nearby monasteries.[45] In Siberia, Tobol'sk had been established as a Muscovite administrative center, but faced danger from both the indigenous populations and local Cossacks on a frequent basis.[46] The Volga itself, particularly south of Saratov, remained in danger from nomadic raids. The pacification of the Nogais in the first half of the seventeenth century only created a new danger in the form of the Kalmyks.[47] Yet the decades of peace in the former khanate did little to reassure tsarist authorities that the local population was not merely waiting for an opportunity to revolt. The increased security policies might have been unnecessary, but the lack of opposition to the security policies was either proof of their effectiveness or of the region's pacification. In either case, greater surveillance of the local population prevented the possibility of a greater uprising in cooperation with the nearby nomads.

The traditions of the Muscovite political system continued to impede the central government's cameralist impulses. At the center of Muscovite politics lay the split authority between church and state. If anything, the Russian Orthodox Church, both inside the Kremlin and outside in the provinces, consistently challenged the agenda of the Prikaz and its officials. At the beginning of the seventeenth century, with Tsar Mikhail Fedorovich and his father holding offices simultaneously, the two institutions cooperated extremely closely. However, this was far from a lasting state of affairs. The conflicts had been obvious in the initial conquests of Kazan, where the Church's narrative of glorious triumph and conversion contrasted with the persistence of Islam and ongoing military resistance. By the seventeenth century, the patriarch of Moscow had his own "chancellery" office, with its own secretariat.[48] This meant another Muscovite office with its own officials with competing directives and interests, which might clash with the Prikaz Kazanskogo dvortsa. Locally, the Church's appointed leader in the region—the metropolitan of Kazan, who sat third in the Church hierarchy beneath the patriarch—had a more immediate connection to the top level of Muscovite society than a *voevoda* could claim. Conflicts between the patriarch's office and the Prikaz Kazanskogo dvortsa would assuredly create trouble for the local administration in Kazan.

In the end, the general trends of the administration are easy to discern but difficult to interpret. There was clearly an expansion of the bureaucracy in size and scope, but the results of this growth were not obvious. Certainly, state officials in the center dedicated themselves to the regularization of authority, information gathering, and record keeping, as the *nakazy* indicate. Moscow needed and expected more responsiveness from the local governors in the countryside. Local governors could attempt to use the conflicted authority in the center to forge a path to independence and relative freedom, but during the seventeenth century this "freedom" was progressively restricted as the Prikaz enumerated the specific powers of the local officials, limiting their ability to act independently. Adding to this tension was the Russian Orthodox Church itself, but without any defined role in the governing structure, its ability to influence events was unclear at best. In other words, the growth of the bureaucracy could hardly be considered a "centralizing" process. As all sides sought information and authority to make decisions, provide direction, and benefit from tax collection, the working system that coalesced among them was not immediately regularized or efficient from the point of view of the tsar, who was increasingly removed from direct control over the government or the periphery. It was not tsarist authority as much as a commitment to the state that held the system together, ultimately.

Local Administrators

The Muscovite state placed the chancelleries between the court and the local representatives of the tsar—the *voevody* and *d'iaki*. These men, as emphasized in the *nakazy*, acted within a gradually shrinking sphere of independent authority. At the top of the local administration, the *voevody* oversaw a staff of bureaucrats to enact daily policies: tax administration, grain requisition, judicial enforcement, military actions, and general surveillance of the population.[49] This staff generally remained small. Underneath them, however, was a larger, and important, professional bureaucratic corps, which carried out the decisions promulgated from Moscow and the local *voevoda*. These secretaries and bailiffs comprised a more experienced but non-elite group, which generally had the professional skills necessary for overseeing trade and the population. This does not imply that they were a disinterested, bureaucratic class acting on behalf of the state. Their self interest was both obvious and expected, and indeed, the growth in size and specificity of the *nakazy* indicates that in fact the Prikaz Kazanskogo dvortsa attempted to regulate local government by decree in response to the growth of local power holders. In this way, authority at the local level gradually came to flow through formal, regularized channels.

Hierarchy determined the structure of local government in Muscovy, driven by its preexisting system of social precedence. For the men who filled administrative posts, this system predetermined many of their career paths. Known as *mestnichestvo*, it precluded the possibility of serving under someone of lesser status. It could happen that the tsar or his government might put someone of inferior status into a ranking post, but that created the possibility of the person "wronged" suing for correction of the situation. It is impossible to be precise in a description of the *mestnichestvo* system, as the official records were destroyed when the system was finally abandoned in the 1670s. Historians have spent a considerable time accurately reconstructing its outline, however. Three family lines were elevated above all else: the ruling families of the Muscovite Rurikids, Poland-Lithuanian Gediminids, and Mongol Chingissids. Connections with these families provided high status; few or no connections to those families left one without precedence or rank. Of course, all military servitors still had "elite" status in Muscovite society, but social rank guided command positions in the army and high office holders, just to name two of the many influential positions at the apex of the pyramid of ranks.[50]

To prevent any disruptions to the system, men from the top rank in society assumed the top posts—as *voevody*—while men of lesser status served beneath them as *d'iaki*. As the top office in the region, it was common for the *voevoda* of Kazan to be chosen from the Duma's ranks, the most elite men of the Muscovite social hierarchy. Ranks in the Duma were characterized by four titles (in descending importance)—boiar, *okol'nichii, dumnyi dvorianin*, and *dumnyi d'iak*. The top three positions were hereditary servitors, with obligations to the tsar based on parentage, carrying the ability to hold military-service land and supervise peasant (later serf) labor. The last position (*dumnyi d'iak)* was a "contract servitor," a political appointment lacking the right to possess military-service land or serfs. Most of these were drawn from the sons of the *d'iaki*, which created an opportunity for a meritorious rise to the upper ranks of society, though of course the position was accorded lesser status. Below the Duma ranks, however, there were further categories of hereditary servitors—including *stol'nik* and *striapchii*—any of whom would outrank a regular, appointed (regular) *d'iak* in government service or in society at large.[51]

Appointments, therefore, had as much to do with familial and individual prestige as qualifications, particularly among the *voevody* expected to administer the frontier.

The tsar's local officials existed in parallel with the political structure at the center of the state. In fact, the *voevody* frequently were members of the same boiar families leading the chancelleries. Younger brothers of members of the boiar council were commonly placed into positions of authority as *voevody*. The men on their staffs, both *d'iaki* and bailiffs, were selected from the lower ranks of the service elites or even from local townsmen. Despite the close relations between chancellery officials and regional governors, the Prikaz Kazanskogo dvortsa monitored the actions of its regional officials as much as possible, and tended to keep *voevody's* terms in office short to limit their influence and prevent them from developing local power bases.

Thus, despite the distance between the tsar's newest possessions and Moscow, and the difficulty of travel between the two, local officials lacked long tenures in office, particularly in the region's most important cities, where the appointment imparted greater political prestige.[52] The more important the post, the more important member of the elite assigned to it, and therefore the greater the potential for insurrection. Undoubtedly, the leadership of the local *voevody* in the rebellions during the Time of Troubles instilled the fear of their revolt.[53] In Kazan, as the most politically and economically important city of the region, one- to three-year terms were standard.[54] Its *voevoda* was in most cases a boiar. Several of these boiars were concurrently members of the tsar's Boiar Duma as well; this included S. V. Golovin in 1625/26, Prince A. Iu. Sitskii in 1627/28–1629/30, G. I. Morozov and Prince N. I. Odoevskii in 1651/52, and Prince G. S. Kurakin in 1664/65.[55] Furthermore, even when the *voevoda* was not a current member of the Boiar Duma, a family member might be. This certainly was the case for the Golitsyn family, who provided four *voevody* from their family during the seventeenth century.[56]

Taking into account the workings of the *mestnichestvo* system, the high status of Kazan's leaders indicates its *voevody* were region's dominant political force. Only Alatyr', which occupied a prominent position as part of the Arzamas Line, had a current member of the Duma ranks assigned as its *voevoda* before 1670.[57] Men holding inferior Duma rank appeared in the region as *okol'nichie*, able to supervise other members of the regional bureaucracy but not to threaten the superiority of the boiars. Before 1670 they appeared only in Alatyr', Saransk, and Simbirsk, which was a sign of the relative importance of those outposts.[58] Few other outposts in the region merited leaders of even this rank. Without question, Kazan dominated the local political map.

In the small towns and outposts, officials typically served a longer term in office because of its lack of influence or desirability. Arsk, Laishev, and Tetiushii eventually lost their own *voevody* by 1651, and Atemar did in 1653, as each fell under the authority of nearby, more prominent (or at least strategically positioned) towns. Several signs point to their diminished size and status. It was not uncommon for local gentry to serve as the political leadership; townsmen from Alatyr' and Kazan held the post in Arsk, townsmen from Sviiazhsk and Kazan served in Laishev, and townsmen from Atemar held office in Tetiushii. Occasionally, they held office for shorter two- and three-year terms, but often for terms as long as twelve or fourteen years, impossible in truly important posts. For Kerensk, Avtamon Semenov syn Bezobrazov served as *voevoda* from the foundation of the city in 1658 until 14 December 1671, when he was removed in office for having failed to respond effectively to local uprisings. His replacement, Dmitrii Kharlamov syn Soimonov, remained in the office of *voevoda* until 1681, but after that year two- to three-year terms became standard.[59] Nor was Kerensk unusual. For example, Arsk, Laishev, and Atemar had remarkably long-term *voevody* during the Time of Troubles: Andrei Aleksandrov syn Nagovo in Arsk (1602–14), Andrei Vasil'ev syn Levashov in Laishev (1601–14), and Danil Ziushin in Tetiushii (1602–14). In that same time period, Kazan had five different *voevody*. While these are some of the longest terms in office on record, the 1630s and 1640s also witnessed long tenures in those cities.

Table 3 provides a clear indication of the prominence of the new towns. Kazan and Arzamas averaged the shortest lengths in office, followed by Sviiazhsk. Kazan and Sviiazhsk were the oldest centers of Muscovite administration in the region, and Arzamas was the stronghold of the first defensive line. Cheboksary, Iadrin, Kerensk, and Tsivil'sk sat either on the Volga or at nearby river crossings. The remainder occupied less strategically important positions, many of which were north of the Volga River, far away from the still dangerous southern frontier. The exception here is quite clearly Penza. However, before the revolt of 1670, Penza only had one *voevoda* for ten years, more typical for a new outpost.[60] The system as a whole was more important to the central authorities than it was useful for local officials. One danger of assigning the shortest terms for the most important sites remained that those *voevody* were the least familiar with the local communities and their issues; certainly the intention was that he would lack the independence to act without direction from Moscow. This history of the *voevody*-led rebellion against Moscow during the Time of Troubles remains the probable cause for this situation.[61]

Table 3 Terms in office of the *voevody*

Town	Voevoda's office active	Number of voevody appointed	Average term in office (in years)
Arzamas	1612–1698	47	1.8
Kazan	1553–1699	72	2.1
Penza	1663–1697	14	2.4
Sviiazhsk	1551–1697	53	2.8
Alatyr'	1602–1682	26	3.1
Simbirsk	1649–1695	15	3.1
Saransk	1651–1691	13	3.2
Atemar	1644–1653	3	3.3
Urzhum	1602–1648	14	3.3
Iadrin	1602–1683	24	3.4
Samara	1602–1698	28	3.5
Tsivil'sk	1601–1697	28	3.5
Cheboksary	1552–1694	38	3.7
Laishev	1575–1651	19	4.1
Tetiushii	1571–1651	20	4.1
Tsarevokokshaisk	1601–1695	23	4.1
Insar	1651–1693	10	4.3
Koz'modem'iansk	1583–1700	28	4.5
Kokshaisk	1574–1681	23	4.7
Temnikov	1614–1693	17	4.7
Arsk	1576–1651	14	5.4
Kerensk	1651–1680	4	7.5

Source: Data drawn from Korsakov, "Spisok nachal'stuiushchikh lits"; and Barsukov, *Spiski gorodovykh voevod*.

Note: It is possible that officials could have been appointed and served without being recorded in the extant documents.

Additionally, governing via the *mestnichestvo* system also supported short terms for prominent posts. These positions were granted based on status gained by birth as much as by experience. Short terms had the benefit of minimizing the damage possible from incompetent supervision. However, this system did not preclude competent men of elite status from gaining prominence through their service. One example is that of Prince Ivan Andreev syn Khilkov, who entered the ranks as a *stol'nik* in 1627, rose to the status of an *okol'nichii* by 1649, serving at that rank in Kazan two years later. In 1655 he was elevated again to the rank of boiar, eventually holding the post of *voevoda* in Astrakhan (in 1667/68) and later in Pskov (in 1673/74).[62] With such a long period of service, and the experience of holding a regional administrator's office, it is likely that even if Khilkov had been unfamiliar with the particular problems in Astrakhan, he could have drawn upon his time in Kazan to make more informed decisions. Still, he would have relied upon the collected wisdom and surveillance of previous office holders and the Muscovite chancelleries to guide his decisions, as would have most administrators. Talented *voevody* were desirable, but the administrative system provided some protection from periods of less capable leadership.

As a result, with the potential of incompetent *voevody*, their staff, comprised of both *d'iaki* and the even lower-status bailiffs, became increasingly important. As the *voevody* rotated, most of the *d'iaki* remained behind. Whereas a *voevoda* might not be literate (and incapable of reading Moscow's directives), literacy was a requirement for the men who would serve as *d'iaki*. Therefore, the danger that new *voevody* lacked experience and ability was ameliorated by the *d'iaki*, who became the professionals who enabled the work of the government to succeed. Of course, there was the potential that this solution replaced one problem with another. *Voevody* arriving in a new position would run the risk of irrelevancy or, worse, a bureaucracy hostile to new policies.

In either case, it is impossible to understand the local government without accounting for the *d'iaki*. As a group, they were vital to any effective administration, but information on the men who served in these positions is significantly rarer than for their superiors. Some conclusions regarding the characteristics of the *d'iaki* serving in the former khanate may be drawn from a list of 331 mentioned in published sources between 1552 and 1671.[63] It was unusual for the *d'iaki* to serve in more than one town in the region—only 32 of 331 did so (9.6 percent). However, over the course of their careers, approximately half of *d'iaki* also served in town or city outside of the former khanate (167, or 50.4 percent). This suggests that regional office work was preparation for similar postings, but there was no particular position carrying the stamp of a "frontier" post. This policy seems to have stemmed from the same rationale for the short terms of office *voevody* enjoyed. In both cases, local officials were prevented from forming long attachments to one community. Of course, supervising a larger non-Russian population with Russian officials also reinforced a divide between the administrators and the local community. While hardly certain, it appears as if non-Russians had nearly no access to employment as a *d'iak*. Only one man, Dzhan Murzin (possibly Janibeg *Mirza*), who served as *d'iak* in Kazan in 1576/77, was likely a Tatar, and no other obvious non-Russian candidates appear on the list.[64]

The *d'iaki* did serve generally longer terms in office than the *voevody*. For example, Aleksei Shapilov, *d'iak* of Kazan at the end of the sixteenth century, was in office between 1596 and 1602, outlasting four *voevody* in that same period, and

A. D. Unkovskii served for three *voevody* in Saratov between 1666 and 1670.[65] Central authorities may have appreciated the benefits of institutional memory on the frontier, or they simply disregarded individual *d'iaki* as potential threats to stability. In the cases in which the length of service can be identified, approximately four years is the average, with frequent longer postings. This included N. M. Shul'gin posted for six years in Kazan followed by a year in Sviiazhsk, F. Starogorodskii's seven years in Tsivilsk, D. Petrov's four years in Arzamas and another three in Temnikov; and S. K. Matchin's five or six years in Cheboksary.[66]

The Moscow chancelleries relied on the experience of these regional *d'iaki*, bringing them into the central bureaucracy: more than half served in a Moscow chancellery (189 or 57.1 percent). However, it appears that experienced *d'iaki* from the former khanate rarely moved into their "home" chancellery: only 39 of 331 (11.8 percent) served in the Prikaz Kazanskogo dvortsa. The Prikaz rarely relied on the skills of the provincial administrators to assist with their decisions. Yet other chancelleries drew more extensively upon the administrative "skills" of *d'iaki* who served in the Volga Region: 28 of 331 (8.4 percent) served in Pomestnyi Prikaz (Service Land) and 26 (7.8 percent) of 331 in the Razriadnyi Prikaz (Military), suggesting military experience of the frontier could assist the central authorities; 24 of 331 (7.3 percent) served in the Bol'shoi Prikaz (Treasury), potentially bringing their experience in regulating trade and tax collection, and another 28 (8.4 percent) served in one of the many Muscovite judicial offices. Although it was more common for a *d'iak* to work in the Prikaz Kazanskogo dvortsa than another Moscow office after service on the Volga, there does not seem to be any particular type of "frontier" *d'iak*. An even smaller number served in "related" offices to the Prikaz Kazanskogo dvortsa, including the older and more prestigious Posol'skii Prikaz (2.2 percent), from whence the Prikaz emerged, or the Sibirskii Prikaz (2.2 percent), which was split from it in 1639. It was possible that some of the *d'iaki* appointed to posts in the countryside lacked sufficient importance to move up the career ladder into a Moscow post. However, it also was possible that experienced bureaucrats were in sufficiently short supply that administrative expertise was as important a criteria for a position in Moscow as "direct" experience on the frontier might have been.

This tentative conclusion is supported by further evidence from the data. Among *d'iaki* who held posts in Moscow, specialization became a hallmark of their service. There are an additional 139 men who served as *d'iaki* in the Prikaz Kazanskogo dvortsa but not in any position in the region. Of this combined sample of 470 men (331 regional plus 139 more from Moscow), 207 of them have documented service in more than one office in Moscow. A pattern emerges from this group of three "career tracks" where specialized knowledge would develop. These included a military track in offices such as Razriadnyi (Military), Pomestnyi (Service Land), Reitarskii (Cavalry), Pushkarskii (Cannon), or Inozemskii (Foreign Mercenaries); a judicial track comprising either the regional court offices or centralized chancelleries including the Chelobitnyi Prikaz (Petition Office); and a financial track in either the Prikaz tainykh del (Privy Affairs) or Bol'shoi Prikaz (Treasury). Of the 207, approximately 123 (59.4 percent) possessed "career tracks" with the following frequency—58 men on the military track (47.1 percent), 39 judicial (31.7 percent), and 26 financial (21.1 percent). It is difficult to conclude that the different percentages indicate the likelihood or popularity of a particular career track. As the "military chancelleries" were by far the most numerous, it was logical that a "military" *d'iak* was the most common. Additionally, because of the published nature of the data on *d'iaki*, favoring the producers of transmitted records, the military and judicial *d'iaki*, definitive conclusions are especially difficult to come by. Caveats aside, it seems likely that *d'iaki* often served in a series of posts linked by certain skills and abilities. Furthermore, there was no clear indication of a "frontier track" composed of offices such as the Prikaz Kazanskogo dvortsa, Sibirskii Prikaz, or the later Ukrainskii Prikaz. This suggests the possibility that the men serving the Prikaz Kazanskogo dvortsa were not chosen based on their local, frontier experiences as much as their knowledge of military, judicial, or economic matters, all of which were responsibilities of the Prikaz for the region.

Even a low incidence of career bureaucrats, represented by the *d'iaki*, indicates a developing professionalization inside Muscovy's bureaucracy in the seventeenth century. Those with the greatest knowledge of the region may not have assisted in its governance directly. Still, those with the appropriate skills acquired over a number of years could be dispatched to places where those skills were in demand. If a *voevoda* lacked judicial or military experience, for example, he could be assigned a *d'iaki* with precisely that experience. This served the interests of the central chancelleries in more than one way. It not only kept the *voevoda* and *d'iaki* detached from the community and dependent on instruction from Moscow, but it also provided the appropriate expertise for the task at hand. This played a factor in the dismissal of Kerensk's *voevoda*, Avtamon Semenov syn Bezobrazov, in 1671. Upon receiving the news of rebellion spreading from the city of Simbirsk, Bezobrazov's indecision forced his *d'iak*, Iakov Timofeev syn Khitrov, to order one thousand men to intercept the rebels before they reached Kerensk. Moscow swiftly reacted by removing Bezobrazov for his incompetence. Khitrov was not rewarded but remained under a new *voevoda*.[67] While there was no guarantee that any *d'iak* in a particular career was in fact skilled, the system was capable of placing a trained official in a necessary office.

This is not to imply this system was so advantageous that it avoided disaster or worked to the benefit of its long-term office holders. It was nearly impossible for a *d'iak* to rise above his position in the administration. While there are examples of *d'iaki* who served as *voevody*, these exceptions were responses to specific pressures rather than social advancement. The first of this small group appeared shortly after Muscovite expansion into the region: Ivan Ivanov syn Bukharin was a *d'iak* in Sviiazhsk in the 1560s, but ended his career as *voevoda* of Kaluga. The rest appeared shortly after the Romanov ascension, when reliable men might have been hard to come by. Petr Grigor'ev syn Zheliabuzhskii served as *d'iak* in Vologda and Turinsk, but also as *voevoda* as Temnikov in 1615. Stepan Osipov syn Karaulov served as *voevoda* of Tetiushii in 1619/20, but later as *d'iak* in Koz'modem'iansk in 1639. Noticeably, Bukharin started as a *d'iak* and rose to *voevoda* at a time when Ivan's faith in the loyalty of the elites was questioned, which could have created opportunity to rise in the system. After the Time of Troubles a similar situation prevailed, but once the system was reestablished, these up-and-comers were no longer necessary. While it remained possible that some successful *d'iaki* could end up as the *voevoda* of very small settlements, it remained unusual. The only example between 1639 and 1671 was Mina Kirillov syn Griazev, who spent time as *d'iak* of Kazan in the 1650s but rose to the position of *voevoda* in both Kaigorodke and Vym Iarensk.

Religious Authorities

The Russian Orthodox Church established a distinct, and parallel, system of authority in the countryside. It began once again with Kazan in the center. The metropolitan, like a *voevoda*, had a staff of trained and experienced professionals to oversee Church lands and agricultural practices, tariff collection, judicial matters, and population surveillance. While always assessing their counterpart's day-to-day authority in the arena of praxis, the local administration and Church officials had more to gain through cooperation than competition. In essence, the Church acted as a virtual "check" on the authority and independence of the *voevody* and the Prikaz Kazanskogo dvortsa by replicating their responsibilities in a parallel system.

As *d'iaki* served both as an integral actuator and brake on the personal authority of the *voevody*, the Russian Orthodox Church evolved into an external check on the general power of the political administration in the region by duplicating its functions. By the end of the sixteenth century, the office of the archbishop of Kazan had been elevated to the rank of metropolitan. Germogen, the first metropolitan of Kazan, was also the most famous. Metropolitan Germogen was an important hagiographical author, producing the texts of the first two miracle cults in Kazan. He later became patriarch of the Russian Orthodox Church early in the seventeenth century, establishing Kazan as his route to high Church office.[68] Though only one other metropolitan in the seventeenth century attained Germogen's national stature (Patriarch Adrian in 1686), Germogen's career influenced the subsequent actions of the metropolitanate and consolidated Kazan's aura of Orthodox holiness.

This aura provided an authority and prestige that the *voevody* of the region simply could not match. Germogen established the precedent of physically marking the countryside with monuments to Orthodoxy and the reputation of his office. He founded the Ioanno-Predtechenskii Monastery in 1595 in Kazan to commemorate German, an earlier archbishop of Kazan. After burning in 1649, it was rebuilt and rededicated to Kornilii, another metropolitan of Kazan.[69] In this way, the metropolitan's authority to reshape conditions on the frontier was closer to the tsar's than to a *voevoda*'s. If nothing else, the Church commanded resources no *voevoda* could match.

Germogen also influenced Russian Orthodoxy throughout Muscovy, which certainly was also more than any *voevody* could aspire too. Germogen was responsible for both the "Life of Gurii and Varsonofii" and the "Tale of the Appearance of Kazan Icon of the Mother of God." Germogen wrote the former either in 1596 or 1597. Germogen may have written the original version of the "Icon of the Mother of God" after its discovery in 1579, but he edited the final version of the tale in 1594 or 1595. Gurii and Varsonofii first appeared in a national *Ustav* (Typicon) for commemoration in 1610, and the Mother of God Icon acquired a national festival on 8 July in 1633, in commemoration of its first appearance. These two miracle tales transformed Kazan's into one of the country's spiritual centers. This reinforced Kazan's (and its metropolitan's) position as the third city in the Russian Orthodox hierarchy and made the city an important pilgrimage site.[70]

As the new miracle cults gained currency, the metropolitan of Kazan also rose in public esteem. The Mother of God Icon received national attention shortly after the commemoration in 1610, when an early copy of the icon was carried into battle against the Poles in 1612, resulting in a short tale, "About the Advance of the Kazan Icon of the Mother of God toward Moscow," which recorded several new miracles affecting Russian troops.[71] Russian Orthodoxy's development on the frontier became important for the entire country.

Germogen encouraged the perception of Kazan as an Orthodox city. He corresponded regularly with the tsar, reminding him of his important connections within the Church, the icons and religious books possessed by the metropolitanate, and the contributions to local defense provided by the region's monasteries.[72]

Figure 2 Copy of a portrait of Patriarch Germogen from the late seventeenth century painted by V. M. Borin in 1913 (Reproduced from Borin, *Sviatieishii Patriarkh Germogen*)

Germogen's contacts and influence in Moscow, particularly with Vasilii Shuiskii, aided his rise through the hierarchy, culminating when he was installed as patriarch of Moscow when Shuiskii became tsar. Germogen gathered support for Shuiskii, but he continued to promote Kazan and its local cults. It was at this time that Gurii and Varsonofii transitioned from local saints into national ones.[73] The Mother of God Icon's role in supporting the Muscovite army against the Poles, in addition to Germogen's martyrdom at the hands of the Poles, reinforced the contribution of Kazan and its local Orthodox faithful in supporting a true Russian tsar against foreign invaders. Germogen also expanded local cults targeted at the conversion of local Muslims into national cults empowering Russian Orthodoxy against all other faiths, including Catholicism.

None of the metropolitans of the seventeenth century matched Germogen's prominence, but each followed his general policies, especially those of promoting the miracle cults of Gurii and Varsonofii and the Mother of God Icon. The icon processed to many of the region's monasteries to remind the public of its power; local churchmen frequently transferred it to Alatyr's Sviiato-Troitskii Monastery, and in 1686 a new church was built inside the Novodevichii Alekseevskii Convent in Arzamas to house the icon as it processed through the region.[74] In the 1670s the Church added German to the *vitae* of Gurii and Varsonofii, bringing new prestige to the city's religious miracle cults and, not coincidentally, its leaders.[75]

The metropolitans found it to their advantage to cooperate with the *voevody*, because of the financial aid the latter could provide. The Russian Orthodox Church in the region had been built initially on Ivan IV's grants of large tracts of land, with the population to work them, and fishing privileges in the Volga River.[76] Archbishop Gurii, the first head of the Orthodox Church in the region, received a stipend of 865 rubles from the tsar, and also 155 rubles, 1800 *cheti* of rye, 1000 *cheti* of other grains, and 50 puds of butter from tariffs from Kazan, Sviiazhsk, and Cheboksary during his tenure in office, in addition to revenues from the lands the archbishopric of Kazan possessed.[77] When the metropolitan and the local church sought further financial support in the seventeenth century, it was the *voevoda* of Kazan who became a tsarlike benefactor, which would have some influence on the balance of power in this unequal relationship. When the lands initially provided by the tsar for the archbishopric were "worn out" by the early seventeenth century, Kazan's *Voevoda* Volodimir Timof'evich Dolgorukov granted new lands to Metropolitan Matfei with land inside the city, fields outside of Kazan, and water rights to the Volga.[78] While it remains possible that such financial support was extended in mid-century, there is no record of such a transaction until the 1690s, when Metropolitan Markel turned to Patriarch Adrian for the 300 rubles needed for repairs to the archbishop's house in Kazan.[79]

Like the *voevody*, in point of fact the metropolitans did not rule alone. Local abbots and parish priests on the frontier limited the vast de jure influence of the metropolitans much as the *d'iaki* did their *voevoda*. An abbot (either a hegumen or an archimandrite), along with his monastery's council of elders, wielded extensive authority over the monastery's estate and its people, possessing the same rights that the metropolitan wielded over the population at large and that the *voevody* held over the urban population. As was generally the case in Muscovy, these lines of authority within governing structures provided the greatest sense of security through cooperative competition, where little could be accomplished without general consensus.

The abbots were not under the supervision of central chancelleries but served them indirectly. In general, abbots served lengthy terms in office, except at the most prominent monasteries. Kazan's Ioanno-Predtechenskii Monastery had eight abbots between its foundation in 1595 and 1736. Abbot Makarii served only from 1613 to 1615, but he was the only abbot in office for less than six years. The longest-serving abbot was Filaret, in office from 1664 until 1702.[80] Alatyr's Sviato-Troitskii Monastery had twelve abbots between its foundation in 1612 and 1720. Abbot Nifont Kabylan was in office from 1650 until 1692, but the monastery had suffered tremendous turnover in its early years. The first abbot, Evfimii, served only fourteen months, from February 1612 until April 1613, and several other abbots who served very short terms, including Iosif Pestrikov from 1618 to 1619, Sevirian from 1627 to 1628, and Vassian from 1697 to 1698.[81] There is no evident link between political or social upheaval in the region and these short terms in office, nor are there indications that these abbots transferred to another institution. Most abbots served until their death.

In the most prominent monasteries of the region, the abbots served short terms in office, as they frequently transferred to other monasteries or into positions within the Orthodox hierarchy. Sviiazhsk's Uspenskii Bogoroditskii Monastery, established in 1555, was one of the region's oldest institutions. In the period between 1555 and 1724, the monastery had twenty-three abbots, for an average of 7.3 years each. Abbot Semën had the longest term in office from 1698 to 1724, but before him there were only two abbots with ten-year, or longer, terms. Its first abbot, German, served a nine-year term before becoming the second archbishop of Kazan in 1564. Several of the abbots after German left the monastery for other positions within the Orthodox hierarchy. Abbot Kornilii became archbishop of Vologda in 1620 after his seven-year term in office; abbot Iosif and Abbot Varfolomei entered the Solovetskii Monastery after the Uspenskii Bogoroditskii Monastery in 1667 and 1669 respectively. Iosif returned to the Middle Volga Region in 1673 to become the abbot of the Spaso-Preobrazhenskii Monastery in Kazan in 1673, which was the

Table 4 Monasteries' villages, households, and people in 1646

Monastery	Number of villages	Number of households/people in villages	Households/people in city	Monastery's total population
Kazan's Troitse-Sergeevskii	4	111/422	8/50	472 people
Kazan's Zilantov Uspenskii	5	159/557	3/5	562 people
Sviiazhsk's Bogoroditskii	6	228/872	0/0	872 people

Source: Information drawn from Pokrovskii, "K istorii Kazanskikh monastyrei."

Notes: Pokrovskii gathered the information from the census of 1646 in Kazan district. He did not include complete information from the census. For Kazan's Spaso-Preobrazhenskii Monastery, he included only the names of the monastery's 29 villages, but did include the 17 households the monastery owned in the city. Similar data does not exist for most of the region's monasteries because of the intermittent record keeping.

most important monastery of the region.[82] With the preferment of so many abbots, the prestige of this monastery was clear. It is notable that even these abbots provided a far more stable presence in the region than the *voevody* with their two- to three-year residences.

With the financial grants to these religious institutions that established their presence in the region came important juridical privileges that tended to undermine one of the powers of the local *voevody*. Abbots held the right to adjudicate all cases except capital crimes for their subjects. Sviiazhsk's Uspenskii Bogoroditsii Monastery had this right in both the city of Sviiazhsk and in the countryside.[83] Kazan's Spaso-Preobrazhenskii Monastery also received exclusive legal privileges over its people in Kazan and all of its villages upon its foundation in 1555.[84] As seen in table 4, monasteries possessed legal privileges for large populations, creating numerous oases of villages free from the control of the local *voevody*.

Throughout the seventeenth century, monasteries accrued additional legal authority over peasants on their lands, as was the case for the Troitse-Sergeevskii Monastery in Arzamas in 1627. At that time, Patriarch Filaret notified the *voevoda* of Arzamas, Vasilii Petrovich Morozov, that jurisdiction over the villages had passed to the monastery.[85] Even monasteries that did not begin with legal control over their peasants could gain it, as was the case of the Saratov's Novospasskii Monastery in May 1652. Its abbot received judicial control for all of his people inside and around Saratov, a loss of authority for the city's *voevoda*, Aleksei Panteleevich Chirikov.[86]

Theoretically, designating legal responsibility for its estate to a monastery was designed to support the Church's conversion efforts, establishing in time an Orthodox population. Many of the region's non-Russian communities lived on Church lands. As a result, legal disputes that included domestic violence, divorce, and robbery (among others), would be resolved by an Orthodox bishop or abbot. How effective this practice was at any particular moment is impossible to know, but it occurred frequently, and many villages in the former khanate found themselves subject to Church justice except in the cases of "red-handed" robbery or murder. These cases remained the responsibility of the local *voevoda*.[87] Sviiazhsk's Uspenskii Bogoroditskii Monastery received the Tatar village of Khoziasheva in 1621, in addition to an earlier grant of the Tatar village of Isakov in Sviiazhsk district. Six Tatar households lived in Khoziasheva, only one of which was Christian at the time.[88] When the Troitse-Sergeevskii Monastery of Arzamas received legal rights over its peasants in 1627, it gained supervision over several villages of non-Christian Mordvins.[89]

It appears clear that in fact the central government found it expedient to split jurisdictional authority among multiple religious and secular officials to maximize its ability to control the countryside and towns with the least expense. Dividing these legal duties between multiple responsible entitles tended to consolidate the authority of the *voevody* by preventing a situation where disputes remained unresolved, or worse, one in which the *voevoda* was unable to enforce a resolution because of overwork, inattention, or lack of resources. Because the *voevoda* retained responsibility for murder cases, the Church was absolved of dealing with capital crimes in a non-Orthodox community, and the two institutions could reinforce their authority by acting in concert. Church officials could also be a valuable auxiliary force for local supervision of non-Russian communities, an important component, it will be remembered, of a *voevoda*'s responsibilities. Since the state had no interest in decisions that failed to maintain peace, and no interest in an expensive, attenuated, judicial bureaucracy on the frontier, by sharing the responsibility for enforcement among Church and state, Moscow increased its control without increasing its payroll.

Dividing legal responsibilities between *voevody* and abbots had the potential to establish firmly their authority over local communities, and aid in bringing Orthodox officials and a non-Russian population into contact, but the system also led to persistent competition over land and resources. Legal authority made claims to tax revenues, tolls, and in-kind contributions much easier to establish, and it was more difficult to command the resources of a village without controlling its legal processes. Several *voevody* of Kazan challenged their local monasteries' claims to populations and lands throughout the seventeenth century, on occasion seeking the right to control the same village time and again. The Zilantov Uspenskii Monastery defended its legal authority over its village of Kinder twice within ten years against the local *voevody*. Each time the monastery was victorious in the dispute.[90] Sviiazhsk's Uspenskii Bogoroditskii Monastery faced at least three challenges to its legal authority by 1650; it was also successful against the *voevody*.[91] The *voevody*'s persistent attempts indicate there was value in holding monastic lands, but the state's support for the rights of the Church over its officials indicates that the chancelleries, at least, were content with the system.

The success of monasteries in the countryside led to the natural development of convents (*zhenskii monastyr'*) which followed monasteries onto the frontier. It was legal to establish new institutions such as these only with state approval, so the establishment of convents was a conscious decision of both state and Church authorities. A greater Orthodox presence on the frontier, and more supervision and development of resources, followed the pattern of state decisions. However, placing Orthodox convents on the frontier involved risks for the women themselves. Could nuns be protected from the non-Russian communities and the continuing dangers of nomadic raiders?[92] The continuous focus on security in the *voevody*'s instructions indicates that there was real concern about the region's safety, especially since convents could not be expected to anchor a defensive position, much less garrison troops.

As a result, the city of Kazan did not receive a convent, the Bogoroditskii Devichii, until after the completion of the first defensive line. By comparison, Kazan's first monastery was built in 1552, and its second followed shortly thereafter in 1555. Officially, the Bogoroditskii Devichii Convent was built to serve only as the home of the miraculous Mother of God Icon, which had recently demonstrated its powers.[93] Later tsars extended additional financial support to the convent, a sign of the state's continuing commitment and a clear sign that the convent war more than a home for the miracle-working icon. Tsar Mikhail Fedorovich assigned the revenue from the rent of four courtyards in Kazan to the convent in 1623 to provide the funds for a new building to house the icon.[94] Furthermore, Kazan became the first city in the region to receive a second convent in 1607, the Troitskii Fedorovskii, built on the instruction of Metropolitan Germogen and the *voevoda* of Kazan, Prince Ivan Ivanovich Golitsyn.[95]

While Kazan was a logical choice for major convents, most new towns and outposts also received them as conditions warranted. For example, in 1584, three decades after the town of Cheboksary was founded, the Nikolaevskii Devichii Convent was created, built to include one of the town's original churches, quite close to the Volga River.[96] In Cheboksary's early years, it was considered a fortress securing the Volga River against the still dangerous local Chuvash and Mari populations. As it grew and became more secure in the decades that followed, Cheboksary gained a cathedral and two churches in addition to its first monastery, but the region was still considered too insecure by the tsar to warrant a convent until the 1580s. It was to this convent that Kseniia Ivanovna Shestova, the mother of the future tsar Mikhail Fedorovich Romanov, was exiled to take the veil in 1601.[97] This was less a sign of the security or prestige of this convent as much as it was a deliberate decision to guarantee Shestova's removal from the seat of government; her husband suffered a similar fate when he was forced into a monastery.

Allowing the convents to follow the defensive line became the pattern in the seventeenth century. Still, construction was slow, and governed by security concerns and limited resources. Construction of the Novodevichii Alekseevskii Convent in Arzamas began only after 1675, despite Tsar Mikhail Fedorovich's decree establishing it forty-one years previously![98] In fact, it was not until the 1670s that there was a genuine boom in convent foundations, with new institutions established in Tsivil'sk, Kerensk, Saratov, and Penza.[99] Nevertheless, convents were important enough as symbols of stability that they were occasionally maintained even near the frontier. For instance, the Kievo-Nikolaevskii Convent was built in Alatyr', farther south than any other convent built to this date, albeit in 1639, twenty years after the town's first monastery and nearly sixty years since the defensive line had been completed. It housed Abbess Elizaveta, her fellow nuns, and their priest, Mefodii, who were refugees from the city of Kiev. The convent burned in 1667, and Tsar Aleksei Mikhailovich ordered it rebuilt and provided all of the necessary funds for the reconstruction, noting that this was a reward for their loyal service on the frontier.[100] Though the convent was exposed, Alatyr', long since a tsarist town, offered more safety than existed in Kiev, a recent battleground in the war with the Polish-Lithuanian Commonwealth.

The limited number of convents played little role in the administrative politics of the region. Neither the Russian Orthodox Church nor the central chancelleries found themselves hampered by the region's abbesses, although in theory they wielded as much authority as an abbot. Abbots acted alongside the *voevody* as an extension of tsarist authority, with an additional focus, that of putting an Orthodox authority in charge of a non-Russian community. An abbess, however, could not exert this authority on the frontier. Orthodox expectations for seclusion necessarily prevented nuns from fulfilling any role in the local administration. Even if a convent had been assigned lands, people, and legal authority to make decisions for that popula-tion, no abbess would have been allowed to see the community.

This is not to say that convents lacked influence. While every convent required a priest to act as an intermediary between its walls and the world at large, they held property, if not lands and people. Most were supported through revenue raised by the ownership of local businesses, in particular mills. These monies were often the sole support for the cloistered communities. Because no one would help them in Alatyr', Abbess Elisaveta of the Nikolaevskii Novodevichii Convent petitioned the tsar on 1 February 1639, demanding funds for the convent's leaking roof and water-damaged cells. She justified the expense claiming that when pilgrims saw the convent they had "great wails and tears" but were unable to offer the convent any assistance. In response, the central government advised the abbess to build a mill and charge for its services, which could finance the repairs, but signally did not offer any funds for construction.[101] Similarly, but more successfully, Arzamas's Nikolaevskii Convent was assigned the revenue from both the land and the mill in a nearby village, Kichazanskii. The revenue from the mill was sufficient that more than one of the *voevody* of Arzamas attempted to seize it to provide for their own coffers in the seventeenth century. Possession of the mills should not be taken as a sign that convents had extensive contact with their financial support. In this case, a priest administered Kichazanskii for the nuns, a typical arrangement.[102] In any town, the grain mill was an essential institution, and a convent's association with it further reinforced the central importance of the business.

Gradually, both types of monastic institution became part of the daily life of the tsar's new lands. As a result, peasants and priests frequently petitioned monasteries for advice or assistance before approaching the local *voevoda* or the central authorities. The exchanges between Arzamas's Troitse-Sergeevskii Monastery and its villages covered a wide field. In 1629, the priest Markel Konstantinovich wrote to the monastery to ask for an explanation of the recent decision of the Council of Elders about the number of days a woman must be secluded after giving birth.[103] The monastery received a petition from one of its villages, sent by the village elder Semën, who asked for assistance during the current famine year (*god goloda*). The monastery denied the petition, asserting that the village had plenty of food.[104] The monastery wrote and validated a contract for a land exchange between the Mordvin Egchaik Kozhilanov and the local *strel'tsy* (musketeers).[105] While the abbot could answer the religious question and write the land contract, he did not have the power to address all petitions. Abbots certainly had no right to grant land, prepare defenses, or ameliorate taxes or tolls, just to name a few possibilities.

As a result, abbots frequently petitioned the central government on behalf of their peasants and even for themselves. Frequently, these petitions were attempts to deny *voevody*'s attempts to seize monastic privileges and property. The abbot of Kazan's Zilantov Uspenskii Monastery protested local bailiffs seizing the carts of the monastery's peasants in 1598. The abbot informed the central government this would prevent the harvesting of the peasants' crops and, subsequently, the monastery's ability to pay the year's taxes. Unsurprisingly the government sided with the monastery to guarantee the tax payment.[106] However, when seeking the assistance of the central government, abbots had no greater a chance of success than *voevody* or *d'iaki*; all three received rejections as often as advice.

There can be no question that both church and state empowered their respective local representatives to manage the day-to-day governance of the region. This was efficient, in a relative sense, depending on which costs the central government, local government, church, and populace were willing to endure. Multiple overlapping lines of authority, both between Moscow and the periphery and between church and state, created opportunities for the local population to find a representative who would take their position, often against church or state interests. The growing professionalization of the *d'iaki*, the presence of powerful and relatively autonomous abbots, and geographic distance checked the *voevody*, as they checked the central government. The judicial authority of abbots provided another set of eyes and ears on the activities of the local population, and the split responsibilities between church and state created a check on the power of any one individual. As in other areas of early modern states, the patchwork of competing interests and institutions with real, if not de jure, administrative power, produced enough fiscal involvement to improve and develop the region, and enough chaos to prevent any true challenge to the tsar.

Cooperative Competition

The Muscovite administrative system was defined by its slowly gestating bureaucracy and practices. While ideologically the tsar ruled as "autocrat and sovereign," his influence depended on the development of his defined channels of power to the countryside. The chancellery system that emerged in Moscow tended to be created and altered in response to the difficulties inherent in maintaining revenues and control during war and simultaneous expansion. When Kazan was conquered, it required governance. When the land east of Nizhnii Novgorod expanded as far as the Pacific Ocean, the Prikaz Kazanskogo dvortsa was split and the Sibirskii Prikaz was created. No one could argue there was a vision or plan for the central government, but despite the competition engendered by the ragged divisions created when the chancelleries were remade, it managed to supervise land, people, and resources, although it is clear that the state depended on quasi-external institutions to fill many deficiencies it could not correct.

This is most evident at the local level on the former frontier of the khanate. The independence of the local Russian Orthodox Church's institutions and its large grants of land gave it an independence that the *voevody* resented. This led to a constant struggle in the countryside. It was impossible to exert the effort necessary to overcome the difficulties of time and distance, and to ensure that the system of social precedence provided competence at every level of the new bureaucracy. The attempted solution, the creation of bureaucratic professionals, as the *d'iaki* generally became, and detailed *nakazy*, worked to make sure a basic system operated reliably, but even then, the Orthodox Church was a necessary adjunct. The administrative system remained unwieldy, impractical, and divisive in multiple ways.

The problems with the system were identifiable to the chancelleries, and they could be overcome. When the interests of the tsar, his chancelleries, local secular and religious officials coalesced on one project, it could be rapidly implemented. This is what allowed the successful construction of a second defensive line. The need for one was always clear. The local nomadic population (Bashkirs, Nogais, and Kalmyks) continued to threaten the region, and increasing population along and behind the Arzamas Line only augmented the danger. A line farther south nearly eliminated the traditional migratory routes of the nomads and increased the available land for Muscovite colonization, creating new "tsarist" territory along the frontier. The position eventually selected allowed the region's defenses to become an extension of the massive Belgorod Line that extended across Left-Bank Ukraine. It was not a quick process. Even in 1618 with the end of the war with Poland-Lithuania, the state was in no position to execute a massive and expensive construction project. Additional losses to Poland-Lithuania in the Smolensk War of 1632–34 hardly improved the situation. However, losses to the west only reinforced the need for a pacified frontier on the remaining borders.

By 1636, construction of the Simbirsk Line was underway. It ran from the outpost of Simbirsk on the Volga due west, eventually connecting to the massive Belgorod project beyond the new outposts of Nizhnii and Verknii Lomov. To mark its success, the former military and trade outpost of Simbirsk was ordered to become new administrative center for the region. Much of this new line was populated with relocated non-Russians, forcibly moved to the south. Insar, for example, was settled by a group of Tatars in Muscovite service. Their first assignment was to build the fort; their second was to live in it.[107] Mordvins were forced south from the lands between Nizhnii Novgorod and Arzamas to settle a new outpost at Kerensk.[108] In both cases, non-Russians were relocated from the forest belt in the north to the mixed swamp and steppe region, where sedentary agriculture would be the only possible occupation. These new colonizers had no experience with "traditional" Russian agricultural practices, having largely relied upon hunting, trapping, fishing, and beekeeping in the north. Though petitions against the process were immediate, the state and its many agents were committed to the process.[109]

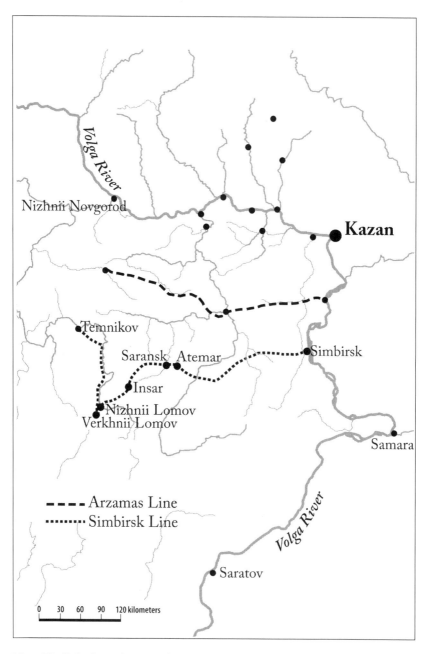

Map 4 The Simbirsk Line (Courtesy of Ev Wingert, University of Hawaiʻi at Mānoa)

Table 5 Outposts and fortifications on the Simbirsk Line

Outposts and towns	Year est.	Monasteries and convents (partial)	Year est.
Nizhnii Lomov	1636	Saransk's Kazanskii Bogoroditskii Mon.	1648
Verkhnii Lomov	1636	Atemar's Voskresenskii Mon.	before 1650
Atemar	Before 1641	Simbirsk's Spaso-Preobrazhenskii Convent	before 1650
Saransk	1641	Atemar's Spaso-Prichistyi Bogoroditskii Mon.	before 1652
Karson	1647	Penza's Spaso-Preobrazhenskii Mon.	1667
Insar	1648	Kerensk's Tikhvinskii Bogoroditskii Mon.	1683
Simbirsk (town)	1648	Saransk's Petropavlovskii Mon.	1684
Kerensk	1658	Penza's Troitskii Convent	1689
Penza	1663	Simbirsk's Pokrovskii Mon.	1698

Source: Data drawn from Romaniello, "Absolutism and Empire," 22, 30, 33.

Following the mechanisms established in the new administration, the new defensive line was a joint project of the central chancelleries, local administration, and various monasteries. Tsar Aleksei Mikhailovich personally assigned a *voevoda* and boiar, Bogdan Matveevich Khitrovo, to transform the former fortress of Simbirsk, outlining in broad strokes the vision of a town with a functioning mercantile district attached to the original fortress.[110] The foundations of new monasteries and their fortifications, as shown in table 5, bolstered the defensive line. Monasteries supervised the non-Russian communities outside of the new outposts, as had been their role in the previous decades. In only a few years, the extended second defenses were complete, and the tsar could successfully claim to have extended his reach further toward the open steppe.

Even though successful, construction on this second defensive line encountered, and created, significant problems. It interfered with the development of the region behind the first defensive construction. Saransk, for example, was built to support a *strel'tsy* outpost as part of the new, southernmost defensive line against nomadic raiders. It replaced an older, nearby town, Atemar, which occupied a less strategic position. With state support behind Saransk, it grew rapidly, reaching a population of more than 600 households within ten years of its foundation. The state also supported Saransk's newer monasteries over Atemar's, transferring the fishing rights of Atemar's Voskresenskii Monastery over the river Inzera to Saransk's Bogoroditsii Monastery. By 1651 Saransk became the administrative center of the region, with responsibility for Atemar and Temnikov, and two years later the *voevoda* of Saransk was also the *voevoda* of Atemar.[111]

The second defensive line became a perfect representation of Muscovite administrative policy. It was more or less successful, though the outcome was not quite what was intended. The conflicting lines of authority—the bureaucratic layers working in cooperative competition—could finish a necessary project for the imperial goals.[112] New land was claimed when the frontier was extended. More trade, more population, and more security could all provide immediate benefits to the people both settled behind the first defensive line. Moscow claimed the right to direct this process—it would not be a natural migration to the south, but a centrally directed, locally enforced drive for control. Like the construction, the results would be uneven.

3

Foreign Interests

The English Merchants themselves in Our Dominions shall sell and Barter their owne Comodities, as also any Russe Comodities. But Russes shall not Trade, nor Barter for them, Also they shall not Convey other Mens Goods for their owne, neither shall they maintain or keep any that belongeth to any other Men, or claim their Goods to be English. . . . And of those Comoditys in all Our Cittys in all Our Dominions, Our Nobles and Governors and all of Our People—authorities shall take noo Toll, nor manner of Custome, according to this Our Princely Gracious Privilidge.

Tsarist Grant of privileges to the Muscovy Company, 1628

Thus the Czar improves the Manufactures of his Countrey, feeds all the Labourers as cheap as we do our Dogs. And lays up the money that comes out of the Cabacks, Bath stoves, Tarr, Pitch, Hemp, Flax, Honey, Wax, Cariare, Sturgeon, Bellusa, and other salted and dry'd fish from Astracan, Cazan, the Lake Belsira, and many other Lakes and Rivers with which the Countrey abounds, especially Syberia in the latter.

Samuel Collins,
The Present State of Russia, 1671

Possession of Kazan and Astrakhan provided Muscovy control over two of the central entrepôts of the Volga River.[1] The first defensive line protected the northern end of the trade route by the 1570s, increasing the ease of merchant travel from Moscow to Kazan (and perhaps as far as Tetiushii, farther south along the Volga). New forts and towns along the length of the Volga, in particular at Samara, Simbirsk, Saratov, and later, Tsaritsyn, provided Muscovy with a set of fortifications, storage facilities, and customs officials up and down the route. European as well as Russian traders understood the opportunities the Volga presented—potential access to the wealth and luxurious commodities of South and East Asia. The river remained dangerous, subject to raids from the still-threatening steppe nomads, but there was no doubt that Muscovite officials believed it was permanently open to trade.[2]

West European merchants had been optimistic about the potential benefits of the Volga route even during Ivan IV's incessant foreign campaigns and Russia's domestic disturbances. English merchants arrived in the 1550s looking for trade opportunities, and the Dutch arrived not long thereafter. The Dutch merchant Isaac Massa, residing in Moscow during the ongoing disaster of the Time of Troubles carefully recorded the potential security and stability of the Volga trade route even as he watched with trepidation the failure of the English merchants then operating in Moscow.[3] An entire decade of domestic and international violence was not sufficient to dissuade competitive merchants from attempting to dominate Muscovite trade. As the Romanov ascension brought a new promise of increased stability throughout the Middle Volga Region and open steppe, Dutch and English merchants remained enticed by hopes of future profits from an Asian trade.[4]

Without exception, traditional interpretations of Muscovy's expansion to the east have offered the long-distance trade potential of the Volga River as one of its central benefits. Kazan, in this interpretation, was the gateway to Moscow's expansion into the global economy. Muscovite authorities and foreign observers expected genuine financial benefits. As was often the case with Moscow's attempts to create an imperial reach, the profits were elusive; it took decades for these aspirations to produce any results. Europeans hoped the Volga would provide a viable alternative to the Ottoman route or the oceanic route to the Indian Ocean. But the success of both the English East India Company and the Dutch India Company avoiding Ottoman-controlled routes during the seventeenth century placed a limit on the Volga's potential utility. However, the greater problem was harder to comprehend in Moscow, London, or Amsterdam. The early-modern world's largest and most robust economies were in the East—particularly in India and China—and the European lack of success in establishing any lasting contacts with them indicated the difficulty of utilizing Muscovy, an insignificant economic power, to create a new, profitable route.[5]

This is not to suggest that Moscow failed to benefit from its new lands, but its profits emerged from its domestic improvements rather than its international position. Considering the general weakness of the Muscovite economy and its particular lack of profitable export products (with the exception of fur), even nominal control over the Middle Volga Region was an economic boon, and internal trade appears to have increased based on a trade in local products.[6] These included honey and wax, salt, and fish, all valuable commodities in the early-modern world. They provided more for Muscovite coffers than the potential cross-continental trade in Iranian silk or Indian spices. Nevertheless, the limits of trade never dissuaded the central chancelleries from pursuing the seductive promise of revenue that might flow from a successful commercial enterprise with Middle Eastern, or South and East Asian entrepôts. Their endeavors, however, never realized large profits.[7] As the Muscovite economy lacked a trade good desired by the international market, it also lacked hard currency for a potential alternative. Indeed, the continuing interest of the English and Dutch in Muscovite trade demonstrates their economic supply weakness in the global economy as well. They also lacked products that could be sold profitably in Asia. Although Muscovy had little to offer Asia, it certainly had products such as hemp, tar, and timber that remained desirable to the West. Adapting to exploit what the region offered, rather than its prospective utility as a trade route, was another lesson of the elusive empire learned only later. Building its presence was Muscovy's success, not generating profits. Since the latter was the goal of economic policy, the creation of a new imperial infrastructure was both of great importance and incidental to the eventual failure of the trade policy.

Economic Opportunities

Economic interests had played an obvious role in the decision to conquer the cities of Kazan and Astrakhan. Trade had, in fact, been one of the earlier tools exploited by Muscovy to dominate Kazan. Ivan IV's father, Grand Prince Vasilii III, forbade Muscovite merchants from engaging in trade along the Volga, and specifically in Kazan, in order to undermine the khanate. Sigismund von Herberstein later commented:

> For Vasiley had, to the great prejudice of the people of Kazan, transferred to [Nizhnii] Novgorod the fairs which it had been the custom to hold near Kazan, in the Island of Merchants, and had proclaimed a heavy penalty upon any of his subjects who should in the future go to the island for the purposes of merchandize, . . . and that being prevented from buying salt, which they received in large quantities from the Russian at that fair alone, they might be induced to surrender.[8]

Even though the embargo was abandoned, it was clear that trade was one of the primary levers Moscow could use to influence Kazan. And with Moscow in theoretical control of both sides of the exchange, profits were guaranteed. As the population of the khanate was largely sedentary and agricultural, the region offered a bounty of production opportunities, in addition to providing greater control over the Volga trade.

After the conquest of the two khanates, English merchants swiftly took the opportunity to travel south from Moscow to test the viability of the Volga as a new route for exchange with the Middle East. Safavid Iran, with its silks and spices, beckoned tantalizingly. Yet when Anthony Jenkinson completed the trip in 1558, the opportunities for trade failed to impress him. Upon reaching Astrakhan, he noted:

> There is a certain trade of merchandise there used, but yet so small and beggarly, that it is not worth the making mention, and yet there come merchants thither from divers places. The chiefest commodities that the Russes bring there are red hides, red sheep's skins, wooden vessels, bridles and saddles, knives, and other trifles, with corn, bacon, and other victuals. The Tartars bring thither divers kinds of wrought silks: and they that come out of Persia, namely from Shamacki, do bring sowing silk, which is the coarsest that they use in Russeland, crasko, divers kinds of pied silks for girdles, shirts of mail, bows, swords, and such like things: and years quantity, the merchants being so beggarly and poor that bring the same, that it is not worth the writing, neither is there any hope of trade in all those parts worth the following.[9]

While Jenkinson was hardly optimistic about the trade potential of the new route, he was clearly aware of Moscow's new connections with South and East Asia. It was only a short time before his Dutch competitors followed suit.

Later, however, Ivan Vasil'evich's domestic and international wars, including some attempts by the Ottoman Empire to expel Muscovite forces from Astrakhan and the lower Volga created continuous disruptions to the Moscow–Europe trade.[10] There were attempts to add security to the Volga River, including the construction of the Arzamas Line, but events generally outpaced development. The additional domestic and international conflicts in the era of the Time of Troubles only magnified the problems. By the time of the Romanov ascension in 1613, Muscovite resources for a sustained period of investment supporting growth in the region, never robust, were exhausted.

The Muscovite state was poorly equipped to pursue the complex task of economic development, no matter its monetary and labor resources. The bureaucratic overlap of the chancelleries was a serious obstacle to the smooth encouraging of increased trade. Security for merchants' safe travel, infrastructure development, and the regulation of trade routes and tolls were under the control of the Prikaz Kazanskogo dvortsa. These could not be implemented from the center, and the

Prikaz relied heavily on its administrators in the countryside to coordinate projects and, frequently, to jury-rig solutions when support from the metropole was not forthcoming. As a result, many of its solutions ultimately involved exploiting the presence of the Russian Orthodox Church in the region, which was an attempt to shift costs onto the Church and increase the effective number of state employees on the ground. Foreign trade, however, remained the province of the Posol'skii Prikaz, not the local administration. The resulting gap in the local supervision of merchants in Kazan created an opportunity for those same merchants to exploit the chancelleries' overlapping powers in the pursuit of commercial advantage. As Muscovite investment in the region progressed, the economic chancelleries, including both the Prikaz Bol'shogo dvortsa (Treasury) and the Prikaz tainykh del (Privy Affairs), pursued their own projects in the regions.[11] Muscovite red tape hindered its own interests as much as the foreign competition did.

Furthermore, even in 1613, after sixty years of Muscovite control, the Volga trade route remained dangerous, had proven expensive to secure, and carried little traffic. In the 1550s, there was little structure to, or security along, the Volga River, other than the cities of Kazan and Astrakhan. For hundreds of miles between the two cities existed mostly hostile nomadic tribes still outside of Muscovite control. Even when trade was worth the risk, it remained only intermittingly possible, because of the nearly constant threat of raids on shipping and transit. As a result, much of what regular commerce developed followed in the shadow of the defensive lines, which offered far better protection than any alternative route. The great distance between the end of the defensive lines to Astrakhan along the Volga remained treacherous throughout the seventeenth century.

The obstacles to a profitable new trade in the region were great, but as in the West, there were many who ardently pursued it. These included the chancelleries, with a dedication lacking in most of their other pursuits. After 1552, it was a natural decision to direct trade to follow the construction of the new defensive lines. The slow-moving Volga River was always the central trade artery when it was secure, but for merchants Muscovy's new outposts along the length increased the ease of transit. From Nizhnii Novgorod, Moscow expected that merchants would travel through Vasil'gorod (later renamed Vasil'sursk), Koz'modem'iansk, Cheboksary, and Kokshaishk to Kazan, then onto Tetiushii, Samara, Saratov, and Tsaritsyn, finally arriving at Astrakhan.[12] However, because the Volga was slow, it remained a tempting target for raids. As a result, Russian merchants frequently opted instead for a partially overland route along the defensive line, moving from Nizhnii Novgorod to Arzamas, then to Alatyr', and ending at Tetiushii, where it reached the Volga River. Only then did merchants travel downstream through Saratov. When the Simbirsk line

Figure 3 Trading vessels on the Volga River outside of Nizhnii Novgorod (Reproduced from Saint-Julien, *Voyage pittoresque en Russie*)

was completed in 1649, overland trade could travel south from Alatyr' to Simbirsk, which was a better port than Tetiushii. Both as a matter of increased safety (traveling through Muscovite outposts) and as an escape from river tolls, the overland routes proved popular with merchants, although they could not avoid the river entirely.

Because of the Volga route's vulnerability, the Prikaz Kazanskogo dvortsa was well aware of the overwhelming importance of security along the trade routes and through Kazan. In 1613, as the state struggled to reestablish itself throughout the kingdom, the Prikaz made the security of its trade routes one of its primary goals. Implementation fell squarely on the shoulders of the *voevody* of Kazan, who were instructed to monitor all trade activity and encourage merchants to wait in the city in order to assemble larger caravans. Without the resources to pay troops to patrol in a sustained manner between Kazan and Astrakhan, the large caravan approach was the best option, even if it never was completely effective. In the *nakaz* of 1613, the Prikaz instructed Kazan's *voevoda* on his new obligations to monitor carefully all merchants along the river. Merchants were held in Kazan in order to maximize the size of the caravans traveling downriver, and forced to wait for a herald's announcement of the departure date of the next caravan to Astrakhan.[13]

Few merchants found it expedient to travel without the protection of the caravan, which ultimately limited both competition and the volume of trade. Later, outposts and towns along the Volga were forced to adopt the same "safety in numbers" approach, with the additional stricture that the Prikaz would hold the *voevody* responsible for the merchants' safety. Nevertheless, raids occurred, and merchant petitions protesting raided caravans and stolen goods became common occurrences in Moscow.[14] New decrees or regulations on transit failed to solve problems that could only be addressed through actual improvements in the region's security.

The Prikaz Kazanskogo dvortsa and its *voevody* consistently applied themselves to improving security for merchants, and gradually an infrastructure developed capable of responding to raids and protecting the flow of trade. A fine example was the new town of Simbirsk. Initially only a nominal outpost along the Volga, when it became the cornerstone of the second defensive line in 1648 it was intentionally upgraded to a trade center providing increased security and traffic along the Volga. Tsar Aleksei Mikhailovich personally assigned the boiar Bogdan Matveevich Khitrovo to transform the former fortress into a caravansary, outlining the necessary buildings to support a new mercantile district along the river.[15] By the end of the seventeenth century, Simbirsk was an influential trade center, complete with its own businesses.

As limited as the progress was with the south, Moscow's officials were aware that the security of the route, and thus its ability to sustain trade, needed improvement. The new infrastructure required a considerable investment of time and money, including diverse projects from storage facilities for goods moved along the river to mechanisms for exploiting the region's natural resources, marketplaces to sell those goods, and administrative structures for monitoring the developing trade system. The Posol'skii Prikaz contributed little to these efforts but was able to look forward to reaping the benefits in the meantime. From Kazan to Astrakhan, the Prikaz Kazanskogo dvortsa struggled to find the resources to manage its "local" projects along the Volga River basin.

The Prikaz's first solution was to place as much of the burden of infrastructure development on the Russian Orthodox Church as possible. For example, as early as 1614, it instructed Arzamas's Spaso-Preobrazhenskii Monastery to construct granaries in two places on its land, one in town and one outside of it, in order to provide a place for merchants to store their goods. The instructions were detailed enough to assign the monastery's village of Strakhov in Arzamas district to provide the revenue for construction. Though the monastery had been tasked with the construction and maintenance of the storage facilities, it would not share the revenue. Any money generated by the silos would be claimed by the government.[16] Nor was this type of decree limited to the smaller outposts. In the 1620s, the Zilantov Uspenskii Monastery in Kazan built ten granaries and two small huts inside the monastery's grounds to provide facilities for traders.[17]

While passing expenses onto the Church, the Prikaz Kazanskogo dvortsa began investing its time and efforts into regulating the trade as it developed. Its best tool was information. The data gathered over time about the workings of the trade network along the Volga, enabled better control over the territory, and, potentially, profits. In the *nakaz* to Kazan from 1649, gathering information on trade became a central piece of the *voevody's* daily responsibilities, as revenue from foreign trade had become a pressing concern. The new *voevoda* was required to inspect all possessions carried by the merchants traveling between Kazan and Astrakhan, making sure that the customs agent (*tamozhennaia golova*) in the city received the appropriate amount for the commodities. After the inspection, the *voevoda* and customs agent were to send a record of the trade goods to the Prikaz Kazanskogo dvortsa.[18] As the number of administrators in the region increased, so did the volume of information. Though the data could not be compiled quickly, among the records held in Moscow by the Prikaz would be complete transit records for all caravans as they moved along the Volga.[19]

More effective protection of traders over the course of the seventeenth century also enabled better customs collection. As the *nakaz* of 1649 implied, the benefit of increased control over the Volga River was cash, collected in the form of tolls and tariffs for transit through the region. All caravans traveling upriver from Astrakhan were stopped and examined in the cities along the Volga River. If the merchants lacked proper permission for trade, or were carrying any banned items, the caravans were seized.[20] Further instructions from the Prikaz required the *voevody* to be wary of merchants who might have fished in the Volga as well as moved goods, and instructed each *voevoda* to watch the customs official in the city to ensure proper taxes were being paid for the goods.[21] The revenue was never large, but the paranoia arising from possible leakages was nearly limitless.

Though not its primary purpose, the *Ulozhenie* (Law Code) of 1649 addressed the regulation of the domestic economy. The two areas of major concern were projects the local administration in the region had been involved with—controlling the toll system and banning illicit commodities and taverns.[22] The inclusion of the tolls reads as an extension of the system that had been developed along the frontier, with an exception that "no one anywhere will collect tolls and ferry fees, and bridge fees from military service people (*sluzhilyi liudei*), from *dvoriane* and *deti boiarskie*, and foreigners (*inozemtsy*)."[23] As every *nakaz* subsequent to the *Ulozhenie* insisted that its principles be enforced, this would seem to eliminate most tolls along the length of the Volga. However, foreign merchants were already greatly restricted, and "foreigners" referred to here were mercenaries in the tsar's army. Similarly, the elites mentioned (*dvoriane* and *deti boiarskie*), generally were not merchants but tsarist servitors; elite merchants (*gosti*) already had tax free status within the kingdom.[24] Therefore, the *Ulozhenie* described a toll system designed to tax local communities: townspeople, local merchants, and peasants traveling to markets.

The revenue raised from the collection of customs was not inconsequential. For example, Simbirsk's customs official collected 129 rubles from tariffs in May 1666 alone, and averaged approximately 100 rubles per month throughout the following summer. During the winter, customs duties dropped to little as 10 rubles per month, but trade duties over the course of one year were more than the money produced from fines in the *voevoda's* court in that same period.[25] Although the Volga trade route never developed to meet the projections of Russian (or English and Dutch) merchants, it produced sufficient customs revenue to subsidize improvements to the security and infrastructure of the region.

Local authorities depended on their church auxiliaries to help maximize the revenue from merchants and the hinterland. Local administrators assigned responsibility for this task to the Russian Orthodox Church itself, and thus monasteries and local *voevody* shared responsibilities for collecting taxes. The Church had the physical presence and staff to make its involvement valuable, and thereby provided a convenient solution for the problem of too few administrators on the frontier. Kazan's Zilantov Uspenskii Monastery, for example, was assigned a section of the Volga River near Tetiushii as early as 1585. The Prikaz informed the *voevoda* of Kazan of the expected fees from the monastery's trade regulation, created by a sliding scale that linked the size of the vessel on the river to its fee. A trading boat (*tovarnii lodok*) paid one *grivna*, while fishing boats in the Volga River paid less for fishing privileges in the same waters.[26] While the fees were nominal, the monastery's fees were not the only ones a boat would pay traveling down the river or over land. Another example was Saransk's Spasskii Monastery, which was assigned a length of the road between Kazan and Saransk. It kept a portion of its assessed fees as an incentive to encourage its vigilance.[27]

The combination of monasteries and *voevody* monitoring merchants and their goods was assembled in an ad hoc manner; it nonetheless functioned as a state-managed toll system. Nor did it assess duties only on goods in transit through the region but also on whatever local commodities were acquired. The best example of this was control over fish taken from the Volga River and its subsidiaries. The Prikaz instructed the *voevoda* of Kazan to maintain records on the volume and price of fish being sold in Kazan, compare that information to previous years, and report any irregularities to the Prikaz.[28] River tolls charged to goods transiting the river and on those goods consumed in transit emphasized the importance of the river to the region's revenue. The *voevoda* needed accurate data to adjust duties yearly, and it served as a check on customs' agents. If fish reached Kazan's market but toll revenues did not corroborate the volume of the catch, the *voevoda* could investigate whether fraud was occurring.

The difficulties of managing local issues reflected the greater challenge of economic development for state and regional authorities. The Volga River was not only a new trade route to control but also an opportunity for Muscovy to position itself within a global economy, in hopes of increasing its profits with new trade relationships in countries that had only ever been indirect contacts.[29] English merchants had arrived in the 1550s and earlier foreign trade had only traveled through the Baltic Sea or overland through Poland. Muscovy's new economic policies were only an assortment of vaguely defined principles, and yet they proved useful for encouraging further investment in the region. Muscovy, like other early modern states, had reached a point when it could opt to direct its economic development, but there was no clear precedent in Russian history or in Kazan's past that resembled this attempt to develop trade.

Domestic Developments

As secure routes and trade infrastructure developed, the regional economy expanded to sustain the growing population on the frontier.[30] Security was the Prikaz Kazanskogo dvortsa's primary regional responsibility, but it still supervised and attempted to regulate this economy, and continued to act in cooperative competition with its administrators and the Russian Orthodox Church. At the same time, local traders and townspeople, who acted first in their own interests rather than at the state's direction, assumed the leading role, fostering the emergence of local markets and products. The region's ability to produce sufficient produce and valuable commodities to sustain its population and export to other regions of Muscovy might be the greatest success of the colonial project. It was, however, as much an accomplishment of the local populace as the state.[31]

The centerpieces of the regional market were new local marketplaces, which arose in all new towns and outposts. In most cases, they emerged inside monastery walls for security. For example, Arzamas's Troitse-Sergeevskii Monastery was the primary market of Arzamas, Simbirsk's market was located in its Troitse-Sergeevskii Monastery, and the Spaso-Preobrazhenskii Monastery served Kazan.[32] The customs house in Kazan, in fact, sat just outside the monastery's walls, in order to register merchants traveling to and from the market.[33] Descriptions of these monastic courtyards depict them as bustling, complete with numerous merchants and a variety of commodities, especially grain, fish, and salt, which were the primary local products.[34] While the cities along the Volga benefited from steady river traffic, even inland cities, such as Saransk, had robust markets visited by merchants from neighboring cities and as far away as Arkhangel'sk.[35]

Though the monasteries offered a safer site for commerce, local secular authorities shared the revenues it generated. Aside from stationing the customs office just outside of the monastic gates as in Kazan, the local *voevoda* and monasteries shared the rent that the monasteries collected from merchants for occupying space in the courtyard. Once again, the Church shouldered responsibility for regulating trade, and the government benefited.[36] The money collected was not inconsiderable, and the competition over space in the monastic courtyards was strong. Meeting the cost of the rents could be difficult, to the point that it was not uncommon for merchants to exchange other property for a small spot in the courtyard. For example, one trader, Andronik Elizarov, petitioned Arzamas's Troitse-Sergeevskii Monastery's abbot for permission to sell goods in the monastery, with the offer of a plot of land in the city as payment in 1618/19.[37] Offering land in exchange became so frequent that some monasteries expressed concern as their income dwindled.[38] From this one perspective, the revived markets could quickly undo their monastic developers. This phenomenon also illustrates that despite the development of a more robust local economy, the lack of currency and a connection to the central economy of Muscovy acted as a retarding factor. Cash was rare—land was not. The state demanded taxes in cash, but the monasteries and merchants could deal most easily in kind, if not in land. This was, for many years, a colonial economy, which slowed economic development and limited the flow of trade. Still, it is difficult to assess how the impoverished center could have perceived, or solved, this problem, without a massive infusion of specie in the form of grants or bounties. Such funds were not forthcoming, and development relied on making something from the land.

Thus it is no surprise that the value of the new trade, and the new lands, was in agriculture and the natural commodities an economy driven by specie-poor commerce could provide. As early as the twelfth century, Moscow had imported grain from Kazan.[39] Grain provided one of the early trade goods for Moscow, as it generally authorized local purchases of grain in order to bring more valuable commodities into the region. It long remained the basic commodity of the region. The Prikaz Kazanskogo dvortsa instructed Sviiazhsk's Bogoroditsii Monastery's to buy up to 264 tons of rye and 85 tons of oats in Cheboksary, for example, and transport that grain to Astrakhan to buy salt and fish, probably a very typical transaction within the region's economy by the seventeenth century.[40]

Grain, fish, and salt, more or less daily necessities, dominated the local markets. Demand was sufficient that several monasteries and local businesses began to commercially produce salt by the later seventeenth century. Other products entered the market as well. Beekeeping, a traditional occupation among the non-Russian populations of the region, produced honey and beeswax, valuable early-modern goods. There was a trade in horses as well, since many of the nearby nomadic tribes, particularly the Nogai Tatars, raised horses. Some of these commodities were sold throughout Muscovy, especially honey, wax, and horses, while the region itself consumed most of its grain and fish.

Of the more valuable and exportable commodities, honey was one of the first that Muscovite authorities attempted to exploit. As early as 1555, for example, local beekeepers paid tribute to the new Muscovite government with their honey production. In a bequest from that year, the early founders of the local Orthodox Church—Archbishop Gurii, Archimandrite German of Sviiazhsk's Bogoroditsii Monastery, and Archimandrite Varsonofii of the Spaso-Preobrazhenskii Monastery in Kazan—received yearly allocations of 500 puds (18,050 lbs.), 200 puds, and 6 puds of honey, respectively. According to the land cadastre of 1623–24, 2,330 Tatar beekeepers lived in the district surrounding Kazan alone.[41]

Honey and wax remained profitable and easily transportable commodities throughout the seventeenth century; honey generally sold for 1 ruble per pud while beeswax could be as much as 9 rubles per pud, and Volga merchants sold both outside the river basin.[42] Fedot Anikeev, for example, a resident of Kazan, arrived in Vologda on 24 September 1634 with three carts of honey and beeswax to sell, and on 26 March 1636 he arrived in Velikii Ustiug with 20 puds of wax and 32 puds of honey.[43] Koz'modem'iansk resident Nikita Terent'ev frequently sold honey in the north, selling 169 puds of honey in Velikii Ustiug on 28 January 1651 and then honey worth 17 rubles, 16 altyns, and 4 dengi in that same city on 15 October 1651.[44]

Though honey and wax were the most profitable products from the region, fish was naturally a source of revenue both as a trade commodity and a consumable along the trade routes, and controlling access to fish was a profitable enterprise in its own right. Kazan's Spaso-Preobrazhenskii Monastery, for example, possessed fishing privileges for a section of the Volga River but charged fees for access in advance of the actual fishing. In 1644, a group Tatars from Sviiazhsk district petitioned the abbot for permission to access the river and the monastery's woods. When permission was granted, the abbot received 200 rubles as an advance payment on the taxes due.[45] Throughout the region, the Prikaz Kazanskogo dvortsa regulated the grants of fishing rights to achieve some balance between the local authorities and religious institutions. Arzamas's Spaso-Preobrazhenskii Monastery had the right to tax its Russian peasants for access to the local rivers Meil' and Avn', but its non-Russian residents paid taxes to the local *voevoda* instead.[46]

The profits from grants of fishing rights provided an incentive for the local *voevody* to push for limiting or eliminating monastic rights. In 1616, Sviiazhsk's Troitse-Sergeevskii Monastery received the right to fish in the Volga within the Kazan district from the tsar, which included, at that time, the right to impose taxes on all men fishing in its new section of the river.[47] Later that year, Kazan's *Voevoda* Volodimer Timof'evich Dolgorukov seized the rights to the Volga near Kazan, and instead extended the monastery those same privileges farther downriver near Samara, with a warning that they should not expect to hold those rights indefinitely.[48] The monastery was forced into an area of fewer profits and greater expenses, supervising the river at a greater distance from the city. The tsar and his government consistently directed that all monasteries in Kazan and Sviiazhsk obtain the right to fish for themselves in the Volga at the very least, though the *voevody* constantly tested this right.[49] As the century progressed, the *voevody* won this battle. Koz'modem'iansk's Spaso-Iunginskii Monastery, for example, was informed in 1663 of the new yearly tax rates for their right to fish the local rivers. The monastery owed the tsar 30 rubles, 14 altyns, and 7 dengi per year, and another 20 rubles, 17 altyns, and 4 dengi for the Koz'modem'iansk's *voevoda*.[50]

Nor was this sort of arrangement limited only to the northern section of the region where Muscovite rule was the most established. In the 1630s, Saratov's Novospasskii Monastery received the right to tax fishing boats, but this grant was because of the monastery's poverty. Were it to increase its income from its other economic privileges, then the tsar's government would rescind the fishing rights.[51] The monastery subsequently bombarded both the tsar and the local *voevody* with petitions to keep its privileges for the next two decades, rather than until it could afford to lose them.[52] It succeeded in 1659. At that time, Saratov's *Voevoda* Aleksei Mikhailovich Khitrovo confirmed the monastery's rights, but increased the amounts collected from tariffs and also increased the tsar's share of the monastery's revenue.[53]

The commodity of most concern to the central chancelleries and the local government was the local horse trade. As horses were of great military value, every agency at every level was concerned about the regulation of the trade. In fact, it was sufficiently important to central authorities that in February 1555, Kazan's *voevoda* received a *gramota* instructing him to welcome Nogai horse merchants into the marketplace at the Troitse-Sergeevskii Monastery. As rent for space in the monastery's courtyard, the monastery received five horses.[54] Even following the construction of the first defensive line in the 1570s, Kazan remained "open" to at least some of the nomads the line was designed to repel—as long as they were trading horses.[55]

The horse trade rapidly expanded after the turn of the century and the region developed into a critical resource for Muscovy. Horses traveled to Muscovy's fairs from a number of sources inside the former khanate. At the Kursk fair, for example, horses were sold from Alatyr' (1677/78), Arzamas (1647/48), Atemar (1660/61), Kazan (1677/78), Kurmysh (1628/29), Simbirsk (1677/78), and Cheboksary (1677/78).[56] During a horse fair in the northern city of Velikii Ustiug between 14 and 19 February 1634, nine residents of Kazan sold a total of eight geldings and two mares. The mares both sold for three rubles, while the average price for the geldings was 3.7 rubles.[57] Two years later, another eleven residents of Kazan each sold a gelding in Ustiug. Five of those merchants were peasants from the estates of Kazan's Spaso-Preobrazhenskii Monastery, one was from Sviiazhsk's Troitse-Sergeevskii Monastery, and two were peasants from the estates of Kazan's metropolitan.[58]

As the profits from the horse trade were considerable, and the military applications made the trade essential, it was an obvious target for increased regulation and state rent-gathering. In the *nakaz* to Kazan in 1649, the Prikaz Kazanskogo dvortsa instructed the *voevoda* to monitor all commodities of military potential. Horse traders needed explicit permission from the Prikaz for any sale. No horses could be sold to either Nogai Tatars or Bashkirs, local nomadic groups threatening Muscovite trade, unless they had demonstrated their loyalty to the tsar.[59] The *nakaz* offered no definition of "loyalty" in this case, and it is difficult to imagine the circumstance in which the Turkic nomads could effectively get around this provision.[60]

Businesses as well as commodity products concerned the Prikaz Kazanskogo dvortsa. Mills, for example, were quite valuable. Establishing new mills was a challenge, as the region's rivers tended to be slow moving, and occasionally dried up, which made working water mills a most precious installation for their owners. The right to own and operate a mill was therefore of enormous value. In most cases, religious institutions obtained the new mills, but the Prikaz Kazanskogo dvortsa instructed monks, nuns, and priests how much their services would cost and who was allowed to use them. Arzamas's Troitse-Sergeevskii Monastery received a mill inside Arzamas for its own uses, but a deed in 1632 ordered the monastery to allow townspeople to use it.[61] Protests against the central authorities' decisions were summarily dismissed. The Prikaz granted the Kievo-Nikolaevskii Convent in Alatyr' a mill in the village of Kichazanskii (in Alatyr' district) as early as 1606/7. The villagers and the *voevody* of Alatyr' contested the ownership numerous times, but the Prikaz kept the mill in the convent's hands.[62]

Of course, with mills so profitable, they were the subject of numerous disputes. One such mill in Kazan district caused years of legal wrangling. The right to run the mill had originally been granted to Iakov Vasil'ev syn Asanov, a Tatar *mirza* in Muscovite service. Kazan's Prechistii Bogoroditsii Monastery claimed the mill so that it could finance its rebuilding following a fire. The Prikaz Kazanskogo dvortsa ruled in Asanov's favor, as he needed the profits from the mill to support the expenses related to his military service for the tsar. Surprisingly, the fact that the monastery had no preexisting claim to the mill was not mentioned in the decision.[63] Two years later, another local Tatar in service with the tsar, Emei Khoziashev, also submitted a claim to the mill. He claimed to possess a grant for the land on which the mill sat, and as Asanov had stopped operating the mill, it was valueless, reverted to the land, and, thus, belonged to him. Asanov responded in court that the mill had been inactive because of level of river had recently been too low, but this did not mean that he had abandoned the enterprise. Both men possessed sets of deeds their respective claims, signed by the Prikaz. With both men holding a claim, the Prikaz refused complete protection of Asanov's rights to the mill. Instead, it decided to divide future profits in half, with each man receiving a share.[64] The simple conclusion, that the Prikaz was concerned mainly with ensuring that both servitors could maintain their households, might well be erroneous. If Asanov required the mill's profits to serve, cutting his income in half would place his ability to do so in jeopardy. If Khoziashev had served without the extra income, there could be little military necessity behind the decision. What was more likely was that the Prikaz was ultimately and fundamentally concerned with operation, not with ownership. Indeed, this judgment makes more sense viewed from the standpoint of an organization that valued the income of such a property working in service to the state as more important than whether any one servitor owned clear title to it.[65]

This makes it clear why the Prikaz regulated mills in the same way it regulated other regional commercial enterprises crucial to the economy, notably taverns and ferries. Taverns were a state-regulated monopoly throughout all of Muscovy, which was further confirmed in law with the promulgation of the *Ulozhenie* of 1649, which outlawed bootlegging and unlicensed taverns.[66] Ivashko Semenov syn Karakashev, a converted Tatar in Muscovite service, petitioned the tsar with his wish to open a tavern on his land along the Ara River outside of Sviiazhsk. He received permission to run a tavern and sell beer.[67] Emei Khoziashev, a Muslim Tatar in tsarist service, had an established tavern and ferry along the Kama River outside of Kazan, but received instructions from Moscow that he must move his businesses farther up the river and away from town.[68] According to the central chancelleries, the ferry was intended to serve Russian, Tatar, Chuvash, and Mari traders, and in its current location it did not. An unwritten reason might have been the state's desire to limit the access of unconverted non-Russians to Kazan, or reserve the better crossing for a Russian, but it also no doubt demonstrates the central government's concern with ensuring its income by manipulating the number of profit-making concerns.

The last major, local trade regulated by the Prikaz Kazanskogo dvortsa was also extremely important in the early-modern era: salt. It was nearly impossible to live or trade without using it to preserve meat and fish. Early salt supplies for Muscovy had traveled up the Volga River from the Caspian Sea. The conquest of Kazan gave Moscow the hope that it could secure to itself this most constant and valuable trade. Salt prices varied in the region throughout the seventeenth century, between 1 pud for .01556 rubles in 1610 to 1 pud for .03125 rubles by the 1665, but the volume of salt steadily increased.[69]

Sviiazhsk's Bogoroditsii Monastery became one of the earliest large-scale salt merchants. The Prikaz Kazanskogo dvortsa instructed the monastery to import 10,000 puds (361,000 lbs.) of salt from Astrakhan. The importation of the salt was not taxed, greatly facilitating the monks' willingness to trade. The salt could be sold in Kazan, Sviiazhsk, or Nizhnii Novgorod for whatever commodities were needed by the monks, including bread, honey, butter, hemp-seed oil, sheepskin, or cloth. In 1613 the Prikaz raised the amount of salt imported by the monastery to 20,000 puds, making the monastery an early center for salt trading in Muscovy.[70] Later records reveal that the monastery imported 33,250 puds of salt in 1621, an increase from the 21,687 puds bought in 1610/11, which had sold for 3,376 rubles.[71]

By the middle of the seventeenth century, Muscovite authorities realized that the region itself could produce salt.[72] Salt refineries became one the most profitable businesses along the Volga within a short period of time. In the 1660s, an official tsarist charter instructed the Savva-Storozhevskii Monastery in Kazan district to establish a salt refinery (*solianyi promysl'*) on their lands in Samara district along the Volga River. The Prikaz Kazanskogo dvortsa granted the monastery the right to hire outside workers for the salt refinery in the 1670s.[73] As was often the case, the Prikaz passed the initial investment costs onto a local monastery, though in this instance there were sufficient profits for all to benefit. In fact, control over the salt refineries became a contentious issue among the central chancelleries. After all, it was infrequent that one of Muscovy's economic projects produced real profits, after sustaining a local institution or the local populace. In the case of the Savva-Storozhevskii Monastery, by the 1680s control over the salt-refining business was seized by Prikaz Bol'shogo dvortsa, even though the Prikaz Kazanskogo dvortsa still received taxes from the monasteries' fishing rights.[74]

There was clear development within the local economy during the sixteenth and seventeenth century, measured by the complexity of the trade network and the increased government interest in regulating it. The Muscovite chancelleries attempted to supervise all commercial traffic along the Volga, developed new businesses, and increased control over the most profitable (and available) products. Local disputes, among individuals or between church and state, were not uncommon, but this did not noticeably impede the rate at which Moscow's influence over commerce increased. In general, it appears that the region did manage to provide for its own needs, which was no small accomplishment. It might be that this was the one area were individual interest and the state's goals most closely coincided— profits were profits—but it was neither quick nor limitless. The economic development of the region was a slow, evolutionary process, achieved by a conscious campaign to gather information and exploit the Russian Orthodox Church's resources. Spectacular profits from international commerce along the Volga River never appeared. Instead, a basic form of economic development, agricultural, practical, and based on primary products that could travel well, was what maintained the Muscovite government in the region. Supplying the local population was the foundation for all other colonial projects.

International Developments

Whereas the local economy was driven by necessity, Muscovy's attempted transformation of the region into a new direct route between East and West was far more enticing, entirely because of the stream of profit it promised. All early-modern governments aspired to a beneficial balance of trade. Muscovy, with its existing trade routes generating only anemic amounts of hard currency, was particularly desirous to generate specie from a new trade with Asian empires. It possessed numerous "naval commodities" (timber, pitch, tar, and flax) that were necessary for the growing navies of Europe, and its hides and furs remained popular throughout Europe and Asia. Unfortunately, it possessed little that would serve as a steady export commodity to the Middle East and Asia. Undoubtedly, the idea of making Muscovy the middleman of Europe was entrancing. It appeared possible: Muscovy held the route, and it would not need a desirable commodity if it could find profits in the transit of goods by foreign merchants. Achieving this goal, considering its limited control over the Volga River and its even more tenuous power over the nomads of the open steppe, was more difficult than early assessments predicted.

Foreign merchants operating inside Muscovy's borders lobbied the government to attempt the opening of an Asian trade route, on the chance that they could more easily tap Iranian and Chinese exports with Russian security protecting their caravans. The English, particularly, pursued the issue despite an absence of experience in managing such an enormous project on either side. The domestic development of the Middle Volga region took decades, yet as early as the 1550s English merchants were attempting to negotiate exclusive privileges for dominating its trade with Asia. With the arrival of West European merchants in Moscow, Ivan IV's government experimented with various regulations to protect Muscovy's commercial interests. In the wake of the English arrival, the chancelleries instituted a higher tax rate on all goods purchased by foreign merchants compared to Russian merchants, with the intent to protect domestic merchants and increase the amount of hard currency foreign merchants would provide state coffers.[75] Given these early restrictions, the initial 1587 agreement between the English "Muscovy Company" and the tsar seemed like a great victory for the foreigners, as the tsar granted English merchants freedom from local tariffs. The Muscovy Company's concession was geographically limited, however, to Muscovy's north, specifically the towns of Arkhangel'sk, Kholmogory, Iaroslavl', Vologda, and Moscow.[76] The Posol'skii Prikaz set the terms of its negotiations with foreign merchants for the next century. It would concede tax privileges to entice merchant spending, and content itself with the introduction of specie into the country, but restricted the foreign merchants' range of action in order to maintain its control over the economy. As long as the English desired access to Iran, India, or even China by traveling along the Volga River, Moscow could dictate the terms.

Queen Elizabeth I's government pursued the goal of unrestricted access for decades, though the English made progress only during the reign of Tsar Boris Godunov at the turn of the seventeenth century. The timing of the appeal worked to the benefit of the English—Godunov was in charge of a cash-strapped government still recovering from the expenses of the Livonian War; Moscow welcomed any promises of foreign-trade revenue. Queen Elizabeth succeeded without making many additional concessions:

> Yett have wee gyven to our said Ambassdor [Francis Cherry] order, to move your Majesty as well for the benefitt of your subjects, and merchaunts, as of ours, to consider of a further discovery, and settling of traffique into Persia, through some part of your Highnes Dominiions, which hee shall more perticulerly open to your Majesty when you shalbe pleased to give hym audience in other matters.[77]

Shortly after this opening accord, the new king James I signed the anticipated agreement, and in 1605 the English finally received a guarantee of access to all Iranian, Indian, and Chinese goods transported through Muscovy.[78] In this instance, the timing was not to England's benefit; the chaos of the Time of Troubles prevented anything like a normal volume of trade from flowing along the Volga for the next decade. Even so, the English continued to pursue access and believed the 1605 accord would allow additional negotiations with the new Romanov government in 1613.[79]

This appeared likely at the start of the Romanov era. The administration needed funds to rebuild the army and repair the state. Muscovy lacked hard currency, and foreign trade could help resolve the problem of the specie shortfall.[80] Indeed, the English were no longer the sole seekers after the Volga trade, which created a potentially lucrative competition for the tsar's approval. Dutch merchants, including Isaac Massa, indicated that real potential existed in trade with the West.[81] Mikhail Fedorovich's government planned, therefore, to use foreign traders to help Moscow construct an ambitious framework—trading embassies with the great empires in Iran, India, and subsequently, China, with the goal of a permanent establishment of commerce through the Volga basin. Establishing relations with the Muslim states was, in any case, a high priority.[82] There is no indication in either English or Dutch records that these merchants understood that Moscow pursued its own interests in the south through foreign traders, although this assuredly occurred to them. Business was business, and mutual interests would be rewarded if the ventures succeeded, even if the Dutch and English served as Muscovite agents.

Of course, Moscow sought a stream of revenue and, in order to secure one, needed to insert itself into the market in order to sequester a portion of the price of imports, preferably by preventing English and Dutch merchants from accessing markets directly. Direct purchase of goods by the Europeans in Iran, for example, was counterproductive.[83] Muscovy's plan was clear, though its execution was somewhat muddy. In theory, elite Russian merchants bought a license for the importation of silk from Iran or India, arranged for transportation along the Volga, and then sold that silk in Moscow to West European merchants. The state benefited from the cost of the licenses and potentially from subsequent duties on transit out of Muscovy. This way, in principle, Muscovy would reap the benefit of its cross-continental trade routes while not alienating foreign traders. This was, after the fact, a continuing rationale for restricting the Dutch and English to the far north of Muscovy, forcing them into compliance with the plan for economic development.

In actuality, Moscow was unsuccessful in establishing a connection between its designated merchants and the Muslim powers, which always hindered its implementation of the plans to make the Volga an international trade route. This failure, often repeated, never deterred successive generations of Western speculators. The negotiations between Muscovite merchants and Iran and India took place away from European notice. And while few Russians may have traveled to Western

Europe, they traveled to the south and east in more significant numbers. For example, between 1590 and 1626, the tsars dispatched at least ten official embassies to Safavid Iran.[84] Ottoman Turkey also received Muscovite emissaries, and Russians crisscrossed the Caucasus region, using it as a (slow) highway and destination throughout the seventeenth century. Many of these travelers were official state embassies, but Russian merchants followed these same routes for their own commercial interests, which, of course, also served state goals.[85]

Though individual Russian merchants made profits, the administration had little success in establishing its vision of a permanent trade delegation or outpost in the south during the seventeenth century despite its persistent efforts. Generating new revenue from foreign trade was an essential mission of Mikhail Fedorovich's new government. With the Europeans still penned in Moscow and to the north, the great hurdle to be overcome before implementing the trade plan for the Volga was the Safavid court in Isfahan. The Posol'skii Prikaz wasted little time in dispatching two embassies to Iran and India following the Romanov ascension: Fëdor Isakovich Leont'ev in 1616 and Mikhail Petrovich Bariatinskii in 1618. Neither succeeded in producing any firm agreement.[86] With these early economic embassies a failure, the Posol'skii Prikaz rethought its strategy and dispatched an information-gathering mission to create the basis for future negotiations. This became the official task of the merchant Fedot Afanasev syn Kotov, dispatched from Moscow in 1623/24.[87] Kotov's journey to Iran traveled along the expected route, down the Moskva River to the Volga all the way to Astrakhan. From Astrakhan Kotov boarded a barge on the Caspian Sea, landing in the Safavid city of Shirvan, and then traveling overland to Isfahan. Isfahan was a great entrepôt, from which Kotov gathered information on the Muslim trading world, with a particular emphasis on Iran and India, the centers of the silk trade that could potentially provide so much benefit to Muscovite fortunes.

Though Kotov made no progress in establishing any formal relationship with Iran, his lack of success did little to dim the optimism of the Posol'skii Prikaz. Kotov hoped that the tense relationship between Mughal India and Safavid Iran could be exploited to produce a more favorable view of Moscow. If Iran was uninterested, then perhaps India could be enticed.[88] Following Kotov's journey, three more embassies from Moscow traveled to Mughal India over the course of the seventeenth century, each carrying a proposal to establish a new overland route from Astrakhan to Bukhara in Central Asia and then south into India.[89] However, by the middle of the seventeenth century, Portuguese, English, and Dutch merchants all had overseas routes to India, which undermined any Muscovite attempt to insert itself into this international exchange. In addition, Muscovy still lacked a viable commodity to sustain a long-term trade with the Muslim world. In 1613, all Moscow had to offer was a route from the Middle East to Europe, in which the Europeans would offer specie for silk and spices. By 1650, Moscow did not even have that.

This does not imply that there was no transit of international goods along the Volga, only that no agency succeeded in establishing a monopoly or a great volume of trade. Individual merchants were potentially the greatest beneficiaries of the Volga trade route, particularly Russian merchants who maintained a freedom of movement denied to their foreign counterparts. One example would be Prokopei Andreev from Kazan. He appears in customs records frequently, buying sable, fox, and bear pelts in Siberia for sales in Velikii Ustiug, Vologda, and Iaroslavl', and purchasing Iranian silk in Kazan for sale in those same places during the 1630s. At one point, he traveled with as much as 150 rubles of silk, which was a considerable investment.[90] At the same time, no Russian or foreign merchant ever received right to an exclusive monopoly. Rather than putting cash directly into state coffers in Moscow, the best the state could hope for was some revenue from tariffs for transportation along the Volga. Though Andreev's trade indicates there was demand for Iranian silk, the fact that he could not purchase the silk in Iran reveals the continuing failure of Moscow's embassies in the south.

What trade there was lay primarily in the hands of Asian merchants who enjoyed access to the Muscovite market even before 1552. The chancelleries chose to risk disrupting this trade after the Romanov era began, and only then did the Posol'skii Prikaz attempt to restrict the ability of Iranian and Indian merchants inside Muscovy's borders to force those men into a similar position as the English and Dutch. For example, in 1638, Kazan's *voevoda* petitioned the tsar concerning the arrival of Iranian and Indian merchants in his city from Astrakhan. The merchants carried gifts for the Posol'skii Prikaz in order to persuade Muscovite authorities to allow them to travel to Moscow with their trade goods. For the moment, they remained in Kazan.[91] While at first this action seems counterintuitive considering the lack of progress Russian merchants had made to the south, the goal for the chancelleries was to place domestic transit in the hands of Russian merchants. Therefore, although relations with these specific merchants might have been improved by allowing their journey to Moscow, this compromise would have done nothing to improve Moscow's position vis-à-vis the Muslim empires and their economies.

Meanwhile, the Posol'skii Prikaz's failure to develop a trade monopoly likely inspired its firm stance on restricting the English presence in Moscow. As early as 1626, King Charles I was making lavish promises to Tsar Mikhail Fedorovich about the potential benefits from allowing English trade along the Volga. Charles promised that he desired that "this Trade of Silk should be settled in your Majesties Dominions rather than in any other Kingdome," while at the same time the English East India Company was already doing just that.[92] No English promise of potential profit, however, would be sufficient to alter the Muscovite policy of banning European merchants from traveling the Volga. Allowing the English access would only have created the possibility that they might succeed where Muscovy failed, and create a situation in which Muscovy would have to settle for English middlemen on a Russian trade route.

Still, resisting English arguments remains a remarkable decision, in light of the Russians' limited profits, the lack of progress in Iran or India, and the continuing security issues. Admittedly, as long as the English believed the Volga offered superior speed and safety to the Middle East compared with traveling through Ottoman Turkey, Moscow maintained a strong hand. In fact, at one point King Charles I sought permission for his ambassador to Iran to travel through Muscovy to Arkhangel'sk for "his speedier returne," arguing that the Volga was far safer than the overseas route.[93] The second, and perhaps more pressing, factor that explains the English persistence was its developing competition with the Dutch over access to the East.[94] Following the English merchants' loss of privileges after the Time of Troubles, the Dutch petitioned the tsar for the right to export Persian silk through Muscovy, guaranteed by a thirty-year monopoly for the Company of Filippo.[95] Although that plan was not successful, Dutch merchants still enjoyed the benefits of their advantageous treaty with the Iranian Shah in 1619.[96] The English hoped to match or exceed its terms. Throughout the seventeenth century, Dutch merchants gained several exclusive export contracts to Russian goods, including important naval commodities such as tar and timber. The English attempts to break the Dutch export monopolies increased the importance of Muscovy and the Volga River for both the English Muscovy Company and East Indies Company.[97] To a great extent, the best way for the Posol'skii Prikaz to continue to receive interesting offers from the English and the Dutch was to use access to the trade route as leverage. It is no wonder that despite the lack of success, the English continued to ardently pursue the goal of foreign trade, particularly focusing on the potentiality of an exclusive monopoly on the importation of silk.

John Hebdon, the English envoy in Moscow during the 1660s, recorded his attempts to persuade the tsar's authorities for an English concession, in hopes of transferring English trade from Ottoman Turkey to Muscovy and undermining the East India Company in the process. Hebdon explained his negotiating tactics in a memo to the Foreign Secretary in London, telling the tsar's officials that the Ottoman sultan attempted to "enriche himselfe and with a great many violencyes and injuries by laying upon then heavy impositions let them passe from himselfe unto Christian Countryes." Furthermore, Hebdon promised that as the English traders would be so much safer traveling through Muscovy than Turkey, that Iran's Shah Abbas would "thank" the tsar for the privilege.[98] The English were trying to exploit Moscow's hope of a permanent trade relationship with Iran but still failed to alter the Posol'skii Prikaz's restrictions.

Informal expedience often trumped the strictest regulation where foreign trade was concerned. Neither the Posol'skii Prikaz nor the Prikaz Kazanskogo dvortsa was entirely successful with either trade regulation or control over merchants' movement. In fact, it would have been nearly impossible for them to manage total control with so many ways for traders to evade tolls and patrols. The chancelleries also compromised their own restrictions in unexpected ways. At least one English doctor resided in Kazan as early as 1622, even though all "Englishmen" had been banned from traveling farther south than Moscow.[99] A similar situation occurred when the Posol'skii Prikaz awarded John White, a member of the English Muscovy Company, the houses of his Russian debtors in Arzamas, creating an English property owner in a city he "officially" could not enter.[100]

In spite of their lack of any notable successes in foreign trade, the Muscovite chancelleries had learned to benefit from stricter controls over the economy by the 1640s. The toll system, in fact, continued to produce specie where other sectors of the economy did not. Increased control created other opportunities as well. Rather than worry if businesses succeeded or failed, selling monopolies provided immediate cash payments up front and placed the risk of the new enterprise on someone other than the government. With a combination of restrictive controls on all commercial exchanges, and use of monopoly licenses to regulate domestic business, the Muscovite government developed in similar ways to most early modern economies— as a mercantilist one. While "mercantilism" as a system is a later identification of these processes, the protectionist and monopolist stance taken by the Muscovite chancelleries to develop the domestic economy and squeeze foreign trade through taxes was not a unique solution.[101]

The *Ulozhenie* of 1649 formalized certain aspects of the domestic economy, but it did not revise, or even address, the role of foreign merchants inside Muscovy's borders. This was left to the revised commercial guidelines published in 1667, which placed a fully protectionist set of controls on all foreign trade. Previously, foreign merchants had been governed by varied regulations controlled by the Posol'skii Prikaz. These ad hoc policies were revised on a case-by-case basis, as when the English Muscovy Company lost its freedom from Muscovite tariffs in 1649.[102] The 1667 *Novotorgovyi ustav* (New Commercial Code) expanded the restrictions for all merchants, not only charging foreign merchants punitive tariffs on all trade goods but also physically restricting all foreign merchants inside the kingdom. Foreign merchants could conduct business only in Arkhangel'sk, Novgorod, Pskov, Smolensk, Putivl', and Astrakhan, severely curtailing their presence in the Muscovite market and preventing any access to the Volga. The English and Dutch were limited to the north, the Swedes to the west, and Indians and Iranians to the far south.[103]

Foreign merchants found the changes significantly more restrictive, but it produced immediate economic benefits for the kingdom in the forms of new fines and new transit opportunities within the country. In Astrakhan, customs officials suddenly gained responsibility for regulating all trade with Asia. The local governor warned the customs officials to watch all "foreigners and Russian people from across the sea."[104] Merchants arriving on Muscovy's shores from the East and West protested the newly invasive inspections but with little result.[105] The new policies remained in force. The reasons were obvious. While some merchants felt wronged by the new procedures, the state had far more to gain by collecting customs duties than it did in accommodating the interest of the merchants. In terms of the long-term attempt to sway Iran or India into supporting contacts with Russian trade interests, this policy could do little but hinder future progress. But only a small trickle of trade was funneled into Russian hands, and Muscovite leverage was still so meager that hindering progress had few consequences.[106]

By this point in the seventeenth century, regulating the movement of foreign merchants was part of the central chancelleries' plan to create a state-managed zone of trade within the interior of Moscow. Foreign goods were still transported along the Volga River, but in well-defined arrangement with specific monopolies. The so-called Armenian Company was established in 1677 to transport goods from Iran and India between Astrakhan and Moscow, having been approved by both the Posol'skii Prikaz and the Prikaz Kazanskogo dvortsa.[107] As a state-sponsored transportation monopoly, the Armenian Company paid for its privilege directly to the central chancelleries, and the local *voevody* and customs officials along the Volga River were forbidden from interfering with the trade. At approximately the same time, the Muscovite government formalized its relationship with Bukharan merchants, who had the exclusive right to transport Chinese goods to Moscow. Bukharan caravans traveled through Central Asia overland, arriving at either Astrakhan or Kazan, and were then expected to travel north along the Volga River, as did the Armenian Company.[108] In this way, the Muscovite government guaranteed itself yearly duties from the exclusive monopolies, resolved the transportation of these valuable goods, and reinforced the ban on foreign merchants traveling inside its borders. If English and Dutch merchants desired Asian commodities, they could be purchased only in Moscow; if Iranian merchants desired Muscovite furs, they could be purchased only in Astrakhan.[109]

The bequest of transportation monopolies to foreign merchants inside Muscovy exasperated English merchants eve more. The trade potential obviously existed, but now it was entirely outside of their grasp. John Hebdon petitioned the tsar several times for the return of the Muscovy Company's "ancient privileges" in the 1670s, but the Muscovite government refused to reinstate them, as a return to tax-free status would undermine its economic accomplishments.[110] For the next few decades, the English never abandoned their hope for a return but had little to show for it. Nor were the English alone. In 1676, the Posol'skii Prikaz notified Hebdon that all foreign merchants in Muscovy "shall come upon their borders no further then such and such places." The English and Dutch remained limited to trading in the north, using only the port at Arkhangel'sk, but in addition the Iranians could trade only in Astrakhan, and the Swedes only in Pskov and Novgorod.[111] These new regulations are a clear statement of the state's mercantilistic policies, enforcing increasing restrictions against foreign merchants and providing the state greater control over all exports. Furthermore, the policies seemed to be producing the appropriate responses from the English. In 1677 Hebdon wrote to London with word of the arrival of Iranian luxuries in Moscow; now available were "severall sorts of Rarities, as Carpets, Severall sorts of Silks, Diamonds, and delicate Horses." While the English remained frustrated yet optimistic, there was no doubt that the Muscovite restrictions seemed effective in regulating their role in the economy.

The English failure was rather a fortunate turn of events for the Dutch. Armenian merchants had established a permanent presence in the Netherlands early in the seventeenth century, and Armenians worked for the Dutch East India Company throughout Asia.[112] Therefore, it was quite likely a natural arrangement for the Armenian Company to make an exclusive arrangement with the Dutch in Moscow, providing the Dutch exclusive access to their Iranian silk.[113] The options for purchasing Asian goods left open to the English were thereby quite severely restricted. Though the English had been the first West European merchants to arrive in Moscow, they were consistently outmaneuvered by the Dutch in the seventeenth century. It must have been quite frustrating for the English to have the Muscovite government remove its economic privileges, and then have lost even more to their closest competitors. By 1681, the Muscovy Company had exhausted all of its proposals and could only exhort its representatives to make whatever promises necessary: "His Majesty is pleased to give leave to you and the rest of the Muscovy Company to offer such proposals as you and they shall think most conducing to the encouragement of Trade and recovery of Priviledges formerly enjoyed by the English in those Countries."[114]

While the English interests had been defeated, Muscovy's mercantilistic turn should not be considered a Dutch victory. The Dutch enjoyed an exclusive right to Armenian-transported silk, but they also had been banned from traveling outside of Moscow like the English. For example, they had been quite active in developing a metallurgy industry inside Muscovy. Some of their new mines and refineries were, in fact, near Kazan. Therefore, the travel ban instituted on foreign merchants in the New Commercial Code restricted their potential access to their own businesses. In 1675 the Posol'skii Prikaz denied the sale of an ironworks between Andrei Andreev syn Vinibsov, Vologda resident Iakov Galaktimov syn Galkin, and Dutch merchant Konrad Filipov syn Nordermann to Peter Meller, who was also Dutch.[115] Whereas Nordermann had entered the tsar's service to gain access to the Middle Volga Region, Meller had not. The Posol'skii Prikaz's intervention followed the common, established economic policies of the later seventeenth century; Russians would control the domestic economy.

In fact, international trade only supplemented the much more significant accomplishment of developing the domestic economy. Regulating trade with local tolls produced tax revenue from local commerce, but foreign merchants did travel in numbers through the region and supplemented the system. Though no formal relationship had been established with Iran or India, the *voevody* had sufficient authority to prevent their access to the interior, while not choking the luxury trade. As the English struggled to regain their early privileges in the seventeenth century, and utterly failed to receive the right to travel to the Middle East along the Volga, their merchants were held in Moscow and points north. Dutch merchants exploited new opportunities, but only in a limited role as defined by the Posol'skii Prikaz. Therefore, while the potential of the trade route had not fully developed, it produced enough revenue in taxes and tolls to finance some of Muscovy's building projects in the region. It was progress, albeit slower than any party expected.

Limited Development

The New Commercial Code of 1667 was a serious turning point for Muscovy's economy, including that of the Middle Volga Region. With this new set of laws, the state formally adopted a mercantilistic set of economic practices focused on guiding domestic development, restricting foreign merchants' access to local goods, and selling monopoly licenses for transportation. All of these principles developed out of the experience gained by regulating the economy over the previous century.

The primary achievements in the Middle Volga Region—security for the trade routes, sufficient products to supply the local residents, and tolls and taxes on all transit—predicted the formal resolutions of 1667.

Even so, foreign merchants loudly protested the "innovations" of 1667, which they must have realized were an extension of preexisting practices but would now be more difficult to evade and more expensive to endure. The Posol'skii Prikaz began receiving protests almost immediately. Now that foreign merchants could not leave the border cities, transit that had been permissible if difficult now was exclusively held by transportation monopolies. Iranian and Indian merchants arriving or living in Astrakhan petitioned Muscovite authorities for permission after travel to Kazan had been restricted. For example, a nephew of the Iranian Shah Mamandu Selbek, Oalarbek, protested the refusal of his request to travel to Kazan from Astrakhan to deliver his goods. In previous years, Oalarbek had traveled to Kazan without hindrance; he protested paying a middleman for that same transportation.[116] An Indian merchant living in Astrakhan, Banda Mingaev, petitioned the *voevoda* of Astrakhan for permission to transport his goods to Kazan. The *voevoda* of Astrakhan wrote to the *voevoda* of Kazan about Mingaev, arguing that Mingaev had obtained permission in the past and only wanted his rights restored.[117] As Astrakhan's *voevoda* was arguing contrary to the policies set by the Posol'skii Prikaz, it seems unlikely that this petition could have succeeded.

As new, or at least explicit, international restrictions were recorded in the New Commercial Code, new domestic controls also arose in the late 1660s. For example, rather than merely observing fish sales in their cities, *voevody* now controlled the fishing rights on all nearby rivers, and were able to tax and, if desired, limit the size of the fish market. This was the case for Simbirsk, which forced residents of the city to petition the tsar for access to the rivers outside of the city. In 1669, urban residents protested *Voevoda* Ivan Ivanovich Dashkov's control. He apparently had blocked their access to the river. The Prikaz Kazanskogo dvortsa agreed with the petition, leaving Dashkov with 900 *cheti* of land along the river and fishing rights to those areas, but granting 3,537 acres of riverbank for the city's *strel'tsy* (musketmen) and service people.[118] This was not an altruistic act. The central authorities decided against the *voevoda* in this case because broader access to the river generated much more revenue from the fishing privileges.[119]

Continuous improvements in infrastructure and security remained important for the enforcement of controls and the collection of revenues until the end of the century. Regulation and surveillance had consistently produced monetary benefits— later *nakazy* changed this policy only by degrees. Ten years after the publication of the 1667 code, three separate articles in the *nakaz* of 1677 warned Kazan's current *voevoda* about the continuing difficulties of transporting goods along the Volga. The first noted the steady Bashkir raids on the caravans traveling from all points north to Astrakhan, which led the Prikaz to warn the *voevoda* to protect merchants more carefully.[120] The second was Moscow's answer to a recent petition from the *voevoda* of Astrakhan concerning merchant protests against the increased duties in Kazan. The Prikaz instructed Kazan's *voevoda* that he was not to impede traffic, but he was responsible for collecting all appropriate duties.[121] The third and longest of the articles summarized all recent decisions affecting the Kazan–Astrakhan trade, highlighting the continuing dangers of raids along the route and the lack of long-term solution. More than anything else, it read as a general reminder that previous *voevody* had protected and supported the Volga trade, and the current *voevoda* must also.[122]

With the West European merchants restricted, and the domestic economy under increasingly effective control, the Posol'skii Prikaz returned to its long-term project of establishing favorable trade terms with Iran and India. Considering that the new initiatives followed the travel restrictions imposed on merchants from the Middle East and Asia in 1667, the Prikaz attempted something different: it relied on Muscovy's Muslim population to create the perception that Moscow would be a suitable trade partner. This happened in 1675 when the Prikaz dispatched Muhammed-Iusuf Kasimov from Astrakhan to India.[123] Unlike the earlier embassies that traveled with Russian documents and a translator, Kasimov was dispatched with letters in Latin and Tatar, and no translator. Moscow expected that Kasimov would be able to communicate with an audience familiar with the Persian language in India and along the trade route.

Despite the new approach, Kasimov's results were much the same as his Russian predecessors. According to Kasimov, poor finances hindered his trade mission. The Posol'skii Prikaz sent Kasimov from Astrkahan to Bukhara with only 711 rubles, more than 1,000 rubles less than the amount with which the earlier embassies had been sent.[124] Kasimov constantly peppered the Posol'skii Prikaz with requests for reimbursement for his out-of-pocket expenses, which apparently went unmet. Upon his arrival in India, Kasimov was more than 2,000 rubles in debt, which undermined his diplomatic efforts to speak to the Mughal Emperor in "love and friendship," much less persuade the Mughals to support the possibility of the new trade route to Bukhara.

The Posol'skii Prikaz, through its own shortcomings, once again failed in its attempt to establish regular trade with Iran or India, but this failure did not affect what had been accomplished in the previous century. State control over the Volga River had been vastly increased, if not perfectly implemented, as a new toll system was created; the *voevody* consistently gathered information on the local economy to adjust tax rates and monitor all transit, and foreign merchants had been restricted to dealing with state-designated monopolies, which guaranteed a flow of revenue for the state, no matter whether they ultimately succeeded or failed to maintain traffic. The financial benefits had been directly applied to construction projects, new defenses, and necessary economic infrastructure, particularly granaries, that benefited the local population. Even with the obvious handicap of domestic commodities ill-suited to international commerce, the Muscovite chancelleries had managed to successfully position themselves within a global economy. Though this never produced the financial windfall some might have predicted in the sixteenth century, the larger project of economic development was no failure, no matter how incidental it was to the elusive goal of a luxury trade with Asia.

By the time the New Commercial Code of 1667 was promulgated in Moscow, the former khanate had been transformed. The hand of the Prikaz Kazanskogo dvortsa guided economic development inside the Middle Volga Region. New towns and outposts had been established, creating new trade routes, markets, and products. The defensive lines were completed, largely securing the region from the continuing dangers of the nearby nomads. *Voevody*, monasteries, and the Prikaz benefited from the toll system, and the combination of their collective interests guaranteed the enforcement of those policies. The *voevody* not only enacted centrally created policies but also provided thorough information to the Prikaz Kazanskogo dvortsa to help maintain and regulate the trade system. By once again exploiting the Russian Orthodox Church as a source of labor and revenue for state projects, the Prikaz minimized the cost of development. The pattern of control over the frontier had been one of strict economy and necessity, determined by the sparse population and poverty of the region. The burden had been placed on the state and the Church, the only two corporate entities capable of commanding the very limited labor and financial resources of the region. The state reaped the benefit.

Thus, even if economic development of the Volga River failed to meet the optimistic assessments of Western merchants, it became one of the more notable successes of the growing empire. For a state that had only limited ability to guide the economy in 1552, it was clear by 1667 that tremendous progress had been made. Not all of that progress was necessarily financial. Using the idea of the Volga as an international trade route, Muscovy also had created an opportunity to negotiate with Western Europe. At the same time, the continuing failures of Muscovy's emissaries to Iran and India provided strong evidence of the weakness of Moscow in the world market. Muscovy never emphasized its true success—instead, it displayed the promise of the new trade route and hid its failures from Western observers. The Posol'skii Prikaz created a far greater impression of improvement than had actually occurred. The English envoy in Moscow during the early eighteenth century, Charles Whitworth, remained convinced that English merchants were just about to reap the financial windfall of Iranian trade along the Volga:

> The English Trade would still increase considerably if any expedient could be found to reconcile the interests of the Muscovite and East India Companys about introducing raw Silk from a Province of Persia calld Chilan, which lyes on the Caspian Sea: This Traffick is now in the hands of some Armenians, who have a permission from the King of Persia, and bring yearly great quantitys hither by Astracan up the river Wolga, Six hundred Bales being either come or expected this Winter, From hence it was usually sent to Holland, but now the Armenians will load two ships for Copenhagen, where they are endeavouring to Settle a Trade and Manufacture.[125]

After far more than a century of restricted travel, increasing taxes, and persistent failure, Western merchants still hoped that the limitless bounties of Asian trade goods arriving in Moscow could be theirs. Whitworth's hope was a victory for the Russian state. Its empire might still have been evolving, but the Western perception of the state proved quite worthwhile.

4

Loyal Enemies

If believers in heterodox faiths [*inovertsy*], of whatever creed, or a Russian, casts abuse on the Lord God and our Saviour Jesus Christ, or on the Lady Most Pure Who gave birth to Him, our Mother of God the Chaste Maiden Mary, or on the Holy Cross, or on His Holy Saints: rigorously investigate this by all methods of inquiry. If that is established conclusively; having convicted the blasphemer, execute him by burning him.

Richard Hellie,
The Ulozhenie of 1649, chap. 1, art. 1

Very true the saying is, "Scratch the Russian and find the Tartar."

James Gallatin,
A Great Peacemaker, 2 January 1823

During the first one hundred years following the defeat of Kazan, Russian plans for the frontier emphasized the establishment of steppe and internal security. Yet even after 1650, internal resistance to tsarist authority, however nominal, and potential raids by nearby nomads tested Russian resilience. Turkic groups threatened both sides of the newly defined border (the Arzamas Line and the later Simbirsk Line). Although some Turkic groups remained animist, Russian administrators between Kazan and the southernmost frontier continually feared a Muslim-Turkic conspiracy supported by the Ottoman Empire. While the two defensive lines aided Russian pacification efforts within the tsarist portion of these lands, they were never as effective as intended. Nomadic raids remained troublesome, and nothing allayed Muscovite fears of a potential Ottoman or Crimean invasion.

The tsar and his government, therefore, relied on a strong cavalry force to defend the frontier, supported by land grants (*pomest'ia*; sing. *pomest'e*). This was in fact nearly the same military-supply system that had been used by the khanate, and the readiest supply of "new" troops for the tsar was Kazan's Tatar elite.[1] These Tatars would retain their traditional estates and peasants as long as they provided military service for the tsar. In this way, with minimal effort and little upfront expense, the tsar made great strides toward stabilizing his frontier. This was not a unique solution for managing frontier security in an early-modern empire. It was an essential tool, in fact, and the Russian state exploited the co-option of local elites across the entire Russian frontier into the twentieth century.[2]

However, this "new" defensive force presented a series of problems for Moscow. The tsar's former Muslim Tatar enemies, who shared neither a language nor a religion with the tsar or his military forces, were now the defenders of the frontier against new Muslim foes. By the 1570s, Ivan IV temporarily added to this suspect population a new, potentially even more dangerous element: a number of exiled Russian elites from the interior, expelled for "disloyalty." Despite the questionable loyalty of both groups, the tsar still expected that they accept their role as the frontier's new gentry, the leaders of his military, and the men now responsible for defeating local rebels and nomadic raiders. While less than ideal, this plan formed one of the foundational pillars of the tsar's elusive empire. It accomplished the goal of providing an inexpensive corps of military forces to secure the region, some with very old roots in the region. Relying as it did on former and current enemies to protect that same frontier, it had the singular virtue of being the only possible way of stabilizing the territory. Ivan's ongoing Livonian War with Lithuania prevented the Muscovite army from ever returning to its southeastern border to restore order in case of some catastrophe.

Demonstrating one's loyalty through military service was the most important way for the local gentry to reinforce their high social status into the seventeenth century. That this policy worked in the long run should not distract from the enormous risks Muscovy took in implementing it. Still, the policy had a certain rough elegance. Without a record of loyal service, frontier elites could have their land seized—if not by the tsar, then by rivals seeking to gain advantage from their own service. For example, Ivan Stepanov syn Vorontsov died performing his obligatory military service in Astrakhan in the late 1630s. As happened elsewhere in Muscovy, his two sons, physically capable of assuming his military duties in the tsar's cavalry, expected to inherit their father's land and his service obligations. Sometime in 1640, though, a local soldier near Vorontsov's estate in Arzamas petitioned the tsar, requesting to inherit it. The sons responded with a petition of their own, highlighting their father's recent death in loyal service to the tsar. They described the solider making the claim, Semën Isupov, "an old enemy" (*staryi nedruzhba*) of the tsar, who had lied in his petition when he said his horse had died.[3] Though the outcome of this petition is unknown, the sons' response followed the form of successful petitions on similar issues. Such disputes were not common, and in general, military service proved loyalty and marked a trustworthy servitor. But because falling short of this standard could result in disgrace and penury, military enlistment across generations became the foundation for maintaining elite status in Muscovite society, both for Russians and non-Russians.

The Russian Orthodox Church had its own test of loyalty: obedient piety. For the Church, a tsarist subject was an Orthodox believer, and service either for church or state was expected. With a large, non-Orthodox population on the frontier, a confessional standard was nearly impossible to meet. Nonetheless, the Church publicized its vision of appropriate behavior and loyalty in its sermons, miracle cults, and saints' lives. Its idealized frontier contained a fully Orthodox community, in which men obediently served the central authorities. Even though the religiosity of the Orthodox message was a challenge to the local community, it reinforced the ideal of loyal service as the prerequisite for all of the tsar's subjects. In this, it served the state very well.

The Church also attempted to define the role of women on the frontier, although secular authorities largely ignored it. Women in the gentry should serve state interests as obedient wives who assisted their husbands' service for the tsar or the Church. From the center, the frontier's new gentry were held to an idealized single standard: all the men served central authorities, and all the women served their husbands. Though this vision of society existed elsewhere in Muscovy, here it was applied uniformly to a diverse community with different backgrounds, lifestyles, interests, and social status, and in seeming ignorance for the reality of frontier society. Ironically, the more the state and the Church committed to a vision of a uniform society of loyal servitors, the more central authorities created opportunities for the gentry to exploit the center's expectations to accomplish personal goals, as was the case for the Vorontsovs.

The relationship between the state and its Muslim servitors was characterized by the negotiations evidenced in the administrative tensions between center and periphery. However, the negotiations worked beneath the rhetoric of the victorious empire. The Russian Orthodox Church had long since proclaimed the destruction of Islam in Kazan and the creation of the new Orthodox city. The need for prosperous, well-armed, and therefore socially preeminent Muslim Tatars on the frontier could hardly be celebrated by Moscow or the Church. States and servitors mediated this seeming contradiction by creating a rhetorical strategy to disguise the true socio-political stage and still satisfy the interests of each party. If Muslim servitors described themselves as loyal allies with generations of tsarist military service, despite their religious nonconformity, then even they could demand concessions from the central authorities regarding the payments for this service.

Because of these similar, yet competing, interests and expectations, Muscovy controlled its expanding frontier only through the joint efforts of both of its centers of elite culture. The tsar and the Russian Orthodox Church could claim success in converting former enemies, Muslim and Orthodox, to the cause of the Muscovite imperial project. The provincial gentry, meanwhile, participated in the state in order to achieve personal goals by nominally conforming to the narrative generated in Moscow's Kremlin. Former enemies became the tsar's loyal subjects. Together, they forged frontier society with this cooperative competition, in which all parties could claim success even if security was incompletely achieved, former enemies continued to be restricted to the frontier decades after the conquest, and the Church supervised a multiconfessional population.

Old Enemies

Officially, the Tatars of Kazan were the villains of the 1552 war. Yet for the generations that followed, even as the Russian Orthodox Church proclaimed the glorious victory of Orthodoxy over Islam, few important structures changed in and around Kazan. The conquest itself had been violent, but within a generation many Tatars simply substituted service to the tsar for service to the khan.[4] Tatar elites, serving in Kazan's army as cavalry, generally retained their positions, lands, and peasants.

The largely seamless maintenance of social order in the region owed its achievement to the *mestnichestvo* system. *Mestnichestvo* influenced Muscovy high social elites more than any other factor in the sixteenth century. As the Mongol Chingissids ranked as one of the highest families of the system, Tatar *mirza*s, each with a plausible claim to Chingissid heritage, maintained social preeminence in Muscovite society.[5] Additionally, *mestnichestvo* recognized the value of a military servitor with a record of loyal service in the tsar's army. Though most members of the broader spectrum of elite society—military servitors, particularly those serving as cavalry—were not ranked as part of the *meschnichestvo* system, the idea of loyalty demonstrated through service affected all elites. Therefore, Tatars and other non-Russians with no claim toward a Chingissid bloodline could overcome their former enemy status by forging a history of loyal service to the Rurikids. These new frontier "gentry" did not rank among the high elites as did the *mirza*s, but their service as cavalry provided them a status clearly superior to the peasants who resided on their estates.[6]

The *pomest'e* system was another Muscovite innovation that became essential to controlling the frontier. *Pomest'e* was a conditional land grant; in exchange for receiving the right to the land and its potential profits, the *pomeshchik* (a title holder) owed military service, usually as cavalry. The system was first implemented after the conquest of Novgorod in the late fifteenth century, when the Grand Prince of Moscow granted new *pomest'e* estates to his military servitors exploiting the seized land from Novgorod. As Moscow acquired more principalities, including Pskov, Smolensk, and Riazan', the pattern was repeated. Hereditary estates held by Moscow's enemies became conditional grants to support Moscow's army.[7] Therefore, Moscow had a proven method of supporting military forces in conquered territory, which Ivan Vasil'evich could implement in Kazan. Before the conquest, Kazan had also begun developing a parallel system of relying upon land grants to support military service, in which its *tarkhans* (military servitors) held hereditary estates.[8] Thus, the territory was already divided into estates designed to support military service as cavalry. Granting the new *pomest'e* estates seized from Kazan back to the local Tatar elites quickly placed this military force under the tsar's control with minimal effort, even as it undermined the *tarkhans*' hereditary privileges. On one hand, relying on the tsar's former enemies as his new military force seems counterintuitive, but, on the other hand, the tsar already had numerous Tatars in his service, some of whom already originated from Kazan.[9] Therefore, Moscow's expectation that the tsar's enemies would serve in his army was not unprecedented.

While the defensive lines were the most visible solution to the tsarist presence in the former khanate, the troops who maintained and provided additional security were more important. Though the defensive lines blocked most nomadic incursions, the domestic rebellions of the 1550s, '60s, '70s, and 1600s all occurred behind the lines among the local population. Clearly garrison forces were required to defend the new towns and outposts from both external and internal threats. Yet, Ivan Vasil'evich's campaigns made protecting the frontier exclusively with Russian troops impossible. While they were spread thin, equipped and trained Tatars were available. Moscow followed its own precedent; it had recruited actively elite Tatars to serve its satellite, the nearby Khanate of Kasimov.[10]

Moscow could not afford to refuse local forces containing Tatars, as there was no apparent alternative and they previously had been considered an essential component of Moscow's defenses against the open steppe. The combination of *mestnichestvo* and the *pomest'e* system provided the best possible solution for managing this population of elite former enemies, allowing Tatars to bear arms but preventing their rise into the upper echelons of Muscovite society. They had considerable status on the frontier but remained inferior to heartland servitors. With only a small group of *mirza*s having any claim to *mestnichestvo* status, the majority of Tatar military servitors, former *tarkhan*s, had no option but to accept tsarist *pomest'e* grants, as without tsarist approval they would possess no rights.

Beyond having few options outside of military service as cavalry, the former elites of Kazan needed financial support, and the tsar needed their cooperation to control the conquered population. All military servitors in the former khanate agreed to a residence requirement as part of their *pomest'e* grant. While Muscovy assigned posts to all of its servicemen, it was not typical for the posts to be the same location as the estates (as became standard in and around Kazan). A Tatar servitor who left his district without permission potentially would forfeit land, people, and status for generations to come. Isennaleevskii, a Tatar holding a *pomest'e* grant, died in service, but his children had left the estate and the district. As a result, in 1622 his village of Beteman on the road to Alatyr' outside of Kazan was granted to another Tatar, Tolubaik Tonashev.[11] Though this represented a small change from the typical conditions for grants elsewhere in Muscovy, the residence requirement severely restricted the mobility of the tsar's former enemies, even as they held "elite" status.[12]

Additionally, the political upheaval of the remainder of Ivan Vasil'evich's reign (known as the *Oprichnina*) generated another potential crop of military servitors—displaced Russian hereditary nobles. The *Oprichnina* began a decade after the conquest, leading a new group of exiled Russian elites to join the Tatars at the apex of the frontier's special pyramid. The causes, processes, and results of the *Oprichnina* are rather a complex subject.[13] However, the *Oprichnina*'s first victims included many members of elite rank who were forcibly relocated to Kazan. R. G. Skrynnikov identified approximately 180 princes and other notables exiled to the region in 1565, primarily from the interior provinces of Iaroslavl', Rostov, Starodub, and Obolensk. Furthermore, Ivan's government seized their *votchina* (hereditary land) and thereby turned them into dependent servitors, reliant upon smaller grants of *pomest'ia* than their original lands.[14] They joined their conquered enemies as the frontier's new gentry. Though many of these exiles were pardoned and allowed to return to the interior, Russian political exiles remained a viable option for adding more cavalry to the frontier defenses. Other portions of the empire, particularly Siberia, relied upon political exiles and foreign prisoners to become new military servitors, following the pattern set in the Volga Region.[15]

Both the Russians and non-Russians needed to demonstrate loyal service in order to maintain or reclaim a semblance of their former status, lost in the reign of Ivan IV. The possibility of redemption through service was easier for the Russian exiles to entertain; for the non-Russians, the tsar's service provided enough consideration for a *pomest'e* grant, but might never develop into a situation in which the state accepted them as true gentry.[16] However, successful long-term service provided status in Muscovy's social system, and while this was the only path to higher rank for Tatars without useful genealogical connections, they could readily adapt to the tsar's "new" military system, and this created a virtuous circle: service, *pomest'e*, and a partial restoration (or the establishment of) status and rank.

The tsar structured the system so as to work more flexibly than that of the old khanate. Muscovy allowed loyal soldiers with a history of service to achieve elite status through grants of *pomest'e*, which opened opportunities for the tsar's new military. Both Iangil'd Enandarov and Bakrach Ianchurin benefited from this more fluid operation, receiving their *pomest'e* in 1595, after enlisting in the tsar's service. Enandarov served longer and thus ultimately obtained more land than Ianchurin.[17] For sons who served after a male relative, greater rewards became possible. Following his father's long career, Nurmamet Nurkeev was awarded hereditary land in addition to his original *pomest'e* in acknowledgment of his second-generation military service.[18]

The system was not without its complications. Muscovy's complex and over-lapping administrative system confused land grants as much as it did economic development or judicial authority. In the sixteenth century, a central military chancellery (the Razriadnyi Prikaz) was established, but military servitors in the region were under the supervision of the Prikaz Kazanskogo dvortsa from its creation. This automatically kept non-Russian servitors from the region outside of the purview of another central agency, but it led to an illogical state of affairs. Theoretically, *pomest'ia* grants were regulated and distributed by the Pomestnyi Prikaz (Service Land Chancellery) for the Razriadnyi Prikaz, but in and around Kazan, the Prikaz Kazanskogo dvortsa generally acted first to assign a grant. Therefore, there was a separate set of procedures established in Kazan for controlling *pomest'e*. This was rather advantageous for the state in the early decades after 1552 when all of the servitors in the region were somewhat suspect.

Even so, because the tsar's former enemies lacked other options that would enable them to enjoy privileges as they had before 1552, great numbers served in the tsar's military forces. The early lists of the cavalry may be divided into two broad categories: "Russians" and "Non-Russians." The "Russians" were Orthodox and held ranks as *deti boiarskie*, *dvoriane*, or *pod'iachie*. "Non-Russians" included three groups: Tatar *mirza*s, non-Russian converts to Orthodoxy (*novokreshchane*), and Muslims. The *mirza*s ranked highest with their Chingissid bloodline in the *mestnichestvo* system. The *novokreshchane* could claim the next best status as their Orthodoxy opened opportunities in Muscovite society, including potential marriage alliances with Russian families. In this system, generally the Muslims had the lowest

Table 6 Comparison of elite servitors

Town	1613/14		1637/38	
	"Russians"	"Non-Russians"	"Russians"	"Non-Russians"
Kazan	100	312	310	300
Sviiazhsk	10	210	121	265
Alatyr'		230	345	456
Arzamas				234
Cheboksary		56	50	
Iarensk		13	13	
Iadrin		17	20	
Kokshaisk			24	
Koz'modem'iansk		22	41	22
Kurmysh			80	162
Laishev				5
Lomov				95
Malmyzh			1	
Temnikov				516
Tetiushii			100	100
Tsarevokokshaisk		28	3	
Tsivil'sk		72	26	
Urzhum			19	22
Total cavalry	110	960	1054	2177

Source: Data drawn from Buganov and Kuz'min, *Razriadnye knigi*, 263–66; and V. I. Buganov, *Razriadnaia kniga*, 118–25.

social status as their religion held them at a distance from Russian Orthodox society. All were "elite" in the sense that they served as cavalry and held *pomest'e* grants.

Table 6 reveals the high number of non-Russians in military service as cavalry throughout the region. The army raised in 1613/14 fought the Polish-Lithuanian army at the end of the era of the Time of Troubles. Though at first glance it appears that non-Russians were overwhelming supporters of the tsarist restoration, those Russians who served might not have been considered recruits from the region, as the Russians were not constrained by a residence requirement as were the Tatars. The registry from 1637/38, a less eventful year, likely was more reflective of the general composition of the frontier elite troops. Elite non-Russians outnumbered Russians approximately two to one, a strong sign of the genuine dependence of regional security on the tsar's former enemies. By comparison, the Tatars comprised only 9 percent of total men in Muscovite military service in 1632, and the total of non-Russians in service was 10.7 percent.[19] In other words, while Kazan remained dependent upon its Tatars, Muscovy did not, which only reinforced the frontier's difference from the heartland.

The singular aspect of the gentry status of Tatars was not their military or social success. It was that they succeeded in doing so as a non-Orthodox, and non-converting, population for more than a century. Until the eighteenth century, the Orthodox Church never succeeded in making conversion a necessity for elite Tatars: the decision to convert was, until then, essentially personal.[20] As a result, new elites from the former enemy appeared on both sides of the religious divide. It is not clear that conversion helped, or that remaining Muslim hindered, the status of Tatars within the elite population. On the one hand, Iakov Vasil'ev syn Asanov, a converted Tatar in service to the tsar and a *mirza*, received extensive lands in Kazan province along the road to Samara in the 1590s. This included the village of Bimer, settled with both Orthodox Russians and converted Tatar peasants. His son maintained possession over the land, received the right to build a mill, and even received more land, taken from the Spaso-Preobrazhenskii Monastery's lands in Kazan in 1616.[21] The family retained possession of that land throughout the seventeenth century, resisting two attempted tax increases and successfully quashing claims against their land by Kazan's Bogoroditsii Convent, and later by a fellow *mirza* family.[22]

On the other hand, the Khoziashev family was another Tatar family from Kazan with extensive landholdings in the province; however, the Khoziashevs remained Muslim. Their *pomest'e* included two villages, Isheevskoe and Taveleva, and a tavern.[23] Another Tatar family, the Enmametevs, repeatedly attempted to claim the Khoziashev's land in the 1630s, which would have dispossessed the original servitor's three children had the attempt succeeded.[24] The tsarist authorities consistently rewarded the loyalty of the Khoziashev family, who defeated at least two more attempts to seize their estates later in the seventeenth century.[25]

The Begishevs were a Muslim Chuvash family with lands in both Iadrin and Sviiazhsk provinces. In 1619 a grant confirmed Ekbulat Begishev's right to his father's land, and he maintained his rights despite attempts to seize the family's land in Sviiazhsk by the *voevoda* of Kazan.[26] The Begishevs' village, Chirkina, was populated by Muslim Tatars. Iambulat Atkeev, an Orthodox Tatar servitor, made at least two attempts to claim the village, but each time the central authorities sided with the Muslim Begishevs, based on their long history of loyal service to the tsar.[27]

Finally, the Andreianovs were another successful Chuvash family, who first received two Chuvash villages in Kazan province in the sixteenth century. In 1613 they received a third Chuvash village as a reward for successfully fulfilling their service obligations.[28] A Chuvash who had converted to Orthodoxy, Boris

Melent'ev, attempted to claim this new grant for himself, but twenty years later the land was still in the possession of the Andreianovs.[29] However, unlike the Begishevs, the Andreianovs converted to Russian Orthodoxy by the 1630s, becoming *novokreshchane*, when the then *syn boiarskii* Smirnoi Men'shov syn Andreianov arranged the marriage of his daughter, Marfa, to Nikita Ivanov syn Brekhov, his new business partner.[30]

The brief histories of these four families demonstrate two aspects of Muscovite *pomest'e* policy in Kazan. Muscovite authorities valued families with long associations of military service as its frontier elites, and they did so to the exclusion of religion. A family with military service over several generations consistently could defeat competing claims to their land, as a further example demonstrates. A Russian servitor attempted to claim the *pomest'e* of Ivan Nekhaev in Alatyr' district, but the Pomestnyi Prikaz kept the grant with Nekhaev based on his two decades of loyal service.[31] Even in cases where Russian Orthodox servitors challenged Muslims, this held true. The Muslim Tatar Arak Kurmanderbyshev, for example, received the grant to the village of Bol'shoi Kuiuk in Kazan province, over the protest of a local Russian military servitor, because the land had been originally granted to Kurmanderbyshev's father. Nearly thirty years later his family remained in control of the land.[32]

However, though loyal service could be convincing in terms of justifying the receipt of *pomest'e* and the resulting elite status, there was evidence that the state did favor Orthodox servitors whenever possible. Two *novokreshchane* servitors, Vasilii and Stepan Timofeev, received new *pomest'e* in 1598 based on their loyal service, a group of Chuvash peasants, their fields, and the stallions they were grooming.[33] To place anyone in charge of the important horse-raising industry was a matter of great trust, but the Timofeevs were not allowed to take up this grant until after their conversion. While Muslims were necessary for frontier defense, and could be rewarded for their service, they were not placed into positions of high authority. This is a reflection of the widespread relevance of *mestnichestvo* among the highest elites. A Muslim was not precluded from joining the ranks of the elite, but there was a limit to their potential status in society. Of course, this limitation was why the Andreianovs converted to Orthodoxy, allowing their rise in status to be capped by the marriage of their daughter to an elite Russian.

Relative success on the frontier also did not translate into any improvement for the Tatars in Muscovite society. Some Tatars might have anchored elite communities on the frontier, but the residence requirement was the first of what became several restrictions upon their advantages. By 1649, the new *Ulozhenie* clarified the distinction between Russian and non-Russian servitors, which created several difficulties for the frontier cavalrymen. *Pomest'ia* belonging to Tatars, Chuvashes, and Mordvins became a separate type of landholding from Russian military service lands: "in the future do not grant the service of lands of Russians to Tatars, or Tatar lands to Russians as service landholdings."[34] In addition, Russians were not allowed to buy or exchange service land from Tatars, Mordvins, Chuvashes, Maris, Udmurts, or Bashkirs, each of whom was named explicitly.[35] If a Russian did "take land on a mortgage or hire for many years" with any of the non-Russians, the lands were to be confiscated. "Moreover, they shall be in disgrace with the sovereign for that."[36] While on the one hand this reflected practices already in place on the frontier, on the other hand it also delimited Russian and non-Russian servitors as fundamentally different types of elites. The consequences could be far ranging. Marriages between Russians and Tatars, for example, were eventually difficult to arrange after land exchanges between the families were declared illegal.[37]

In addition to recognizing a formal legal distinction between Russians and non-Russian servicemen, the *Ulozhenie* reflected a growing concern that Muslim Tatars (and not their converted brethren) would likely attempt to escape from their service obligations. "Mirzas and Tatars shall not lay waste to their own service landholdings. They shall not flee from those service landholdings of theirs into other towns. . . . They shall not abandon service."[38] Russian servitors were not mentioned as likely flight risks, though of course land grants lacked residence requirements. Even before the *Ulozhenie*, limiting non-Russian servitors to the frontier had been a priority, but in 1649 it was limited to specifically to Muslims.

The *Ulozhenie* was not simply discriminatory. It also acknowledged Muscovite society as diverse in terms of both ethnolinguistic and religious differences, and established a legal precedent that tsarist subjects need not be Orthodox to exercise privileges effectively. For example, the courts relied primarily upon oral testimony, with the reliability of testimony being assured by an oath. Russians and converted non-Russians would kiss the cross as a sign of their trustworthiness, while Muslims and animists were required to "take an oath . . . according to their creed." After testimony had been provided to the court, it needed to be signed for validation: "Tatars who are literate in the Tatar language [would sign] over their signatures," and illiterate non-Russians would sign over their mark.[39] Most importantly, "Tatars and any other foreigners" (*ili Tatarovia ili inye vsiakie inozemtsy*) had the legal right to sue a Russian.[40] This law allowed non-Russian elites the same right to contest their rank and privileges in the court, which was essential to maintain their status in society.

The *Ulozhenie*, therefore, encapsulated the equivocal status of non-Russian elites in Muscovite society. Diversity was acknowledged, even among Muscovy's elites, and yet Muslims faced new restrictions. Conversion to Orthodoxy was encouraged, if only minimally. However, the *Ulozhenie* did not immediately inspire a set of conversions or legal victories for Orthodox claimants. Neither was ethnolinguistic nor religious difference the only distinction between the frontier and the heartland after 1649. Whereas military servitors with *pomest'ia* in the central provinces frequently found themselves with several small grants distributed among a geographically diverse area, not only were single-estate grants more common among the non-Russian servitors but those holding more than one estate found them clustered on the frontier. In the Saransk muster roll for 1670, for example, 39.4 percent of the servitors had single-district *pomest'e*, and the remainder had possessions in nearby districts.[41] Among Russian military servitors, distributing land grants among several districts prevented the gentry from developing close connections in one particular district. It was the military equivalent of the administrative practice of rotating officials in and out of regional positions. The military elites were intended to serve in the tsar's army, not at home. Of course, this had never been the practice for the tsar's former enemies, and it was clear that no adjustment was forthcoming. Local Tatars remained connected to their communities.

With the local practices from the region codified in 1649 or otherwise apparently institutionalized from decades of practice, Tatar elites had little option other than remaining in the tsar's service and accepting the very same land grants their ancestors had held. On the surface, it was a stagnant situation, with very little overt change even after more than one hundred years of tsarist rule. However, the evolution of military technology during the seventeenth century would do irrevocable damage, permanently reducing the importance of elite cavalry. Beginning as early as the 1620s, the tsarist army began to include new musket-wielding infantry. Cheaper to supply and easier to train, the numbers of infantry steadily escalated throughout the century.[42] As the relative need for cavalry diminished, so too did the ability of non-Russians, including Muslims, to maintain their value in Muscovite society.

Yet, as the century progressed, the numbers of non-Russian military elites steadily gained numerical dominance among the local forces. In Kokshaisk, for example, twelve military servitors were registered in 1668/69. Three were Russian, one was non-Russian (*inozemets*), and eight were *novokreshchane*.[43] As seen table 6 in this chapter, fifty years earlier there had been no non-Russians in service there. In Sviiazhsk, non-Russians were nearly 75 percent of the servitors in 1669, and they remained primarily Muslim (82 Muslim, 28 *novokreshchane*, and only 39 Russian). However, the Russians held significantly larger estates, between 300 to 700 *cheti* (405–945 acres), while almost all non-Russians held estates less than 100 *cheti*.[44] With the new land-grant restrictions created in 1649, non-Russians should not have been able to receive land that had belonged to Russians. This new law may have affected the disparity among the estate sizes. Russians may have also acquired land from other Russians who had abandoned the region, while non-Russian estates might have be divided to accommodate more servitors, in order to maintain numbers of troops without granting Russian land to non-Russians. A third possibility is that Russian estates were transferred—but only to Orthodox converts among the non-Russians, who also appeared in greater numbers. A fourth possibility is that the law was simply not applied at all. Likely all were true at one time or another. But the lesson was clear—as military service became an unattractive option for Russian elites, it more or less simply absorbed more non-Russians, confirming their lesser status in society and legally binding them to their residence on the frontier.

Ironically, 1552 was less of a disruption of frontier elite society than was the slow technological transformation of the army. For more than a century, former conquered elites enjoyed much of their status and prestige in a foreign environment, without the pressure to convert to Russian Orthodoxy. After 1649, however, with *mestnichestvo* becoming less relevant (and ending by the 1680s), the military recruitment system it fostered had become obsolescent. It was a remarkable evolution. All military servitors held high social status in the sixteenth century. After 1649, elite non-Russians, particularly Muslims, could have foreseen only a steadily diminishing status, regardless of their heretofore (and still) valuable service to the tsar. This meant that after a century, the Muslim elites of Kazan had truly been defeated. This was certainly not an indication that the region had become fully "assimilated" within Muscovy than it had been during the previous century, but only that conversion to Orthodoxy would now mark the only path leading to social and political status.

Orthodox Exemplars

Tsar Ivan Vasil'evich's need for all possible military servitors during his reign provided protection for Muslims and animist men capable of defending his new claims. Yet the Russian Orthodox Church never lacked influence. It built infrastructure and played a central role in economic development. As the tsarist institutions of *mestnichestvo* and *pomest'e* guided frontier military service, so did the religious reforms of the 1550s affect the role of provincial elites. In 1551, the Church officially promulgated a widespread set of reforms designed to uphold the authority of Russian Orthodox bishops and standardize all aspects of Orthodox liturgy and practice.[45] When the conquest opened the frontier to Russian Orthodox settlement, Russian settlers, primarily the political exiles, had to contend with multiple pressures. The Russian Orthodox hierarchy expected a rigorous morality based on these recent reforms while the state expected a stable Tatar and settler community of military elites to hold an insecure frontier. These two visions differed on the role of Orthodoxy, but both church and state held obedience to authority as the ideal virtue of the frontier community. If conversion efforts might well have been destabilizing, and thus not integral to the state's interests, the Church invested much greater effort in influencing the behavior of its own believers than on risky effort to convert Muslims. This was to some degree an extension of the state's own policies concerning its military servitors. Not until 1649 at the earliest was there any particular effort to encourage the conversion of Muslims in law, although some *novokreshchane* Tatars saw value in converting without being compelled to do so. Nevertheless, the need for cavalry placed the development of an entirely Orthodox community in a subordinate position.

There are several difficulties with examining the Russian Orthodox Church's policies toward the Orthodox community on the frontier. The state tended to observe and regulate the newly conquered and occasionally rebellious non-Orthodox populations rather than those presumed to be loyal, but the Church's policies are harder to document. There are no extant records of confessions, church attendance, or even entry into local monasteries and convents. Yet there were clear signals that official expectations for behavior existed. The Orthodox hierarchy recorded its image of proper Orthodox behavior on the frontier through local miracle cults and saints' lives. More importantly, unlike state plans into which they rarely figured, women were an integral component of a Russian Orthodox society on the frontier.

Central to the development of a model for Orthodox behavior was the creation of local Orthodox saints. Of course, the emergence of both new saints and miracle-working icons reflected the victory of Orthodoxy over Islam, a narrative the Church had been recording since 1552. The canonization process was a bit haphazard in late-sixteenth century Muscovy, before becoming more formalized over the course of the seventeenth century. Generally, the local community discovered the existence of a saint or miraculous icon. The miracle worker could be revealed through visions or by miraculous cures. As belief and proof of the miraculous nature of the saint or icon grew, the Russian Orthodox Church hierarchy officially investigated and recorded the miracles. When the evidence was convincing, local or national commemoration would follow; outright dismissal of unconvincing miracle cults was possible. Therefore, the miracle cults emerged "naturally" from the local community, and inclusion in the official miracle cycle of a new saint or miracle-working icon also marked an official endorsement of the local community and its

Figure 4 Kazan's miracle-working Mother of God Icon (Reproduced from the author's collection)

Orthodox believers.[46] In recording the process of discovery, Church officials also described an Orthodox life on the frontier.

As part of the "Life of Gurii and Varsonofii," sixty-six miraculous cures were recorded by the early seventeenth century. Most of those cured by the relics were clergy, townspeople, and men in tsarist service. Most of the sixty-six were from Kazan district with the furthest afield arriving from Arzamas, Vologda, Viatka, and Rostov, all towns with trade connections to Kazan, and thus all "local" themselves. The second local miracle cult was established in connection to the miracle-working icon of the Mother of God. By the early seventeenth century, its official "Tale of the Appearance of Kazan Icon of the Mother of God" included fourteen miraculous cures, eleven affecting men, three for local women, and not a single person affected by a miracle was a non-Russian.[47] Had the purpose of the miracle cults been to inspire conversions, evidence that the local Muslims noticed the miracles might be expected, but these two cults were clearly linked solely to local Orthodox men and women.

There were only two officially adopted and endorsed miracle cults, but together they presented eighty individual examples of appropriate Orthodox behavior. The "Tale" reinforced its edifying miracles with an explicit exhortation to emulate these behaviors in daily life, emphasizing above all that each "Christian must imitate Christ with both words and deed . . . and with righteousness and without vice."[48] Though this would seem like sensible advice for all Christians, the miraculous recipients had provided a very specific template of what constituted righteousness: all men and women demonstrated obedient submission to political and religious authority.

With a few exceptions, only local elites received miraculous cures. The majority fell into one of four occupations—tsarist officials, Orthodox priests, military servitors, and the wives of men in those three occupations. For example, the *syn boiarskii* Ivan Kuzmin'skii went to the shrine of the Icon of the Mother of God and prayed for his wife to be healed of her leg injury. After his prayers, "his house was made joyous."[49] Similarly, Elena Itagasheva, the wife of the priest Grigorii, also needed the support of her husband to provide her a miraculous healing. Her eyes had been ill for three years, but once her husband arrived at the monastery housing the icon in Kazan, she was also cured.[50] An exception to these four categories was a man named Aleksei from the town of Mozhaisk. He suffered from demon possession, and, after traveling to the saints' shrine, promised to labor on behalf of the saints for one year in order to receive their blessing. During his year of service, he received a vision, in which he was told that God had allowed him to become possessed because he had left his home without his father's permission. After proving obedience in a year of service, he was healed.[51] Many of the miracle cures possessed similar features: men in service to the state or the Church, their obedient wives, and the necessary demonstration of Orthodox piety, although usually the tales lacked the details of Aleksei's story.

Men in the military formed a large group of the miraculously cured, but also comprised a large portion of the Russian population on the frontier. Their healing narratives also appeared very similar to one another: the tsar's military servitors, protected by Orthodoxy, would be healed, or their families cared for, following their demise (usually campaigning). Aleksei Fëdorov syn Orelov, a *strelets* (musketeer) in the tsar's service in Kazan, fell victim to demon possession. After being placed under St. Varsonofii's chains, he received a vision of both saints interceding on his behalf against a group of three demons who were banished. After his healing, he returned to the tsar's service.[52] In another, a woman sent myrrh from St. Gurii's tomb to her daughter to restore the eyesight of her grandson; once his mother anointed his eyes, the boy was cured. Shortly after this miracle, the daughter received the news that her husband had died while on campaign for the tsar's service, and she was overcome with confusion. To restore her, her family rubbed her body with the myrrh, and she was also healed.[53] Though Russian military personnel in Kazan were only a small portion of the tsar's forces, they dominated these stories.

When women appeared in the miracle cycles, all were married, and their husbands were uniformly worthy of a miraculous cure, because each was loyal to his wife and his superior, either in the Church or in the state. For example, a *d'iak* in Kazan, Aleksei Agramakov, received a letter that his wife had fallen ill in Moscow. He traveled to the saints' shrine and asked the archimandrite of the monastery for myrrh, which he sent to his wife, who was healed.[54] Similarly, Akilina, the wife of a priest, was healed after her husband traveled to the shrine, prayed, obtained myrrh, and returned home to rub her body.[55]

One of the longest tales in the miracle cycle involved Varvara, the wife of a soldier from Kazan. Varvara fell ill from a head injury; after she prayed to Gurii and Varsonofii, they appeared to her in a vision. Gurii instructed her to become a nun. Varsonofii interceded on her behalf with Gurii, arguing that it was not necessary for her to become a nun yet. When Varvara awoke, her illness was gone, and she traveled to the shrine to give thanks. Shortly thereafter, her husband was sent off to duty "in distant cities," and told his wife to go to the shrine and pray for him. However, Varvara became wrapped up in her family life "in the way of the simple people" and forgot her promised prayers. Then she became severely ill, and had a second vision of the saints. Gurii raised his hand to strike her, but Varsonofii once again interceded and asked Gurii for forgiveness on Varvara's behalf. When Varvara awoke, she was once again healed.[56] In Varvara's case, the saints even took care to instruct her in proper Orthodox comportment—a strict commitment to piety and obedience to all authority, including her husband. These miracles reinforced an image of the frontier with a stable, settled, married population. In such tales, the frontier was no longer populated by rebellious, animistic, non-Russians, even as they constituted the overwhelming population of the region.

Both the "Life of Gurii and Varsonofii" and the "Tale of the Appearance of Kazan Icon of the Mother of God" presented the centrality of personal religious experiences in relating the history of the Russian Orthodox Church along Muscovy's frontier, as well as the importance of presenting a positive, constructed image of Kazan as a holy, Orthodox city. The miraculous cures of the local population magnified the holy aura of the saints and the icon, which would (hopefully) inspire the conversion of the local non-Orthodox population. Both of these cults developed after the Muscovite conquest of the region, but they were not the only local saint cults. For example, Makarii Zheltovodskii was another saint in the region, who became the patron saint of a monastery near Arzamas.[57] During his life, Makarii lived on the edge of Muscovite territory, at a time when the Khanate of Kazan was still a hostile enemy. His death early in the sixteenth century preceded Muscovite success in the area by a few decades. Tales of Makarii's miraculous cures provide a comparison to those in later reports, though from an earlier era, and they reflect a different attitude toward the Tatars of Kazan, who are prominently featured and unquestionably hostile.[58]

In the ten miracles recorded during Makarii's life and after his death, six affected men and four, women. No uniform image of frontier society, as presented in Kazan's miracle cults, existed. Men and women fought, revealed their moral failings, and society appeared less exemplary. In one miracle, the saint was responsible for freeing a "beautiful and virtuous" unmarried woman from captivity and protecting her virtue from a raid by the Tatars of Kazan. She prayed to the saint for her release and the preservation of her "bodily purity," and dreamed of Makarii, who told her twice to get up and return home, which she did. When dawn arrived, she found herself outside of her city gates. She knocked, and when questioned by the guard, could not answer him because of her sobs, but she was soon returned to her family.[59] Another miracle involved a husband suffering from "the drunken illness," which had rendered him blind. Because of the demonic influence of alcohol, he beat his wife Elena and "broke her bones." The very pious Elena considered leaving her husband, but then decided to drown herself in a nearby well. Before throwing herself into the well, she prayed to Makarii, who then appeared to her and changed her suffering to joy. Having experienced this miracle, she then told her husband and her neighbors.[60] Whether her husband was cured of his drunkenness does not appear in the miracle cycle, but the saint successfully restored Elena's obedience to her husband.

Not only are the details of these two miracles significantly different from the others seen in the "Tale of the Icon" or "Gurii and Varsonofii" but they also revealed concerns of Orthodox society before the conquest. Living on the edge of the steppe frontier remained dangerous, including the continuing fear of being taken captive and sold into slavery. Not all men and women were married, and marriages were fraught with social problems, including drunkenness, abuse, and rape. The eighty-eight miraculous healings from Kazan in the "Tale of the Icon" and "Gurii and Varsonofii" were more obviously tales of exemplary behavior, whereas "Makarii Zheltovodskii" recounted daily life and all its sordid dilemmas.

With the establishment of the new bishopric of Kazan in 1555, if not before, the Russian Orthodox Church had constructed a triumphant narrative of the Church Militant. The reality of the region was that Muslims and animistic non-Russians were the tsar's new subjects. Whereas an earlier miracle cycle such as "Makarii Zheltovodskii" could reflect lived experiences on the frontier, it was impossible for the Church to allow miracle tales to do so after they had constructed an image of victory. As a result, it was only logical that later miracle cycles portrayed an idealized community that did not reflect the current composition of frontier society. All the men were obediently serving some central authority, albeit the Church or the state, all of the women were married, and no one appeared who was not Orthodox. It was a vision of a desirable, but elusive, frontier life.

Of course, the Russian Orthodox Church's vision of an exemplary society was inaccurate. The Church predicted an Orthodox society with its public proclamation of Islam's defeat in the 1550s; well into the seventeenth century this Orthodox frontier simply did not exist. The tsar was content with military service. The prominent Muslims in the region, including many of the local elites, demonstrated on a daily basis the limits of the Church's success. In the "Tale of the Icon," the miracle-working icon reveals its powers as a reward for the faithful in their struggle against the heterodox (*inovertsy*), but there was no other mention of the majority of the population. In "Gurii and Varsonofii," the only mention is that the Tatars "were awed" by the miracles of the saints.

This Orthodox vision of frontier society served the interests of the state as well. As the miracle cycles were read, distributed, and repeated in churches and monasteries, the Church effectively propagandized the state's expectations as much as its own. The Church's message neatly reinforced the tsar's expectation of loyalty. All men should serve the tsar in loyal (military) service. Their wives had an obligation to support their husbands, and could do so without fear, knowing the state would provide for them.

After 1649, when the state moved toward more restrictive policies for Muslims specifically and non-Russians in general, the vision of the Church was no longer a collection of exemplary men and women but rather a blueprint for the future. Elite Tatars increasingly needed to convert to Orthodoxy in order to maintain their privileges and social status. The expectations for their behavior, service to the state and the Church, and relationship with their wives had already been explained, and in detail. The uniformity of society depicted in the miracle tales was now more ominous than inclusive. For a century, state tolerance had maintained religious diversity in service to the tsar's interests, but it was a transitional era, not a permanent one.

Petitioning Authority

Using the tsar's former enemies as his new frontier gentry was necessary, but as already evident from the relative size of *pomest'e* grants, it did not mean that the state treated Russians and non-Russians, Orthodox and Muslim, equitably. Furthermore, the moral lesson of the Russian Orthodox Church was that Islam was undesirable and simply did not exist in Kazan. However, there were great numbers of elite Muslim Tatars in Russian service for the century after 1552, and non-Russians continued to serve for the remainder of the seventeenth century, even if conversion became more likely among the elites. The *Ulozhenie* of 1649 enacted the first restrictions on Muslims holding *pomest'e* grants, but further restrictions followed as service landholding became less desirable. Even so, the process of granting land for military service remained flexible enough to allow negotiations between central authorities and frontier elites. As long as military service was required for local security, elites could barter with the state in order to maintain their lands and status. As a result, most of the specific terms of military service—the length of military duty per year, the size of the estates, and even possible tax obligations—all became negotiable. Furthermore, all elites bargained with the state to protect their families' inheritance, provide their daughters dowries, sell or swap land, and even avoid service obligations. In other words, frontier elites were active participants in the development of the empire's structure.

These negotiations were not revealed in the formal records of the state or the Orthodox Church but rather in the innumerable petitions of military servitors to the central government. However, these petitions used the chosen language of the state and the Church. The elite men were the loyal military servitors of the tsar, obedient and pious. Muslim servitors may not have been able to appeal to the same Orthodox expectation of piety, but always stressed their generations of loyal service. As early as the 1560s, petitions argued that there were no enemies on the frontier, only loyal "slaves." Using a consistent, subservient rhetoric in petitions to the tsar was hardly a new phenomenon in Muscovite history. In the sixteenth century, Western visitors were all struck by the Muscovite court's willingness to describe themselves as the tsar's slaves, which partially inspired the Western idea of the tsar as an "Oriental despot."[61] As recent work has shown, the tsar was not the only figure who expected this treatment; nearly all other Muscovite elites used language as a tool to inflate tsarist authority.[62] It was merely one more example of the ways in which multiple levels of the state and society, in the heartland and the frontier, willingly participated in the construction of the empire. This time, of course, it was also for the servitors' personal interests.

At the heart of most petitions from Kazan to the tsar lay the fate of an entire family. When no man from the family could provide service, theoretically the land could be seized and granted to another able-bodied man, rendering his family dispossessed. Fortunately for the frontier gentry and their families, the state's need for cavalry placed its and their interests in tandem. The gentry often petitioned for the right to protect their wives and children by holding the land in the family. If the servitor was survived by a son of age to provide military service, then allowing him to keep his father's land guaranteed military service and tax revenue without difficulties. But sometimes a servitor petitioned to allow a widow or a minor son to reside on the land until the son was ready to serve, or to divide the estate in order to provide a dowry for a daughter. Therefore, it was a typical bequest in 1646 when the Pomestnyi Prikaz granted Aleksei Bogdanov syn Dubrovskii the land in Arzamas district that his father had been granted in 1626/27.[63] While there was no express legal precedent for these actions, such requests could be approved if the servitor was willing to follow the accepted forms of negotiation.

Partible inheritance among all the heirs was common in Muscovy, including provisions for providing for widows and daughters, each of whom was to receive a portion of the estate for their provision.[64] If there was only one heir, inheritance followed a direct line. If, however, multiple heirs succeeded their father, there was no single pattern for inheritance. This variability extended to the frontier, and to *pomest'ia*. For example, the eldest of three Kozlov brothers, Nikita, had inherited all the *pomest'ia* of his father in 1666, which included several villages in both Nizhnii Novgorod and Alatyr' districts. His brothers attempted unsuccessfully to claim a portion of land for themselves.[65] Conversely, the next year in Kerensk, one family's estate was divided into three to provide for two brothers, Bekbulat and Uraz Makmametev, and their cousin Shmamet Lasaev syn Shukinchev.[66]

Minors keeping the *pomest'ia* of their departed fathers was not uncommon in the sixteenth century but became rarer in the seventeenth century, at least in the central provinces.[67] On the frontier, it persisted into the late seventeenth century, likely because the population density was low enough that the state attempted to make sure that families could inherit land de facto. The minor Ivan Alekseev syn Alenin received the land of his recently deceased father in Saransk district on 18 April 1654, because the Pomestnyi Prikaz concluded "it was necessary" for the city to keep its residents.[68] The youngest children in the Alferov family, gentry of Saransk and Penza districts, received all of the family's *pomest'ia* despite the claims of their elder cousins, Dmitrii and Vasilii. The latter did not remain on the frontier, but had returned to the central provinces.[69] This grant kept the land with the members of the family with the greatest commitment to service. More importantly, this sort of familial inheritance worked in the long-term interest of the state by keeping the tsar's former enemies on the frontier with a minimum of year-to-year migration and a low incidence of flight from the land.

Yet even though servitors benefited by providing for their families though bequests of *pomest'e*, they could not alter the legal fact that it was not a possession of the gentry. As a result, residents could not resolve all transfers of land related to family business. This was a recurring problem for fathers wishing to provide their daughters with a dowry of land. The equal exchange of *pomest'ia* between servitors was legally permissible (and of course required approval from Moscow), but land could not be granted without equal exchange (for instance, to a future son-in-law). Still, the gentry often tried to use *pomest'ia* as dowries even if they were never able to bank on the success of the gambit. Such were occasions for intense negotiations with the central authorities as a military servitor attempted to win approval for his illegal action.[70]

It is not possible to estimate with perfect accuracy how often the gentry successfully utilized land as the dowry for their daughters' marriages. However, the attempts were not uncommon. The crucial variable, of course, was whether the new son-in-law could provide military service, which would make a dowry of *pomest'e* desirable for central authorities, especially if there was no male heir to claim the grant. Although notable families like the Andreianovs mentioned above likely had an easier time arranging dowries for their daughters, gentry of the lower ranks also gave land for their daughter's marriages. Fëdor Prokof'ev syn Derevii gave the village Zhrikhinoi in Elnattskaia hamlet along the Volga to Vasilii Nikoforov syn Kokorin as a dowry for his daughter's marriage in 1654, and Boris Gavrilov syn Ostrovskii's daughter received the village of Levasheva in Arzamas district and peasants from his estates in Vologda to marry Leontii Aleksov syn Kopnin in 1683.[71] This was the argument for a dowry carved from a *pomest'e* grant that most often succeeded. The new husband benefited the state by ultimately providing a fighting man and thus supported the land grant. The woman (presumably of child-bearing years) was not the beneficiary of this transaction. As a tactic, this did not always work, but frontier gentry appear to have been more successful than their counterparts in the interior.

A second reason for a the incidence of successful petitions requesting the division a grant for a dowry was the Muscovite chancelleries' atypical regulation of *pomest'ia* in the region. Dividing a *pomest'e*, even for a dowry, was traditionally within the purview of the Pomestnyi Prikaz, but in the frontier regions *pomest'ia* were supervised by the Prikaz Kazanskogo dvortsa. While there is insufficient evidence to conclude that the Prikaz Kazanskogo dvortsa considered dowry arrangements more favorably than the Pomestnyi Prikaz, servitors did attempt to utilize the interchancellery competition to their advantage, seeking permission from any or all parties who could possibly approve the transaction. While Fëdor Maksimov syn Dement'ev received permission from the Prikaz Kazanskogo dvortsa to turn 130 *cheti* of his land in Alatyr' district (out of 360 *cheti* combined in Alatyr' and Arzamas) over to Bogdan Volokitich Nesterov as a dowry, Grigor Petrov syn Evlashchev in Kurmysh obtained permission for the transfer of his daughter's dowry from the Pomestnyi Prikaz.[72]

Servitors throughout Muscovy also had success negotiating dowries or assuring their sons' inheritance, but those on the frontier had unique advantages, not the least of which was the competitive chancelleries themselves. After all, as long as the state remained dependent upon the local population for military service, the Prikaz Kazanskogo dvortsa was likely to accept at least a portion of the local servitors' petitions. Guaranteeing that service was maintained reinforced the local policy of keeping the local elites, primarily Tatars, living on the frontier. Therefore, those successful petitions that might appear to be concessions to the interests of local elites, in fact kept non-Russian servitors at a marked distance from Moscow, which may not have been an explicit policy enforced by the chancelleries, but was indeed a fact. Local Russian servitors also benefited from this lenience, as some had originated from a suspect population of exiled elites. The ability of frontier elites to provide for their families was surprisingly beneficial, a confluence of their interests and those of the state, lubricated by the inconsistency of the early-modern Russian bureaucracy.

This should not imply that all issues raised in elite petitions received as favorable a hearing. When servitors attempted to mitigate the conditions of their grant, either by reducing the number of days of service or lowering their potential tax obligations, the state's responses varied widely. Servitors had three major approaches for achieving their personal goals: outright rejection of a land grant in hopes of receiving better or more land, claiming the land was of poor quality and insufficiently productive to meet the service or tax expectations, or simply requesting boundary adjustments or a reduction of service obligations based on a history of loyal service. Whereas rejecting a dowry petition, for example, could undermine frontier security by removing a servitor from the frontier, these other issues were less pressing, involved more bluff on the part of the servitor, and, therefore, were less likely to be accommodated.

Not surprisingly, tax obligations seemed to have been a chronic area of complaint for the local administration and the servitors, and generated considerable correspondence. When a new land registry was created, petitions could arrive from nearly every servitor, for the new dimensions of their land and estimates of their productivity would establish their future tax rates and possibly their service obligations. An early register for Kazan district in 1567, for example, inspired numerous petitions from both servitors and several newly established local monasteries. Nikita Fedorov syn Ol'gov complained to the tsar that the correct boundary of his *pomest'e* included all of the territory between the Chuvash village on the estate of Azeleev Rogil'dei Meev up to the forest by the Mordvin village held by Naratleev Kurlik Kudashev.[73] If protesting the amount of tax failed to inspire an adjustment, servitors simply opted to not pay the yearly fees, much to the displeasure of the local *voevody* who were responsible for collecting the taxes. Yet, the local *voevody* usually sent only a steady stream of reminders to the servitor to fulfill his obligations. These tax reminders were practically form letters, sent with regularity. The *voevoda* would notify the individual servitor of his expected payment, and that it was a condition of holding his *pomest'e*, and then suggest he immediately pay it.[74] No explicit consequences for failure were mentioned, no punishment threatened, and, moreover, there are no records of a *voevoda* seizing the estate of a recalcitrant taxpayer.

While the assessment of taxes was a local concern, other economic petitions needed decisions from more central authorities. Ivan Semenov syn Karakashev, a *novokreshchanin*, petitioned the tsar for the right to operate a tavern on his land along the Ara River outside of Sviiazhsk. In 1622 he received a favorable reply from Moscow, granting him the right to open a tavern, but he was limited to selling mead and beer, but no wine.[75] Averkii Fedorov syn Bolshin received an additional 130 *cheti* of land in Arzamas in addition to his original holdings in Zvenigorod district in response to his petition to the tsar.[76] The fact that his original holdings were outside the district, and the new bequest was a large estate in Arzamas, indicates Bolshin was rather important, or at least, significantly more so than the local Tatars. Without a direct comparison to failed petitions asking for similar privileges, it is hard to be certain why these requests succeeded while so many others did not.

In this broader negotiation process involving a wide set of issues, except for the elite *mirza*s, non-Russians were at a disadvantage compared with elite Russians. Russians might have familial connections elsewhere in the kingdom that could assist their negotiations, or a history of ties to the crown that provided a demonstration of loyalty. The only mechanism that allowed non-Russians to petition for, and to obtain, land, was loyal military service. The standard could be quite high. A Tatar, Teregul Aginev, had been in military service for thirty years when he petitioned the tsar asking to improve his grant. He desired a piece of land along the Sviiaga River where a tavern was currently located.[77] Since the local taverns had been the possessions of elite families such as the Asanovs, this petition appears unlikely to have been fulfilled, despite Aginev's the long years of military service. Non-Russians who served in a tsar's administration as bailiffs or translators did not even meet the military service expectation, but many still desired land. Unable to obtain it by other means, it was these non-Russians who petitioned for it. Ivashka Khvotsov and Granushka Machekhin, two Tatar bailiffs of Kazan in the 1580s, were both denied land in spite of several years of service in the *voevoda's* office.[78] Denying the requests of non-Russians in administrative service created a pool of potential recipients for the land that had been rejected by Russian military servitors. The quality or location of the land was less important to this group, which had no alternative.

As a result, Russian servitors had some ability to be more selective in the process of receiving *pomest'e*. Those unwilling to accept offers of land tended to face increasing pressures from both the Prikaz Kazanskogo dvortsa and the local *voevody* who were dependent upon their potential service. In the sixteenth century, they increased land offers to entice agreement. In 1583, for example, a resident of Kazan, Deviatii Volkov, was instructed to accept the offer of "only 200 *cheti*," which he had previously turned down, even though it was more than a non-Russian would have been offered.[79] But by the seventeenth century, when more men were present on the frontier, the offers became less extravagant. As a result, both outright rejections and petitions for the receipt of previously rejected land were common. Davyd and Mikhail Zherebtsovykh petitioned Tsar Mikhail Fedorovich for the right to receive the *pomest'e* that had been rejected by Nikita Kudrin in Arzamas and Nizhnii Novgorod districts.[80] Boris Morozov petitioned for land in Alagorenskii hamlet in

Alatyr' district on 1660. Artemii Ivanov syn Agibalov rejected this land the previous year; Morozov hoped to add this *pomest'e* in Alatyr' to his hereditary estate in Arzamas.[81]

If one servitor rejected an estate, local authorities would grant the land to any willing servitor. Frequently, these secondary bequests were beneficial to the local servitors who remained in the district. For example, the *voevoda* of Alatyr' offered land rejected by Grigor Nekliudov to Kozan Pushechnikov, arguing that Pushechnikov's *pomest'e* laid alongside the rejected land, therefore Pushechnikov would want the rejected land "for his family."[82] Bogdan Matveevich Khitrovo and Petr Shapilov rejected some land in Nizhnii Novgorod district in 1677, because they believed the land to be of poor quality. The then *voevoda* of Nizhnii Novgorod, Boris Vasil'evich Gorchakov, petitioned the Pomestnyi Prikaz for the right to grant the land to different servitors. The Prikaz agreed, believing *Voevoda* Gorchakov's claim that Khitrovo and Shapilov already had "too much land," and relying on the opinion of the local village elders, who assured Gorchakov that the land was good.[83] Khitrovo, one of Muscovy's most prominent boiars, lacked a pressing need for new land as he certainly had other possessions throughout Muscovy. However, unoccupied, arable land was a concern for frontier authorities, who always pursued maximal numbers of military servitors in order to maintain security.

While the outright rejection of a land grant was possible before a servitor received an estate, once accepted, he was obligated to work the land. However, servitors could still claim that the land was of poor quality and demand that it be exchanged, or even sold, in order to adjust the military service or tax conditions of the grant. Some of the claims that the land had deteriorated and was no longer arable would have been valid. During the sixteenth and seventeenth centuries, peasants in the Middle Volga Region used field rotation to improve crop yields, but some still relied upon slash-and-burn agriculture. Claims of poor soil quality were likely based on the inevitable results of slash-and-burn production, which produced rich soil initially, but much lower yields after several years. When Ivan Romadinovskii of Atemar petitioned the tsar in 1652 for permission to sell his *pomest'e* to the local monastery, the Spaso-Prichistaia Bogoroditsaia, he begged the tsar to allow the sale, because "nothing grows on" the *pomest'e*, and "there is certain death from hunger."[84] While it is possible that the monastery would pay for depleted land, it is equally possible that Romadinovskii was using this trope to escape the tsar's service. Poor land frequently appeared as a reason to avoid yearly tax duties, as was the case for Merkulii Osip syn Pobedanskii, who petitioned the tsar that he would not be able to pay his full tax bill for the year, because his village of Khudoshyna in Arzamas district was "not worth much" and "provided little." The central government's response to his petition was that his land and village were fine, and he was expected to fulfill all his obligations.[85]

There is no way to judge the truthfulness of these petitions, but it is important to note that petitions for new lands based on poor soil quality were not limited to the region's servitors. For example, Metropolitan Matfei of Kazan successfully petitioned the tsar in 1616 for new land, because the metropolitanate's lands were "used up."[86] Local priests relied on this trope as well. Markel Konstantinovich made three separate attempts to buy land from Arzamas's Troitse-Sergeevskii Monastery. In his second attempt, he claimed that his family's land "had served long enough" and that his children "had fallen out over it," and for their "future happiness" he wanted to acquire some new land from the monastery.[87] Neither his first attempt nor his last referred problems with his children or the quality of his land, suggesting that his land was not, in fact, exhausted. Rather, this argument was a mere convenience.[88]

If a history of service, rejections of grants, or a claim that land was inadequate failed to motivate a favorable response from the central government, servitors resorted to asking local authorities for dispensation. With Muscovy's system of competitive cooperation, there was always another authority upon which to impose. Legal disputes among servitors, local administrators, and Church officials all occurred with some regularity. In general, the verdicts tended to favor whoever was in current possession of a parcel of land, especially a servitor residing on *pomest'e*. Sviiazhsk's *voevoda*, Petr Ivanovich Rostovskii, warned Sviiazhsk's Bogoroditsii Monastery to stop claiming the village of Beshbotman in Sviiazhsk district in 1583. The monastery's lands entirely surrounded the village, rightfully the *pomest'e* of Nikita Fedorov syn Ol'gov, and it recently had attempted to rule Ol'gov's peasants as its own.[89] Similarly, the Troitse-Sergeevskii Monastery of Sviiazhsk lost its battle in a dispute over a village of "tsarist peasants" against the *voevoda* of Kazan in 1669. While the *voevoda*'s office received the rights to the village in 1618, the monastery claimed it in 1652. After each side presented its claims, the Prikaz Kazanskogo dvortsa decided in favor of the *voevoda*, but the crops from the current year's harvest would be turned over to the monastery first.[90] After all, reassigning land that currently produced military service would have potentially endangered frontier security.

From the perspective of the local elites, the process of accepting *pomest'ia* was fraught with more complexity than the obvious state need to place troops on the frontier, or its desire to keep Tatars away from Moscow. To a degree, every condition of the grant was negotiable, but not every negotiation was successful. When servitors sought to protect their families' interests or to use their land as a dowry, as long as family remained on the land there was a high chance of success. The pursuit of goals lessening the burden of the grants offered less predictable results, but the willingness of all the regional actors to file petitions and go to court in order to resolve local issues indicates that there were few passive participants where land, the law, and economic gain were concerned. If a petition failed, perhaps a lawsuit might work, or petitioning the local *voevoda* instead of Moscow.

Local elites, therefore, were active participants in this most fundamental aspect of frontier security. The central and local authorities required a strong military presence to secure the region from external threats and the potential of internal revolts. Elites exploited this opportunity to maintain their social status, alleviate tax obligations, and potentially expand their estates or run new businesses. As servitors accomplished personal goals, they also confirmed the image of frontier society created by the Russian Orthodox Church. All the men were loyal, obedient servants of central authorities, and their wives and daughters were accessories needing protection. An unitary image of frontier society emerged from secular and religious authorities and the documents from the servitors themselves. The empire might have accommodated diversity, but all men served the tsar. The state's success was that by participating in the system, all parties potentially had something to gain.

Diminishing Status

In many ways, everything that occurred on the frontier demonstrated the limits of state control, but, at the same time, its successes. Military servitors successfully negotiated with the state in order to secure and protect land for their families, and yet the state kept them on the frontier without suffering regular revolts or losing population. Each party could be happy with the outcome.

It would not be a permanent state of affairs. By the 1670s, families began to lose control over the lands they had held for generations, and the state was the cause. In 1676, the Kazan resident Andrei Vasilev syn Elagin bequeathed his father's land in Arzamas to his nephew, Fëdor Petrov of Sviiazhsk. Petrov was a relative and lived within the Middle Volga Region. When the governor of Arzamas was asked to approve this exchange, he notified Elagin and Petrov that a boiar, Iakov Nikitich Odoevskii, already had rights for the land.[91] The reaction of Elagin cannot be determined, but obviously the high status of Odoevskii must have influenced this break from the traditional pattern seen above, but it was also noteworthy that an elite member of the court sought land in the region, another shift from traditional grants. Though it had taken more than a century, the relationship between frontier gentry and the central authorities was no longer a balance between the chancelleries' need and the gentry's less desirable origins. Now, the situation clearly favored those in the center, and the frontier was settled by a population that the state began to push out from their traditional settlements.

Less surprising was the declining status of non-Russians, particularly Muslims, during and after the 1670s. After the "Orthodox conquest," necessity had outweighed ideology, and relying upon preexisting structures rather than developing new schema was the quickest resolution for a difficult defensive situation. When Tsar Ivan Vasil'evich consistently engaged his neighbors in successive conflicts in the sixteenth century, the former elites of the khanate and his own political exiles were the only available forces to secure his new possessions along his exposed frontier. As security in the region improved with the construction of the defensive lines and with the transformation of an army no longer dependent upon cavalry, the compromise struck in the sixteenth century became increasingly less desirable in the seventeenth. This change allowed the state to move forward with the elimination of this group from the ranks of the social elite, particularly after 1649. The narrative of the conquest of Kazan, constructed by the Russian Orthodox Church after 1552 and confirmed with the creation of the new miracle cults and their highly restricted view of frontier society, moved closer to reality. The short-term co-option of the tsar's former enemies could be slowly erased, even if the transformation took several generations.

The century following 1552 was in many ways an elite Muslim "golden age" within the Muscovite Empire. The state's dependence on its old enemies created opportunities for both parties. Muslim Tatars received land grants, maintained elite status, and proved loyalty to the state over generations. In return, they could protect their families' fortunes. While the Russian Orthodox Church created an image of an Orthodox exemplar serving the state in pious obedience, the tsar's Muslim servitors continued to prosper, unaffected by an Orthodoxy aimed only at Russians. By 1670 this era of accommodation was eroding. Incentives to convert to Orthodoxy became law, and discriminatory practices became more acceptable to central authorities. The transformation was unavoidable as military technology changed. As cavalry became less essential to tsarist security practices, so did the Muslim servitors who fulfilled those roles. It may have taken more than a century, but Muslim Tatars were no longer valued enemies but rather local undesirables.

5

Irregular Subjects

The *Cheremisin Tartar* [Maris], that lieth betwixt the *Russe* & the *Nagay*, are of two sorts, the *Lugavoy* (that is of the valley) and the *Nagornay*, or of the hilly countrey. These have much troubled the Emperours of *Russia*. And therfore they are content now to buy peace of them, under pretence of giving a yeerly pension of *Russe* commodities, to their *Morseis* [*mirza*s] or *Divoymorseis* [*divei-mirza*s] that are chiefe of their tribes. For which also they are bound to serve them in their wars, under certain conditions. They are saide to be just & true in their dealings: and for that cause they hate the *Russe* people, whom they account to be double, & false in all their dealing.

Giles Fletcher,
Of the Russe Commonwealth, 1591

[The Maris] live mostly in wretched huts, rather than houses, and subsist by raising cattle, collecting honey, and hunting game. They are excellent archers and teach their children to be the same. They are a disloyal, thieving, and superstitious people.

Adam Olearius,
The Travels of Olearius in Seventeenth-Century Russia, 1636

Muscovy's frontier required labor to function economically and militarily. Merchants and long-distance trade provided some of the economic resources necessary, but the new towns and settlements required agricultural labor. This labor also supported the Russian Orthodox Church, the local administration, and supplied the garrisons. While the cavalry served as the elite troops of the army, infantry was always its larger counterpart. Cheaper to equip and supply, the Muscovite soldiery was recruited from the peasantry throughout the country. As important as the local elites were to the functioning of the frontier military force, the local population, though different than those in Muscovy proper, provided the backbone of the regional economy.

The local peasantry was far more diverse than the gentry, and its ethnolinguistic and religious geography was much more complex. Turkic Tatars and Chuvashes, some Muslim but most animist, were settled closest in and around Kazan. Along the Volga were Finno-Ugric Mordvins and Maris, and north of the river were groups of Udmurts. Some Russian slaves held by the Khanate of Kazan chose to remain on the frontier as free men after their rescue in 1552, and other Russians fled from the interior and settled in the region, particularly during the chaotic era between the Livonian War and the Time of Troubles. Most of these settlers farmed, either with field-rotation or slash-and-burn agriculture, although a sizeable proportion became hunters, trappers, fishermen, and beekeepers.[1] For both the new local government and that in Moscow, language, religion, and occupation divided the population in confusing and unexpected ways, which they found difficult to classify. For decades they worked to distribute this population's labor among the landowners in the gentry, administration, and the Orthodox Church. The general goal of the state was clear: allow no alternative sources of authority in the form of cohesive ethnolinguistic communities. It reinforced ethnolinguistic and religious divisions and isolated individual communities, leaving Muscovite rule as the only common denominator among a subject population split by religion, ethnolinguistic identity, and social status.

Much as the region as a whole needed to be secured and made productive, so did the population. The small revolts after 1552 disrupted the early attempts, but construction of the Arzamas Line, with its earthworks, settlements, and forts, stabilized the border, physically (and symbolically) containing the population. It remapped the ranges of those nomad groups still outside of Muscovy's borders, where it failed to exclude them. It also impeded any potential flight by Muscovite subjects attempting to escape the reach of the authorities. The ongoing project of dividing the population settlement by settlement, community by community, into Muscovite service proceeded as the borders were defined and secured.

During this early postconquest period, the central government divided the local populace into one of three legal categories: monastic peasant, servitor's peasant, or *iasachnye liudi* (people who pay tribute). To one degree or another, most of the populace in the region would not have noticed much of an immediate difference in their standing relationship with a landlord, but there existed distinctions among the categories having more far-reaching consequences. Monastic peasants were under the direct supervision of the Orthodox Church. Servitors' peasants were under the direct supervision of a gentry landlord, who in some cases remained the same as before the conquest but in others was a newly arrived Russian military servitor, separated from their workforce by language and religion. *Iasachnye liudi* were defined by the yearly payment of a tax (or tribute).

However, in placing the khanate's peasantry under new ecclesiastical and military landlords, the state constructed a nascent framework for transforming the region's populace. All military servitor peasants belonged to a new legal category, which was demonstrated once they became serfs in 1649. After enserfment, these non-Russian, non-Orthodox peasants were most directly under state authority, as this population was attached formally to state land. The Russian Orthodox Church also benefited from its new peasants but swiftly discerned that if monasteries converted animists to Orthodoxy, the local governor might reclassify and reassign the population to an Orthodox military servitor, who would now find them more suitable. The *iasachnye liudi*—diverse, distinct, containing as a group individuals with many skills and few common connections—found itself threatened and pressured by new Russian settlements populated by refugees from the interior. It was not surprising that petitions for adjustments in land grants, tax bills, and military service arrived in Moscow from all groups, along with pleas for changes in status and protests against government practices. Nor was it surprising that the late 1500s witnessed a series of revolts, but after the Romanov ascension an unexpected period of relative peace and stability prevailed, despite a new legal system, a continuously expanding empire, and the relatively dangerous border with steppe nomads.

When serfdom was finalized in Muscovy in 1649, it immediately affected military servitors' peasants, but it soon would affect all segments of the frontier populace. When the first tsarist commissions arrived a few years later to recover runaway serfs, serfdom became the problem of everyone in the region as they were suddenly investigated, and, in some cases, incarcerated. At the same time, the movement of populations became more attractive to the tsarist authorities, who experimented with the forcible relocation of the Mordvins to the south, from the region around Arzamas, to the new Simbirsk Line. The Mordvins, like the new Russian settlers around Kazan, were forced to adopt grain agriculture in the new fields on the edge of the steppe, though for centuries they had only been trappers, fishermen, and beekeepers in the northern forest. It was not a relocation for which they were particularly suited, and it inspired consistent resistance to tsarist authority, but the Mordvins had little chance of successfully resisting the weight of a far more entrenched state presence than had existed in 1552.

By 1670 in fact, most of the local populace had reasons to resent tsarist rule and violently resist it. Non-Russian military servitors had maintained a portion of their social status in the 120 years following the conquest. The true transformation of the region is more evident when examining the peasants. Non-Russian peasants consistently and steadily lost rights, land, and socio-religious autonomy in what was arguably the most successful implementation of imperial policy in the region. That success for the Muscovite government was possible because of the peasants' inability to resist state power over time. The construction of workable control mechanisms over the peasantry had been slow to evolve, which reflects the incremental development of administrative, economic, and military policy. The local population had begun as diverse groups with little in common. Tsarist categorization, the reduction of peasant legal privileges, investigations, and forced relocation atomized them further, but it also created a known, common adversary—the tsarist government. The widespread revolt of 1670, therefore, was a logical explosion following a century of steadily imposed tighter restrictions. Its easy suppression, however, indicated how successfully the state had managed the task of imposing its power over its tsarist subjects.

Questionable Peasants

In the early sixteenth century, the Muscovite legal system was a loose compilation of individual decrees. Both the *Sudebnik*s of 1497 and 1550 were short documents that failed to address innumerable legal issues. Perhaps the most glaring omission was the absence of a legal definition of the rights and obligations of the social category of "peasant" (*krest'iane*).[2] In 1552, it had yet to be clearly defined. Therefore, the concept of a "peasant" must be inferred from extant administrative, economic, and military practice. For a non-Russian population, Michael Khodarkovsky suggested there were four central components: loyalty to the tsar, language (Russian), lifestyle, and religion (Orthodox).[3] Clearly, then, in the central provinces a "typical" peasant was an Orthodox, Russian-speaking subject of the tsar, who lived in a settled community that practiced traditional agriculture. This is not to imply that this was the situation of all peasants in Muscovy, but rather that the state preferred these features to others. In the lands of the former khanate, there was a non-Russian-speaking, non-Orthodox population, some practicing grain agriculture, others of whom were hunters, beekeepers, or fishermen. No later than 1571, however, they were subjects of the tsar, defined by the demarcation of the newly constructed Arzamas Line, and they lived in settled communities and engaged in some type of agricultural production. Clearly, these non-Russians were not pastoral nomads as the other Turkic groups of the steppe still were, but were they "peasants"? It was the work of more than a century to arrive at a serviceable answer.

The region around Kazan was agriculturally productive long before Muscovy's occupation of the city in 1552. It produced sufficient excess grain to export to the Slavic principalities in the medieval era.[4] It was planted in the same system as in the Muscovite heartland, despite its different environment. Moscow lay for the most part within a forested belt, allowing the widespread use of "slash-and-burn" style agriculture, which required new fields to be taken under cultivation once the previously cleared land had been exhausted. By the sixteenth century, Muscovite peasants were practicing a three-field rotation system, but for some it still began with slash-and-burn practices. Kazan and its hinterland were a mix of oak and birch forests and open steppe grasslands, and appeared to have used a two- or three-field rotation system. There is some archaeological evidence that the Udmurts, situated farthest to the north and inside the forests, likely relied upon slash-and-burn agriculture instead of any rotation.[5] Though the systems may have been similar, there is no question that the former khanate had a variety of agricultural systems in place, suited to its different environments.

However, the most notable feature in the region was that it produced numerous local products that were more profitable than grain. This included honey and wax, collected in large volumes along the Volga River, but especially by the Mordvins and Maris. Fishing in the numerous rivers, as well as fur trapping, was common throughout the region. Many of the non-elites of the khanate paid their yearly tribute to the khan in kind, including wax, honey, fish, fur, and grain. Therefore, many of the people in the countryside were not "peasants" in the strictest sense as they did not produce grain or produced it only intermittently, yet their labor supported the local administrators, churchmen, and military servitors all the same.

The majority of non-Russian peasants became *iasachnye liudi* under Muscovite rule—the category defined their relationship to the state through their tax-paying status. *Iasachnye liudi* status allowed non-Russians to maintain their traditional lifestyles as farmers, trappers, beekeepers, or fishermen, and limited almost entirely their contact with Muscovite officials to their yearly tribute payments. A small number of non-Russians, however, found themselves placed into a new relationship with their conquerors, because they were assigned to work either for a monastery or for the Muscovite military servitors. Though *iasachnye liudi* made up the largest percentage of non-Russians within the former khanate, as time passed more non-Russians found themselves redesignated as peasants attached to a military servitor's land.

The *iasachnye liudi* existed within the most ambiguous legal category of the three but, as a result, endured the easiest transition to the tsar's rule. *Iasachnye liudi* lived largely independent lives, separate from the local government and the newly arrived Russian Orthodox Church, which usually ignored them except when they made yearly tribute payments to the tsar. Communities or villages, rather than individuals, held collective responsibility for meeting their tax obligations.[6] There was no question that the *iasachnye liudi* were the largest portion of typical local populations, and newly established outposts and towns profited from the large numbers of tribute-paying villages in their districts. In the oldest Muscovite town bordering the region, Nizhnii Novgorod, there were nearly one hundred Mordvin villages paying yearly *iasak* (taxes, tributes) to the city's coffers.[7] In Koz'modem'iansk, the Prikaz Kazanskogo dvortsa monitored the yearly *iasak* from the local Maris, the amount of which was set both in cash and in kind, preferably in fish.[8] In Simbirsk, the yearly *iasak* from twenty-eight villages of *iasachnye liudi* contributed more into the city's coffers than did trade tariffs between June through August, the three months of highest volume.[9]

As the relationship between the *iasachnye liudi* and the local authorities was so limited, they experienced few pressures designed to alter their traditional agricultural practices. This also no doubt had much to do with the value of their production. Beekeeping, in particular, was among the region's most valuable trades, and as early as 1555, for example, the Muscovite government guaranteed the Russian Orthodox Church that local beekeepers in Kazan province would pay the Church their yearly tribute in honey and wax. In a land cadaster from Kazan of 1623–24, there were at least 2,330 Tatar beekeepers living in the province.[10] In the tax records from 1614–15 from Nizhnii Novgorod province, Finno-Ugric Mari and Mordvin beekeepers alone paid the city a total of just over 167 rubles, about 50 percent of the total amount paid by the twenty-eight *iasachnye* villages of Simbirsk.[11] The financial benefits for the local authorities were so obvious, they rarely pressured the *iasachnye* to adopt Russian peasant grain agriculture.

Economic production set the *iasachnye liudi* at a legal distance from Russian peasants, and before 1649 they accrued further benefits, which emphasized their unique status. If a non-Russian village demonstrated its loyalty to the tsar with consistent tribute payments over several generations, it received the legal right to its ancestral lands. This was the case for the *iasachnyi* Tatar Aladiachek Bivaev syn Isheev, an elder of Nirkov-Amachev, a village in Sviiazhsk province, who, in the name of the inhabitants, accepted the rights to his village's land in 1625, bequeathed to the villagers in honor of the loyalty of their ancestors.[12] Once the process was established, some non-Russians attempted to preempt the decision of the state by entering Muscovite service in order to receive their villages as *pomest'e*. This was the case for the *iasachnyi* Tatar Enbai Teregulov, who received the Tatar village of Bylgan in Kazan province as his *pomest'e* in 1639, and for the *iasachnye* Mordvins

Boiiashka Arzamasov and Lukashko Khudiakov, who received the Mordvin village of Rizovatovo in Arzamas province in 1642.[13] In a sense, this was similar to the policy of rewarding loyal elite with grants of *pomest'e*, even though these men emerged from more humble origins. However, the primary effect of granting *iasachnye liudi* property rights was to differentiate them legally from Russian peasants in the heartland, who generally did not own land. Of course, the "black" peasants of the Russian north were also small property holders, but they did not own property collectively as a village.[14]

Entering Muscovite service or making tribute payments consistently, however, were not the most common strategies adopted by *iasachnye liudi* to support their position inside Muscovy. Some *iasachnye liudi* simply failed to pay their yearly *iasak*, which generated a response from the central authorities, though usually little more than a firm reminder to fulfill their obligations. At times, *iasachnye liudi* deployed the refusal as a deliberate rebuke to authorities. In 1629, for example, Mordvin and Mari peasants living in Alatyr' province protested the recent arrival of Russian peasants by withholding tax payments. The central chancelleries responded with a decree instructing the non-Russians to fulfill their duty and accept the arrival of Russians into the area.[15] The awareness that the community could alert authorities to their grievances in this way indicates that *iasachnye liudi* understood their legal privileges as tsarist subjects, and were willing to use the Muscovite legal system to their advantage.

Iasachnye status was more of a transitional state than it might first appear. On the one hand, formal acknowledgement from the state kept the non-Russians at a distance from local and central political authorities, and separate from the Russian Orthodox Church. The economic benefits to the local administration inspired their commitment to maintaining the system as it existed. Further, the *iasachnye liudi* were willing to use the tsarist subject's traditional right to petition to protest changes to this relationship and gain legal rights through service and their tribute as well. On the other hand, this was an era of increasing taxes, which fell on peasants throughout Muscovy. For example, the tax reforms in the reign of Mikhail Fedorovich placed tax assessment on a per household basis instead of per plot of land, requiring more intensive surveying and accounting in the local communities in order to produce the greater revenue it predicted.[16] *Iasachnye*, however, were not directly affected, protected by their status. Certainly the *voevody* could, and perhaps did, attempt to extract greater tribute, but the *iasachnye liudi*'s yearly tribute was calculated on a different basis, not that of land held. Yet, every time groups of *iasachnye liudi* petitioned the tsar to confirm their separate status from other peasants, they emphasized their status as his subjects. In other words, both *iasachnye liudi* and the Tatar gentry relied on their utility to the state in order to preserve what few privileges they held, but this dependence could never maintain their status before 1552—it could only retard the erosion.

Meanwhile, the position of *iasachnye liudi* was still more independent than that of the other peasants. Muscovite authorities had greater control over the monastic peasants than the *iasachnye*, even if those peasants were supervised directly by ecclesiastical officials. Non-Russians who resided on newly assigned monastic estates were transformed overnight into the labor force of the Russian Orthodox Church. While many performed their traditional trade (usually farming or fishing), monasteries had both economic and legal control over their non-Russian peasants, and more closely managed their activities compared to the local government's supervision of most *iasachnye liudi*. The first grant of a non-Russian village to a monastery occurred shortly after the occupation of Kazan, and monasteries received non-Russian villages steadily throughout the sixteenth and seventeenth centuries. Kazan's prestigious Spaso-Preobrazhenskii Monastery, established within Kazan's kremlin, possessed several villages in the countryside. On 15 June 1586, Prince Mikhail Bitiagovskii, then *voevoda* of Kazan, informed the central government that he granted the village of Iakovlevskoe, with its lands and peasants, to the monastery to fulfill Kazan's tithe. Bitiagovskii then ordered Iakovlevskoe's Tatar peasants to plow the monastery's fields so that its taxes could be paid.[17] In 1595 another decree by the *voevoda* gave the monastery ownership of the village of Polseka with its land and peasants, and then the village of Sukhaia, granted in 1601.[18] By 1621 Sviiazhsk's Bogoroditskii Monastery possessed at least two Tatar villages, Khoziasheva and Isakov.[19] By 1646 the region's three oldest monasteries (Spaso-Preobrazhenskii, Bogoroditskii, and Kazan's Zilantov Monastery) oversaw a total of fifteen villages with a combined population of 1,851 non-Russians.[20] This evidence supports E. L. Dubman's study of monastic landholding in Simbirsk and Samara provinces, in which he argues that non-Russians worked all the land granted to monasteries in those regions.[21]

This was a great increase in the power of the state to control peasants compared to the relationship between the two during the khanate's life, but monastic peasants gained some distance from secular authorities because of their new ecclesiastical intermediaries. Monastic landlords had the closest contact of any Orthodox institution to the region's non-Russian peasants. For the next century, abbots regularly intervened on behalf of their non-Russian peasants, generally in order to defend their own economic privileges. The abbot of Kazan's Zilantov Monastery, for example, protested to the central government in 1598 that the bailiffs of Kazan's *voevoda* had seized his peasants' carts, which would prevent the harvest. The central government sided with the monastery over the bailiffs in this instance, in order to guarantee payment of the monastery's tax bill.[22] While the abbot's action was largely self-interested, this petition demonstrated an advantage gained by the new monastic peasants that the *iasachnye liudi* lacked—a more effective intermediary with the Muscovite government. While non-Russian petitions might be ignored, it was far harder to dismiss the abbot of one of the region's most prestigious monasteries.

There was no guarantee that abbots would willingly defend all of the protests of their peasants. However, it is hard to overemphasize how well financial concerns could bring abbots and peasants together in a common cause, overriding the distinction between Orthodox landlord and non-Orthodox peasant. This was the case for the Muslim Mordvin Gerasim Onanin, who reported to his landlord, Abbot Kornilii of Arzamas's Spaso-Preobrazhenskii Monastery, that his fellow villagers, the Muslim Tatars of Cherny Khrety, had fled the area and were not returning. Onanin hoped to avoid responsibility by fulfilling the Tatars' obligations in addition to his own.[23] In 1678/79 the peasants of Chernukha, a Mordvin village, petitioned Tsar Fëdor Aleksevich to be returned to the Spaso-Preobrazhenskii Convent of Arzamas, which had been granted the village more than fifty years earlier, in 1626/27. The villagers preferred the convent as a landlord to their current one, a Russian servitor. The petition was returned to the convent, the likely source of the petition, without an answer.[24] Direct financial interests might have united monastery and village, but could only sometimes succeed against state interests.

Indirect economic interest, however, was much more important to the relationship between the peasant and his abbot. Here the tensions between state and monastic interests dissuaded abbots from pursuing the conversion of non-Russian peasants.[25] The explanation was simple. If a monastery succeeded in converting its own village to Orthodoxy, then that village and its people could be re-granted to a military servitor. The state would not allow Muslim or animist peasants to serve Russian gentry, but Orthodox peasants were suitable. Furthermore, monasteries were not allowed to possess villages of Russian peasants; as more Russians settled in the region, often displacing non-Russians, monasteries lost control over their earlier possessions.[26] With two such potentially avoidable disasters threatening monasteries and their labor forces, it was no surprise that they came to view unconverted non-Russians settled on monastic land as an asset, especially in land disputes. In other words, the Russian Orthodox Church supported confessional plurality throughout the region for many years. This is not to imply that the relationship between the local Church and its labor force was benign, but it may have been less adversarial than other places in Muscovy.[27]

Existing at a legal distance from the institutions of the Muscovite government was not always an advantage. As was case of the *iasachnye liudi*, this new monastic labor force was not a traditional community of Russian, grain-producing peasants. They were tsarist subjects, and considered the property of the Russian Orthodox Church, but few, if any, were Orthodox. These non-Russians also reaped real benefits from belonging to the monasteries. They possessed an advocate against both central and local authorities, and even if they could not always rely on the intervention of the Church in disputes, when Church officials saw fit to act they were more effective than non-Russians acting on their own. As telling was the evidence that the Russian Orthodox Church essentially ignored its mission to convert the peasants to Orthodoxy. Well into the eighteenth century, the local monasteries possessed vast estates of non-Russians who remained non-Orthodox. When abbots defended their non-Russian peasants, they defended Muslims and animists against the Orthodox tsar. The slight protection offered by monastic peasant status created some security for non-Russians residing on monastic estates that the other peasants in the region, including *iasachnye luidi*, did not possess.

The peasants facing the greatest change, and diminution of status, were those who resided on the new estates of military servitors after the conquest. This was because they shared the general loss of privileges suffered by Russian peasants on military servitor estates during the sixteenth century.[28] Initially, most of those servitors were in fact the former military elites of the khanate. However, by the 1560s, some Russian political exiles and other servitors began to arrive and receive sizeable land grants, including a peasant labor force residing on those estates. The numbers of non-Russians living on the lands of Muscovite servitors was quite small, but grew in the seventeenth century as *pomest'ia* became more common, and Russian peasant migrants and local converts to Orthdoxy could become a viable labor force. The percentage of non-Russians that became servitors' peasants varied from province to province inside the former khanate, though the number was highest in Arzamas, the province closest to Muscovy's heartland. The Mordvins, the primary group in that region, formed a larger percentage of this category of peasants when compared to Tatars or Chuvashes, for example, who generally remained *iasachnye liudi* and were less likely to be converts to Orthodoxy.[29]

Military servitors' peasants had several obligations to their landlords. These were similar to those some of the peasants would have experienced in the khanate, which also maintained its cavalry with the support of peasant labor. However, as *pomest'e* was only temporarily held by the military servitors and remained the property of the state, these lands belonged to the government. Restrictions on their movement increased in the sixteenth century, ultimately producing a series of laws enabling landlords to reclaim runaway peasants. As early as the *Sudebnik* of 1497, peasants living on gentry estates were only allowed to migrate from the estate on St. George's Day in the fall. As the Muscovite economy suffered throughout Ivan IV's Livonian War, military servitors were offered greater privileges in exchange for their continued service. By the end of the sixteenth century, the use of the "Forbidden Year," in which the peasants were prevented from exercising their right to leave on St. George's Day, had become standard. The "Forbidden Years" produced a de facto serfdom, though it was not yet law. In 1597, the government legalized a five-year time limit for the recovery of runaway peasants; this was extended to ten years in 1642. The 1642 law also allowed a fifteen-year recovery period for peasants "taken by force" from their landlord's estate.[30] Even with the gentry's increased power to restrict peasant movement, servitors continued to press the tsar's government, seeking the unrestricted right to reclaim runaway peasants during the first half of the seventeenth century, succeeding in 1649 with changes to the law included in the *Ulozhenie*.[31]

Before 1649, this legal relationship between the peasantry and the gentry, de facto serfdom, was obviously the greatest burden on non-Russians in any of the categories. Nor were Russian peasant refugees fleeing from the interior provinces enjoying greater freedom on the frontier, as they became the preferred peasants for military servitor estates. Although it did not affect a large portion of the local population, those who had been peasants in the khanate but were now closer to serfdom consistently protested their loss of privileges under Muscovite rule. Frequently the central government's sole response to protests was the publication of a charter instructing villagers on their responsibilities to their new landlord, as was the case when a group of peasants living in Kudeiarovskaia village in Alatyr' province were reminded of their legal obligation to their servitor landlord, Dmitrii Kuroedov.[32] However, these sorts of complaints might have been the result of the process of transferring both *iasachnye liudi* and monastic peasants from their previous landlords to the authority of servitors. This situation would have further removed non-Russians from their traditional sociopolitical relationships or lifestyles, in particular, the stark transition from *iasachnye liudi* to something much closer to a traditional Russian agriculturalist.

The relationship between the state and its new peasants was highly variable, given the three distinct relationships that determined a peasant's relationship to the central and local government. Throughout the region, any of the local non-Russians (Chuvashes, Maris, Mordvins, Tatars, Udmurts) were equally likely to become one of these three new types of peasant, according to their population's density in any locality. However, it was not a question of convenience, or even geography. Local divisions among the peasant community, created by either language or religion, could be reinforced by separating villages into different legal categories, or at least among different landlords. For example, the Asanovs, a family of converted Tatars in service, received a village in Kazan province settled with both Russians and Tatars, but all were Orthodox.[33] Nearby, the Chuvash Andreianov family received their third Chuvash village as part of their land grant in 1613, and the Khoziashev family of converted Tatars possessed two villages of Tatars during the seventeenth century.[34] However, the Orthodox village of Beshbotman in Kazan province was granted to the Orthodox Russian Nikita Fedorov syn Ol'gov, in order to separate the Muslim Chuvash village belonging to Azelei Rogil'dei Meev on one side from the animist Mordvin village of Naratlei Kurlik Kudashev on the other.[35]

In this way, each religion, and often each ethnolinguistic population, was divided not only by distance but also by property lines. Because the local population contained only a small population of Russian servitors, this system tended to work to the advantage of non-Russian *pomest'e* holders, rather than their Russian counterparts. While it was true that Russian elites possessed larger estates in terms of land area, for example in Sviiazhsk province, most of the villages were assigned to Tatar servitors.[36] This is likely the origin of the policy of assigning converted non-Russians to Russian servitors. Without a ready supply of Russian peasants, at least the Russian servitors could have some connection with an Orthodox village, even if Russian was not their daily language.

Therefore, it seems almost certain that the government pursued a "divide-and-conquer" strategy in assigning the local populations to their future landlords. In the 1550s and again in the 1570s, the non-Russian population revolted against tsarist rule, still seemingly connected enough to Kazan's memory and retaining mechanisms that overcame religious and ethnolinguistic obstacles, to rise effectively (if not successfully) against Muscovite rule. By the end of the century, this had become more difficult. Not only were there the obvious ethnolinguistic and religious divisions among the diverse population but now well-established legal differences split the population along lines of economic interest. While the village belonging to one landlord might protest increased taxes, it was unlikely that their neighboring village had identical burdens. To take just one possible example, monastic peasants saw their abbot defending them against the local *voevody*, and therefore, they might be unwilling to join protests by villages under a servitor's control. The new legal system almost certainly discouraged conversion or assimilation, but the multiple categories were in fact an effective mechanism of colonial rule. Standardized social categories remained elusive, but the complicated system proved administratively advantageous, as the state required religious and ethnolinguistic difference to maintain control. But it hardly fit any model matching the glorious "Orthodox" conquest proclaimed in 1552.

The division of the local community was an effective policy for the state in the century following the occupation of Kazan. While the Chuvashes, Maris, Mordvins, Tatars, and Udmurts were not traditional Russian peasants, their settled agricultural practices generally made them suitable as the labor force and tax base for the new settlements. And though the majority of the population remained *iasachnye liudi*, they still received new legal rights and some privileges, which allowed them to protest further changes to their relationship. Monastic peasants gained an intermediary with the local and central authorities. Military servitor peasants may have faced the greatest immediate supervision, but in theory this did not mean they were at a comparative disadvantage in this new legal system. This colonial policy adroitly undid one of the factors facilitating revolt, while successfully maintaining local agricultural production.

Suspect Recruits

Each of the three distinct new classes of peasant in the Middle Volga Region possessed advantages and disadvantages, and non-Russians enjoyed varying amounts of success in mitigating or altering the terms of their legal status, depending on place and circumstance. This makes it difficult to generalize about "peasants" as a social group. At the same time, the state's attitude toward the former subjects of the Khanate of Kazan remained largely constant—suspicion. From the conquest until the promulgation of the *Ulozhenie* in 1649, both the central chancelleries and the local administration remained alert to the threat of future insurrections. The Arzamas Line in 1571 limited the danger of nomadic incursion, and inasmuch as it kept the tsar's subjects out of the steppe, it did not suddenly pacify a region possessing a history of periodic resistance to the tsar's government.

Non-Russians were included in only one clause of Kazan's *nakaz* of 1613, though admittedly the document itself was quite short. "If there will be Russians, Tatars, Udmurts, Bashkirs, Chuvashes, or Maris who think about instability or trouble," the *voevoda* was required to "investigate" them and "bring them to court," followed by interrogations to uncover the source of the problems.[37] There was no mention of their tax or tribute payments, their potential military service, or their situation on Orthodox lands, among the other topics that might have been a concern. While the chancelleries may have supplied supplemental information to the local *voevody*, this document conveyed the clear message—the *voevoda* must be prepared at any moment to stop any revolt before it started. It would be difficult, but, despite non-Russian participation in the life of the region, this effort would dominate the next century.

The *voevody*'s vigilance did not prevent a brief revolt in 1615. During 1614, as the Muscovite army traveled through the region on campaign against the Crimean Tatars who were raiding farther south, it requisitioned grain from the local population in excess of their yearly taxes. The following year, with grain probably in short supply from the requisition, Tatars, Chuvashes, Maris, Udmurts, and Bashkirs rose against the local garrisons.[38] However, both the scale of the event and the specific causes remain unknown. Local forces had little difficulty pacifying the region, and from 1616 until 1670, there was no general revolt or protest throughout the entire region.

In this period, Moscow addressed security by adjusting its military presence in the area. In the late 1640s, Muscovy completed the construction of the second defensive line, the Simbirsk Line. During this generation, new musket-wielding infantry (*strel'tsy*) arrived, shifting local garrisons away from their previous reliance on gentry cavalry toward non-elite formations, who were easier to equip and support. Even if the unsuccessful 1632–34 Smolensk War against the Commonwealth of Poland-Lithuania embarrassed the tsar's new gunpowder army, the transition was unstoppable. Certainly, the greater security against the steppe nomads created by the second defensive line, coupled with new military forces equipped in ways rebels could not match, may have discouraged insurrection.

As in the case of the region's cavalry, the overwhelming majority of the local infantry garrisons were drawn from the non-Russian population. This was traditional in Muscovy, with infantry recruited from the peasantry across the kingdom. While seemingly ironic, since the local administration continued to suspect non-Russians of disloyalty, the necessity for easily recruitable local garrisons trumped Moscow's unease. One of the *voevoda*'s core functions was to inspect the local non-Russians to warn the chancelleries of potential revolts, but there was no other source of garrison troops: the result was a major recruitment drive among this suspect population.

As indicated by tables 7 and 8, the military transition resulted in a very real increase in garrison strength. But was the increased strength reliable? It is quite clear that in 1637/38, the local garrisons were filled with some *strel'tsy*, very few Russian townsmen, and large numbers of local non-Russian infantry. It was far more practical to recruit troops from the surrounding countryside than to move men across the entire state (as the border with Poland-Lithuania remained insecure), but it remained

Table 7 Comparison of recruits from town and countryside

| Town | 1613/14 | | 1637/38 | | |
	Townsmen	Non-Russians	Strel'tsy	Townsmen	Non-Russians
Kazan		1,563	2,228	1,197	9,949
Sviiazhsk		712	500	305	3,955
Cheboksary		667	300	262	1,993
Koz'modem'iansk		428	300	53	1,902
Iarensk		290	200	45	1,304
Tsarevokokshaisk		241	200	20	917
Tsivil'sk		559	200	24	2,032
Urzhum			200	25	1,235
Alatyr'			100	22	871
Kokshaisk		104	100		333
Kurmysh			100		1,036
Iadrin		297	50	111	1,025
Temnikov			50	88	1,120
Tetiushii			50	117	100
Malmyzh			40	43	
Laishev			20	122	
Total	**0**	**4,861**	**4,638**	**2,434**	**27,772**

Source: Data drawn from Buganov and Kuz'min, *Razriadnye knigi*, 263–66; and Buganov, *Razriadnaia kniga*, 118–25.

true that the local *voevody* were protecting their settlements with the same people their fortresses had been situated to control. Any revolt that might have occurred in the early decades of the seventeenth century would have been suppressed by its own communities, in essence. It is impossible to consider the tsar's defense policy in Kazan as simply one of Russian settlers defending against a steppe inhabited by indigenous non-Russians.

Furthermore, the composition of the regional forces, primarily Tatar servicemen including *mirzas* and the *novokreschane*, existed only as a fraction of the number of their peasant counterparts. Throughout the new settlements established in the lands of the khanate, Chuvashes, Maris, and Udmurts dominated. Since these troops would have been identified as "*novokreschane*" if they had been converted to Orthodoxy, it is likely they remained animist. It is also important to note that Mordvins comprised part of the frontier military forces, though their service typically was confined to the region's western edge, near their traditional homeland.

Local infantry recruits, in fact, played a decisive role in the Muscovite expansion signaled by the establishment of the second defensive line at Simbirsk. While the

Table 8 Comparison of Tatars vs. other non-Russians in 1637/38

Town	Tatars, *Mirzas, Novokreshchane*	Other non-Russians
Kazan	300	9,949 Chuvashes, Maris, Udmurts
Sviiazhsk	265	3,955 Chuvashes, Maris
Alatyr'	170	871 Mordvins
Cheboksary		1,993 Maris
Iadrin		1,025 Chuvashes, Maris
Iarensk		1,304 Maris
Kokshaisk		333 Chuvashes, Maris
Koz'modem'iansk	22	1,902 Chuvashes, Maris
Kurmysh	162	1,036 Maris
Laishev	5	
Temnikov	516	1,120 Mordvins
Tetiushii	100	
Tsarevokokshaisk		917 Maris
Tsivil'sk		2,032 Maris
Urzhum	22	1,235 Maris
Total	1,562	27,672

Source: Data drawn from Buganov and Kuz'min, *Razriadnye knigi*, 263–66; and Buganov, *Razriadnaia kniga*, 118–25.

first defensive line ran through well-settled territory, this new defensive line was on the northern edge of the steppe, and had no settled populations nearby. The problem of finding a population to man the Simbirsk Line developed into a serious challenge for Moscow. While some Russians settled in the area, it primarily was drawn from the aforementioned forced settlement of the Mordvins.[39] Moving the Mordvins made logical sense, however much they would inevitably resist. From the vantage point of the Muscovite court, restated in Kazan's *nakazy*, Muslim Tatars remained potential supporters of the Crimeans or the Ottomans. Mordvins were not Muslim, which made them implicitly more loyal, as a population, than the Tatars. Furthermore, out of all the ethnolinguistic groups of the former khanate, the Mordvins had the longest history of contact with Muscovy and were settled closest to the preconquest borders. As a consequence, as Mordvins moved south, Russians moved into formerly settled Mordvin territory, which provided Russian settlers a remarkably convenient opportunity to colonize new lands and readily reestablish their traditional agrarian lifestyle on land environmentally similar to that of their former homes. Meanwhile, the Mordvins struggled to adapt to the different climate of the steppe, placing the greater burden of migration on them. The

Mordvins, their former monastic landlords in the north, and the local administrators in the south all petitioned the central chancelleries to stop the relocation throughout the century, but it continued. It would not be a peaceful process for any party.[40]

In order to achieve its goals of generating sufficient Mordvin settlement for the south, the state relied on both "push" and "pull" factors. The state did not directly move Mordvins south—to do so was beyond Moscow's capabilities. Unfortunately, no document has been found that explicitly summarizes the government's blueprints, but the scheme unfolded in an organized way; some planning was evident. At the beginning of the seventeenth century, most Mordvins still lived on their ancestral lands. The state first assigned their ancestral lands to Russians, either peasants who were encouraged to settle there, or military servitors who received the land as *pomest'ia*. Then, as compensation, Moscow offered the Mordvins new lands in the south, in newly created outposts like Kerensk, Saransk, and Insar. It was not uncommon for the Mordvins to refuse to move, or return to the north after having been forced to settle along the Simbirsk Line. However, the state's most effective tool was persistence. Even from a halting beginning, eventually the Mordvins had to accept their relocation, as state officials offered no leniency or amelioration of the land transfers.

While complete certainty regarding the scale of the deportations is impossible to attain, the extant land cadastres provide a sense of the activity's scope. One demographic reconstruction by A. Geraklitov, based on records from three hamlets in the Alatyr' district, between 1624–26 and 1721, showed a 33 percent decline in the number of Mordvin households.[41] Archival documents provide anecdotal evidence that relocation was responsible, but a plague in the 1650s could also have affected the population and number of households.[42] However, the study covered a long span of time, the decline continued long after the plague, and it was constant and persistent. These relocated Mordvins were assigned to the new southern defensive line, in sufficient numbers that many of the new outposts were in fact named by the Mordvins. For example, Kerensk was named for the Mordvin word for "forest" (*keren*), a somewhat ironic choice for an outpost on the open steppe.[43]

The Mordvins protested this relocation process at every step. When new settlers arrived or their land was reassigned to a military servitor, Mordvins petitioned the tsar first, and then the local *voevoda*. The Mordvins of the village of Troetskii in Temnikov district, for example, complained to the *voevoda* of Arzamas about the arrival of Russian settlers, which was "shrinking their lands." The *voevoda* denied their petition entirely, including a pointed addendum that they were already assigned new lands near Mokshalev village in Saransk district.[44] If they accepted their loss and moved south, the Mordvin settlers frequently tried more petitions. Some of the more confrontational would avoid the state's plans and settle where they could, either choosing to flee back north or farther south, possibly joining the nomadic populations on the steppe, and yet others decided on a different location along the Simbirsk Line from their assigned lands. The *voevody* along the Simbirsk Line were expected to monitor this population movement, and encourage the Mordvins to accept their proper assignments. When one group of Mordvins lead by Rozan Siavashev decided to settle in Atemar rather than in Saransk, its *voevoda* had to act, though he chose the carrot rather than the stick, and sent Siavashev a glowing description of the beautiful lands that awaited their arrival.[45]

If the Mordvins accepted their new lands along the Simbirsk Line, they still confronted tremendous difficulties. They needed new skills to master farming on the steppe, quite unfamiliar to people at home with hunting, fishing, and trapping in the forested regions of the north.[46] If they did manage to produce grain, some now owed a portion of it to the local administration on the Simbirsk Line as well as needing to pay their financial obligations to their former monastic landlords. And, of course, they were also obligated to serve in the new garrisons defending the Line against nomadic raids. The best that local officials could offer the Mordvins, like Siavashev, and the monasteries, was an optimistic sales pitch. The *voevoda* of Penza, for example, assured the abbot of Arzamas's Troitse-Sergeevskii Monastery that the newly arrived Mordvins had been given enough land to farm the steppe, pay taxes, assume new militia duties in town, and fulfill their financial duties to the monastery.[47] He did not mention how those duties would be managed, or offer any support or assistance to the new residents.

Ecclesiastical authorities had no greater success in halting the Mordvin relocations, which indicates how important this process was to the state and how damaging it was to the monasteries. The Troitse-Sergeevskii Monastery in Arzamas held the most complete set of documents concerned with this relocation process. The reason for this concentration of correspondence was because the monastery's Mordvins were among the first targeted for relocation, which led the monastery to compile a large dossier of evidence of the depletion of its workforce.[48] As late as the 1630s, the Troitse-Sergeevskii was still receiving land and people to support its establishment; the region was no longer part of an exposed frontier, as Muscovite settlement had moved well to the south.[49] As a result by 1646, the monastery's Mordvin peasants were being instructed to travel south to their new lands. The abbot wrote two separate petitions for the Mordvins from the village of Bazkov, one to the tsar and the other to the local *voevoda*, requesting (on their behalf) the right to remain on the monastery's land. Both petitions included several small maps to demonstrate how the Russians already had begun to build their homes on the Mordvins' traditional lands.[50] Though the dossier contained no specific response to their petition, the losses recorded in the file over the next fifty years indicated there was no adjustment of state policy.

Nor was the Troitse-Sergeevskii Monastery the only wealthy church organization affected by the resettlement, or which questioned its purpose. Moscow's Novodevichii Convent, the most prominent women's institution in Muscovy, suffered from the Mordvin relocation as well, resulting in its abbess joining the chorus of protests against the policy's continuation. The convent lost a village in Simbirsk district, despite all of its influence. In fact, the government's commitment to relocating the Mordvins' land led them to the seizure of the convent's entire estate, which it gave as *pomest'e* to a military servitor.[51]

Neither petitions from the Mordvins and religious authorities nor concerns reported by local *voevody* altered the state's commitment to the policy. The region's security was the first priority, and everyone was expected to support the state's efforts. The easy colonization on the freed land to the north must have been an important secondary consideration. Aside from the demographic and security issues, the Muscovite administration itself made altering the policy nearly impossible once it had begun. The overlapping administrative roles among the Novgorodskaia chetvert', supervising much of the original Mordvin territory around Arzamas, the Monastyrskii Prikaz, supervising monastic lands, and the Prikaz Kazanskogo dvortsa, now supervising the Mordvins located along the Simbirsk Line, required consensus among all parties to adjust decisions. The Monastyrskii Prikaz might have been appeased by the requirement that Mordvin settlers fulfill their yearly financial obligations to their former monastic landlords, but this practice was a "double burden" for the settlers, who now paid two landlords with the revenue from one plot of land. Possibly the Novgorodskaia chetvert' was appeased by the increased security in the north created by the new defensive line farther to the south. Nothing was ever offered to the Mordvins to offset their sacrifice.

Furthermore, the state was assisted in the relocation by the Russian colonists, as when Russian peasants accused the Mordvins of practicing witchcraft. Whether there was actual evidence of wrongdoing or this was just a strategy to seize the Mordvins' land is impossible to know, and these accusations were uncommon but not unusual. Even before the Mordvin resettlement became a large-scale project, Russian settlers, newly arrived on the frontier, complained to the local *voevody* in the north about Mordvin witchcraft practices. But the official response to an accusation was quite serious because witchcraft was a crime in Muscovy, as it was everywhere in Europe during the early-modern era.[52] A village of Mordvins living on an estate held by the Pecherskii Monastery in Nizhnii Novgorod faced this trial in

1629. Their new Russian neighbors first petitioned the local *voevoda* of Arzamas, the closest judge to the village, and when this failed to motivate an investigation, they complained to the monastery.[53] At that point, the monastery investigated the case, and the Mordvins were ultimately cleared. In this instance, investigating the accusations provided some security for the monastery against the possible intervention by the *voevoda*. Had the abbot not investigated, and subsequently the *voevoda* did, then the village might have been seized. Once the state began forcing the Mordvins south, these accusations tended to gain more traction as the state now had another reason to pursue presumptions of Mordvin guilt. Accusations against another group of Mordvins were made in Alatyr' in 1650, and then again in Kurmysh in 1658.[54]

Witchcraft accusations in Muscovy, as elsewhere, fell on local healers.[55] When medical treatment failed, frequently the grieving family or its elders accused the practitioner of witchcraft. This is the most commonly documented type of accusation against Orthodox men and women in Muscovy. Most also used Orthodox prayers to assist in treatment, which provided some protection against witchcraft accusations. However, if the healer was a non-Orthodox, non-Russian, Orthodox rituals would not be used as part of the treatment. The result in such a case was a danger of witchcraft accusations in any medicinal treatment. As Russian settlement accelerated in the seventeenth century, accusations increased. Unsurprisingly, most of these accusations arose from the regions where Russians were replacing the displaced Mordvins. Because the state's interest was served by driving the Mordvins from their northern homes, the investigations were not surprising. The Mordvins largely remained animist, and witchcraft was an acceptable rationale for demanding their removal from their traditional lands.

The resettlement of the Mordvins contrasts rather dramatically with the settlement of the Belgorod Line across Muscovy's extended Ukrainian border. At the same time the Simbirsk Line was being populated, so was the much larger Belgorod project.[56] In each case, the challenge for the state was finding a settler population, quite difficult in a state that restricted most movement. The Mordvins selected for the Simbirsk Line were generally forced from monastic estates, which did not endanger the estates of the region's military servitors. As with the northern towns and outposts, the new garrisons therefore were largely peasant infantry. The Belgorod Line was quite different. The state recruited former military servitors who had lost their estates due to economic or other deprivations, or the younger sons and siblings of military servitors, to serve as *strel'tsy* in the forts. This was a novelty; *strel'tsy* had only comprised small numbers of the military forces in either the Arzamas or Simbirsk Lines. The Belgorod men were also given financial incentives, and usually received small estates to provide for themselves. There was a clear attempt to entice settlement, even though former servicemen accepting posts as *strel'tsy* would be declining in social status. On the Simbirsk Line, Mordvins were forced to accept punitive conditions, such as double taxation. Muscovite authorities were aware throughout the entire process that the Mordvins might not be reliable, but a lack of available population for settlement left the state without other options.

The Prikaz Kazanskogo dvortsa, at least, had little faith in the loyalty of the population. The *nakaz* to the *voevoda* of Kazan sent in the spring of 1649 (before the promulgation of the *Ulozhenie*) reflects the steady increase in state concerns about the reliability of the non-Russian population after 1613. There were five clauses laying out immediate measures to control the local non-Russians. One clause replicated the earlier general instruction to the *voevoda* to investigate and interrogate non-Russians, and prevent future instability.[57] However, the specific language of this later version changed. It warned the *voevoda* against service Tatars (the local gentry), Chuvashes, Maris, and Udmurts. Bashkirs were no longer listed among the suspect peoples in Kazan, although it was not entirely clear why; by 1649 the new fortress of Ufa had been completed, built largely to control them.[58] Furthermore, the *nakaz* stated that Russian soldiers, specifically, should be dispatched to prevent any potential revolt. This might have been a practice established earlier, but in the 1613 *nakaz*, Russians ranked among potential rebels, not as a preventative measure. Considering that Kazan's garrison troops were Chuvash, Mari, and Udmurt peasants, it seems that this directed the *voevoda* to first dispatch his Russian *strel'tsy*, as they would been Russian, available, and less sympathetic to local grievances than the rest of the garrison.

In addition to using the now traditional practice of detentions and interrogation, the Prikaz warned the *voevoda* to prevent all sales of implements useful as weapons to any Chuvash, Mari, or Udmurt community, suggesting investigations into local villages to uncover possible caches. The list was rather detailed—no "helmets, sabers, iron muskets," or any goods made by "blacksmiths or silversmiths."[59] It is impossible to know whether this instruction responded to a recent event or not, as there had been no large uprising since 1615, but its prophylactic intent was of a piece with the other clauses.

A long clause outlined the necessity for controlling all movement within the district. The *voevoda* was required to monitor all people arriving in Kazan, and forbade departures without his express permission. It instructed the *voevoda* to prevent any potential departure that would reduce the size of the garrison. Anyone leaving town without his permission was to be arrested and imprisoned. As with the other clauses, this one also expressly identified likely violators: potential mercenaries in service, including "Litva" and "Nemtsy" (Lithuanian/Belarusian and German, but generally applied to west European soldiers), the tsar's own military servitors, including *novokreshchane*, *mirza*s, and other Tatars, and finally all *iasachnye liudi*, particularly Chuvashes, Maris, and Udmurts. The clause ended with a final admonition, that the *voevoda* was "to guard closely the non-Russians, so that those who asked for leave did not deceive [the *voevoda*] with their treachery."[60] As the people involved were the tsar's own troops, this level of "directed suspicion" implied persistent problems with the local garrison, persistent fears about armed revolts, or a combination of both, liberally sprinkled with the paranoia imparted by Kazan's distance from Moscow.

This institutional paranoia was evident in the clause of the 1649 *nakaz* directing hostage taking to prevent disorder. This, the chancellery stated, was of great importance. If the *voevoda* could believe non-Russians who "claimed" to have a family, he was instructed to take a hostage from that family, keeping the "best people" (*samykh luchnykh liudei*) in Kazan at the "hostage house" (*amanaty dvor*).[61] The suspect groups once again were Tatars, Chuvashes, Maris, and Udmurts. Taking hostages to guarantee good behavior had been a steppe practice for centuries. The Muscovite government used it already to influence the steppe nomads still outside its borders.[62] In Kazan, the hostages taken were likely from the families of the tsar's garrison troops, used as a tool to guarantee their loyalty.

A later clause of the *nakaz* addressed the steps necessary to ensure consistent tribute payments from the local *iasachnye liudi*. The *voevoda* was instructed as before to investigate the local communities, but in 1649 the intent of the *nakaz* was to establish the residence of any individual family, and, more importantly, to track runaway peasants. If the *iasachnye liudi* in question were from Kazan or its surrounding districts, they must pay the *voevoda*. If inquiries revealed runaway peasants, they must be held in Kazan's prison and returned to their original district.[63] While Muscovy's laws at this time allowed landlords to reclaim runaway peasants within a limited time frame, Kazan's *nakaz* reflects a different concern—very close supervision over the entire population. The state, not the individual landlords, led the charge to uncover runaway peasants. In general, runaways would have contributed to the development and the security of the region with their labor. However, the chancelleries apparently feared that Kazan was vulnerable enough that a few extra peasants might foment instability, not to say rebellion.

At the same time, there is very little evidence that the Russian Orthodox Church possessed the same mistrust of its non-Russian peasants, even without their conversion to Orthodoxy. In the witchcraft cases, the Church usually exonerated its Mordvin peasants. In the relocation efforts, the Church, as landlord, always protected its peasants even if it generally failed to alter the state's plans. And while individual abbots might have questioned the ability of the Mordvins in the south to continue to meet their financial obligations to their former monasteries, there is no evidence that any abbot forgave those financial obligations after he lost his Mordvin villagers (nor that any received payment).

This toleration may have been the result of the leadership of the metropolitans of Kazan in the seventeenth century. Without a doubt, there was no coordinated attempt to impose baptisms upon the local non-Russian community in his region. However, just outside of the metropolitanate's territory, there was at least one attempt to target non-Orthodox peasants. This occurred in the 1650s among the Mordvins residing near the new settlements at Shatsk and Tambov (farther west than the end of the Simbirsk Line). Archbishop Misail of Riazan' appears to have instigated the program in the early 1650s. Using force, he violently baptized the local Mordvins, possibly "converting" as many as 4,000 by 1655. However, the Church's use of involuntary baptisms inspired a strong reaction; those Mordvins killed the archbishop while he was on procession through the region that year.[64]

The violence and the attempted mass conversion were quite distinct from anything that occurred in the territory under the Metropolitan of Kazan, which was coterminous with much of the Prikaz Kazanskogo dvortsa's administrative region. In the area where the non-Russians lived in the greatest numbers, the Russian Orthodox Church was unwilling to employ the conversion methods seen in Shatsk and Tambov. The Mordvins living under Kazan's metropolitans, tellingly, did not revolt against the Church's authority. Local authorities, so intent on observing the populace, could hardly have failed to note that forced conversions did not produce the desired result of a loyal, Orthodox population. For the Church as landlord, labor dues and the payment of taxes were the only impositions onto the non-Russian villages they controlled. Indeed, the greatest nuisance for the Church on the frontier often appeared to be the state's goals for the region, removing the Church's peasants to concentrate more land and people in the lands of military servitors. The state might benefit from a larger military presence in the region, but the Church had more to gain by defending non-Russian peasants against the interests of local administrators.

Chuvashes, Maris, Mordvins, Tatars, and Udmurts, therefore, were protected from some of the state's policies while still exploited for their labor. The central chancelleries cautiously created as many internal, controllable divisions as possible by using three distinct legal categories for its new peasants, and involved the local administration, the Russian Orthodox Church, and Russian and non-Russian military servitors in the process of supervising the communities. Unquestionably, the Prikaz Kazanskogo dvortsa still viewed the population as potentially hostile during the first half of the seventeenth century, as it enacted new security policies designed to prevent or control future violence. At the same time, generally, the Russian Orthodox Church's leadership avoided conversion and tended to protect its animists and Muslims against local interference from secular authorities. This type of conflicted authority within Muscovy did not always produce opportunities for the local population, but there was at least always a chance to appeal to some authority to soften unpopular decrees.

The decisions of the Muscovite authorities were logical in a colonial context, but seemingly contradictory. Without other options, the state turned to its non-Russian peasants to defend the region, first creating the infantry garrisons in the north and then forcing the settlement of the Mordvins in the south. The Prikaz Kazanskogo dvortsa, in fact, could not have functioned without non-Russian recruits. Yet, much of its actual security procedures involved investigating and interrogating that same population for fear of potential revolts. The possibility that its frequently harsh treatment of the non-Russians, such as taking hostages or forced relocation, would encourage disloyalty, never inspired the reconsideration of such policies. Conversely, the Church, no less dependent on non-Russian peasants for its financial well-being, used what influence it had to defend its peasants against the state. Though each institution was making rational choices from their own perspective, the non-Russians were far likelier to support the Church than the state. The final enserfment of military servitors' peasants in 1649 was hardly likely to improve the situation.

Regular Serfs

As demonstrated earlier, an evolution took place between 1552 and 1649 that created the legal categories necessary to absorb a large population of local non-Russians within the Muscovite state. Each category carried a different legal and economic status and connection to the local authorities. Dividing the population into three separate legal categories (*iasachnye liudi*, monastic, and military servitor peasants) was an undeniably complex change that required administrators and peasants alike to learn and adapt to the new structures. This was the inherent cost to creating the categories that the chancelleries deemed essential to weld multiple religious groups and ethnolinguistic populations into a Russian Orthodox state. The *Ulozhenie* of 1649, however, was a legal change of a more dramatic character and marked a turning point for the empire. The government expanded and clarified the Muscovite legal system, and the status of the tsar's non-Russian peasants was transformed not because of a recent military defeat but because they had been subjects for a century. The transformation of their lives, accomplished without war or revolt, was perhaps the best proof of the success of the Muscovite colonial project.

Muscovy had been progressing toward serfdom since the sixteenth century. During the reign of Ivan IV, landlords, both military servitors and the remaining hereditary elites, pushed the government for the unrestricted right to pursue "runaway peasants" (*beglye krest'iane*). This was a reaction to the increasing demands the tsar placed upon them, while peasants fled the land, often for the eastern frontier. A 1642 law extended the time limit for reclaiming runaways to ten years (fifteen years if removed by force), but this failed to quell the protests. In the 1648, following the tsar's recent economic decrees, which included indefinitely delaying payment to the army, urban protests in Moscow against the tsar took place. In response, elites pressured the government to allow the complete enserfment of their peasants in exchange for their continued support.[65] The *Ulozhenie* of 1649 was, in part, the product of this elite pressure on the tsar's government. It would affect uniformly the entire kingdom, immediately transforming the legal status of all peasants in the Middle Volga Region residing on military servitor estates. In the former khanate, it affected a small portion of the population, but one spread throughout the territory. The limited extant records make a direct estimate difficult, but there were 31,260 serfs in Kazan and Simbirsk provinces in 1662–72 compared to 176,580 *iasachnye luidi* in 1678.[66] Even while the majority of peasants remained *iasachnye*, serfdom inspired a new set of administrative practices that ultimately affected every resident.

The *Ulozhenie* eliminated the statute of limitations on reclaiming runaways, essentially giving the tsar, hereditary elites, and service landholders the unrestricted right to reclaim all peasants who had been registered on their lands at any time. The language was clear: "[if] . . . those fugitive peasants or their fathers were registered [as living] under the sovereign: having hunted down those fugitive peasants and landless peasants of the sovereign, cart them [back] . . . to their old allotments as [registered in] the cadastral books, with their wives, children, and with all their moveable peasant property, without any statute of limitations."[67] It was the first time that a serf's entire family would be forced to return. The *Ulozhenie* also outlined the process by which peasants would be returned to their former masters. The landlord petitioned the Pomestnyi Prikaz, which turned the petition over to the Razriadnyi Prikaz for enforcement. The Razriadnyi Prikaz notified one or more of the local *voevody* to investigate. They then claimed and returned the peasant to his or her original landlord. Because the *voevody* became agents of enforcement, the Prikaz Kazanskogo dvortsa involved itself because of its supervisory role over the *voevody* in the region.[68] In general, after a landlord petitioned the Pomestnyi Prikaz for the return of his peasant, that Prikaz instructed the Prikaz Kazanskogo dvortsa and its *voevody* to investigate, bypassing the involvement of the Razriadnyi Prikaz entirely.

Even before 1649, landlords had frequently petitioned the Pomestnyi Prikaz for the return of their runaway peasants but before the *Ulozhenie*, bureaucratic inertia stymied most. For example, in 1626, Archimandrite Iosif of Murom's Troitse-Sergeivskii Monastery petitioned for his peasant's return in an attempt to reclaim the man, who fled to the village of Selitsa in Arzamas district. Following the rhetoric of such petitions, the abbot claimed the monastery suffered great hardship from the loss of its peasants; only the tsar could rectify the situation.[69] In 1642 Ivan Semën syn Karachev, a *novokreshchanin* servitor, petitioned the Pomestnyi Prikaz for the return of his runaway peasants, Sten'ka Titov and his sister, from Kazan district.[70] However, because of the statute of limitations, *voevody* were often uninterested in enforcing these petitions. A *voevoda* desiring the increase of his local population for taxes, for example, could, and did, ignore requests, and the statute would expire without action on his part, or he would transfer out of office, making the problem concern of the next *voevoda*.

However, after 1649 this unofficial loophole closed, and, correspondingly, the number of petitioners and requests grew. The number of peasants who fled to the Middle Volga Region is uncertain, though the Muscovite government considered it to be large, and focused much of its reclamation efforts in the region.[71] Vasilii Mikhailovich Lunevskii, a military servitor in Kurmysh district, petitioned the Pomestnyi Prikaz in 1659/60, asking for the return of his peasants from the village of Sasuyonka in Saransk district on the *pomest'e* of Grigor Mikhailovich Ziminiskii.[72] In 1669, *Voevoda* Ivan Danilov syn Myshchetskii of Alatyr' petitioned at least twice for the return of his peasant Fëdor Ivanov, who had fled his village of Borzhoto in Alatyr' district.[73]

After the petitions were filed, the Prikaz Kazanskogo dvortsa or the Pomestnyi Prikaz instructed the region's *voevody* to investigate. For example, Nizhnii Novgorod's *voevoda* notified the Pomestnyi Prikaz in 1661 about the successful return of Marfa, a peasant woman who had fled from Ivan Ivanovich syn Chemodanov's village of Vodovstoe in Arzamas district to the *pomest'e* of Silvian Vorontsov in Nizhnii Novgorod district.[74] Not all petitions were successful, especially if the original petition failed to specify the current whereabouts of a runaway peasant. In one case, one of Sviiazhsk's bailiffs spent most of 1666 trying to locate a single peasant fleeing from

Iakov Nikitich Odoevskii. The bailiff reported on his searches of numerous villages in Sviiazhsk district, but could not find any evidence of the runaway. The *voevoda* of Kazan then began to search in his own district.[75]

Despite the sometimes expensive and time-consuming searches, filing petitions remained the best option for a landlord to reclaim his lost peasant. After 1649, the Pomestnyi Prikaz added a second option. It began sending commissions into the region, which systematically examined the entire peasant population to uncover runaways. This process did not involve landlords petitioning specifically, and generally had a high rate of success. All peasants who could not establish that they belonged to the region were seized and returned to their original owners. The first Muscovite commission of this type arrived in Kazan in 1658, and several more followed in the 1660s, searching Arzamas, Alatyr', Penza, Sviiazhsk, Simbirsk, and Saransk.[76]

In general, the commissions uncovered more runaway peasants along the Simbirsk Line and farther south than in the older settled territory along the Arzamas Line and points north. The investigation in Penza district in 1664/65 found 1183 runaway peasants in the district, and 77.6 percent were returned to their original land.[77] These 1183 peasants comprised as much as 10 percent of the total peasant population in the district.[78] By comparison, the commissions sent to Arzamas and Alatyr' districts in 1665–66 uncovered 283 runaway peasant households, which comprised at most 1 percent of the total peasant population.[79] In both cases, however, the peasant commissions proved highly successful in reclaiming runaway peasants when compared with the individual attempts made by local *voevody*, especially the pre-1649 efforts, which were indifferently executed. The conflicting authority of the involved chancelleries certainly encouraged the success of the commissions. The Pomestnyi Prikaz gained by returning peasants no longer on military servitor estates to their former landlords, while the *voevody* would no longer avoid implementing Pomestnyi Prikaz requests. The Prikaz Kazanskogo dvortsa, the beneficiary of the former inefficiency, now lost population, having no protection from a policy designed to break the impasse caused by the bureaucracy.

The commissions were also important for generating demographic data about the origins of runaway peasants, with whom they traveled, and the length of their residence in their new homes. In Penza for example, 42.9 percent of the peasants arrived with their families. Runaway peasants in Penza had arrived from Arzamas, Alatyr', Riazan, Kasimov, and Kadom.[80] It was typical for the region that many of the peasants arriving had arrived from nearby provinces; few if any traveled across the country to settle on the frontier. Even short distances, however, did not make it easy to track fugitives. Most runaway peasants had been long settled in their new homes: 111 of the 283 runaway peasant households in Arzamas and Alatyr' (approximately 40 percent) had been settled in the district for more than ten years, and twelve of those households had in fact been settled there for more than forty years.[81]

Given the pressure from elites in the Muscovite metropole, and the apparent number of runaways, the state had no obvious interest in utilizing the data gained by the commissions to modify the policy of returning runaway serfs. On the contrary, the commitment of state resources to reclaiming runaway peasants from the interior indicates at least that the Pomestnyi Prikaz believed in the seriousness of the problem. The state dispatched four commissions to Alatyr' in the 1660s, which produced minimal returns despite the ongoing interrogations of the entirety of the peasant population. The runaways uncovered by the commissions were not a restless population endangering the countryside but were established families contributing to the settlement of the frontier, especially in the sparsely populated south; this reality had little impact on the Pomestnyi Prikaz's attitude toward runaway peasants. It was as successful as it could be in reclaiming runaways, but this success came at the potential expense of weakening Muscovite presence along its exposed frontier, and certainly undermined the Prikaz Kazanskogo dvortsa's garrisons.

Furthermore, the commissions investigated all communities in the region, not just those on military servitor estates. In this way, enserfment rapidly affected all non-Russians in the region, who were subjected to a new round of interrogations. Even the monastic peasants could not turn to their landlords for protection against another state investigation. However, enserfment was not the final legal change of the century, as the *Ulozhenie* marked a turn in Muscovy toward the standardization of the legal system and social status. After 1649, the Muscovite government steadily worked toward crafting a legal category for its other peasants, who eventually would be classified as "state peasant" in the eighteenth century. This would encompass both the *iasachnye liudi* and monastic peasants, the remaining 80 percent of the local population.[82] It took nearly as long to develop this category as had the creation of legal serfs (which took most of a century from the first restrictions on leaving a landlord's estate to formal enserfment). The time taken to create the category implied how massive its effects on the economic and social life on the region. It changed as much as had the recategorization of peasant into serf in 1649.

However, the transition from *iasachnye liudi* to state peasants was only beginning, and it proceeded incrementally. Non-Russians attempted to preserve as much of their land and traditional way of life as they could, but in doing so served the goals of the state's shifts in policy. In particular, more and more non-Russians formally entered the tsar's service as both *strel'tsy* and military servitors in order to maintain possession of their village's traditional lands. Typically, after a village's men entered service, they would petition the central authorities to award their village to the entire community and not hold it as their individual service land. In 1664, four Tatars in service from the village of Elkovka in Simbirsk received the right to their village, which they attempted to bequest to the village's remaining *iasachnye* Tatars. The petitioners wrote that they only entered the tsar's service to be awarded land, so the village Tatars would no longer be "exiled or convicted," and no longer "be questioned" by Muscovite authorities.[83] In 1662, an entire Tatar village in Simbirsk received the rights to their village and its lands because all forty-one men in the village entered the tsar's service; in 1663, a nearby Chuvash village of Khirkhosa and its seventeen men also enrolled in the tsar's service to retain their village.[84] It is possible that this movement was a response to the arrivals of the peasant commissions, but it was more likely an attempt to resist the local *voevody*'s regular investigations and interrogations. As military servitor landlords, these new non-Russian servicemen could potentially prevent the intrusions in a way a village of *iasachnye liudi* could not. However, the result was that throughout the 1660s non-Russians began to voluntarily change their status from *iasachnye* to serf in order to remain on their ancestral lands, the first of many ways in which the population of *iasachnye liudi* would diminish over the next century.

Furthermore, after 1649 more *iasachnye liudi* sought legal recourse for protecting their traditional economic privileges. Those whose livelihood produced goods of lesser value were far more exposed to potential losses from economic disruption or policy changes. For example, fishermen among the Mordvins in Alatyr' province and Maris of Iadrin province lost their livelihoods when they lost their access to the Sura River in 1667, which they had utilized since the sixteenth century.[85] Though not stated explicitly in documents, it is likely the economic deprivation was intended to force their migration. However, beekeeping remained a right of many indigenous apiarists well into the eighteenth century, because it was the most valuable of the traditional occupations among the non-Russian populations. In 1663 local bee-keepers in Nizhnii Novgorod, Koz'modem'iansk, and Kurmysh provinces petitioned their landlord, the Makar'evskii Zheltovodskii Monastery in Nizhnii Novgorod, asking for the privilege to pay their tribute in cash rather than honey. The bee-keepers wanted to sell their honey directly to merchants, rather than allowing the monastery to profit as the middleman.[86] In fact, unlike most of their *iasachnye* brethren, Mordvin, Tatar, Chuvash, Mari, and Udmurt beekeepers of Arzamas province successfully petitioned the tsar to retain their *iasachnye* status in 1682, whether "of different faiths, newly baptized, or Orthodox Christian." This decision from the central chancelleries exempted these non-Russians from paying the traditional peasant poll tax to the local *voevoda*, and instead they continued to pay yearly tribute in honey and wax.[87] With the high cost of honey and wax, it was likely more profitable for the state to receive these commodities than the normal taxes. Even so, this was a rare example of non-Russians maintaining *iasachnye* status at a time when the state was removing this status from many of their neighbors.

While the steps were small, each was a change to a century-old set of policies. The underlying goal for the Russian state was the standardization of the legal privileges among the largest segment of the local population. Each group of *iasachnye liudi* had individually negotiated tribute payments, different access to lands and fields, and different legal obligations to the local *voevody*. As seen above, these were often hard to suborn. However, the state's interests were fulfilled by the division of all land among military servitors and monasteries, which simplified a complex system, thereby guaranteeing regular taxes, easier access to recruits, and greater vigilance in the countryside. The non-Russians paid the price for the state's achievements with losses in terms of their legal independence and economic freedom. Nor were the *iasachnye liudi* alone. By the eighteenth century, monastic peasants endured a set of legal changes that would also move them into the broader category of "state peasant."[88] The diverse categories and local flexibility that had accommodated so many different groups from 1552 until 1649 were not desirable in a state that continued to define and "modernize" legal categories. In this way, the process of relocating the Mordvins to the south, and the peasant commissions arriving in the 1650s and 1660s, were just the first signs of a serious and long-term transformation of society in the frontier. From then on, all groups of society could be inspected, reorganized, and validated, and that power now belonged to the central government, not the local administration.

Rebellious Subjects

Tatars, Chuvashes, Mordvins, Maris, and Udmurts were difficult to manage and challenging even to define. These non-Russians comprised the majority of the local population, were suspected of seditious activity and hiding runaway peasants, and yet formed the majority of the local garrisons and also fortified the Simbirsk Line. Though not "traditional" Russian Orthodox peasants, the state could not exist in the region without their labor and taxes. As the state increased restrictions on their movement, freedoms, and legal privileges, it seemingly only increased its own fears of the potential consequences. Despite the tensions created by its greater power, the state ultimately transformed the legal status of the non-Russian population, and resultantly changed their lives, lifestyles, and residences. It was a notable accomplishment for a cameralist state.

At the same time, relocating the Mordvins and encouraging settlement to the south, while simultaneously removing runaway peasants to the interior, was another act central to the construction of Muscovy's elusive empire. On the one hand, the state demonstrated its firm control over its population, and exploited this labor to serve imperial needs, by claiming space, cultivating new lands, and securing the new frontier. On the other, the state bowed to the interests of its elites, removing population that was needed to produce on, and defend, its new possessions. This conflict was enabled by the competing chancellery offices. As the Pomestnyi Prikaz succeeded in pacifying military elites with the return of their runaway peasants, it left the Prikaz Kazanskogo dvortsa in a lurch as it drained the manpower so necessary to defend the region. This might have inspired the Prikaz Kazanskogo dvortsa's increasing fear of its population, but it certainly undermined its security policies. As was so often the case, the state's aspiration to hegemonic control over its frontier fell short as it addressed short-term demands rather than long-term stability.

The shortcomings of the growing empire also inspired the limited attempt of the Russian Orthodox Church in the region to resist state policies. Undoubtedly, monastic estates fell victim to both loss of the Mordvins and the arrival of the peasant commissions. The fact that even witchcraft accusations did not motivate a conversion mission, perhaps from fear of a violent response from local communities, indicates that when it came to the Church's peasants, at least, it did not share the state's interest. Its ability to resist the plans of the central chancelleries was small, but there clearly was no longer any consensus between local Church officials and the state.

At the same time, the development of the *Ulozhenie* of 1649 eroded, or ended, many of the central tenets of the transitional policies in Muscovy that had existed since 1552. As the *Ulozhenie* played a critical role as an instrument breaking down the old system grafted to the former khanate's social and economic framework, the colonial system that had served Muscovite interests for nearly a century was less necessary. The *Ulozhenie* was followed by a number of legal innovations, which foreshadowed the creation of a broad category of "state peasant," and continuous attacks on traditional society in the region resulted. Undoubtedly, the local population had cause for discontent, but so did the Church and its monasteries, the *voevody*, and even local landlords. As the invasive practices continued, the likelihood of rebellion only rose. The state policies designed to control the population succeeded, but encouraged great discontent at great expense, ultimately serving as midwife to the rebellious population the state always feared would be born of the non-Russian subjects of the tsar.

6

Subdued Rebels

The Grand Prince cannot get reinforcements except by forcing his peasants into military service; but they are not armed, as are all peasants in the Christian world, and they know nothing about war.

Heinrich von Staden,
The Land and Government of Muscovy, 1578–82

Therefore the *voevoda* sent a boatload of *streltsi* [musketeers] to meet us near Mokrits Island, three versts from the town [Cheboksary], to investigate and see what sort of people we were. The soldiers circled the boat at some distance and then hurried back to town. . . . Here, as in neighboring towns on the Volga, though not inland, the *voevoda* has at his disposal a goodly number of Russian soldiers; so if the conquered Tatars should rebel, an army can easily be collected to subdue them.

Adam Olearius,
The Travels of Olearius in Seventeenth-Century Russia, 1636

By 1670, the Muscovite government, despite setbacks, had made considerable progress toward pacifying the Volga basin. Moscow increasingly had constrained the local administration with a strict set of proscriptions against their discretionary authority, reducing the *voevody* to agents, record keepers, and functionaries, greatly diminishing their former independence. Both domestic and foreign merchants recoiled from the imposition of the New Commercial Code when Moscow finally seized active control over most aspects of the economy, but could not easily avoid its regulations nor abandon the growing trade along the river. The frontier's gentry, who enjoyed some successes in negotiation with the central authorities, including the right to keep their Muslim faith without coercion, had watched those privileges erode since 1649. Meanwhile, the local populations outside the town walls suffered under the authorities' militant vigilance, which suspected them of a myriad of crimes. They faced accusations of witchcraft, and, in the case of the Mordvins, suffered a devastating relocation south onto the open steppe, which ravaged the population. The process of creating an empire, which had been so illusory in 1552 and proven so difficult to build, was a reality more than a century later despite its many problems.

One primary theme links each of the component narratives. Whereas accommodations with local groups had been beneficial to the stability and security of the frontier after 1552, the state deemed it no longer desirable, or in some cases even necessary, to allow variances and decentralization as formerly enemy territory was now firmly within the tsar's grasp. The tsar's administration and the Russian Orthodox Church now sat at the center of every new town and outpost. Beyond the region, the expansion into Ukraine accomplished during the Thirteen Years' War (1654–67) had strengthened Muscovy against Poland-Lithuania, the Crimean Tatars, and the Ottoman Empire, and turned the Left-Bank Cossacks into the tsar's new border guard.[1] Politically, economically, and socially, the Volga basin from Kazan to Simbirsk was no longer an exposed frontier. Now it was largely an extension of the interior with minimal differences in the treatment of the local population, compared to the rest of the tsar's realm. This was a remarkable transformation.

For most of the seventeenth century, the local accommodation of diverse interests in the Volga had been a successful formula for avoiding the domestic conflicts that raged throughout central Muscovy. Since 1613, the country had been challenged by the unsuccessful Smolensk War, the widespread urban riots of 1648–49, an outbreak of the plague in the 1650s, and the "copper riots" along the southern frontier, which followed the currency devaluation in the 1660s. But civil stability endured in the Middle Volga Region, because Kazan and the Volga were insulated from Muscovite politics. Eventually, the long-term effects of these disasters penetrated the Volga in the form of the new restrictions in the *Ulozhenie* in 1649. New instructions to the *voevody* increased oversight from the center, and the new trade regulations demonstrated that Moscow's concern was originally, and continued to be, revolt. Nevertheless, non-Russian peasants did not revolt in the 1630s, '40s, '50s, or '60s.

As later events in the region demonstrate, the long-term stability of the region's population did not mean that insurrection was improbable. Every segment of the population had been adversely affected by some part of the new restrictions enacted throughout the state by the 1660s. The 1670 revolt should not have surprised Muscovite authorities, but by the same token it was not the inevitable conclusion to growing resentment among the populace. It is hard to determine whether the revolt in 1670 would have begun without the outside stimulus from the steppe, though neither the Nogais in the late sixteenth century nor the Kalmyks in the early seventeenth century inspired revolts when they arrived to pressure Muscovite defenses.[2] When Stepan Razin and his Cossacks turned from attacking Iranian shipping in the Caspian Sea to raiding tsarist cities in 1670, Razin was likely the spark set to a powder keg of latent hostility arising from Muscovite administrative, economic, and social policies. When his emissaries traveled throughout the region seeking local support, they were greeted by towns and outposts already in chaos. He provided the inspiration, but the tsar's changing policies had provided the motivation.

The last remnants of the rebellion were suppressed early in 1671, but the legacy of the revolt would inform administrative and religious policy decisions for many decades. The actual invasion of Razin's Cossacks never threatened Kazan or any city in Muscovy proper. The ease with which his forces were beaten indicated that the security policies developed since 1552 to secure the tsar's land against nomadic invasion had been well implemented. All of the sacrifices, investigations, and paranoia, had finally proven valuable. The remaining problems were more troubling. The domestic revolt, separate from Razin's raid, lasted longer and caused far more devastation in the local region, including the loss of almost the entire Simbirsk Line for months in 1670. If strategy and policy changes were to be made in the wake of the unrest, the very first priority had to be the security of the Simbirsk Line. It needed to be as secure as its northern counterpart. Of course in 1670, the Simbirsk Line had only been complete for a generation, and the state was still in the process of forcibly resettling population to man it, unlike the Arzamas Line, which was a century old and had always been situated among a settled population. As the measures already in place had defeated the steppe invasion, the preferred method for fixing the southern defensive line was clear—enforce the established procedures. There would be no major revision or alteration of policy. When changes did occur, they emerged as part of the reorganization of tsarist government, not in response to the violence of 1670. Without question, the former khanate was now integrated into the tsar's kingdom, without any distinction or acknowledgement of its diverse population or distance from the center.

This was the one of last acts of the elusive quest for empire. In 1552, based on meager accomplishment, the tsar and the Russian Orthodox Church proclaimed a glorious victory and the recovery of Orthodoxy versus Islam. This rhetorical façade deterred attacks of all kinds, while the tsar relied extensively upon the cooperation of the local Muslim and animist population to erect a foundation capable of re-placing the mock-up. With decades to study, define policy, and correct missteps, by 1670 the state was entrenched in the region and well prepared to impose a less flexible system. By the time of the Razin's arrival the Volga basin surrounding Kazan was merely a rebellious province, and it would be treated no differently from any part of the Muscovite heartland. The suppression of the revolt, and the lack of subsequent aftershocks, demonstrated the tardy but real assimilation of the Khanate of Kazan into the Muscovite Empire.

The Revolt

Between 1615 and 1670, the Middle Volga Region was relatively peaceful. Even the construction of the Simbirsk Line failed to incite a revolt (as the construction of the Arzamas Line had in the 1570s). The domestic disturbances of the seventeenth century, the urban revolts of 1648 and 1649, the international conflicts (including the Smolensk War in the 1630s and the Thirteen Years' War), and the copper riots of the 1660s, all left the region unaffected. Nomadic raids from the steppe, which continued to plague merchants along the Volga, never coalesced into a persistent military challenge. The Simbirsk Line was Muscovy's declaration of ownership over all of the land behind it, some of which lay along traditional steppe migration routes, yet Muscovy's construction was unchallenged. This fact, rather than the quality of Muscovy's administration, was the key to the quiescence. Yet Moscow did not itself challenge the steppe nomads to the south, along either bank of the Volga; because the security of trade and communications necessitated the suspicious supervision of non-Russians, the regulations laid down by documents like the *nakaz* of 1649 persisted despite the fortifications. Since these laws also effectively asserted control over the regional *voevody*, even in the absence of threats like the Kalmyks and Bashkirs, no more liberal regime would have developed.

In the fall of 1670, the region was suddenly overwhelmed by two events: a local revolt against Muscovite rule, and an invasion of a band of raiders from the steppe, Stepan Razin and his Cossacks.[3] Though traditionally the event has been simplified as the "Razin Revolt," the insurrection and invasion were connected but not mutually dependent.[4] Razin's arrival at the southern point of the defensive line at Simbirsk simply created the opportunity for the local revolt. Upon his arrival, Razin dispatched emissaries to gather support from the local region, but his men found towns and outposts where news of his arrival had already run ahead of his agents, and they had risen. The chaos created by these simultaneous challenges caused extensive damage. Rebels burned Alatyr' to the ground and killed several *voevody*, numerous local officials, and one priest. The entire event was short-lived, beginning in September and completely suppressed by January 1671. Though the folk legends surrounding Stepan Razin have obscured the complex interactions between revolt and invasion, the relatively quick success of the local administration in ending both events proved the expensive and repressive preparations had proven their utility.[5] The feared steppe invasion was effectively deflected, without any damage to the "interior" regions behind the Simbirsk Line.

Stepan Razin led a Cossack band that started off raiding shipping along the southern portion of the Volga, downriver from his home on the river somewhere between Saratov and Tsaritsyn. By early 1668, he led as many as three thousand Cossacks south to the Caspian to raid Safavid shipping with at least the tacit support of local tsarist officials. With the Thirteen Years' War having ended only in 1667, hard currency was both in short supply and desperately needed for rebuilding projects in Ukraine. Razin's probable arrangement with Muscovite officials likely involved turning over part of his loot to the crown. Over the next two years, Razin won a series of victories against both Caspian merchants and eventually Safavid forces, from whom he seized as many as thirty-three cannons in June 1669. By August 1669, Razin was greeted in Astrakhan as a great hero, at least according to the legends. Perhaps spurred on by his success or, at least, by his growing reputation, Razin and his Cossacks returned to the Volga River, raiding Tsaritsyn in March 1670. By June 1670, when Razin left Tsaritsyn to proceed north along the Volga, his troops numbered six thousand, larger than any individual garrison farther north, but considerably fewer than the total of troops the tsar had under arms in and around Kazan. Over the course of the summer, Razin sacked Saratov and then Samara, finishing his conquest of every Muscovite outpost between Simbirsk and Astrakhan. These forts were constructed to defend Muscovite merchants against nomadic raids along the Volga, but were too small to slow his advance up the river.[6]

By 4 September 1670, Razin's siege of Simbirsk had begun. Estimates of his troop strength at that point range between five thousand to twenty thousand men, with up to fifteen thousand local peasant infantry supplementing his five thousand Cossacks.[7] It is unlikely that his new recruits would have possessed gunpowder weapons, or indeed, any form of weapon more sophisticated than wooden farming implements, since sales of all metal objects to the countryside had been illegal for some time.[8] Simbirsk's *voevoda*, Ivan Bogdanovich Miloslavskii, had prepared for Razin's arrival by gathering between three thousand to four thousand men under his command, including his garrison of *strel'tsy*, local military servitors, and infantry.[9] Unfortunately for Razin, Simbirsk was a well-fortified city, well-garrisoned and well-supplied. This was Razin's first attack on the Simbirsk Line, one of the state's best defensive positions. Miloslavskii held the city with few problems until Muscovite forces arrived from Kazan on 1 October. The combined pressure of the garrison and its relievers successfully broke the siege on 5 October. Razin himself was injured during the fighting and retreated with his forces down the Volga.[10]

Judged in terms of successfully repelling an invasion from the steppe, the Razin siege proved to be the finest hour of the region's forces. While the Volga fortresses Razin had sacked had also been fortified, Simbirsk proved to be a stronghold of a different order. The smaller regional fortresses may never have held even with extensive preparations, but Simbirsk required organized formations to reduce. It had not been built solely to protect merchants along the Volga but as an administrative center capable of marshalling the defensive line's resources in the territory between the Simbirsk and Arzamas Lines. When Stepan Razin arrived, the deficiencies of his numerically large force precluded any attempt to storm the city. This was unquestionably a victory for the local garrisons, and, once again, offered some evidence that despite the many disaffected peasants who joined the rebels, the non-Russian population of the region was uninterested in joining Razin's forces and fighting the tsar. Kazan's garrison, after all, was filled with Chuvashes, Maris, and Udmurts; Russians comprised less than 10 percent of the force.[11] With Razin's defeat, the Prikaz's defensive contingency planning was validated.

However, Razin's strikes served to enable opportunistic uprisings all over the region, between the two defensive lines. The insurrectionists may not have been interested in Razin's Volga campaign, but they were intent on attacking the local government. This second, domestic upheaval in the fall of 1670 was less easily resolved and far more damaging than Razin's raiding. While the fortress at Simbirsk held, many of the settlements along the Simbirsk Line rebelled. The revolts spread farther than just along the southern defensive line, occurring at both Alatyr' and Arzamas (on the northern defensive line), and even farther up the river at Tsivil'sk and Koz'modem'iansk along the Volga's northern run. This "local" revolt took longer to suppress than Razin's, but while it lasted some months, it had been contained and the towns pacified by the spring of 1671. While Razin's invasion fell into the long-established pattern of nomadic raids on merchant shipping, albeit writ large, the local revolts emerged, fundamentally, from an entirely separate issue—local grievances against the Muscovite administration. In many cases, word of the siege of Simbirsk had preceded "official" word from Razin himself. As was the case in innumerable revolts in the early-modern period, information about them tended to incite further uprisings.[12] Information had far more power than Razin himself, and it is this legacy that was so damaging to the region.

The spread of the 1670 revolt along the Simbirsk Line and beyond appears attributable to one primary cause. The consequences of the forced migration of the Mordvins encouraged the grievances that turned the region's populace toward

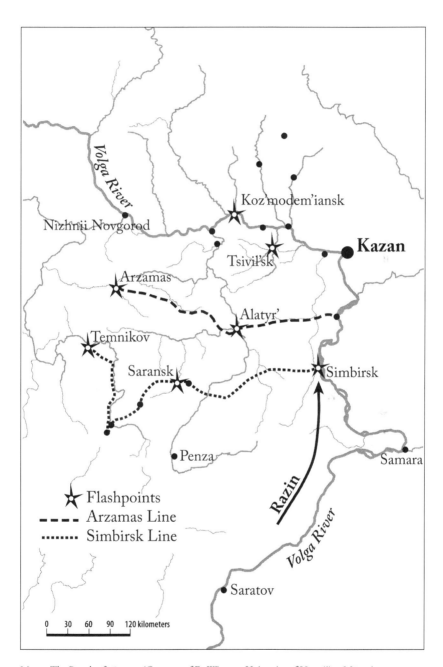

Map 5 The Revolt of 1670–71 (Courtesy of Ev Wingert, University of Hawai'i at Mānoa)

rebellion. The peasant commissions had removed a sizeable portion of its Russian peasant population (who had been runaways from the interior), leaving the line settled almost exclusively by Mordvins, who were still struggling with their double burden of paying both local state officials and their former monastic landlords. Additionally, the extent of the northern revolt encompassed Arzamas and Alatyr', which lay within the Mordvins' traditional homeland. The correlation of the revolt to the area of forcible population transfers is impossible to ignore. In the parts of the region where the revolt did not spread, like Kazan and Tetiushii, the population had remained stable for the previous one hundred years. In those places where the population had been resettled or removed in the previous two decades, the revolt spread like wildfire.

The victims of this revolt were primarily the *voevody*, the men holding the office that enforced this policy. Rebels killed several *voevody*, and on more than one occasion replaced the *voevoda* with a council, elected by the townspeople and rebels, to rule their district. There was no corresponding record of attacks on the official of the Russian Orthodox Church, suggesting that the long-term relationship between Church and populace was more favorable. One church was burned in Alatyr', but that town's *voevoda* had sought sanctuary in the building, rendering it a target.

Some details of the unfolding revolt exist. The Alatyr' revolt was among the first, beginning almost immediately upon the heels of Razin's arrival at Simbirsk. On 6 September, *Voevoda* Akinfii Buturlin of Alatyr' reported information gathered by one of his *d'iaki*, Iakov Lukin syn Panov, about the spread of Razin's influence into the countryside. Panov had sent a trusted man, Lar'ka Khrenov, south to Simbirsk to discover what was happening to the city. After ten days of travel, Khrenov returned to Alatyr' having failed to reach Simbirsk. Panov had ended his trip 32 kilometers (30 versts) from Simbirsk at the Tatar village of Gorenko. The village had already been visited by five Cossacks from Razin's army. The Tatars informed Panov that once Razin took the city, he would move into the countryside with the support of military servitors, *strel'tsy*, and the peasantry.[13]

By 10 September, overwhelmed by the scope of the rebellion and its rate of expansion, *Voevoda* Buturlin wrote to Moscow, pleading for assistance. He informed the tsar that Alatyr' had taken in refugees fleeing from Razin's siege. This included *deti boiarskii*, *mirzas*, other Tatar military servitors, and numerous townspeople from the surrounding regions.[14] But the *voevoda* already had made a critical error: he did not gather local military forces to defend Alatyr', believing that the nearby Muscovite army under the command of Fëdor Ivanovich Leon'tev would protect the city. However, when the latter received word of the size of Razin's army, he abandoned Alatyr' district and departed for Arzamas. Buturlin decided to retreat to the center of town to await his fate, lacking enough men to protect his city.[15]

Local rebels attacked Alatyr' on 16 September. Without reinforcements or hope of relief, the *voevoda* and his garrison were unable to prevent local Mordvins, Maris, and Chuvashes from burning the town's walls and towers. The next day the rebels proceeded into the town, discovered the *voevoda*, his family, and his officials seeking refuge in the town's cathedral, and burned it to the ground.[16] After burning the town, the rebels abandoned it. One group of the rebels moved toward Arzamas, inspiring a nervous report from its *voevoda*, Lev Shaisupov, who clearly believed he would share his fellow *voevoda*'s fate.[17] Some of the rebels moved northward toward Kurmysh, participating in that town's rebellion against its own *voevoda*, which resulted in his death. The Prikaz Kazanskogo dvortsa became increasingly alarmed when a former resident of Alatyr', currently in Kurmysh, predicted the rebels' success in the Volga presaged the fall of Moscow.[18]

The sack of Alatyr' provides the clearest narrative episode of the revolt's progress; events before and after are more difficult to track. No other attack produced as much physical damage, though throughout the region rebels killed several other *voevody*. However, there were other clear indications of the scope of the revolt. When Razin's agents investigated the recently established outpost of Penza on 30 September, they discovered that it was already under the control of local rebels. *Voevoda* Elisei Lachinov, his *d'iak* Aleksandr Telepov, and a priest, Luka, already had been "beaten to death" (*pobili do smerti*). Furthermore, the rebellion had proceeded eastward ahead of Razin's agents. The *voevody* of Nizhnii and Verkhnii Lomov were dead, and the local rebels were on the march to Kerensk.[19] This was, remarkably, only a week before Razin withdrew from Simbirsk. In order to concentrate its forces to raise the siege, Moscow was compelled to let the disorder spread, and had lost control over the entirety of the southern defensive line. It is unlikely, however, that officials in Kazan could have been aware that as its garrison marched south on Simbirsk, the rest of the line had already been lost. Razin's inspiration of the revolt outweighed his actual success in the region by an order of magnitude, and that revolt outran temporarily both his influence and Kazan's.

The greatest danger in the northern region was the mass of peasant rebels who had destroyed Alatyr'. Razin's emissaries provided some military guidance to the rebel force, although how much is debated. This was certainly the case in Koz'mo-dem'iansk. On 1 or 2 October, between twenty and thirty local Maris and Chuvashes under the leadership of two of Razin's Cossacks arrived at the town gates. According to later reports, town residents willingly opened the gates to the rebels, and then assisted the outsiders in killing their *voevoda* and *d'iak*, Ivan Pobedinskii and Vasilii Bogdanov. After the execution of the *voevoda*, a local group claimed the town for Stepan Razin, obviously unaware that his retreat from Simbirsk had begun, and established themselves as the new town council. This council was comprised of two of the town's residents, Ivashka Shust and Zamiatenka Laptev, one of its *strel'tsy*, Mit'ka Kholelev, and the two Cossacks, Ivashka Soroka and Ivashka Pronek.[20] Although non-Russians had a prominent role in the revolt, in this case, at least, Russians placed themselves in positions of authority.

Koz'modem'iansk was perhaps the most unusual revolt in the entire region. At least a part of the town's garrison participated in the revolt, making it the only known town or outpost not on the Simbirsk Line where the garrison supported the rebels. More typical of the northern region was the city of Tsivil'sk. On 30 September, a Tatar from Sviiazhsk, Almakaiko, led local Tatar and Chuvash peasants against the town. The local garrison and townspeople came together to defend the town, with Russian Orthodox residents fighting alongside its *mirzas* and other Tatars. By 2 October, the peasant rebels had managed to encircle the city, beginning a long siege. On 23 October, a part of the garrison from Kazan arrived and drove off the insurrectionists, but throughout the three-week siege the local garrison held the town securely.[21] By this point, with the Kazan garrison in the field, the central government's forces had swiftly broken the momentum of the larger rebellion. The successful defense of Arzamas, which proved capable of defeating the rebel forces with Leon'tev's troops arriving from Alatyr', prevented the spread of the revolt into the central regions of Muscovy. On 26 September, a new army had joined with Leon'tev under the command of Iurii Dolgorukov. When Dolgorukov updated the central government on that day about the current situation, he reported that Saransk, Kurmysh, Tsivil'sk, and Temnikov were all occupied by rebel forces. To protect Arzamas and the central provinces, Dolgorukov established his camp with eight hundred men to the east of Arzamas on 27 September.[22]

Fortunately for Dolgorukov and the Muscovite government, the state's forces never faced a coordinated attack within the town district. By the beginning of October, there were three separate groups of rebels operating around Arzamas. The first of these was defeated on 6 November to the south.[23] The northernmost group, under the command of the Cossacks Vas'ka Tikhonov and Vas'ka Petrov, led a group of peasants from the Pecherskii Monastery's estate against the Makarev Zheltovodskii Monastery outside of Nizhnii Novgorod on 7 October. The Monastery withstood the assault and refused to open its gates, even after the rebels bombarded the walls with stolen cannon. A portion of Dolgorukov's army arrived and easily broke the siege.[24] After brief battles on 20 October and on 22 October, Dolgorukov's forces defeated all remaining rebels along the western frontier of the Middle Volga Region, securing Arzamas and Nizhnii Novgorod.[25]

So while some rebels continued to vex Muscovite authorities until January 1671, Dolgorukov had defeated its main forces by the beginning of November 1670.

The non-Russian peasants of the region had been quite active in the rebellion, but of course fought on both sides. The garrison troops in the region, overwhelmingly non-Russian, successfully defended the northern cities and the Arzamas Line (with the exception of Alatyr'), and the forces gathered at Kazan defeated multiple rebel bands in addition to Razin himself. It was not just the garrison, fortifications, and supplies that provided the key to Muscovite victory. The Prikaz Kazanskogo dvortsa had instituted a set of information-gathering procedures that warned the authorities, proving their worth. The Prikaz first received word of Razin's presence on the Volga River as early as 1667, shortly after his campaigns began. The *voevoda* of Saratov wrote immediately to Moscow of his fears. Moscow took these fears seriously, allowing more than enough time to make preparations.[26] While it has been traditional to argue that Razin's victories in Astrakhan, Tsaritsyn, Saratov, and Samara provided a great challenge to Muscovite authority, the reality is that the state and its officials focused on defending its more valuable, settled territory.[27] Once Razin moved against tsarist officials, the military response would take time to prepare, but of course this response was fastest and most efficient inside the tsar's borders, not in its distant outposts.

In retrospect, the 1670 revolt appears significant for several reasons. One noteworthy aspect of the violence was its targets. Military servitors' peasants had only recently been enserfed, but there was little evidence of serfs rising against their landlords. Equally, the Russian Orthodox Church was spared, only suffering some property damage. Every town had a church; most had monasteries and convents. Numerous monasteries were established throughout the countryside, and many peasants resided on Church estates. The exception was the Makarev Zheltovodskii Monastery outside of Nizhnii Novgorod, but it was not attacked by the peasants from its own land. One conclusion, therefore, appears to be clear—the revolt was not a reaction to the changing legal and economic status of the local population, despite how popular this theory had been with Soviet historians.[28] Nor does it appear that this was an exclusively "non-Russian revolt" against the Muscovite government and the Russian Orthodox Church, as non-Russians both participated as the rebels and as the state forces, just as local Russians did.

There was a common target for the rebels' attention, of course, and it was the local administration. It is hard to know whether the death toll in Alatyr' would have been as high had the *voevoda* had not sought the protection of the town's cathedral. Additionally, with the exception of Alatyr' and Koz'modem'iansk, the towns and outposts from the Arzamas Line to the north all functioned well while under siege. Most significantly, the violence was generally concentrated on the Simbirsk Line. All outposts except Simbirsk overthrew their *voevoda*, and nearly all acted in advance of actual communication with Razin or his troops. Along the southern defensive line, then, there was a general and popular revolt in the fall of 1670 against the Muscovite administration. It was largely spontaneous and relatively quick, having spread down the line in less than a month. It took the local administration by surprise, but, in the end, even with Razin's support and a number of stolen weapons, it was no match for the tsar's local forces.

The differences between this line of settlements and the interior region are not hard to discern, and the causes of the revolt are linked to these differences. These new outposts and towns were settled by a population still recently dislocated from the north; the oldest settlement along the line was only around three decades old by 1670. The settlers included the Mordvins from Arzamas and Alatyr' districts, who most probably struggled to thrive on the alien steppes. However, aside from the fact that many Mordvins attempted to depart from these new settlements, there is a lack of direct evidence depicting discontent along the defensive line before 1670. Still, it is unlikely that the Mordvin settlements on the Simbirsk Line were spared economic hardship, famine, and disease. These likely had an impact on the morale and fitness of the population, as well as their satisfaction with the regional administration. Therefore, while the "spots" of revolt in the north indicate a general discontent throughout the region, the concentration of flashpoints along the southern defensive line reveals, indirectly at least, the primary causes of discontent among the rebels. This was a protest against Muscovite colonial policy, led by its most recent (and continuing) victims. The violence in the north was on a smaller scale, because the region had been long since settled, with communities there more than a century old. In the south, however, the settlers used Razin's arrival as an opportunity to expel the government which had so recently victimized them.

Vigilant Policies

During the revolt, Muscovite authorities endured the destruction of Alatyr', the loss of parts of the southern defensive line, and the deaths of several of its *voevody* and other local officials. The murders of officials are readily explicable—the *voevody* led the peasant investigations, enforced restricting trade policies, took hostages, and enforced migration orders. In the wake of the revolt, therefore, the state focused its response on these peasant rebels, particularly the dangerous groups of forced migrants and runaway peasants from the interior. The settled populations were not the same kind of threat. Later, when a religious upheaval signaled new dangers, they too would receive attention. However, the state saw no reason to alter the majority of its administrative policies which had largely proven effective.

Not surprisingly, one state response to the revolt was an increased emphasis on control over population movement. It expanded the scope of its security policies, for the scale and speed of the revolt had revealed some weaknesses. The *nakaz* to the *voevoda* of Kazan in 1677, for example, contained thirteen clauses related to security, an increase from the nine clauses of 1649; some were identical, including the ban on selling arms to local non-Russians, a demand for constant supervision of the non-Russians, checks on anyone arriving in or leaving from the district, and the continuation of the practice of taking hostages from non-Russian families. However, new clauses reflected the state's experiences during the revolt. Two clauses demanded the immediate fulfillment of all instructions from the Prikaz Kazanskogo dvortsa: one was targeted at *voevody* who had failed their directives, the other instructed the *voevoda* to oversee the lieutenant of the *strel'tsy* and guarantee that he acted upon all his orders.[29] There were warnings to use only "good and trust-worthy people" at the city gates and during fires.[30] Although Kazan had not fallen during the rebellion, several other Volga cities had been betrayed by their gate-keepers, and assuring the loyalty of the cities' troops became a greater concern, especially since the *strel'tsy* had been instrumental in breaking the siege of Simbirsk. Another clause warned the *voevoda* to monitor alcohol sales in the city's taverns. According to recent information gathered by the Prikaz Kazanskogo dvortsa, after the siege of Simbirsk, its inhabitants consumed much more alcohol than before.[31] Another clause reiterated an early warning about the danger of fires, but specifically instructed Kazan's *voevoda* to locate the grain silos away from cathedrals, because the cathedral in Alatyr' had been the main target during the revolt.[32]

The chancelleries did not overlook the Mordvin relocation in the wake of the revolt. The forced migration was not abandoned, as the state lacked an alternative population to settle its southern frontier. The Prikaz instead turned toward its preferred solution to security issues—more vigilance. In 1682, 1688, and 1697, it instructed the *voevoda* of Kazan to investigate specifically all Tatar and Mordvin villages in the district, in expectation that the villagers were hiding Mordvins fleeing from the southern frontier.[33] The additional investigations were not overkill; evidence accumulated quickly that the Mordvins were not yet accepting their role as colonists. In 1676, for example, the *voevoda* of Kerensk notified the Prikaz that some of the local Mordvins were fleeing south to join the Don Cossacks, both reducing the labor supply and reinforcing the rebellious Cossacks.[34] In 1684 the Mordvins settled outside of Temnikov revolted again, but it was quickly suppressed by the *voevoda* and his garrison.[35] With this record of obvious continued resistance, the Prikaz's commitment to this policy may appear counterintuitive. However, the Mordvin unrest also demonstrated that the local administration's greater concern and closer supervision of their fractious colonists was logical and, if consistently applied, would work, given enough time.

To supplement the actions of its *voevody*, the Prikaz Kazanskogo dvortsa dedicated itself to recruiting more military servitors, particularly along the southern frontier. Many of the original Mordvin settlers had been monastic peasants, who were freed from their monastic landlords (if not their obligations) to serve to the local administration in the south. With more servitors, these peasants would now be serfs. In general, the new military servitors were veterans of the tsar's army, or dedicated administrators with long careers in the government. In other words, they were the sort of "loyal" men the state always had wanted for this region, and who had been notably absent in the original settlements of the Simbirsk Line. For instance, on 2 November 1682 the Prikaz instructed Saransk's *Voevoda* Ivan Pavlov syn Iazykov to reward all of the Tatar and Mordvin cavalry serving with Mevtsapin Kutsiazkov syn Eushev with military service land in the district.[36] While a logical choice for this region, this turn toward more military servitors was occurring while the state as a whole was turning away from adding cavalry.[37] Similarly, some of the new *d'iaki* in the region were pensioners from the army. This was the case in 1680 when the Prikaz Kazanskogo dvortsa ordered Dmitrii Grigorev syn Azter'ev to become a *d'iak* in Saransk because his recent injury prevented further military service. In order for Azter'ev to keep his service land in the district, the career change was necessary.[38] More importantly, the Prikaz guaranteed the small outpost of Saransk received the specialist knowledge of an experienced veteran, improving its defensive value. Azter'ev's appointment may have been atypical, as *d'iaki* had to be literate, and few soldiers could meet that standard.

This is not to imply that this was a golden era for military servitors on the frontier. The demand for more servitors created opportunities for Muscovy's military elites to attempt to bargain for better lands or terms of service, but they were not exceptionally successful. One example would be the Russians, Boris Matveev and Fëdor Sychov, who rejected land an offer of land in Arzamas and then again in Alatyr' in 1673, as the Pomestnyi Prikaz attempted to entice them to an offer of frontier service.[39] While men newly in service might have an advantage in their negotiations with the state, those already in service did not gain new privileges. For example, Mikhail Mikhalov syn Oshcherin gave his future son-in-law forty-seven acres of his land in Arzamas district in 1675/76, and sought approval after the fact from the Pomestnyi Prikaz. Not only was the petition for approval denied but the Prikaz instructed the *voevoda* of Arzamas to seize the entire estate forthwith.[40]

The willingness of the region's military servitors to press for greater privileges likely contributed to the largest change in security policy in the 1670s, the recruitment of nomadic mercenaries. The first instance of this change came in 1674, when the Posol'skii Prikaz paid the Kalmyks with muskets and gunpowder to reestablish order in Simbirsk after a small revolt.[41] In principle, Simbirsk existed to defend the region against the steppe nomads, including the Kalmyks. Based on recent events, however, it must have been more expeditious to hire fresh, experienced mercenaries than turn to the depleted and exhausted garrisons that had survived the revolt. This incident was not an abandonment of the old system but rather an exception, recognizing that the serious, immediate threat to Muscovite control over its southern frontier was not necessarily external. It was also evidence that the nearby steppe nomads were slowly transforming from the main Muscovite enemy in the region into a potential client group and resource.

There was one enormous exception to the post-revolt emphasis on greater security and supervision of the population. This was the gradual abandonment of the runaway peasant commissions into the Middle Volga Region. There must have existed some understanding in the Prikaz Kazanskogo dvortsa of the consequences of the relocation policies and the imposition of serfdom in setting the stage for the 1670 revolt, because the chancellery allowed this policy to lapse, despite its high rate of success. This was the most conspicuous administrative change in Muscovite policy. Only one commission arrived between 1670 and 1700, at Arzamas in 1692/93, though at least eight had arrived in the 1660s.[42] It is probable that the commissions caused serious disruptions in the countryside, which were undesirable in the wake of a widespread revolt. It is also possible that the runaway peasants became a desirable population in the region, perhaps considered more loyal than the non-Russians throughout the region. In either case, even with occasional investigations from *voevody*, runaways continued to settle in the Middle Volga Region. For example, in the records of the estates of the Samara's Spaso-Preobrazhenskii Monastery in 1723, 60 percent of the peasant households were comprised of runaway families from Alatyr' and Kasimov districts.[43]

As the laws concerning runaway peasants had not changed, it was still possible for elites and military servitors to pursue individual requests for specific peasants. The gentry did petition the tsar for the return of their runaway peasants, just as before 1649, but the end of the commissions was more than a simple return to the pre-*Ulozhenie* state. Now it became the gentry's responsibility to investigate the region to uncover the current location of their runaway peasants, for the state no longer invested time or effort in tracking them. Sometimes the region's *voevody* still took action. In 1672/73, Moisei Matveev syn Shchukin received word of this imminent return of his peasant Aleksei from Arzamas district where he had been residing on the estate of Petlin Selaminulin.[44] In 1680, the Prikaz Kazanskogo dvortsa notified *okol'nik* Ivan Ivanov syn Chaadaev to expect the return of all of his peasants from Kazan and Simbirsk districts, where they had been found living among local Maris.[45]

It did appear that servitors and other landlords had to make the investigations themselves, and successes were much rarer. Family members might get involved in such attempts, questioning neighbors in their area for the origins of newly arrived peasants. This was case for Ivan Ivanov and Nikofor Ivanov deti Aristov in 1685, who wrote to their brother Fëdor Ivanov syn Aristov, currently residing in Kazan, to ask him to find two runaway peasants, Ioshka Mikhailov and Iosof Pietrov who might be living in Kazan province.[46] Another Aristov, Ivan Andreev syn Aristov, petitioned the tsar in 1699/1700 for the return of his runaway peasant, who was currently residing on the estate of Grigor Fedorov syn Griboedov in Saransk province, indicating once again that the family had conducted its own investigation.[47]

While wealthy families such as the Aristovs conducted private investigations, those with fewer resources found themselves frequently failing to recover runaways. Local landowners once again could protect their labor supply in court. Aleksei Durov from Penza petitioned the Pomestnyi Prikaz for the return of his peasant from Grigor Timov's lands outside of Nizhnii Novogorod. Timov responded by bringing Durov to court in Nizhnii Novgorod for slander, which he won (perhaps because Timov was a bailiff of that court).[48] Even more telling, runaway peasants now sometimes responded to a petition demanding their return with a petition to remain. For example, Grigor Ivanov syn Zakharov was notified in 1672 that the petition from Simai Semenov for his family had been granted, and they were not to return to Zakharov in Arzamas.[49] When the subjects of a petition were not serfs, any attempt to recover them was even less likely to succeed. This was the case for Petr and Naum Narmukimov, who were townsmen of Kazan. They filed several petitions in the early 1690s to reclaim their runaway debt slave, Petrushka Zakharin syn Aprov and his wife, from Saransk. The first investigation in Saransk did not discover the debt slave; after more petitions, the Aprovs were found on the estate of the current *voevoda* of Saransk. The Narmukimovs did not regain their lost debt slave, but instead the Prikaz Kazanskogo dvortsa paid compensation and let the *voevoda* of Saransk keep Aprov and his wife.[50]

Though the laws for the reclamation of runaway peasants remained intact following the revolt, there was a clear change in the enforcement of the laws. In essence, the Prikaz Kazanskogo dvortsa unofficially condoned runaway peasant settlement in the region. Yet it was still possible for individual landlords to obtain assistance from local officials to reclaim their peasants. This mixed policy demonstrates some equivocation on the part of the central authorities. Certainly, the earlier commissions had been markedly invasive, but it remained the case that the commissions themselves had never inspired an immediate revolt. As the state seemed to have turned toward the expectation that more military servitors residing on the southern frontier would be beneficial, the maintenance of a larger peasant population in the region became more important than ever before. While not an explicit policy, it was clear that the state supported further settlement from all ranks on the unreliable Simbirsk Line, no matter what their origins were.

The mixed message of the new runaway policy was mirrored by a new concern for the religious affiliations of the local elite population. However, it was the secular and not the religious authorities who adopted the conversion of non-Orthodox servitors as a state aim. The first method used was financial. In 1680 the Prikaz Kazanskogo dvortsa enacted its first incentives, a grant of land, for the conversion of Muslim Tatars of Kazan.[51] In 1681 the Mordvins were offered financial rewards for conversion to Orthodoxy, becoming the first peasants in the region to be made such an offer.[52] Considering their very public participation in the revolt of 1670–71, this decision was not surprising. Even so, the state largely remained focused on elite conversion, granting the *voevody* the authority to seize *pomest'ia* from Muslim Tatars in order to provide more service land for converted Tatars, extending the repercussions for failing to convert that had begun in 1649.[53]

The Russian Orthodox Church lacked the state's interest in conversion, however. In 1690, a long pastoral missive from the current patriarch sent to the Metropolitanate of Kazan and Sviiazhsk enumerated a long list of instructions for the clergy's role in the region, but this list notably did not include conversion of non-Russian animists or Muslims as one of those responsibilities.[54] Conversion was mentioned as a concern of the Russian Orthodox Church only in the context of its fears that non-Russians who had converted to Orthodoxy might not have been practicing their new faith correctly. In 1687, for example, Metropolitan Adrian of Kazan warned Archimandrite Misail of the Spaso-Iunginskii Monastery in Koz'modem'iansk to monitor all of the converted peasants on the monastery's estates for fear of improper practices.[55]

It is hard to state conclusively that the Church was uninterested in the issue of conversion, but it may have directed its attention elsewhere by the 1660s. It experienced a schism among its believers during these decades, with the Russian Orthodox hierarchy endorsing a set of "corrected practices," which some among the faithful denounced as immoral innovations. Those refusing the changes were eventually identified as "Old Believers," though in the late seventeenth century they were generally labeled schismatics (*raskol'niki*). The reason why the Metropolitan of Kazan was concerned about the Orthodox practices among the peasants of the Spaso-Iunginskii Monastery was from a fear of schism, not paganism. The first hint that the region had been affected was in 1670, but not until later in the 1670s was the first report of schismatic activity among the local Orthodox peasantry sent to Moscow.[56] The Church discovered Old Believers first in the northwest portion of the region, between Nizhnii Novgorod and Arzamas, with a second group later identified in and around Penza.

As was true throughout Muscovy, the earliest proponents of the schism were ecclesiastical men and women who were the first to learn of Nikon's reforms of Church practices. There is one report of a sermon given in 1670 at a cathedral in Kazan where the priest recalled the "old times," but there is little other evidence of anyone supporting the schism until 1675.[57] By then, the situation had changed, and Archimandrite Antonii of Sviiazhsk's Bogoroditsii Monastery was accused of maintaining a correspondence with a community of Old Believers in the Blagove-shchenskii Monastery in Viaz'ma, and then again in 1676 of communicating with the Vvedenskii Devichii Convent.[58] The Bogoroditsii Monastery was the region's third oldest and among its wealthiest because of its salt-refining manufactory; the discovery that its abbot was an Old Believer was a serious problem for the local Church hierarchy.

Had the schism remained only a religious issue, its consequences might have been more circumscribed. While the Bogoroditsii's abbot was involved in a religious dispute, the spread of the schism to the local communities turned a religious debate into another potential cause of unrest. This fear revealed itself in 1675, when the *voevoda* of Arzamas sent his first reports of Old Believer peasants to Moscow. Neighboring Nizhnii Novgorod district was a developing Old Believer center, and so the presence of schismatics in Arzamas was predictable, but still disconcerting for authorities observing the southward spread of the schism. Court documents filed in Moscow in October 1675 recorded that Mamon Sergeev, a peasant living outside of Arzamas, burned his neighbor Vasil'ev, his wife, and their children to stop the spread of their "fascination" (*prelest'*) with the schism.[59] In response to this report, the Novgorodskaia chetvert' (its supervisory office in Moscow) instructed the local *voevoda* that if any other "schismatics or deceitful people" (*raskolniki i prelesnye liudi*) were uncovered doing "an evil thing" (*zloi del*), then they should be imprisoned in an isolated cell.[60] By the spring of 1676, Arzamas's *voevoda* reported with alarm the discovery of more Old Believers in his district, which was leading toward more violence among the local peasantry.[61]

For the Russian Orthodox Church and the central administration, this was more than sufficient evidence of the schism's dangerous potential. The effects were immediate and unnerving. The Church's own archimandrites were willingly turning away from the hierarchy, and the local Orthodox community had been provided a new reason for violence. This was a danger that the region's security policies could not counter. These were geared toward the non-Orthodox peasants but slow to adapt to policing a fractious Orthodox population. In this sense, the schism was an odd confirmation of the region's integration—this was a Russian Orthodox crisis, not a frontier threat.

The revolt of 1670–71 was proof of the success of Muscovite policies in the former khanate. The security policies developed over the course of more than a century proved successful, even if it was more so in terms of the steppe nomads rather than domestic revolts. However, both were resolved fairly expeditiously. Security policies were adjusted in the 1670s to incorporate recent lessons, but these were more evolutionary than entirely new. There was no cessation of the Mordvin resettlement to the south, despite the warnings from local *voevody* and another small revolt in 1684. The state planned for more military servitors along its southern frontier, to reinforce both security and supervision of the local population. This was a time in which the state was generally turning away from military servitors due to the transformation of military technology, but they had long since proven their ability to monitor and control the local population. The resistance north of the Simbirsk Line to the revolts, the reliability of most towns, the lack of evidence of revolts against landlords, all argued that military servitors remained a valuable form of control.

Negotiated Adjustments

One hundred and twenty years after the conquest of Kazan, the Muscovite administration of the Middle Volga Region had enjoyed the luxury of gradually building an effective defensive apparatus, which never faced an enemy capable of overwhelming it. While both the tsar and the Russian Orthodox Church still fell short of the triumphant claims of victory after 1552, by 1671 the region was Muscovite. The administrative, economic, and social policies that the chancelleries adjusted in the last quarter of the seventeenth century reflected general changes in Muscovy, not specifically local issues in Kazan.

Most of these changes occurred during the reign of the new tsar, Fëdor Aleksevich, who inherited the throne from his father in 1676. Fëdor's reign may have been short, lasting only six years, but his government succeeded in instituting some of the most important reforms in Muscovite history. The new tax system (assessed on the basis of household rather than by land area) was completed in 1679, the product of nearly a generation of work. The household assessment could only work in a state with adequate record keeping at the local level, a bureaucratic achievement accomplished after decades of improvement in local governance and information gathering. However, the most radical change to the structure of the state was the abolishment of *mestnichestvo* in 1682. As this system of social precedence had conditioned numerous aspects of administrative and social interactions among all elites, its abandonment marked a significant caesura in the politics of the Muscovite elite.

Nor was the end of *mestnichestvo* the only major transformation of the era. The chancellery system had been slowly evolving, adding new offices, eliminating old ones, and reorganizing administrative responsibilities among the remaining *prikazy*.[62] Certainly there was no lack of evidence that changes would improve the chancelleries' efficiency. One example would be the plight of a non-Russian in service, Matvei Stepanov syn Pushkin, who had been taken hostage by the Bashkirs in the early 1670s. The Posol'skii Prikaz's authority to manage all affairs with the Bashkirs prevented the Prikaz Kazanskogo dvortsa from resolving a situation involving one of its own people. Since hostage ransoms were paid by the Posol'skii Prikaz, the Prikaz Kazanskogo dvortsa sent a note on 25 September 1675 to remind it to pay the ransom in order to release Pushkin back to the service of the Prikaz Kazanskogo dvortsa. On 21 December 1676, the Prikaz Kazanskogo dvortsa wrote again to the Posol'skii Prikaz, to remind its officials of the situation, since more than one year later the ransom had still not been paid.[63] While Pushkin was just one servitor, his captivity (and inability to serve) reflected the general complexity of the overlapping authority of the chancelleries.

Situations such as these indicated that resolving the conflicting lines of authority would have military and administrative benefits. In 1680, the Razriadnyi Prikaz was assigned control over all military servitors, including those that had been in the service of the Prikaz Kazanskogo dvortsa. Theoretically, this provided one central registry of military servitors, now all under the control of the only chancellery responsible for all military matters in the region. However, all non-Russian military servitors, approximately two-thirds of the men in the region, were placed under the control of the recently established Inozemskii Prikaz (Foreigners' Service Chancellery), which was also responsible for foreign mercenaries in the tsar's service.[64] The Prikaz Kazanskogo dvortsa delayed implementing the change of command, but could not resist repeated commands from the tsar, and by the end of 1681 the transfer was largely accomplished. It was hard to see this change as an improvement or simplification of military service in the region. It was also difficult to argue that this was a decision primarily targeting Kazan or the Tatars in military service, as it was part of ongoing, comprehensive military reforms.

But now two chancelleries, one brand new, with little experience supervising men in the region had gained authority, and the Prikaz Kazanskogo dvortsa no longer possessed the ability to control its own security procedures.[65] Furthermore, military servitors had a long history of appealing to multiple chancelleries when necessary to accomplish their own goals; adding chancelleries increased this tendency.

With the transfer of authority over local military elites to two different chancelleries, combined with the abolition of *mestnichestvo* in 1682, numerous issues were thrown into confusion. Petitions from military servitors to the central chancelleries only escalated after 1680. The process for dowries or inheritance had generally fallen into a common pattern during the previous century, but the new chancelleries created new opportunities and difficulties for land transfers. Judicial matters were now considerably less clear, as social precedence was not necessarily a factor in determining the outcome of legal disputes.

The greatest change from the earlier system was that accepting military service and acquiring status in society thereby became a less popular option, since status was no longer guaranteed. Not frequently, but certainly more often, potential servitors began to turn down estates to avoid military service. One of their goals might have been to improve the government's offers, but for Russian servitors with other options, accepting the condition of local service and the expectation of residence may have become unappealing. As an example, in 1690 the Russian servitor Fëdor Stilenev died, leaving his land in Kazan district without a familial heir. As after 1649, Russian service land legally could not be given to a non-Russian, the *voevoda* tried to entice another Russian to accept the land and service conditions. The *voevoda* offered the land to Lov Zhukov, who examined the land but rejected it as "untrustworthy." Apparently there were no other viable candidates, because the *voevoda* then offered the land to a Tatar, Elbno Fedorovshii, who accepted the estate in 1690.[66] This transaction was illegal, of course, but the need for a military servitor in the countryside was no less in 1690 than it had been in 1649. Zhukov's report on the land was included in Fedorovshii's offer, so he certainly knew that the land was suspect. Whereas a Russian facing fewer constraints in society could find a better offer elsewhere in the state, for a non-Russian to be offered a Russian estate was impossible except in this region. Non-Russians remained a largely captive labor force for government military needs, even if the system had become unbalanced.

This is not to say that non-Russians servitors were desperate—they also rejected land grants. Converted Tatars, and cousins, Mikhail Petrov and Ivan Semenov deti Beklemeshev, rejected estates at least twice in the 1680s, forcing the Pomestnyi Prikaz to continue to search for an estate that would entice them to remain on the frontier.[67]

It is possible that the Beklemeshevs were displeased with the estates in Nizhnii Novgorod or Alatyr' province, preferring to stay closer to their homes or in another district. There was an increase in petitions from servitors in this era attempting to move from one district to another. Savva Vasil'ev syn Dulov, for example, attempted to move to Saransk in 1689, petitioning both the Prikaz Kazanskogo dvortsa and the Posol'skii Prikaz. His family had held their estates outside of Kazan for nearly a century, but he wanted to move south to Saransk. The petition was denied, unsurprisingly, as all of the chancelleries' policies were designed to prevent such relocation.[68] Refusing an initial offer from the government became a tool to negotiate the location of one's estate (even if it was not always successful). Though there was no guarantee that another estate would be offered, the state's increased recruitment of servitors in the wake of the revolt of 1670 created new opportunities. It seems probable that it must have happened often enough that servitors expected this possibility, because few non-Russians would run the risk and potentially reject elite status.

The need to keep servitors on the land, and appeased, also seems to have led to an easing of dowry exchanges. Of course, it was not a simple matter, as military elite service was still monitored by multiple chancelleries even after 1680. The Pomestnyi Prikaz, for example, endorsed Pëtr Gavrilov syn Domozhirov's petition to the tsar to give a portion of his lands in Zaiudemskii hamlet in Nizhnii Novgorod district to Ivan Rodinov syn Zheriskii, his son-in-law, and then resident of nearby Alatyr', in 1685/86. Mikhail Alekseev syn Vosukii similarly received permission for a transfer of land to Iakov Ivanov syn Shakhov in Arzamas as a dowry in 1689/90. However, servitors also sought permission from other chancelleries when their first attempts failed, but these tended to address chancelleries that had not been involved at all in the early part of the century. This second or third attempt could also be successful, as when the Prikaz Bol'shogo dvortsa (Treasury) approved the petition of d'iak Petr Grigor'ev syn Ramodanovskii for a dowry exchange in Arzamas district.[69]

Servitors filed more petitions to reduce their service obligations, in addition to their petitions for other privileges. Kondratei Filimonov, for example, managed to lower his yearly tax payments for his fields in Simbirsk district in December 1682.[70] Nikita Semenov syn Bolkovskii attempted far more, writing several petitions in the 1690s to persuade the central authorities that he should keep his service land in Arzamas without fulfilling his military service obligations.[71] This seemingly amazing request, to abrogate his military service, might have been an assertion that by the end of the century the role of landlord was more useful and important than the role of cavalryman. The rejection of his petitions, however, indicates that the local authorities did not agree with Bolkovskii's unique assessment of his service obligations.

In general, even with the new chancelleries involved, much of the correspondence resembled earlier petitions and their responses. If a dispute arose among potential recipients for service land, the claimant with both familial connections to the land and current residence in the region usually defeated unrelated petitioners. In July 1681 Mikhail Ruzhevskii and one of his neighbors, Aleksei Stepanov syn Khlopov, both filed claims for Ruzhevskii's father's large estate in Simbirsk district. Ruzhevskii's petition focused on both his father's and his own loyal service to the tsar, including their long residence on the estate. With this argument, it was not a surprise that Khlopov failed.[72] In 1692, Kazan's *Voevoda* Dmitrii Vasil'ev syn Urakov tried to seize the lands of Stepan and Fedia Levashev for himself. The Levashevs presented eight deeds to demonstrate their claim to their estate, beginning with the original grant from 1646. With this evidence and proof that they had paid their taxes, the Levashevs defeated the *voevoda*.[73] If only one of the potential heirs had remained on the land, he was likely to inherit the entire estate even if it disinherited his relatives. For having left the region, they lost their privileges. Konstantin Miakin, for example, received all the land held by his uncle in 1686, distributed among Arzamas, Alatyr', and Kurmysh districts, because his cousins had abandoned the region.[74]

If there was a notable change for military servitors after 1670, it was that the state would break with its informal inheritance practices to punish families who abandoned the region. This should not have been a surprise to the disinherited men, as the region had never tolerated military servitors leaving their estates, much less at a point in time when the state was pursuing a goal of increasing military servitors' numbers throughout the region. Semën Ivanov syn Bogtachevskii lost the village of Kamenii Brod in Simbirsk district in 1686 to Savva Timofeev syn Voronkov, then living in Simbirsk, even though the village had been the estate of Bogtachevskii's family for two previous generations. Bogtachevskii, however, had left Simbirsk. He petitioned the tsar to be given the land, but his petition was rejected.[75]

Thus, changes at the margins of practice had the effect of loosening old patterns, even if the relationship between military servitors and the central chancelleries largely remained as it had been before 1670. Potentially rejecting a grant outright created new ground for negotiation, but it is just as possible that military service itself was becoming less appealing to Muscovy's elites. Non-Russian elites, of course, still held fewer options than Russians. New laws pressured them to convert to Orthodoxy, and elite status was no longer guaranteed by entering service to demonstrate loyalty. The relationship that had been built over generations between families and the Prikaz Kazanskogo dvortsa was ended, as Russian military servitors now belonged to the Razriadnyi Prikaz and the non-Russians to the Inozemskii Prikaz. As each group performed their military service locally, and neither gained the right to leave their estates, in many ways the situation resembled its earlier incarnation. The local *voevody* remained important, because they continued to monitor military service, and, on occasion, distribute service land in order to keep the ranks full. The administrative apparatus for military service functioned according to a new structure, but its template remained the same.

Economic changes progressed in a similar fashion to the security adjustments, as the Prikaz Kazanskogo dvortsa's ability to monopolize affairs in the region diminished. As the region's production and revenue increased, more and more state chancelleries became involved in exploiting its potential. In March 1676, for example, the Prikaz tainykh del (Privy Affairs) instructed a Tatar merchant, Mamatagei Zamanov, to establish a new silk factory in Simbirsk, from which revenue would be given to the Prikaz Kazanskogo dvortsa to support its local officials. Zamanov had already completed a similar project in Kazan, also at the instruction of the Prikaz tainykh del. However, the responsibility for enforcing this instruction fell to the Posol'skii Prikaz, because the new factory would be producing cloth from imported silk, which remained under its control.[76]

The increasingly developed local economy was still tightly controlled by the chancelleries. Foreign merchants still found themselves discriminated against, and tariffs along the Volga remained high. The New Commercial Code and its enforcement policies remained fully in effect, and frequently protested. The merchant Klima Kalmykov petitioned the tsar in 1676 for freedom to move salt along the Volga between Saratov and Astrakhan. The local *voevody* were collecting tolls, which Kalmykov believed should not have been charged.[77] Similarly, Petr Gudumov and Terchanin and Semën Gruzin complained in a petition that they were being stopped on the overland trade route between Arzamas and Simbirsk and being held until they paid tolls, even though they were not merchants. Gudumov and the Gruzins sent their complaint to the Posol'skii Prikaz, which was responsible for monitoring foreign trade, suggesting that despite their disclaimers they were transporting imported commodities through the region.[78] In 1682 the English agent in Moscow, Thomas Meverall, petitioned Tsar Fëdor Alekseevich to resolve numerous difficulties the English continued to face in Muscovy, including invasive searches of English vessels, denying bills of sale so that goods could not be exported, and, perhaps most surprisingly, denying Englishmen bought out of Turkish slavery the right to return to London by traveling through Muscovy. Summing up his grievances, Meverall was quite forceful, arguing that the tsar's behavior was "contrary to ye Usage of all Christian Prince."[79] None of these attempts, however, were successful, since profits from tariffs were an important source of revenue for the state.

Even as the Prikaz Kazanskogo dvortsa lost much of its control over the military and the economy, it gained greater judicial authority to resolve local disputes without guidance from Moscow. In 1693 the tsar transferred to the Prikaz Kazanskogo dvortsa judicial rights over cases involving dishonoring boiars' or *mirzas'* reputations in any part of the territory under its jurisdiction, removing that right from the Sudnyi Prikaz (Judicial Chancellery).[80] As a result, there does seem to be an increase in cases reaching court, or, at least, that the Prikaz became more likely to intervene in cases that might otherwise have slipped through the cracks, or involved lengthy and expensive trips to Moscow. For example, on 10 August 1681, Aleksei Ivan syn Mukhanov petitioned Arzamas *d'iaki* Timofei Isaakov syn Kuz'min and Bet'iand Pelageno Grigor'ev to begin an investigation. Mukhanov had recently been attacked with a sword by one of his peasants, Efrem Issev, and Mukhanov expected the *d'iaki* to resolve the matter.[81]

All legal issues among servitors would now be resolved at the local level, which enhanced the administration's influence and authority. However, motivated servitors still attempted to induce the involvement of the central chancelleries, especially if the local *voevoda* lacked interest, or was unwilling to act against his own interests. This happened regularly, as in 1685, when the *voevoda* of Saransk investigated Matvei Erlov, a military servitor residing on his estate in the district. According to Timofei Iachont'ev syn Karazulov, a resident of Simbirsk, Erlov arrived on Karazulov's service-land estate, and "broke him," seizing his land, and forcing him to move to the city. When the *voevoda* interviewed Erlov, Erlov explained that there had been no violence, and that Karazulov willingly dealt away his land. According to Erlov, Karazulov's plan was to meet with the tsar at the Pomestnyi Prikaz by arranging an illegal exchange of service land. Amazingly, Saransk's *voevoda* found this explanation plausible enough to petition the Prikaz on Erlov's behalf. However, it seems more likely that bribery was the reason for the *voevoda*'s action. In any case, the *voevoda* did not address the illegality of the alleged "deal," for when the Pomestnyi Prikaz finally sent its verdict to Saransk in 1686, it found Erlov guilty and fined him for the attack, but allowed him to keep the land he had seized.[82] While this outcome seems unfair to Karazulov, now deprived of his estate, the verdict was in keeping with rewarding those servitors who remained in the district and punishing those who abandoned it. It is not known whether Karazulov met with the tsar.

This type of case reveals the continuing tension among the chancelleries. Their functions might slowly have been rationalized, but competitive cooperation endured. No *voevoda* was likely to sacrifice his own servitors when regional security was dependent upon these men. The central chancelleries in general preferred to keep servitors on their estates, even unjustly seized, rather than reduce their number. As long as the *voevody* received instructions from the Prikaz Kazanskogo dvortsa, the Prikaz could influence any number of issues regardless of the other chancelleries' legal rights.

To an extent, the central government implicitly supported the Prikaz Kazanskogo dvortsa's rights to most aspects of regional control. The Prikaz Kazanskogo dvortsa gained control over monastic lands throughout all of the territory under its supervision when the Monastyrskii Prikaz was dissolved in 1678, although throughout the rest of Muscovy's monastic estates were given to the supervision of the Prikaz Bol'shogo dvortsa (Treasury).[83] Local security issues were clearly the rationale for this exception. With control over monastic estates, the Prikaz Kazanskogo dvorsta gained immediate control over monastic taxes and the recruitment of peasants residing on monastic estates.

The legal change only followed preexisting practice. Monasteries and convents had begun losing control over their estates since the 1660s, particularly after the Razin invasion and local revolt. There was a need for more military servitors and larger garrisons, and local ecclesiastical institutions remained the best source of new, well-tended, arable land that the state could convert into servitor estates. The large monastic estates existed originally to maintain turrets and watchtowers that had served as integrated parts of the defenses against steppe nomads, and which were now obsolete. Therefore, the state's resource, the land, was reallocated without reference to monastic privileges or Church interests. A fine example was the resolution of the long-standing dispute began between Simbirsk's Spaso-Preobrazhenskii Convent and the *voevody* of Arzamas. In 1672, *Voevoda* Mikhail Brevich Tagishchev finally won his claim to the monastery's village of Cherukha. The *voevoda* wanted the village to provide more land for more *strel'tsy*.[84] Over the next two decades the convent attempted unsuccessfully to reclaim its lost village, using different justifications as its appeals failed.[85] By this time, such a loss for the convent was not atypical; Arzamas's Troitse-Sergeevskii Monastery lost its village of Slotnik to the local *voevoda* in 1686, and Arzamas's Makar'evskii Zheltovodskii Monastery lost its village of Kolovek to a servitor, Mikhail Andreev syn Shaimotov, in 1694.[86]

At the same time, the construction of monasteries of the type built during the previous century commenced again, this time in the south. In 1670 the Simbirsk Line had been overrun, and would remain of limited utility while supported by an unreliable population. After 1670, many monasteries and convents were founded to add to the number of strongholds, including potential observation posts, as seen in table 9. New outposts were constructed south of the line, including Syzran,

Table 9 New monastic foundations

Monasteries and convents	Year est.
Saratov's Spasopreobrazhenskii Monastery	1680
Saratov's Krestovozdvizhenskii Convent	1680
Syzran's Voznesenskii Monstery	1683
Kerensk's Bogoroditskii Convent	1683
Saransk's Petropavlovskii Monastery	1684

Source: Data drawn from Romaniello, "Absolutism and Empire," 22, 30, 33.

established in 1683. The construction of monasteries and convents to supplement the defensive line had been long-standing practice, and certainly had accompanied the construction of the Simbirsk Line itself. At a time when some of the convents and monasteries to the north were losing estates to military servitors, these new institutions were supported with lands and were as important for the future success of the region as the older ones had been in the north. Older monasteries in the south were resupported with new villages as well, including Saransk's Kazanskii Bogoroditsii Monastery, which received the Mordvin village of Bogoslovskoe in 1686.[87] Similarly, when a Tatar village, Voznesenskoe, petitioned the tsar in 1686 to be freed from its landlord, the Savvo-Storozhevskii Monastery of Simbirsk, the Prikaz Kazanskogo dvortsa's denied their petition, reminding them they had been bequeathed to the monastery in 1674/75 in memory of Tsar Aleksei Mikhailovich.[88] While the Prikaz offered the argument that "freeing" the village would dishonor the tsar's memory, in truth, it had no desire to undermine a monastery in Simbirsk at a time when all of its efforts were dedicated to expanding the role of monasteries along the southern defensive line.

The "migration" of monasteries south was not an explicit policy, nor did northern monasteries lose all of their possessions, because they continued to hold and gain donated lands. The new laws were not designed to eradicate monasteries, just to provide greater resources to support more military servitors, or at least more troops in general. This did not stop secular authorities from attempting to grab as much as they could—the struggles were often protracted and expensive. These legal battles continued throughout the century, as *voevody* tried to block any acquisitions of land by monasteries, even donations. In 1676 Arzamas's Spaso-Preobrazhenskii Monastery prepared an itemized list of all of its donations, including courtyards, buildings, fields, and villages, in order to prepare to defend itself against the *voevoda*'s ongoing attempt to seize its estates. It highlighted its donors, and the reasons the land was donated, using the donors' status as a shield.[89] This appears to have worked; throughout the next decade, after the Prikaz gained its authority over monastic estates, the monastery continued to thwart the *voevoda*'s attempts to seize any part of the donations.[90]

As evident as was the tsar's quest for greater efficiencies in administration, the functions and practices followed in the Middle Volga Region by his officials and servitors flowed as it had before 1670, albeit in different channels. The Prikaz Kazanskogo dvortsa was concerned to maintain or increase its military strength in the region (although it then lost its ability to command those forces), and there was a definite commitment to maintaining the residence requirement for military servitors in the region. The involvement of new chancelleries, however, meant that the business of the region remained complicated, inefficient, and exploitable by savvy individuals. The greatest changes, in fact, involved no chancellery directly, but impacted all equally. The end of *mestnichestvo* was obviously the most important; it was an enormous shift in society that would ultimately transform many features of both Muscovite administrative and military service. Thus, the quality of the change in administrative practice was more significant than the structural changes in and of themselves. Kazan and the Volga now fell under universal state rule, and were no longer subject to a specific "colonial" regime of laws targeting the frontier. The former khanate, therefore, slowly shed its frontier past even as it adjusted to its new position as an integrated region of the Muscovite state. This new status had been constructed so gradually, and so incrementally, that only by the 1680s or 1690s were newer policies reinforcing or replacing the older "colonial" policies. The latter had been predicated on the government's interest in surveillance and security. As long as the region could be influenced by outside powers (even if rarely the case) or was defended by non-Orthodox, non-Russian subjects, this could hardly be otherwise. The shift in policies was definite proof this region was no longer an exposed frontier, but a province within a new Russian Empire.

Imperial Evolution

The revolt of 1670–71 confirmed the success of the previous centuries' policies and demonstrated that while the revolt's scale appeared vast, the government's response could be swift and efficient. In its wake, administrative, military, and economic policies were adjusted, but could be structured in accordance with the ongoing transformation of the Muscovite government, with the exception of the ending of runaway peasant commissions. In the main this represented a jettisoning of its general policies during the previous century. The decision to reduce the Prikaz Kazanskogo dvortsa's control over its territory could be taken because the territory's character had changed, and efficiencies (hopefully) harvested from a revised chancellery structure. Like most bureaucratic organizations, the Prikaz Kazanskogo dvortsa refused to accept that it had fulfilled its purpose and was no longer necessary. But viewed from the late seventeenth century, without the investments, and the application of over a century of time, on the part of the Prikaz Kazanskogo dvortsa itself, this achievement and the integration of the territory, could not have taken place.

These successes were based on the evolutionary nature of the Muscovite empire. By proclaiming victory so publicly in the 1550s, both the tsar and the Russian Orthodox Church created the space to slowly implement and tailor local policies to specific circumstances. Distance prevented Moscow's enemies from affecting its rule and created the space to accommodate the government's incompetence. There was no way for the state to hold Kazan without the participation, either forced or by tacit consent, of the local population, both elite and peasant. The Muscovite Empire therefore was built as much by Tatars, Chuvashes, Maris, Mordvins, and Udmurts as by Russians. It was firmly established as an empire of diversity, in terms of ethnolinguistic identity, religious confession, and economic production. All of the practical accommodations that enabled the empire to function on the local level were neatly disguised by the rhetorical structure of empire constructed after 1552. In Moscow, foreigners observed the glorious monument to the victory over Kazan—St. Basil's Cathedral—without any impulse to question whether the victory meant in terms of the state's actual power and wealth. Until 1670, in this context, the non-Russian population appeared to be the primitive subjects of an empire, compliant within the existing order. This façade of success created the appearance of a strong state holding valuable territory, while Muscovy continued to pursue the difficult task of obtaining hegemonic control over the empire.

With enough gestation, however, the fantasy of 1552 in several areas approached reality after a century. By 1649 the Muscovite government was sufficiently stable to impose the new law code upon Kazan's population as well as Moscow's. The New Commercial Code was equally applied throughout the state and disrupted the established trade on the Volga as much as it regularized revenues and participants. Even considering the rebellion and invasion of 1670, the tsar's chancelleries were confident enough to hire Kalmyk mercenaries to attack their own subjects in Simbirsk in 1675. At this point, the only threat to the state's control was revealed to be along its southern defensive line, which became the subject of coordinated development in the 1670s and '80s. Kazan and its environs were long since secured. Control over the region, the elusive work of a century in the context of the conquest of 1552, had been successful.

Afterword

The mode of men and women, rich and poor, are all one, all over the Empire, from the highest to the lowest, and their Language one, yea and Religion too, which certainly must hugely tend to their peace and preservation.

Samuel Collins,
The Present State of Russia, 1671

Considering the vast Extent of the Russian Empire and that many parts of it are almost inaccessible, it was no wonder that so many of those Heathen Nations remain unconverted: However that his Czarish Majesty had made already a Beginning of their Conversion, and was resolved to continue in his Zeal for propagating the Christian Religion all over his Dominions.

Friedrich Christian Weber,
The Present State of Russia, 1723

Most of the colonies which originated in the center and extended like radii to the periphery of the empire were formerly spontaneous undertakings brought about by the natural instincts of the people and the interests of the seigneurs. They were carried out privately and the government simply allowed them. . . . But by no means did the government plan or supervise the entire enterprise. Prior to Peter I the government was, moreover, not organized in such a manner that it could have carried out a large and systematic economic project of this nature.

August von Haxthausen,
Studies on the Interior of Russia, 1847

In European Russia the struggle between agriculture and nomadic barbarism is now a thing of the past, and the fertile Steppe, which was for centuries a battle-ground of the Aryan and Turanian races, has been incorporated into the dominions of the Tsar. The nomadic tribes have been partly driven out and partly pacified and parked in "reserves," and the territory which they so long and so stubbornly defended is now studded with peaceful villages and tilled by laborious agriculturists.

Donald Mackenzie Wallace,
Russia, 1886

Contemporary foreign observers habitually observed and considered Russia's expansion and tsarist rule in only one dimension. Not surprisingly, many viewed Russia through the lens of "orientalist" ideas.[1] They assessed it to contrast its ways with the more familiar traditions of their own countries; viewed it as an Asiatic monolith, uniform and ruled absolutely by the tsar; or imposed on it systems and schemes resembling the ideas of utopian socialists or other theoreticians. They were confounded. The state was too large, too empty, too "foreign" to be easily categorized, especially given the distinction drawn between "Western" and "Eastern" Europe during the Enlightenment, which only added to the sense of estrangement for foreign arrivals in Moscow.[2] Even the most dedicated scholars studying Russia did not complicate their view of Russia with discussions of its regional particularisms, even though they were undoubtedly familiar with those of their own countries. Nor were Russian scholars immune to these intellectual traps. When V. O. Kluichevksii rather infamously wrote in the nineteenth century that the history of Russia was "the history of a country colonizing itself," an empire delineated by the footsteps of Russians expanding across empty lands, he was as much reacting to foreign observations as he was expressing nationalist pride.[3] The reality, as the previous chapters indicate, was messy, unsystematic, and not dissimilar to the history of other early-modern empires.

The Muscovite Empire gave birth to modern Russia by integrating diverse lands and peoples through a system best described as "composite sovereignty." Due to the limitations of time and distance, coupled with a lack of population, wealth, and other resources, innumerable administrative variations based on adaptations to local conditions dotted the landscape of the tsar's territory. Different regions developed very different methods to maintain military, economic, or social systems. Imposing uniformity was tremendously difficult, and until the eighteenth century served no great purpose compared to the trouble it took to accomplish. The various imperial networks connecting the frontier to the metropole, particularly the Russian

Figure 5 Kazan before the conflagration of 1842 (Reproduced from Sears, *An Illustrated Description of the Russian Empire*)

Orthodox Church's apparatus, allowed the state to manage these many interests and adapt its machinery to defend, exploit, and control different populations without the expense associated with imposing a bureaucracy onto unsettled territory. The benefit of this lack of a single system was that given sufficient time, incremental steps toward increasing the tsar's authority over his people could work. This is not to imply that there were not significant leaps toward greater centralization, break-throughs such as the *Ulozhenie* of 1649, but these unquestionably built on the smaller accomplishments of previous decades, and the lack of coordinated changes in the wake of the revolt of 1670–71 was far more typical. The cogs of the administration largely worked independently even when the tsarist government attempted to streamline itself. The Russian Orthodox Church generally followed its own, not dissimilar, interests as it too spread throughout the growing empire. The cooperative competition among central and local administrators, working for both the state and the Church, created flexibility rather than uniformity, which ultimately served imperial interests. That this was the only realistic path for a poor state lacking any other resource but time only reinforces the significance of the accomplishment. The empire neither built itself nor was it directed from a central bureaucratic node and based on a strategic blueprint. The truth lay in between, even into the eighteenth century. Peter the Great may have reframed the state as the "Russian Empire" and revamped its symbolic and ideological trappings in the early eighteenth century, but he only renovated the existing structures of the empire.[4]

Even with the benefit of visits to the countryside and long study, contemporary observers could hardly have been expected to fully grasp the complexities and confusion of Russian rule. Neither the Muscovite nor modern Russian Empire ever achieved the uniformity of language or religion that Samuel Collins discussed in the seventeenth century and Friedrich Christian Weber saw in the eighteenth. Nor was the empire peaceful, although the state certainly managed to redress challenges to its authority. Most observers failed to notice that the strength of the tsar's army was not his "Russian" troops but his diverse military forces, as was proved in the response to the Razin invasion and the subsequent revolt of 1670–71. Haxthausen's suggestion that the settlement of the Muscovite Empire occurred independently of the state was also highly equivocal. After all, in a state utilizing different regional accommodations at different points in time, multiple paths to empire and types of population control were possible. However, it was certain in the Middle Volga Region that the state was an invested participant, directing as much as possible from the center but having to rely on the interests of local authorities to accomplish any of its goals. Only Donald Mackenzie Wallace's observations from later in the nineteenth century accurately reflect some of the transformative processes of empire, yet while applicable to the Volga, they were off the mark regarding the ongoing expansion farther south and east into Central Asia.

With the combination of erroneous observations and the variable imperial practices of a composite sovereign state, it is not surprising that the legacy of the Muscovite Empire also remains rather elusive. The territory and the peoples acquired in the sixteenth century still remain within the borders of the Russian Federation, but no longer as scattered ethnolinguistic groups sharing space, unified by a connection to the metropole. The Tatars, Chuvashes, Maris, Mordvins, and Udmurts are now national groups residing in autonomous republics within the Russian Federation's borders, each with its own relationship to the center. At the same time, each of these national groups possesses only a slim majority, if that, in their own autonomous republics. Though Chuvashia might have been created as a Soviet autonomous region for the Chuvashes, sizeable Russian and Tatar minority populations exist within its borders. Much like the sixteenth century, when examined closely, local identities are still hard to define and categorize.

Furthermore, the interactions among these modern national groups, their autonomous republics, and the Russian Federation are as complex and varied as they were during the early-modern era. As the Tatars remain numerically the largest of these national minorities, residing in the largest republic in the region, they remain the central focus of the Middle Volga Region's relationship with Moscow. It began early in the twentieth century, when the Tatars led a relatively successful (and independent) revolt against the tsar, attempting to remain separate from the emerging Soviet government during the revolutionary era.[5] Though independence was short-lived, the Tatars preserved this legacy of resistance in numerous Soviet-era histories, which reframed the Tatars history as an endless struggle against the tsar.[6] This type of narrative served Soviet interests, as it demonstrated the Communists' support for their "national minorities," who prospered in the Soviet Union when compared to the centuries of tsarist exploitation.[7] However, by the end of the Soviet era, this narrative had largely been simplified to an understanding of continuous Tatar resistance to Moscow's dictates since 1552, eliding any difference between the tsarist and Soviet eras. As a result, it was not a complete surprise that the new republic of Tatarstan announced its independence from the Soviet Union on 30 August 1990, preceding the dissolution not only of the Soviet state itself but also the creation of the new (post-Soviet) Russian Federation. Even after Mikhail Gorbachev recognized the collapse of the Soviet state in the fall of 1991, Tatarstan continued to pursue total independence. In 1992 Tatarstan's government adopted its own constitution.[8] In a treaty signed 15 February 1994 Tatarstan agreed to "rejoin" the Russian Federation, but only after large concessions from Moscow, including guarantees of civil freedoms far greater than those protecting the rest of Russia:

> The plenipotentiaries of the State Bodies of the Russian Federation and the State Bodies of the Republic of Tatarstan: empowered by the Constitution of the Russian Federation and the Constitution of the Republic of Tatarstan; based on the universally recognized right of all nationalities to self-determination and the principals [sic] of equality, voluntariness and free will; having the aim to guarantee the preservation of territorial integrity and the common economic interest; wishing to promote the preservation and development of historical and national customs, cultures, languages; being concerned about ensuring civil peace, international accord and national security; acknowledging the priority of basic human rights and freedoms regardless of nationality, religion, location of habitation and other differences.[9]

Any cooperation with Moscow was, however, an uneasy proposition among Tatar nationalists. In 1998, R. M. Amirkhanov wrote that "the Tatars and other non-Russian peoples are again placed by 'democratic' Russia in an epoch of the colonial autocracy, being deprived even the right to self-determination proclaimed by the Bolsheviks."[10] In many regards, the 1994 agreement was a tremendous statement of quasi-independence, recognized by the new Russian government, yet the "historical" legacy of Russian domination was not eradicated by these new concessions.[11]

In recent years, the political climate in Russia and Tatarstan has not resembled the chaotic condition of the 1990s. Certainly Moscow has pushed for greater uniformity in provincial rule. Tatarstan extensively revised its constitution in 2002 and signed a new version of the 1994 agreement on 26 June 2007 (both reflecting Moscow's interests).[12] As a result, Tatarstan was largely unified with the Russian Federation. But even as Tatarstan lost the quasi-independence it possessed in the 1990s, it has also emerged as a model of cultural plurality within the Russian Federation, with both Tatar and Russian as its official languages, and an education system based on Tatar-language instruction.[13] Considering the fate of other Turkic Muslim regions of Russia, including Chechnia and Dagestan, it is not hard to understand why the peaceful reintegration of Tatarstan, and the maintenance of cultural diversity, is widely admired, both inside Russia and by foreign dignitaries.[14]

The current situation of the Tatars and Tatarstan should not obscure the complex ways in which history has been exploited throughout the region for contemporary political agendas. As much as the Tatars constructed a narrative of centuries of resistance to Moscow's influence, its neighbors, both in the Chuvash and Mari-El Republics, have forged their own historical narratives where the Tatars, not Moscow, remain the enemy. For example, a folktale exists, "How the Maris Went to Moscow," which relates Ivan IV's invasion of Kazan in 1552. In the tale, the Maris were the vanguard of the invasion force. The famous Cat of Kazan overheard the Mari battle plans to sap the kremlin's walls, and warned the khan to flee the city with his wife and daughter before the final siege. For the Maris, the lesson is that only the intervention of the cat saved Kazan from utter devastation, though their own loyalty to their new tsarist allies was unquestioned.[15] Similarly, in 2001 the Chuvash Republic celebrated (in elaborate fashion) its 450-year "union" with Russia. According to the republic's official narrative, in 1551, the Chuvashes petitioned Ivan IV to save them from Tatar oppression.[16] Neither the myth nor the "history" accurately records the events of the sixteenth century, discussed in the previous chapters. Each group had a far more equivocal relationship with the Russians, and each other, than their current narrative presents.

All of these constructed narratives have political repercussions and influence on the emergent nationalist (and potentially separatist) movements among these peoples. However, none of them are historically accurate. Just as the tsar forged an image of a successful, expansionist empire to cover the limitations and local accommodations that pervaded within his realm, modern Tatars, Chuvashes, and Maris have presented an image of cooperation with Moscow or resistance of Russian colonialism to serve their current political interests.[17]

Figure 6 Cat of Kazan, woodcut from the eighteenth century (Reproduced from Bakhtin, *Russkii lubok, XVII–XIX vv.*)

None of the "historical" narratives these groups muster resemble their true position in Muscovite Russia. There was little difference in the treatment of any of the region's non-Russian groups, except perhaps for the Mordvins, who were the most victimized by Muscovite colonialism. For the Tatars, Chuvashes, and Maris, a common narrative largely describes all of their experiences. They were conquered, their elites co-opted into the Muscovite social hierarchy, and the remaining population was exploited for their labor in exchange for minor concessions (or none at all). Elite Chuvashes also accepted tsarist *pomest'e* grants; this was not an exclusive privilege of the Tatars. Elite Russians and the Russian Orthodox Church relied on the peasant labor of the entire local population, making any argument that Russia offered protection to the Maris or Chuvashes hard to accept. At the same time, each group did benefit to some extent from the state's local accommodations. While the tsar's new peasants were not saved from labor or tax obligations, there was little pressure to adopt new agricultural practices (at least until the establishment of the southern defensive line), nor did the Russian Orthodox Church pursue a conversion mission in the region. Though this remained an exploitative system, it was no worse than what Russian peasants faced in the heartland, and keeping local languages, customs, and religious practices preserved non-Russian traditions within the framework of the elusive empire. In a limited sense, these groups held greater independence from Moscow in the seventeenth century than in the twenty-first.

Historical distortions are not an innovation of the modern era; the Muscovite Empire was also built upon a symbolic foundation to disguise its genuine limitations. Following the events of 1552, the Russian Orthodox Church and the tsar constructed a narrative of triumphant expansion and Islam's defeat. It was popularized with the construction of St. Basil's Cathedral in Moscow. The fictionalized account of conquest was far more interesting than the slow, incremental stages that would take more than a century to succeed. At the same time, the public presentation of empire also created the time and space needed for Muscovy's slow development to bear fruit. By creating a system that could allow local accommodation, the empire did expand, becoming something more like its initial claims over time. For an early-modern state, lacking technology, transportation, education, wealth, or prosperity, it was a remarkable achievement.

Muscovy's long experience governing the populace of Kazan and the Volga shaped the creation of Russia. The development of a system of composite sovereignty, not the quest for uniformity within the tsar's borders, facilitated imperial governance. The construction of the defensive lines, the creation of new settlements, the enlistment of the local population, and the regulation of local and international trade were all necessary steps, but none could be completed in the decades immediately following 1552. It would take more than a century. The seemingly decisive turning points, such as the *Ulozhenie* of 1649, the abolishment of *mestni-chestvo*, and the military reform reducing the state's reliance on its cavalry, appeared as dramatic events in the short-term, but reflected decades of adjustments by administrators on the periphery and in the central chancelleries. The state's pursuit of sovereign control over its populations was achieved not by outright dominance but rather long-term persistence and incremental policy adjustments. It is a lesson that the Russian Federation could benefit from, as the ongoing struggle in Chechnia demonstrates that political and military control remain elusive goals, whereas local accommodations and limited acceptance of cultural pluralism in the Middle Volga Region produced far more stable relationships, even if they remain somewhat uneasy.

Notes

Introduction

1. This chapter's second epigraph comes from "Catherine to Voltaire, Kazan, 29 May/ 9 June 1767," in *Voltaire and Catherine the Great: Selected Correspondence*, ed. A. Lentin (Cambridge, 1974), 48.

2. For an overview of Russian expansion, see Andreas Kappeler, *The Russian Empire: A Multi-Ethnic History* (Harlow, Essex, 2001).

3. "Middle Volga Region" refers to the land alongside the Volga River between Nizhnii Novgorod and Saratov, as opposed to the "Upper Volga" lands, which were Muscovite possessions before 1552.

4. For an introduction to the population of the region, see R. G. Ganeev, M. V. Murzabulatov, and L. I. Nagaeva, *Narody Povolzh'ia i Priural'ia: Istoriko etnograficheskie ocherki* (Moscow, 1985); Bulat Khamidullin, *Narody Kazanskogo Khanstva: Etnosotsiologicheskoe issledovanie* (Kazan, 2002).

5. For the Muscovite explanation of right by conquest, see Jaroslaw Pelenski, *Russia and Kazan: Conquest and Imperial Ideology (1438–1560s)* (The Hague, 1974), 88–91. For a comparative discussion, see Sharon Korman, *The Right of Conquest: The Acquisition of Territory by Force in International Law and Practice* (Oxford, 1996).

6. For a discussion of the difficulties of communication in early-modern empires, see Fernand Braudel, *The Mediterranean and the Mediterranean World in the Age of Philip II*, trans. Siân Reynolds (Berkeley, 1995), 2:355–94; and Tonio Andrade and William Reger, eds., *The Limits of Empire in the Early Modern World* (forthcoming).

7. Here I borrow from Clifford Geertz, "Centers, Kings, and Charisma: Reflections on the Symbolics of Power," in *Culture and Its Creators: Essays in Honor of Edward Shils*, ed. Joseph Ben-David and Terry Nichols Clark (Chicago, 1977).

8. For the use of "institutional bricolage" in the creation of the Ottoman Empire, see Karen Barkey, *Empire of Difference: The Ottomans in Comparative Perspective* (Cambridge, 2008), esp. 7–8.

9. Laura Benton discusses layered sovereignty in her *A Search for Sovereignty: Law and Geography in European Empires, 1400–1900* (New York, 2010), esp. 30–39. See also Charles Tilly's discussion of "fragmented sovereignty" in early-modern states in his *Coercion, Capital, and European States, AD 990–1992*, rev. ed. (Malden, MA, 1992). For a discussion of another "imperial network," see Kerry Ward, *Networks of Empire: Forced Migrations in the Dutch East India Company* (Cambridge, 2009).

10. For a broader discussion of composite states, see H. G. Koenigsberger, *Politicians and Virtuosi: Essays in Early Modern History* (London, 1986), 1–25; J. H. Elliott, "A Europe of Composite Monarchies," *Past and Present* 137, no. 1 (November 1992); and Daniel H. Nexon, *The Struggle for Power in Early Modern Europe: Religious Conflict, Dynastic Empires, and International Change* (Princeton, NJ, 2009), esp. chap. 2.

11. Conceptualizing imperial space as both an ideological construct, and a social and political sphere of interaction, follows the work of Edward W. Soja, *Postmodern Geographies: The Reassertion of Space in Critical Social Theory* (London, 1989), and Henri Lefebvre, *The Production of Space*, trans. Donald Nicholson-Smith (Malden, MA, 1991).

12. See, for example, Pelenski, *Russia and Kazan*; S. Kh. Alishev, *Kazan' i Moskva: Mezhgosudarstvennye otnosheniia v XV–XVI vv.* (Kazan, 1995); D. M. Iskhakov, *Tiurko-tatarskie gosudarstva XV–XVI vv.* (Kazan, 2009).

13. See, for example, I. P. Ermolaev, *Srednee Povolzh'e vo vtoroi polovine XVI–XVII vv. (Upravlenie Kazanskim kraem)* (Kazan, 1982); A. G. Bakhtin, *XV–XVI veka v istorii Mariiskogo kraia* (Ioshkar-Ola, 1998); Damir Iskhakov, *Ot srednevekovykh tatar k tataram novogo vremeni* (Kazan, 1998); E. P. Lezina, *Goroda na territorii mordovii v XVI–XVII vv.* (Saransk, 2002). For other regional studies, see a special issue of *Forschungen zur osteuropäischen Geschichte* 63 (2004), edited by Andreas Kappeler, *Die Geschichte Russlands im 16. und 17. Jahrhundert aus der Perspektive seiner Regionen*, though the individual articles tend to treat each group in isolation.

14. However, several of these studies still make noteworthy contributions. See, for example, S. Kh. Alishev, *Istoricheskie sudby narodov Srednego Povolzh'ia XVI–nachalo XIX v.* (Moscow, 1990); Aidar Nogmanov, *Tatary Srednego Pololzh'ia i Priural'ia v Rossiiskom zakonodatel'stve vtoroi poloviny XVI–XVIII vv.* (Kazan, 2002).

15. In addition to those mentioned above, see E. L. Dubman, *Khoziaistvennoe osvoenie Srednego Povolzh'ia v XVII veke: Po materialam tserkovno-monastyrskikh vladenii* (Kuibyshev, 1991); A. Akhmetov, *Agrarno-krest'ianskie otnosheniia i sotsial'no-politicheskoe razvitie simbirsko-ul'ianovskogo zavolzh'ia v XVII–XX vekakh* (Ul'ianovsk, 2004).

16. The exception is Andreas Kappeler, who took a broad view of the region, but considers the era between 1552 and the eighteenth century one of "status quo." See his *Russlands erste Nationalitäten: Das Zarenreich und die Völker der Mittleren Wolga vom 16. bis 19. Jahrhundert* (Cologne, 1982), 137–243.

17. Michael Khodarkovsky, *Where Two Worlds Met: The Russian State and the Kalmyk Nomads, 1600–1771* (Ithaca, NY, 1992); Michael Khodarkovsky, *Russia's Steppe Frontier: The Making of a Colonial Empire, 1500–1800* (Bloomington, IN, 2002); Willard Sunderland,

Taming the Wild Field: Colonization and Empire on the Russian Steppe (Ithaca, NY, 2004); Brian J. Boeck, *Imperial Boundaries: Cossack Communities and Empire-Building in the Age of Peter the Great* (Cambridge, 2009).

18. Valerie Kivelson, *Cartographies of Tsardom: The Land and its Meanings in Seventeenth-Century Russia* (Ithaca, NY, 2006); Christoph Witzenrath, *Cossacks and the Russian Empire, 1598–1725: Manipulation, Rebellion, and Expansion into Siberia* (London, 2007); Andrew A. Gentes, *Exile to Siberia, 1590–1822* (Houndsmills, Basingstoke, Hampshire, 2008).

19. Among the works on these regions, see Edward C. Thaden, *Russia's Western Borderlands, 1710–1870* (Princeton, NJ, 1984); Sean Pollock, "Empire by Invitation? Russian Empire-Building in the Caucasus in the Reign of Catherine II" (PhD diss., Harvard University, 2006).

20. For the changing imperial framework, see Richard Wortman, *Scenarios of Power: Myth and Ceremony in Russian Monarchy*, vol. 1 (Princeton, NJ, 1995), esp. 43–83.

21. For a survey of the literature on the "modern" empire, see Nicholas Breyfogle, "Enduring Imperium: Russia/Soviet Union/Eurasia as Multiethnic, Multiconfessional Space," *Ab Imperio*, no. 1 (2008).

22. Throughout the text, I have used terms such as "bureaucratization," "centralization," "cameralism," and "mercantilistic" in order to highlight the parallel developments in Muscovy with those in Europe more generally. I am not arguing that these ideas were universally applied or understood. Instead, my hope is to enable a broader discussion about the more general processes and transformations of the early-modern world.

Chapter 1. Imperial Ideas

1. For an introduction to the "new" monarchs, see Hendrik Spruyt, *The Sovereign State and Its Competitors: An Analysis of Systems Change* (Princeton, NJ, 1994).

2. For an introduction, see Alan Fisher, *The Crimean Tatars* (Stanford, CA, 1978), 1–57.

3. A. S. Morris, "The Medieval Emergence of the Volga-Oka Region," *Annals of the Association of American Geographers* 61 (1971).

4. Sergei Bogatyrev, "Reinventing the Russian Monarchy in the 1550s: Ivan the Terrible, the Dynasty, and the Church," *Slavonic and East European Review* 85 (2007); V. V. Trepavlov, *Belyi Tsar': Obraz monarkha i predstavleniia o poddanstve u narodov Rossii XV–XVIII vv.* (Moscow, 2007).

5. This idea appears in the first paragraph of Kotoshikhin's description of the Muscovite government. G. K. Kotoshikhin, *O Rossii v tsarstvovnanie Aleksei Mikhailovicha* (Moscow, 2000), 22.

6. For an introduction to identity in the Muscovite empire, see Michael Khodarkovsky, "Four Degrees of Separation: Constructing Non-Christian Identities in Muscovy," in *Culture and Identity in Muscovy, 1359–1584*, ed. Ann Kleimola and Gail Lenhoff (Moscow, 1997).

7. For an overview of Ivan IV's reign, see Andrei Pavlov and Maureen Perrie, *Ivan the Terrible* (New York, 2003); Isabel de Madariaga, *Ivan the Terrible: First Tsar of Russia* (New Haven, CT, 2006); Alexander Filjushkin, *Ivan the Terrible: A Military History* (London, 2008).

8. For a discussion of the legal issues of non-Russians in the empire, see Matthew P. Romaniello, "Ethnicity as Social Rank: Governance, Law, and Empire in Muscovite Russia," *Nationalities Papers* 34 (2006).

9. Geertz, "Centers, Kings, and Charisma."

10. The symbolic importance of claiming space has been a useful category of analysis in recent work. See Lefebvre, *Production of Space*; Soja, *Postmodern Geographies*; James C. Scott, *Seeing like a State: How Certain Schemes to Improve the Human Condition Have Failed* (New Haven, CT, 1998); Paolo Squatriti, "Digging Ditches in Early Medieval Europe," *Past and Present* 176, no. 1 (August 2002).

11. For other European contexts, see Korman, *Right of Conquest*.

12. Judith Herrin, *Byzantium: The Surprising Life of a Medieval Empire* (Princeton, NJ, 2008); Sarolta A. Takács, *The Construction of Authority in Ancient Rome and Byzantium: The Rhetoric of Empire* (New York, 2009).

13. For an engaging discussion of the legacy of Vladimir's conversion, see Francis Butler, *Enlightener of Rus': The Image of Vladimir Sviatoslavich across the Centuries* (Bloomington, IN, 2000).

14. John Fennell, *A History of the Russian Church to 1448* (Harlow, Essex, 1995), esp. 132–47. For the impact this had upon the emerging monarchy, see David B. Miller, "The Cult of Saint Sergius of Radonezh and its Political Uses," *Slavic Review* 52 (1993).

15. For a traditional interpretation of the acquisition of Byzantine culture, see Dmitri Obolensky, "Russia's Byzantine Heritage," *Oxford Slavonic Papers* 1 (1950); and Michael Cherniavsky, "Khan or Basileus: An Aspect of Russian Medieval Political Theory," *Journal of the History of Ideas* 20 (1959).

16. For a discussion of the debate over the use of the double-headed eagle, see Gustave Alef, "The Adoption of the Muscovite Two-Headed Eagle: A Discordant View," *Speculum* 41 (1966). For the use of this culture, see Michael Flier, "The Iconography of Royal Ritual in Sixteenth-Century Muscovy," in *Byzantine Studies: Essays on the Slavic World and the Eleventh Century*, ed. Speros Vryonis and Henrik Birnbaum (New Rochelle, NY, 1992); David B. Miller, "Creating Legitimacy: Ritual, Ideology, and Power in Sixteenth-Century Russia," *Russian History/Histoire Russe* 21 (1994); and Russell E. Martin, "Gifts for the Bride: Dowries, Diplomacy, and Marriage Politics in Muscovy," *Journal of Medieval and Early Modern Studies* 38 (2008).

17. There is a large debate on the legacy of Mongol influence in Muscovy. See Charles J. Halperin, *Russia and the Golden Horde: The Mongol Impact on Medieval Russian History* (Bloomington, IN, 1987); Donald Ostrowski, *Muscovy and the Mongols: Cross-Cultural Influences on the Steppe Frontier, 1304–1589* (New York, 1998); the debate among David Goldfrank, Halperin, and Ostrowski, in *Kritika* 1 (2000): 237–304; and Marlies Bilz-Leonhardt, "Deconstructing the Myth of the Tatar Yoke," *Central Asian Survey* 27 (2008).

18. For a discussion of Mongol administrative structures, see Thomas T. Allsen, *Mongol Imperialism: The Policies of the Grand Qan Möngke in China, Russia, and the Islamic Lands, 1251–1259* (Berkeley, 1987). For a study of the continuity among the Mongol successor states, see Mansura Haidar, *Medieval Central Asia: Polity, Economy, and Military Organization (Fourteenth to Sixteenth Centuries)* (New Delhi, 2004); Anne F. Broadbridge, *Kingship and Ideology in the Islamic and Mongol Worlds* (New York, 2008).

19. David DeWeese, *Islamization and Native Religion in the Golden Horde: Baba Tükles and Conversion to Islam in Historical and Epic Tradition* (University Park, PA, 1994).

20. For the history of this early period, see Robert O. Crummey, *The Formation of Muscovy, 1304–1613* (London, 1987).

21. Elliott, "A Europe of Composite Monarchies." See the discussion in Koenigsberger, *Politicians and Virtuosi*, 1–25.

22. Jan Glete, *War and the State in Early Modern Europe: Spain, the Dutch Republic, and Sweden as Fiscal-Military States, 1500–1660* (New York, 2002); Chester Dunning and Norman S. Smith, "Moving Beyond Absolutism: Was Early Modern Russia a 'Fiscal-Military' State?" *Russian History/Histoire Russe* 33 (2006).

23. Ann Kleimola, "Status, Place, and Politics: The Rise of Mestnichestvo during the *Boiarskoe Pravlenie*," *Forschungen zur osteuropäischen Geschichte* 27 (1980); Iu. M. Eskin, *Ocherki istorii mestnichestva v Rossii XVI–XVII vv.* (Moscow, 2009), esp. 138–90. For its implementation in the sixteenth and seventeenth centuries, see chaps. 2 and 4.

24. Horace W. Dewey, "The 1497 Sudebnik: Muscovite Russia's First National Law Code," *American Slavic and East European Review* 15 (1956).

25. Elliott, "A Europe of Composite Monarchies."

26. Pavlov and Perrie, *Ivan the Terrible*, 26–40.

27. Olga Novikova, "Le couronnement d'Ivan IV: La conception de l'empire à l'Est de l'Europe," *Cahiers du monde russe* 46, no. 1/2 (2005).

28. Works on this subject include Paul A. Bushkovitch, "The Epiphany Ceremony of the Russian Court in the Sixteenth and Seventeenth Centuries," *Russian Review* 49 (1990); Michael Flier, "Breaking the Code: The Image of the Tsar in the Muscovite Palm Sunday Ritual," in *Medieval Russian Culture*, vol. 2, ed. Michael S. Flier and Daniel Rowland (Berkeley, 1994); and Flier, "Golden Hall Iconography and the Makarian Influence," in *The New Muscovite Cultural History*, ed. Valerie Kivelson et al. (Bloomington, IN, 2009). For a recent revision of Ivan's court symbolism, see Bogatyrev, "Reinventing the Russian Monarchy."

29. A. A. Zimin, *Reformy Ivana Groznogo* (Moscow, 1960); Horace W. Dewey, "The 1550 Sudebnik as an Instrument of Reform," in *Government in Reformation Europe*, ed. Henry J. Cohn (New York, 1972).

30. For a discussion of the reforms, see Pavlov and Perrie, *Ivan the Terrible*, 55–78.

31. Paul Bushkovitch, *Religion and Society in Russia: The Sixteenth and Seventeenth Centuries* (New York, 1992), 22–26.

32. R. G. Skrynnikov, "Ermak's Siberian Expedition," *Russian History/Histoire Russe* 13

(1986). For a general history, see W. Bruce Lincoln, *The Conquest of a Continent: Siberia and the Russians* (New York, 1994).

33. Daniel B. Rowland, "Did Muscovite Literary Ideology Place Limits on the Power of the Tsar (1540s–1660s)?" *Russian Review* 49 (1990); Nancy S. Kollmann, "Pilgrimage, Procession and Symbolic Space in Sixteenth-Century Russian Politics," in Flier and Rowland, *Medieval Russian Culture*, vol. 2.

34. This is typical for early-modern monarchs. See Paul Kléber Monod, *The Power of Kings: Monarchy and Religion in Europe, 1589–1715* (New Haven, CT, 1999). For a discussion of this phenomena in Muscovy, see Valerie Kivelson, "Merciful Father, Impersonal State: Russian Autocracy in Comparative Perspective," *Modern Asian Studies* 31 (1997); and Donald Ostrowski, "The Façade of Legitimacy: Exchange of Power and Authority in Early Modern Russia," *Comparative Studies in Society and History* 44 (2002).

35. Donald Ostrowski, "The Mongol Origins of Muscovite Political Institutions," *Slavic Review* 46 (1987). For a more critical assessment of the Mongol legacy, see Horace W. Dewey, "Russia's Debt to the Mongols in Suretyship and Collective Responsibility," *Comparative Studies in Society and History* 30 (1988).

36. Trepavlov, *Belyi tsar'*. For a critique of this theory, see Charles J. Halperin, "Ivan IV and Chinggis Khan," *Jahrbücher für Geschichte Osteuropas* 51 (2003).

37. For recent histories of Muscovite geopolitical concerns, see Carol Stevens, *Russia's Wars of Emergence, 1460–1730* (New York, 2007), and Brian L. Davies, *Warfare, State, and Society on the Black Sea Steppe 1500–1700* (New York, 2007).

38. For an introduction into the competitive claims over the former Kievan lands, see Jaroslaw Pelenski, "The Incorporation of the Ukrainian Lands of Kievan Rus' into Crown Poland (1569)," in his *The Contest for the Legacy of Kievan Rus'* (Boulder, CO, 1998), 151–87.

39. For an introduction, see Alan Fisher, "The Ottoman Crimea in the Sixteenth Century," *Harvard Ukrainian Studies* 5 (1981).

40. For these early relations, see Edward Keenan, *Muscovy and Kazan' 1445–1552: A Study in Steppe Politics* (PhD diss., Harvard University, 1965); Pelenski, *Russia and Kazan*; and Alishev, *Kazan' i Moskva*.

41. Janet Martin, "Muscovite Frontier Policy: The Case of the Khanate of Kasimov," *Russian History* 19 (1992); Bulat Rakhimzianov, *Kasimovskoe khantsvo (1445–1552 gg.): Ocherki istorii* (Kazan, 2009).

42. For an introduction to the Tatars, see F. M. Sultanov, *Islam i Tatarskoe natsional'noe dvizhenie v Rossiiskom i mirovom musul'manskom kontekste: istoriia i sovremennost'* (Kazan, 1999); S. Kh. Alishev, *Ternistyi put' bor'by za svobodu (Sotsial'naia natsional'no-osvoditel'naia bor'ba Tatarskogo naroda. II polovina XVI–XIX vv.)* (Kazan, 1999).

43. V. D. Dmitriev, *Chuvashiia v epokhu feodalizma (XVI–nachale XIX vv.)* (Cheboksary, 1986); Masanori Goto, "Metamorphosis of Gods: A Historical Study on the Traditional Religion of the Chuvash," *Acta Slavica Iaponica* 24 (2007).

44. This certainly is the modern conception of the Chuvash nation, as seen in the celebration of Chuvashia's "union" with Moscow in 1551. Torrey Clark, "Chuvashia Fetes 450-Year Union with Russia," *Moscow Times*, 25 June 2001.

45. M. G. Ivanova, ed., *Finno-ugry Povolzh'ia i Priural'ia v srednie veka* (Izhevsk, 1999).

46. Ivanova, *Finno-ugry Povolzh'ia*, 115–60; and Ivan Smirnov, *Mordva: Istoriko-ethnograficheskii ocherk* (Saransk, 2002).

47. *Polnoe sobranie russkikh letopisei* (hereafter cited as *PSRL*), vol. 13, *L'vovskii letopis'* (St. Petersburg, 1862), 457–58, 460–61.

48. Filjushkin, *Ivan the Terrible*, esp. 92–112.

49. For a brief introduction to the Muscovite army and its limitations, see Thomas Esper, "Military Self-Sufficiency and Weapons Technology in Muscovite Russia," *Slavic Review* 28 (1969); Dianne L. Smith, "Muscovite Logistics, 1462–1598," *Slavonic and East European Review* 71 (1993); Michael C. Paul, "The Military Revolution in Russia, 1550–1682," *Journal of Military History* 68 (2004).

50. For a discussion of transformation of logistics and its consequences, see Geoffrey Parker, *The Military Revolution: Military Innovation and the Rise of the West, 1500–1800* (Cambridge, 1996).

51. The following narrative of the conquest is based on the later accounts written by one of Ivan's military commanders, as well as religious chronicles. J. L. I. Fennell, ed. and trans., *Prince A. M. Kurbsky's History of Ivan IV* (Cambridge, 1965), and several volumes of the *PSRL*.

52. This strategy resembled Timurid siege practices, another Mongol successor state. Haidar, *Medieval Central Asia*, 321–52.

53. *PSRL*, 13:505–6; Fennell, *Kurbsky's History of Ivan IV*, 54–55.

54. Heinrich von Staden, *The Land and Government of Muscovy: A Sixteenth-Century Account*, trans. and ed. Thomas Esper (Stanford, 1967), 56–57.

55. See the account of the battle in Fennell, *Kurbsky's History of Ivan IV*, 59–71; and *PSRL*, vol. 13, pt. 1, 251.

56. *PSRL*, vol. 13, pt. 1, 251.

57. In particular, see Pelenski, *Russia and Kazan*.

58. Makarii Veretennikov, *Moskovskii mitropolit Makarii i ego vremia* (Moscow, 1996). For Makarii's specific plans for Kazan, see Pelenski, *Russia and Kazan*, 177–96. *PSRL*, vol. 29, *Letopisets nachala tsarstva tsaria i velikogo kniazia Ivan Vasil'evich* (Moscow, 1965), 58.

59. *Dopolneniia k aktam istoricheskim, sobranniia i izdaniia arkheograficheskoiu kommisseiu* (St. Petersburg, 1846), 1:27–30, no. 28, 25 March 1534.

60. *PSRL*, 29:58.

61. *Akty istoricheskie, sobrannye i izdannye arkheograficheskoiu kommissieiu* (St. Petersburg, 1841), 1:287–90, no. 159, 25 May 1552; see also a later epistle, 1:290–96, no. 160, 13 to 20 July 1552. In addition to the metropolitan, Archbishop Fedosii of Novgorod called a campaign against the Tatars as early as 1545/46. *Dopolneniia k aktam*, 1:38–40, no. 37.

62. Kollmann, "Pilgrimage, Procession," 177.

63. Saratov State University Library (hereafter cited as SGU), SGU 1073, *Sbornik*, 1630s–1650s, "Life of Gurii and Varsonofii," ff. 156r.–167r., available on microfilm at the Hilandar Research Library, Columbus, OH.

64. *PSRL*, 29:234–35.

65. Apollon Mozharovskii, "Izlozhenie khoda missionerskago dela po prosveshcheniiu khristianstvom kazanskikh inorodtsev s 1552 do 1867 god," in *Chteniia v imperatorskom obshchestve* (Moscow, 1880), 11. A short version of these events stressing the procession of Makarii, Ivan IV, and Gurii with important icons to the Frolovskii gates is found in *PSRL*, 29:240.

66. For a discussion of the independence of Russian Orthodox bishops in the Muscovite era, see Georg B. Michels, "Rescuing the Orthodox: The Church Policies of Archbishop Afanasii of Kholmogory, 1682–1702," in *Of Religion and Empire: Missions, Conversion, and Tolerance in Tsarist Russia*, ed. Robert P. Geraci and Michael Khodarkovsky (Ithaca, NY, 2001); and Georg B. Michels, "Ruling Without Mercy: Seventeenth-Century Russian Bishops and Their Officials," *Kritika* 4 (2003).

67. *PSRL*, vol. 20, *L'vovskaia letopis'*, 481–82; *PSRL*, vol. 21, *Kniga stepennaia tsarskogo rodosloviia*, pt. 2, 650–51.

68. SGU 1073, ff. 156r.–158r.; Mozharovskii, "Izlozhenie khoda," 12–13.

69. SGU 1073, ff. 160r.–163r.; Mozharovskii, "Izlozhenie khoda," 13–14.

70. For a thorough analysis of this icon and the development of Orthodoxy's Church Militant, see Daniel Rowland, "Biblical Military Imagery in the Political Culture of Early Modern Russia: The Blessed Host of the Heavenly Tsar," in Flier and Rowland, *Medieval Russian Culture*.

71. For a discussion of the Church, see Michael S. Flier, "Filling in the Blanks: The Church of the Intercession and the Architectonics of Medieval Muscovite Ritual," *Harvard Ukrainian Studies* 19 (1995).

72. *PSRL*, vol. 19, *Istoriia o Kazanskom tsartsve* (Moscow, 2000); a full description of its publication history is in D. S. Likhachev, ed., *Slovar' knizhnikov i knizhnosti drevnei Rusi*, vol. 2, *Vtoraia polovina XIV–XVI v.*, pt. 1, *A–K* (Leningrad, 1988), 450–58. For a discussion of the religious imagery in the text, see Daniel Rowland, "The Memory of St. Sergius in Sixteenth-Century Russia," in *The Trinity-Sergius Lavra in Russian History and Culture*, ed. Vladimir Tsurikov (Jordanville, NY, 2005), esp. 59–60.

73. Hilandar Research Library, Columbus, OH, Aronov Collection, no. 18, *Chronograph*, last quarter of the seventeenth century. The text from ff. 10r.–722v. closely resembles the *Stepennaia kniga* of the sixteenth century, published in *PSRL*, vol. 21, pts. 1 and 2 (St. Petersburg, 1908–13).

74. *The Voyage of Master Anthony Jenkinson*, http://depts.washington.edu/silkroad/ texts/jenkinson/bukhara.html#moscow, reproduced from Richard Hakluyt's *The Principal Navigations, Voyages, Traffiques and Discoveries of the English Nation*, 12 vols. (Glasgow, 1903–5), 2:449–79.

75. The traditional narrative of Russia's eastward expansion can be summed up as "first Kazan, then the Pacific." This argument was first suggested by V. O. Kliuchevskii in his *Kurs russkoi istorii* (reprint, Moscow, 1956), and repeated often in English-language literature. See, for example, Robert Kerner, *The Urge to the Sea: The Role of Rivers, Portages, Ostrogs, Monasteries and Furs* (New York, 1942), and Joseph Wieczynski, *The Russian Frontier: The*

Impact of the Borderlands upon the Course of Early Russian History (Charlottesville, VA, 1976).

76. See chap. 4.

77. Michael Khodarkovsky, "Not by World Alone: Missionary Policies and Religious Conversion in Early Modern Russia," *Comparative Studies in Society and History* 38 (1996): 273; Madariaga, *Ivan the Terrible*, 239 and 266–67. For an example of the conciliatory language of the tsar, see F. Lashkov, ed., *Pamiatniki diplomaticheskikh snoshenii Krymskago khanstva s Moskovskim gosudarstvom v XVI i XVII vv.* (Simferopol', 1891), 31–34, no. 129, 1593.

78. For a history of the Khanate of Astrakhan before its conquest in 1556, see I. V. Zaitsev, *Astrakhanskoe khanstvo* (Moscow, 2004).

79. Part of the Ottoman response was military. See A. N. Kurat, "The Turkish Expedition to Astrakhan in 1569, and the Problem of the Don-Volga Canal," *Slavonic and East European Review* 40 (1961); Allan Fisher, "Muscovite-Ottoman Relations in the Sixteenth and Seventeenth Centuries," *Humaniora Islamica* 1 (1973). In addition, the conquest of Astrakhan added to the ongoing tensions between the Ottomans and Safavids. See Carl M. Kortepeter, "Ottoman Imperial Policy in the Black Sea Region in the Sixteenth Century," *Journal of the American Oriental Society* 86, no. 2 (1966).

80. See Matthew P. Romaniello, "Mission Delayed: The Russian Orthodox Church after the Conquest of Kazan," *Church History* 76 (2007).

81. Alishev, *Ternistyi put' bor'by*, 12–21; Sultanov, *Islam i Tatarskoe natsional'noe dvizhenie*, 50–56.

82. Kurbskii's account is reprinted in N. L. Rubinshtein, ed., *Istoriia Tatarii v materialakh i dokumentakh* (Moscow, 1937), 124–25.

83. *PSRL*, 13:269–70, 281–82.

84. At the end of the sixteenth century, a mosque still sat outside of Kazan's walls. *Akty, sobrannye v bibliotekakh i arkhivakh Rossiiskoi Imperii Arkheograficheskoiu ekspeditsieiu* vol. 1, *1294–1598* (St. Petersburg, 1856), 436–39, no. 358, 18 July 1595.

85. The Tatar district was established at least by 1565. See S. G. Tomsinskii, ed., *Materialy po istorii Tatarskoi ASSR: Pistsovye knigi goroda Kazani 1565–68 gg. i 1646 g.* (Leningrad, 1932), and I. P. Ermolaev's analysis of the data in his "Gorod Kazan' no pistsovoi knige 1565–1568 godov," in *Stranitsy istorii goroda Kazani*, ed. M. A. Usanov (Kazan, 1981).

86. For a discussion of the ethnolinguistic minorities and the new towns, see A. N. Zorin, *Gorozhane Srednego Povolzh'ia vo vtoroi polovine XVI–nachale XX v.: Istoriko-ethnograficheskii ocherk* (Kazan, 1992); Lezina, *Goroda na territorii mordovii*. For a general discussion of town fortifications in Muscovy, see N. F. Gluiantskii, ed., *Gradostroitel'stvo Moskovskogo gosudarstva XVI–XVII vekov* (Moscow, 1994).

87. *Akty Moskovoskago gosudarstva*, vol. 1, *Razriadnyi prikaz, Moskovskii stol', 1571–1631* (St. Petersburg, 1890), 1–2, no. 1, 1 January 1571.

88. For an estimate of the expenses involved in a later defensive line, see Richard Hellie, "The Costs of Muscovite Military Defense and Expansion," in *The Military and Society in Russia, 1450–1917*, ed. Eric Lohr and Marshall Poe (Leiden, 2002), 41–66.

89. By the seventeenth century, these decisions were fully documented, whereas the sixteenth century records are much rarer. See the instructions to the first governor of Simbirsk, established as the final settlement of the region's second (more southern) defensive line. M. F. Superanskii, *Simbirsk i ego proshloe (1648–1898 gg.)* (Simbirsk, 1898), 3–7.

90. D. J. B. Shaw, "Southern Frontiers of Muscovy, 1550–1700," in *Studies in Russian Historical Geography*, vol. 1, ed. R. A. French and James Bater (London, 1983).

91. For example, the archbishop of Kazan was assigned responsibility for maintaining the stone towers of Kazan's two oldest monasteries, the Zilantov Uspenskii and the Spaso-Preobrazhenskii. Russian State Archive of Ancient Acts, Moscow (hereafter cited as RGADA), f. 281, Gramoty kollegii ekonomii, op. 4, d. 6432, 25 January 1595.

92. Monasteries' ability to connect towns and their hinterlands have been explored in Ross Balzaretti, "Cities, Emporia and Monasteries: Local Economies in the Po Valley, c. AD 700–875," in *Towns in Transition: Urban Evolution in Late Antiquity and the Early Middle Ages*, ed. N. Christie and S. T. Loseby (Brookfield, VT, 1996).

93. In one study of monastic landholding in Simbirsk and Samara districts, E. L. Dubman claims that all land granted to monasteries in those regions was settled with Tatars and Mordvins peasants. Dubman, *Khoziaistvennoe osvoenie srednego Povolzh'ia*, 13.

94. K. Nevostruev, comp., *Istoricheskoe opisanie byvshikh v gorode Samara muzheskogo Spaso-Preobrazhenskago i zhenskago Spasskogo monastyrei* (Moscow, 1867), 3.

95. RGADA, f. 281, op. 1, d. 260, 24 March 1630.

96. These arrangements were reviewed in a document sent to Metropolitan Germogen later in the sixteenth century. RGADA, f. 281, op. 4, d. 6432, 25 January 1595.

97. A. Vladmirskii, ed., *Tserkovniia drevnosti g. Kazani* (Kazan, 1887), 21–28.

98. E. A. Malov, *Kazanskii Bogoroditskii devich' monastyr': Istoriia i sovremennoe ego sostoianie* (Kazan, 1879), 3. For more on this icon, see chap. 4.

99. A. V. Khlebnikov et al., eds., *Istoriia Mariiskoi ASSR*, vol. 1, *Sredneishikh vremen do Velikoi Oktiabr'skoi sotsialisticheskoi revoliutsii* (Ioshkar-Ola, 1986), 66–73; G. N. Aiplatov, "'Cheremisskie voiny' vtoroi poloviny XVI v. v otechestvennoi istoriografii," in *Voprosy istorii narodov Povolzh'ia i Priural'ia*, ed. Iu. P. Smirnov (Cheboksary, 1997); Bakhtin, *XV–XVI veka v istorii.*

100. N. F. Akaemov, "Gorod Kurmysh v XIV–XVIII vekakh," *Izvestiia obshchestva arkheologii, istorii i etnografii pri Kazanskom universitete* 11, no. 6 (1894).

101. *PSRL*, vol. 14, *Nikonskaia letopis'—ukazateli v IX–XIV vv.* (Moscow, 1910), 34.

102. For one description of the construction of a new outpost, see A. A. Andreianov, *Gorod Tsarevokokshaisk: Stranitsy istorii (Konets XVI–nachalo XVIII veka)* (Ioshkar-Ola, 1991), 15–17.

103. For a comparison to other monarchies, see Patricia Seed, *Ceremonies of Possession in Europe's Conquest of the New World, 1492–1640* (Cambridge, 1995).

104. See, for example, Alton S. Donnelly, *The Russian Conquest of Bashkiria, 1552–1740* (New Haven, CT, 1968); B. A. Kochekaev, *Nogaisko-Russkie otnosheniia v XV–XVIII vv.* (Alma-Ata, 1988); and Khodarkovsky, *Russia's Steppe Frontier.*

105. For a history of the entire era, see Chester S. L. Dunning, *Russia's First Civil War: The Time of Troubles and the Founding of the Romanov Dynasty* (University Park, PA, 2001).

106. Work on the Bolotnikov revolt includes I. I. Smirnov, *Vosstanie Bolotnikova, 1606–1607* (Leningrad, 1951); A. I. Kopanev and A. G. Man'kov, eds., *Vosstanie I. Bolotnikova: Dokumenty i materialy* (Moscow, 1959); Paul Avrich, *Russian Rebels 1600–1800* (New York, 1972), 1–49; Maureen Perrie, *Pretenders and Popular Monarchism in Early Modern Russia: The False Tsars of the Time of Troubles* (Cambridge, 1995), 120–81; Dunning, *Russia's First Civil War*, 261–384.

107. Dunning, *Russia's First Civil War*, 287–91. For a contemporary report of the effort needed to reclaim Cheboksary from Tatar and Mari rebels, see Rubinshtein, *Istoriia Tatarii*, 367, 1 January 1609.

108. Isaac Massa, *A Short History of the Beginnings and Origins of These Present Wars in Moscow under the Reign of Various Sovereigns down to the Year 1610*, trans. and ed. G. Edward Orchard (Toronto, 1982), 164.

109. *A Chronicle of the Carmelites in Persia and the Papal Mission of the XVIIth and XVIIIth Centuries* (London, 1939), 1:104–13; P. Pierling, *La Russie et le Saint-Siège: Ètudes diplomatiques* (Paris, 1901), 3:237–39; P. Pierling, *Iz smutnago vremeni: Stati i zametki* (St. Petersburg, 1902), 64–66; Perrie, *Pretenders and Popular Monarchism*, 132, 144–49.

110. I. E. Zabelin, *Minin i Pozharskii: Priamye i krivye v Smutnoe vremia* (Moscow, 1999).

111. V. D. Dmitriev, "Uchastie naseleniia Chuvashii v bor'be protiv Pol'skoi i Shvedskoi interventsii v nachale XVII veka," *Voprosy drevnei i srednevkovoi istorii Chuvashii* 105 (1980).

Chapter 2. Conflicted Authorities

1. This chapter's first epigraph comes from Russian State Archive of Ancient Acts, Moscow (hereafter cited as RGADA), f. 16, Gosudarstvennyi arkhiv, r. XVI, vnutrennee upravlenie, op. 1, d. 709, ll. 40b.–5, copy from 1720. There are five extant *nakazy* for Kazan from the seventeenth century: the first four are reprinted in V. D. Dmitriev, ed., "Tsarskie nakazy Kazanskim voevodam XVII veka," *Istoriia i kul'tura Chuvashskoi ASSR: Sbornik statei* 3 (1974); the fifth is reprinted in *Polnoe sobranie zakonov Russiskoi Imperii* (hereafter cited as *PSZ*), series 1, vol. 3 (St. Petersburg, 1830), 284–303, no. 1582, 22 April 1697.

2. For a thorough examination of the transformation during the Time of Troubles, see D. B. Liseitsev, *Prikaznaia sistema Moskovskogo gosudarstva v epokhu Smuty* (Tula, 2009).

3. Glete, *War and the State in Early Modern Europe*, 10–41; Dunning and Smith, "Moving Beyond Absolutism."

4. V. D. Dmitriev, "Vosstanie iasachnykh liudei Srednego Povolzh'ia i Priural'ia 1615–1616 godov," *Voprosy drevnei i srednevkovoi istorii Chuvashii* 105 (1980); Alishev, *Ternistyi put' bor'by*, 27–28.

5. Braudel, *Mediterranean*, 2:355–94.

6. The argument for "consensus politics" in Moscow is extensive. Sergei Bogatyrev, *The Sovereign and His Counselors: Ritualized Consultations in Muscovite Political Culture, 1350s–1570s* (Helsinki, 2000).

7. For an overview of the chancelleries, see Michael Rywkin, "Russian Central Colonial Administration: From the *prikaz* of Kazan to the XIX Century, A Survey," in *Russian Colonial Expansion to 1917*, ed. Michael Rywkin (London, 1988).

8. N. F. Demidova, *Sluzhiliia biurokratiia v Rossii XVII v. i ee rol' v formirovanii absolutizma* (Moscow, 1987); L. F. Pisar'kova, *Gosudarstvennoe upravlenie Rossii s kontsa XVII do kontsa XVIII veka: Evolutsiia biurokraticheskoi sistemy* (Moscow, 2007), 27–84.

9. This is how the government is explained, for example, by Giles Fletcher after his visit to Moscow in 1588–89, Fletcher, *Of the Russe Commonwealth* (1591), repr. in *Rude and Barbarous Kingdom: Russia in the Accounts of Sixteenth-Century English Voyagers*, ed. Lloyd E. Berry and Robert O. Crummey (Madison, 1968); see esp. 146–53. This has become the traditional narrative of the bureaucracy, as noted in Rwykin, "Russian Central Colonial Administration," 8.

10. The estimate of the chancelleries in 1647 comes from *The Travels of Olearius in Seventeenth-Century Russia*, trans. and ed. Samuel H. Baron (Stanford, 1967), 218–32; and the number in 1667 was given by G. K. Kotoshikhin before his death in Sweden, in his *O Rossii v tsartvovanie Alekseiia Mikhailovicha*, 107–47.

11. For a brief discussion of the fluctuating number of chancelleries, see Peter B. Brown, "Muscovite Government Bureaus," *Russian History/Histoire Russe* 10 (1983): 272–73, esp. n.7.

12. *Akty istoricheskie*, 3:398–99, no. 240, 13 March 1645.

13. *PSZ*, vol. 1, 499, no. 282, 12 September 1660.

14. I. P. Ermolaev and D. A. Mustafina, eds., *Dokumenty po istorii Kazanskogo kraia: Iz arkhivokhranilits Tatarskogo ASSR (vtoraia polovina XVI–seredina XVII): Teksty i komment* (Kazan, 1990), 135–36, no. 60, no earlier than September 1641.

15. Ibid., 44, no. 10.

16. Ibid., 45, no. 11, 25 August 1585. The year 1585 proved to be an unfortunate one for Istomka Khvostov, who was informed that his request for *pomest'e* was denied on 13 September, and was instead offered six rubles as compensation for his service. See Ermolaev and Mustafina, *Dokumenty po istorii Kazanskogo kraia*, 46, no. 12.

17. For example, see the instruction to Kokshaisk for 1634, repr. in *Nakaz gosudaria, tsaria Mikhaila Fedorovicha, dannyi na upravlenie g. Kokshaiskom s uezdom, chuvashskimi i cheremisskimi volostiami*, ed. I. D. Preobrazhenskii (Kostroma, 1913). See also the discussion in Ananii Ivanov, "Razvitie regiona Mariiskogo Povolzh'ia v sostave Rossiiskogo gosudarstva vo vtoroi polovine XVI–XVII vv.," *Forschungen zur osteuropäischen Geschichte* 63 (2004).

18. All are found in RGADA, f. 16, op. 1, d. 709, copy from 1720.

19. With the exception of different names in the first clause concerning the arrival of the new *voevody*, these two *nakazy* are comprised of the exact same articles. RGADA, f. 16, op. 1, d. 709, copy from 1720; ll. 36–111 is from 1677, ll. 1150b.–181 is from 1687.

20. Both topics were included in all of the *nakazy* to Kazan, except for the one from 1613, which did not include an article reminding the *voevoda* of his loyalty to the Prikaz. In 1613, power was given to *Voevoda* Iurii Petrovich Ushatyi and *d'iak* Stepan Dichkov. RGADA, f. 16, op. 1, d. 709, copy from 1720, l. 3a. In the *nakaz* for 1649, the first article (f. 16, ll. 6–60b.) is the direction for turning over the keys to the new *voevoda*; the second article (f. 16, ll. 60b.–8) is the article directing all residents to give their loyalty to the new *voevoda*; and the third article (f. 16, ll. 8–80b.) reminds the new *voevoda* that his loyalty belongs to the tsar and the Prikaz Kazanskogo dvortsa. For 1677, the first three clauses cover the same instructions as 1649, f. 16, ll. 360b.–38.

21. Ermolaev and Mustafina, *Dokumenty po istorii Kazanskogo kraia*, 54–55, no. 19.

22. RGADA, f. 16, op. 1, d. 709, ll. 380b.–390b.

23. RGADA, f. 16, op. 1, d. 709, ll. 3a–5, 16 April 1613.

24. RGADA, f. 16, op. 1, d. 709, ll. 3a. ob.–4.

25. RGADA, f. 16, op. 1, d. 709, ll. 40b.–5.

26. G. N. Anpilogov, "Polozhenie gorodskogo i sel'skogo naseleniia Kurskogo uezda nakanune vosstaniia 1648 g.," *Vestnik Moskovskogo universiteta*, series 9, *Istoriia*, no. 5 (1972); N. N. Pokrovskii, *Tomsk 1648–1649 gg.: Voevodskaia vlast' i zemskie miry* (Novosibirsk, 1989); Valerie A. Kivelson, "The Devil Stole His Mind: The Tsar and the 1648 Moscow Uprising," *American Historical Review* 98 (1993).

27. Though the rebellion in Astrakhan has not been studied, the Swedish envoy in Moscow recorded the departure of troops for Astrakhan, indicated the scope of the rebellion was more than local authorities could handle. K. Iakubov, "Rossiia i Shvetsiia v pervoi polovine XVII vv., VI: 1647–1650 gg. Doneseniia koroleve Khristine i pis'ma k korolevskomu sekretariu shvedskogo rezidenta v Moskve Karla Pommereninga," *Chteniia v imperatorskom obshchestve istorii i drevnostei rossiskikh pri Moskovskom universitete* 1 (1898): 430, no. 13, 14 November 1648.

28. RGADA, f. 16, op. 1, d. 709, ll. 10–11, 16 May 1649, copy from 1720.

29. Ibid., ll. 9–12. The same articles were included in the *nakaz* from 1677 (f. 16, op. 1, d. 709, ll. 390b.–420b., 570b.–61), but added several more restrictions discussed below.

30. Ibid., ll. 11–12, 270b.–28.

31. Ibid., ll. 12–130b.

32. Ibid., ll. 22–24.

33. Ibid., ll. 21–210b., 240b.–26, 30.

34. Ibid., ll. 270b.–28. An account of the fire and its destruction of the monastery can be found in the monastery's official history, P. Azletskii, comp., *Opisanie Ioanno-Predtechenskogo muzhskogo monastyria v gorode Kazani* (Kazan, 1898), 4–7.

35. For example, the original site of the Zilantov Monastery outside of the city suffered regular floods, forcing the abbot to seek permission to move its church. G. Z. Kuntsevich, comp., "Gramoty Kazanskogo Zilantova monastyria," *Izvestiia obshchestva arkheologii, istorii i etnografii pri Imperatorskom Kazanskom universitete* 17 (1901): 270–72, 19 June 1560.

36. See chap. 3.

37. RGADA, f. 16, op. 1, d. 709, ll. 12–140b., 140b.–21, 270b.–28, and 320b.–350b. By comparison, the *nakazy* of 1613 only had one clause on tax or trade, and it included these specific instructions. RGADA, f. 16, op. 1, d. 709, ll. 4–40b.

38. Anyone caught selling such liquor was to be jailed. RGADA, f. 16, op. 1, d. 709, l. 140b.

39. RGADA, f. 16, op. 1, d. 709, l. 3a ob.

40. The *nakaz* claimed the ability to settle boundary disputes for the tsar, but, in actuality, the "tsar" would mean the Sudnyi prikaz, the Pomestnyi prikaz, or the Prikaz Kazanskogo dvortsa, depending on their specific claims of authority against one another. RGADA, f. 16, op. 1, d. 709, l. 24.

41. Also, if a person claimed land from a monastery, that was for the monastery to settle and the *voevoda* should not be involved. RGADA, f. 16, op. 1, d. 709, ll. 30–320b.

42. Although Arzamas was outside the authority of the Prikaz Kazanskogo dvortsa, its *voevoda* had similar judicial authority. See Nancy Shield Kollmann, "Judicial Authority in the Criminal Law: Beloozero and Arzamas," *Forschungen zur osteuropäischen Geschichte* 63 (2004), esp. 64–68.

43. For a discussion of the transition to cameralism, see Michel Foucault, *Power/Knowledge*, ed. Colin Gordon (New York, 1980), 78–108.

44. This article had the benefit of not only stopping raiding nomads but also providing a mechanism for finding and capturing runaway peasants. This clause first appeared in 1649's *nakaz*, and then in the remainder of the *nakazy*. RGADA, f. 16, op. 1, d. 709, l. 30.

45. Donnelly, *Russian Conquest of Bashkiria*, 19–33.

46. See, for example, Witzenrath, *Cossacks and the Russian Empire*, 45–49, 70–78.

47. See, for example, Khodarkovsky, *Where Two Worlds Met*, 74–99.

48. For a discussion of the Russian Orthodox Church hierarchy, see Bushkovitch, *Religion and Society*, 51–73.

49. For the biography of a sixteenth century *voevoda*, see E. L. Dubman, *Kniaz' Grigorii Zasekin (Khronika zhizhni i deiatel'nosti stroitelia volzhskikh gorodov)* (Samara, 1995).

50. For a more thorough description, see Robert O. Crummey, *Aristocrats and Servitors: The Boyar Elite in Russia, 1613–1689* (Princeton, NJ, 1983), 34–64; Nancy Shields Kollmann, *By Honor Bound: State and Society in Early Modern Russia* (Ithaca, NY, 1999), esp. 131–67; Eskin, *Ocherki istorii mestnichestva*, esp. 281–348.

51. For a discussion of the Duma ranks and the possibility of a meritocracy, see Marshall T. Poe, *The Russian Elite in the Seventeenth Century*, vol. 2, *A Quantitative Analysis of the 'Duma Ranks' 1613–1713* (Helsinki, 2004), esp. 24–30.

52. For a discussion on the evolution of the office of *voevoda* in the sixteenth century, see Brian L. Davies, "The Town Governors of Ivan IV," *Russian History/Histoire Russe* 14 (1987), esp. 107–19.

53. For these revolts, see chap. 1.

54. S. I. Porfir'ev, "Spiski voevod i d'iakov po Kazani i Sviiazhsku, sostavlennye v XVII stoletii," *Izvestiia obshchestva arkheologii, istorii i etnografii pri Imperatorskom Kazanskom universitete* 27 (1911).

55. Marshall T. Poe, with Ol'ga Kosheleva, Russell Martin, and Boris Mironov, *The Russian Elite in the Seventeenth Century*, vol. 1, *The Consular and Ceremonial Ranks of the Russian "Sovereign's Court" 1613–1713* (Helsinki, 2004), 107, 111, 113, 115, 161, 199.

56. The four are Ivan Ivanovich Golitsyn (1602), Ivan Andreivich Golitsyn (1639–41), Aleksei Andreivich Golitsyn (1670–73), and Andrei Ivanovich Golitsyn (1682). V. D. Korsakov, comp., "Spisok nachal'stuiushchikh lits v gorodakh tepereshnei Kazanskoi gubernii: S 1553 g. do obrazovaniia Kazanskoi gubernii v 1708 g.," *Izvestiia obshchestva arkheologii, istorii i etnografii pri Imperatorskom Kazanskom universitet* 24 (1908): prilozhenie, 4.

57. Prince Iu. A. Dolgorukov in 1669/70; Poe, *Russian Elite*, 1:215.

58. All in 1669/70. See Poe, *The Russian Elite*, 1:215-16.

59. G. P. Peterson, *Istoricheskii ocherk Kerenskogo kraia* (Penza, 1882), 78.

60. Aleksandr Barsukov, comp., *Spiski gorodovykh voevod i drugikh lits voevodskago upraveleniia Moskovskago gosudarstva XVII stoletiia* (St. Petersburg, 1902), 169–70. Also, Barsukov's data produces a low average for "Lomov": 1.3 years, or 38 *voevody* from 1644 to 1693. However, Barsukov combined Nizhnii and Verknhii Lomov as one site, though it was two outposts in the seventeenth century. Therefore, the average should be 2.6, more in keeping with the other outposts.

61. As discussed in chap. 1.

62. Poe, *Russian Elite*, 1:456.

63. The data set has been compiled from S. V. Veselovskii, *D'iaki i pod'iachie XV–XVII vv.* (Moscow, 1975). This is an incomplete listing. The conclusions reached are indications of a pattern, not numerical absolutes.

64. Thanks to David Goldfrank for the suggested identity of Janibeg Mirza. It is impossible to be 100 percent accurate in uncovering ethnolinguistic identity from registry lists. All last names were "Russianized" with at least an "-ov" ending, though certain names, such as Rakhimgullov might appear Tatar, Asanov less so. Frequently, non-Russians adopted place names (such as Arzamasov or Kazantsov), but Russian peasants could just as easily do so.

65. A. A. Geraklitov, "Spisok Saratovskikh i Tsaritsynskikh voevod XVII v.," *Trudy Saratovskoi uchenoi arkhivnoi komissii* 30 (1913): 81.

66. Veselovskii, *D'iaki i pod'iachie*, 324–25, 410, 489, 585.

67. Peterson, *Istoricheskii ocherk Kerenskogo kraia*, 14–19.

68. E. Cherkashin, *Patriarkh Germogen: K 300 letiiu so dnia smerti 1612–1912* (Moscow, 1912); and Vasilii Borin, *Sviateishii Patriarkh Germogen i mesto ego zakliucheniia* (Moscow, 1913).

69. Azletskii, *Opisanie Ioanno-Predtechensoi muzhskogo monastyria*, 4–7.

70. The authorship of the tales and their development into national cults is briefly discussed in Pelenski, *Russia and Kazan*, 269–75; Bushkovitch, *Religion and Society*, 87–88, 108–10, and 214–15; and R. G. Skrynnikov, *Gosudarstvo i tserkov' na Rusi XIV–XVI vv.* (Novosibirsk, 1991), 248–50.

71. The tale is published in *Polnoe sobranie russkikh letopisei*, vol. 14, *Nikonskaia letopis'* (St. Petersburg, 1910), 132–33. The tale is briefly discussed in Pelenski, *Russia and Kazan*, 273.

72. RGADA, f. 281, Gramoty kollegii ekonomii, op. 4, d. 6432, 25 January 1595; and RGADA, f. 281, op. 4, d. 6432, 25 January 1595. Germogen also received updates from Patriarch Iov concerning current political developments in Moscow. RGADA, f. 156, Istoricheskie i tseremonial'nye dela, d. 76, 1598.

73. Gurii and Varsonofii were not included in the *Ustav* of 1602 but were included in 1610 after Germogen's tenure as Patriarch. Bushkovitch suggests it that the inclusion was to bolster support in the Middle Volga Region during the Bolotnikov Revolt, but Germogen's inclusion of local saints whose cult he established should also be considered a factor. See Bushkovitch, *Religion and Society*, 87–88.

74. I. F. Tokmakov, comp., *Istoriko-statisticheskoe i arkheologicheskoe opisanie Sviato-Troitskogo muzhskogo monastyria v gorode Alatyre, Simbirskogo gubernii* (Moscow, 1897), 10–16; I. N. Chetyrkin, ed., *Istoriko-Statisticheskoe opisanie Arzamasskoi Alekseevskoi zhenskoi obshchiny* (Nizhnii Novgorod, 1887), 7.

75. While the date of German's addition to the miracle cult of Gurii and Varsonofii is uncertain, it was completed by 1678. In a letter to Metropolitan Ioasaf of Kazan in 1678 concerning the construction of a new cathedral for the Kazan Mother of God Icon, thanks are given to "Gurii and Varsonofii and German Kazan miracle workers." *Akty iuridicheskie, ili sobranie form starinnago deloproizvozstva* (St. Petersburg, 1838), 400–401, no. 380, 12 August 1678. For a discussion of German's career before and during his time as archbishop until his death during the *Oprichnina*, see A. A. Zimin, *Oprichnina* (Moscow, 2001), 157–59.

76. On 13 August 1555, the tsar granted Gurii 2,000 *cheti* of land, fishing rights, and the villages of Kadysh, Karaish, and Karadulat for the financial security of the bishopric. *Akty istoricheskie*, 1:298–99, no. 162.

77. S. Nurminskii, "Vliianie monastyrei na raselenie narodnoe v Kazanskom krae," *Pravoslavnyi sobesiednik* 1, no. 2 (1864): 184.

78. RGADA, f. 281, op. 4, d. 6451, August 1616; and RGADA, f. 281, op. 4, d. 6452, 10 May 1618.

79. I. M. Pokrovskii, "K voprosy o naspedstvennom prave tserkovnykh uchrezhdenii, v chastnosti Kazanskago Arkhiereiskago doma, v kontse XVII veka," *Izvestiia obshchestva arkheologii, istorii i etnografii pri Imperatorskom Kazanskom universitete* 18, nos. 1–3 (1902): 4–5.

80. Azletskii, *Opisanie Ioanno-Predtechenskogo muzhskogo monastyria*, 46.

81. Tokmakov, *Istoriko-statisticheskoe opisanie Sviato-Troitskago monastyria*, 17–18.

82. A. Iablokov, *Pervoklassnyi muzhskii Uspensko-Bogoroditskii monastyr v gorode Sviiazhske, Kazanskoi gubernii* (Kazan, 1907), 157–58.

83. Ermolaev and Mustafina, *Dokumenty po istorii Kazanskogo kraia*, 28–29, no. 1, 16 May 1555.

84. Episkop Nikaron, ed., "Vladennyia gramaty Kazanskago Spasopreobrazhenskago monastyria," *Izvestiia obshchestva arkheologii, istorii, i etnografii pri Imperatorskom Kazanskom universitete* 11 (1893): 357.

85. RGADA, f. 281, op. 4, d. 6457, 5 March 1627.

86. RGADA, f. 281, op. 7, d. 10797.

87. This was the specific condition of the legal authority of the Kazanskii Zilantov-Uspenskii Monastery over its village of Kinder, from a *gramota* granting its legal privileges on 28 February 1585. Kuntsevich, "Gramoty Kazanskogo Zilantova monastyria," 272–74.

88. Ermolaev and Mustafina, *Dokumenty po istorii Kazanskogo kraia*, 84–92, no. 38, 24 February 1621.

89. RGADA, f. 281, op. 1, d. 277, is a dossier of the relationship between the monastery and its Mordvins.

90. The monastery was notified of its victory on 3 August 1613 and 26 February 1621. Kuntsevich, "Gramoty Kazanskogo Zilantova monastyria," 281–90.

91. Ermolaev and Mustafina, *Dokumenty po istorii Kazanskogo kraia*, 32–36, no. 3, no later than August 1567; 84–92, no. 38, 24 February 1621; 161–62, no. 74, 31 May 1649.

92. There is little work specifically on convents before the eighteenth century. The exception is Marie A. Thomas, "Muscovite Convents in the Seventeenth Century," *Russian History/Histoire Russe* 10 (1983). See also Alice-Mary Talbot, "Women's Space in Byzantine Monasteries," *Dumbarton Oaks Papers* 52 (1998), for a discussion of the importance of female seclusion in Orthodox convents.

93. Malov, *Kazanskii Bogoroditskii devich' monastyr'*, 3. By the eighteenth century, the convent had nearly 6,000 women residing within its walls. See Angelika Schmähling, *Hort der Frömmigkeit—Ort der Verwahrung: Russische Frauenklöster im 16.—18. Jahrhundert* (Stuttgart, 2009), 51, 86.

94. Mikhail Fedorovich gave four courtyards in Kazan to the Bogoroditskii Devichii Convent in 1623 for a new building to house the Mother of God Icon. RGADA, f. 281, op. 4, d. 6456, 29 October 1623.

95. L. I. Denisov, *Pravoslavnye monastyri Rossiiskoi imperii: Polnyi spisok* (Moscow, 1903), 253.

96. Ioann Barsov, "Nikolaevskii devichii monastyr' v g. Cheboksarakh," *Izvestiia obshchestva arkheologicheskii, istorii i etnografii pri Imperatorskom Kazanskom universitete* 14 (1898): 520–21.

97. Ibid., 519–20.

98. Chetyrkin, *Istoriko-statisticheskoe opisanie*, 1–15.

99. See chap. 6.

100. V. E. Krasovskii, comp., *Kievo-Nikolaevskii byvshii Pokrovskii Ladinskii Todrovskii Novodevichii monastyr' Simbirskoi eparkhii (Istoriko-arkheologicheskoe opisanie)* (Simbirsk, 1899), 16–20. The departure of these nuns from Kiev's Ladyn Convent is noted in Sophia Senyk, *Women's Monasteries in Ukraine and Belorussia to the Period of Suppressions* (Rome, 1983), 161.

101. Evgeniia Aleksovicha Notariusa, ed., *Istoricheskoe opisanie Alatyrskago Kievo-Nikolaevskogo zhenskogo monastyria* (Alatyr', 1997), 9–11.

102. The challenges were made in 1606/7, 1608/9, 1614/15, 1615/16, and 1632/33. RGADA, f. 281, op. 1, d. 317, 13 January 1688.

103. RGADA, f. 281, op. 1, d. 262, September 1629.

104. RGADA, f. 281, op. 1, d. 264, 19 April 1630.

105. RGADA, f. 281, op. 1, d. 276, 27 February 1633.

106. Kuntsevich, "Gramoty Kazanskogo Zilantova monastyria," 279–81.

107. N. I. Sugonin, *Insar: Dokumental'no-istoricheskii ocherk o gorode i raione* (Saransk, 1975), 5–7.

108. Peterson, *Istoricheskii ocherk Kerenskogo kraia*, 10. Similarly, Penza was established with a large non-Russian population in 1663. A. F. Dergachev et al., eds., *Ocherki istorii Penzenskogo kraia: S drevneishikh vremen do kontsa XIX veka* (Penza, 1973), 19–26.

109. This will be discussed in detail in chap. 5.

110. I. S. Romashin, *Ocherki ekonomiki Simbirskoi gubernii XVII–XIX vv.* (Ul'ianovsk, 1961), 5; Superanskii, *Simbirsk i ego proshloe*, 3–7.

111. I. D. Voronin, *Saransk: Istoriko-dokumental'nye ocherki* (Saransk, 1961), 23–24, 50–53.

112. This conclusion agrees with Peter B. Brown's assessment of the chancellery system. See his "Bureaucratic Administration in Seventeenth-Century Russia," in *Modernizing Muscovy: Reform and Social Change in Seventeenth-Century Russia*, ed. Jarmo T. Kotilaine and Marshall Poe (London, 2004).

Chapter 3. Foreign Interests

1. The chapter's first epigraph comes from the National Archives, Kew, Great Britain (hereafter cited as TNA), SP 91/2, Secretaries of State: State Papers Foreign, Russia, "Emperor Michael—grant of privileges to the Muscovy co.," ff. 139 r.–145 r., 13 June 1628, quote from 142–142v.

2. For an introduction to the Volga trade route under Muscovite rule, see J. Kaufmann-Rochard, *Origines d'une bourgeoisie Russe (XVIe et XVIIe siècles)* (Paris, 1969), 93–154; Maxine Siroux, "Les caravanserais routiers safavids," *Iranian Studies* 7 (1974); Paul Bushkovitch, *The Merchants of Moscow 1580–1650* (New York, 1980), 92–101; Chantal Lemercier-Quelquejay, "Les routes Commerciales et Militaires au Caucase du Nord aux XVIème et XVIIème siècles," *Central Asian Survey* 4 (1985); Janet Martin, "Muscovite Travelling Merchants: The Trade with the Muslim East (15th and 16th Centuries)," *Central Asian Survey* 4 (1985); L. K. Ermolaeva, "Krupnoe kupechestvo Rossii v XVII–pervoi chetverti XVIII v. (po materialam astrakhanskoi torgovli)," *Istoricheskie zapiski* 114 (1986); Stephen Frederic Dale, *Indian Merchants and Eurasian Trade, 1600–1750* (New York, 1994), 78–127; S. M. Kashtanov, "K istorii Volzhskogo torgovogo sudokhodstva vo vtoroi polovine XVI v.," in *Voprosy istorii narodov Povolzh'ia i Priural'ia*, ed. Iu. P. Smirnov et al. (Cheboksary, 1997); Stefan Troebst, "Die Kaspi-Volga-Ostsee-Route in der handelskontrollpolitik Karls XI: Die Schwedischen Persien-missionen von Ludvig Fabritius 1679–1700," *Forschungen zur osteuropäischen Geschichte* 54 (1998).

3. Massa, *Short History of the Beginnings*. For a brief introduction to the Anglo-Dutch rivalry, see Jonathan Israel, "England, Dutch, and the Struggle for Mastery of World Trade

in the Age of the Glorious Revolution (1682–1702)," in *The World of William and Mary: Anglo-Dutch Perspectives on the Revolution of 1688–89*, ed. Dale Hoak and Mordechai Feingold (Stanford, 1996).

4. For an introduction to the Muscovy's foreign trade and domestic economy, see Joseph T. Fuhrmann, *The Origins of Capitalism in Russia: Industry and Progress in the Sixteenth and Seventeenth Centuries* (Chicago, 1972), and J. T. Kotilaine, *Russia's Foreign Trade and Economic Expansion in the Seventeenth Century: Windows on the World* (Leiden, 2005).

5. Andre Gunder Frank, *ReORIENT: Global Economy in the Asian Age* (Berkeley, CA, 1998); Kenneth Pomeranz, *The Great Divergence: China, Europe, and the Making of the Modern World Economy* (Princeton, NJ, 2000); R. Bin Wong, "The Search for European Differences and Domination in the Early Modern World: A View from Asia," *American Historical Review* 107 (2002); and David Washbrook, "India in the Early Modern World Economy: Modes of Production, Reproduction and Exchange," *Journal of Global History* 2 (2007).

6. For a discussion of early-modern economic development, see J. N. Ball, *Merchants and Merchandise: The Expansion of Trade in Europe 1500–1630* (London, 1977). For Russia, see Jarmo T. Kotilaine, "Mercantilism in Pre-Petrine Russia," in *Modernizing Muscovy: Reform and Social Change in Seventeenth-Century Russia*, ed. Jarmo T. Kotilaine and Marshall Poe (London, 2004).

7. Kotilaine estimates the value of the total trade with Asia (both South and East) averaged approximately 10 percent of the trade in Arkhangel'sk with the West. See Kotilaine, *Russia's Foreign Trade*, 442–95, and his conclusions on 494.

8. Sigmund von Herberstein, *Notes upon Russia*, trans. Richard Henry (London, 1852), 2:73. For a discussion of this quote, see Pelenski *Russia and Kazan*, 37.

9. "Anthony Jenkinson's Explorations on the Land Route to China, 1558–60," http://depts.washington.edu/silkroad/texts/jenkinson/bukhara.html#kazan, accessed 4 September 2009.

10. Hélène Carrère d'Encausse, "Les routes commerciales de l'Asie centrale et les tentatives de reconquête d'Astrakhan d'après les registres des 'Affaires importantes' des Archives ottomanes," *Cahiers du monde russe et sovietique* 11 (1970); Alexandre Bennigsen and Chantal Lemercier-Quelquejay, "La poussée vers les mers chaudes et la barrière du Caucase: La rivalité Ottomano-Moscovite dans la seconde moitié du XVIe siècle," *Journal of Turkish Studies* 10 (1986).

11. See chap. 6.

12. The state treated these cities as a functioning trade route. For example, in a charter to the Astrakhan's Troitse-Sergeevski Monastery on 8 July 1578. Kashtanov, "K istorii Volzhskogo," 49.

13. Russian State Archive of Ancient Acts, Moscow (hereafter cited as RGADA), f. 16, Gosudarstvennyi arkhiv, r. XVI, Vnutrennee upravlenie, op. 1, d. 709, ll. 140b.–16, 16 May 1649, included advice on controlling the merchants' travel. By 1677, the announcement of the herald of the next departure state had been elevated in importance to become its own clause in the *nakaz*. RGADA, f. 16, op. 1, d. 709, ll. 52–530b., 22 March 1677.

14. For example, see the discussion in Kaufmann-Rochard, *Origines d'une bourgeiosie Russe*, 100–102; or the protest of a Russian merchant along the Volga, K. A. Antonova and N. M. Gol'berg, eds., *Russko-Indiiskie otnosheniia v XVII v.: Sbornik dokumentov* (Moscow, 1958), 40–43, no. 15, between 1 March 12 and 12 July 1639.

15. Romashin, *Ocherki ekonomiki Simbirskoi gubernii*, 5; Superanskii, *Simbirsk i ego proshloe*, 3–7.

16. RGADA, f. 281, Gramoty kollegii ekonomii, op. 1, d. 246, 12 April 1614.

17. Kuntsevich, "Gramoty Kazanskogo Zilantova monastyria," 294–98.

18. RGADA, f. 16, op. 1, d. 709, ll. 300b.–35, from 1649.

19. For example, Saratov's *voevoda* also tracked customs owed in his city, in a similar manner to Kazan's *voevoda*. Two of these records are published in Antonova and Gol'berg, *Russko-Indiiskie otnosheniia*, 93–94, no. 42, 7 December 1649; 94, no. 43, 7 December 1649.

20. RGADA, f. 16, op. 1, d. 709, ll. 140b.–16, 16 May 1649.

21. Ibid., ll. 320b.–35, 16 May 1649.

22. Richard Hellie, trans. and ed., *The Muscovite Law Code (Ulozhenie) of 1649*, The Laws of Russia 1, Medieval Russia, vol. 3, pt. 1, *Text and Translation* (Irvine, CA, 1988), chaps. 9 and 25. Hereafter cited as Hellie, *Ulozhenie*.

23. Ibid., 18–19, chap. 9, art. 1.

24. The *gosti* were the elite merchant class of Muscovy and have received much attention from historians, including Bushkovitch, *Merchants of Moscow*; Samuel H. Baron, "The *Gosti* Revisted," *Explorations in Muscovite History* (Hampshire, 1991); A. A. Timoshina, "Raselenie gostei, chlenov gostinoi i sukonnoi soten v russkikh gorodakh XVII v.," in *Torgovlia i predpreinimatel'stvo v feodal'noi Rossii*, ed. A. Iu. Karlov (Moscow, 1994).

25. A. N. Zertsalov, *Materialy dlia istorii Sinbirska i ego uezda (Prokhodo-raskhodnaia kniga Sinbirskoi prikaznoi izby) 1665–1667 gg.* (Simbirsk, 1896), 94–95, 98–100. About that time 100 rubles might have purchased one boatload of salt, or as many as 25 horses, based on the other sales in the region discussed below.

26. This information was included in a *gramota* sent to Kazan's *voevoda*. An ocean-going boat (*plavnyi lodok*) paid two *dengi*, while a small fishing boat (*botik*) paid only one *dengi*. Rubinshtein, *Istoriia Tatarii*, 156, 26 February 1662. These rights had been granted as early as 1585, when Kazan's *voevoda* instructed the Zilantov Monastery of its responsibilities for merchants transporting salt and fish from Astrakhan to the north. *Arkhiv P. M. Stroeva*, Russkaia istoricheskaia biblioteka 32 (Petrograd, 1915), 1:626–29, no. 323, 22 July 1585.

27. For example, Ovam Voroblevskii wrote to Archimandrite Avram of the monastery after paying the toll for transportation of salt. He told the archimandrite that he was paying the toll only because it was the tsar's command. RGADA, f. 281, op. 7, d. 10828, 1686.

28. RGADA, f. 16, op. 1, d. 709, ll. 160b.–21.

29. Russian merchants had been trading in South Asia since at least the fifteenth century. See J. Martin, "Muscovite Travelling Merchants," and Mary Jane Maxwell, "Afanasii Nikitin: An Orthodox Russian's Spiritual Voyage in the Dar al-Islam, 1468–1475," *Journal of World History* 17 (2006).

30. Different aspects of the local economy have been studied in several works. These include I. M. Pokrovskii, *K istorii pomestnogo i ekonomicheskom byta v Kazanskom krae v polovine XVII veka* (Kazan, 1909); N. A. Baklanova, *Torgovo-promyshlennaia deiatel'nost' Kalmykovykh vo vtoroi polovine XVII v.: K istorii formirovaniia Russkoi burzhuazii* (Moscow, 1959); Romashin, *Ocherki ekonomiki Simbirskoi gubernii*; N. B. Golikova, "Torgovlia krepostnymi bez zemli v 20-kh godakh XVIII v. (Po materialam krepostnykh knig gorodov Povolzh'ia)," *Istoricheskie zapiski* 90 (1972); and Aleksandr Andreev, *Stroganovy* (Moscow, 2000).

31. The discussion of trade in this chapter is built upon extant records, generally merchant transactions. As a result, the local market will appear merchant dominated, though certainly peasants did in fact engage in their own unrecorded commercial activities. For a discussion of peasant traders in Muscovy during the seventeenth century, see V. R. Tarlovskaia, *Torgovlia Rossii perioda pozdnego feodalizma: Torgovye krest'iane vo vtoroi polovine XVII–nachale XVIII v.* (Moscow, 1988).

32. Contracts signed by these monasteries and merchants prove the importance of these courtyards. For example, the merchants Fëdor Lukochnov syn Sibiriak signed a contract with the elder of Simbirsk's Troitse-Sergeevskii Monastery for space in its courtyard. RGADA, f. 281, op. 8, d. 11534, 9 June 1656.

33. This location was described in the *pistsovaia kniga* of 1565–68. Rubinshtein, *Istoriia Tatarii*, 234.

34. In the records of Nikita Vasil'evich Borisov and Dmitrii Andreevich Kikin, written between 1565 and 1568, described Kazan's Spaso-Preobrazhenskii Monastery's courtyard with numerous secular and ecclesiastical merchants. Tomsinskii, *Materialy po istorii Tatarskoi ASSR*, 14, 32.

35. This is recorded in a later customs book. A. I. Iakovlev, *Saranskaia tamozhennaia kniga za 1692 g.* (Saransk, 1951).

36. Both the central government and local officials would remind monasteries if they fell into arrears. For example, Prince Ivan Mikhailov syn Vorotinskii wrote from Moscow to remind Archimandrite Arsenii of Kazan's Spasopreobrazhenskii Monastery of its outstanding tax bill due to the tsar. RGADA, f. 281, op. 4, d. 6436, 18 May 1596. *Voevoda* Ivan Vasilevich Morozov wrote to the archimandrite of Sviiazhsk's Bogoroditsa's monastery to remind him of the yearly payment of 4 rubles and 5 grivnas still due. RGADA, f. 281, op. 45, d. 6468, 19 July 1637.

37. RGADA, f. 281, op. 1, d. 249, 1618/19.

38. In a letter from the Arzamas's Troitse-Sergeevskii Monastery's cellarer to Archmandrite Deonisii in 1632, the cellarer informed the abbot that instead of the expected 30 rubles from this year's rent, there would instead be 16 rubles this year and another 16 rubles in two years. RGADA, f. 281, op. 1, d. 270, 16 March 1632.

39. Morris, "The Medieval Emergence."

40. S. I. Arkhangel'skii and N. I. Privalova, eds., *Nizhnii Novgorod v XVII veke: Sbornik godumentov i materialov k istorii Nizhnogo Novgoroda i ego okrugi* (Gor'kii, 1961), 68–70, no. 35, 18 March 1627.

41. I. M. Pokrovskii, "Bortnichestvo (pchelovodstvo), kak odin iz vidov natural'nago khoziaistva i promysla bliz Kazani v XVI–XVII vv.," *Izvestiia obshchestva arkheologii, istorii i etnografii pri Imperatorskom Kazanskom universitete* 17 (1901).

42. These were the exact prices of the sales of Koz'modem'iansk resident Mikifor Grigor'ev in Velikii Ustiug in 1651. Grigor'ev sold 15 puds of wax and 148 puds of honey. I. Iakovlev, ed., *Tamozhennye knigi Moskovskogo gosudarstva XVII veka*, 3 vols. (Moscow, 1950–51), 2:34, 11 January 1651. These prices are consistent with Hellie's observations of prices during the seventeenth century. Richard Hellie, *The Economy and Material Culture of Russia, 1600–1725* (Chicago, 1999), 93–94, 123–24.

43. M. Ia. Volkov and E. B. Frantsuzova, eds. *Tamozhennaia kniga goroda Vologdy, 1634–1635 gg.* (Moscow, 1983), 45, 24 September 1634. In Velikii Ustiug, Anikeev also carried some silk and leather with him. The honey, wax, silk, and leather were sold for a combined 171 rubles. Iakovlev, *Tamozhennye knigi*, 1:184, 26 March 1636.

44. On the later date, Terent'ev arrived in the city with Mikifor Grigor'ev, another resident of Koz'modem'iansk, who carried wax and honey worth 36 rubles. Iakovlev, *Tamozhennye knigi*, 2:39, 28 January 1951; and 2:131, 15 October 1651.

45. Ermolaev and Mustafina, *Dokumenty po istorii Kazanskogo kraia*, 143–45, no. 65, 13 June 1644.

46. During the Time of Troubles, a confirmation of fishing rights were given to the monastery over its villages for those rivers. RGADA, f. 281, op. 1, d. 243, 21 March 1608. Another confirmation followed after the villages' refusal to pay. RGADA, f. 281, op. 1, d. 244, 6 May 1608. However, after the Time of Troubles the monastery's fishing rights were restricted to only Russian peasants living in its villages. RGADA, f. 281, op. 1, d. 245, 27 March 1614.

47. RGADA, f. 281, op. 4, 4 March 1616.

48. RGADA, f. 281, op. 4, d. 6449, 26 March 1616. Later that same year, the privileges for the Volga River outside of Samara were extended until 1621, warning the monastery that their privileges might not be renewed after that point. RGADA, f. 281, op. 4, d. 6450, 5 August 1616.

49. *Arkhiv P. M. Stroeva*, vol. 2, Russkaia istoricheskaia biblioteka 35 (Petrograd, 1917), 638–39, no. 337, 8 May 1624.

50. G. I. Aiplatov and A. G. Ivanov, eds., *Monastyrskaia kolonizatsiia Mariiskogo Povolzh'ia: Po materialam Spaso-Iunginskii monastyria Koz'modem'ianskogo uezda, 1625–1764 gg.* (Ioshkar-Ola, 2000), 100–103, no. 19, 8 March 1663.

51. RGADA, f. 281, op. 7, d. 10794, 26 December 1631.

52. Their petitions proved successful. This included *Voevoda* Grigor Ivanovich Fefilaev agreeing to leave the privileges intact. RGADA, f. 281, op. 7, d. 10795, 22 March 1635. A longer letter to the monastery one year later reiterated the history of its fishing privileges, allowing it to keep them for another year. RGADA, f. 281, op. 7, d. 10796, 22 March 1636. *Voevoda* Aleksei Panteleevich Chirikov extended the monastery's privileges again. RGADA, f. 281, op. 7, d. 10798, 6 April 1653.

53. RGADA, f. 281, op. 7, d. 10799, 3 March 1659. *Voevoda* Mikhail Ivanovich Glebov left those tariffs in place, but also required the monastery to regulate the local fish market in Saratov. RGADA, f. 281, op. 7, d. 10800, 2 June 1674.

54. *Akty, sobrannye v bibliotekakh i arkhivakh Rossiiskoi imperii arkheograficheskoiu ekspeditsieiu imperatorskoi akademii nauk*, vol. 1 (St. Petersburg, 1836), 1:239, no. 235.

55. For a broader discussion of Muscovy's relationship with the Nogai, see Kochekaev, *Nogaisko-Russkie otnosheniia*).

56. A. I. Razdorskii, *Torgovliia Kurska v XVII veke (Po materialam tamozhennykh i obrochnykh knig goroda)* (St. Petersburg, 2001), 246–49.

57. Iakovlev, *Tamozhennye knigi*, 1:134–35, 14–19 February 1634. Hellie's median price for geldings (*meriny*) was 4 rubles, and for mares (*kobyly*) was 2.3. Hellie, *Economy and Material Culture*, 39–45. Between 17 March and 30 March 1634, eleven residents of Kazan sold 9 geldings for an average of 3.17 rubles and 2 mares for 2.5 rubles. Iakovlev, *Tamozhennye knigi*, 1:136–37, 17–30 March 1634.

58. Iakovlev, *Tamozhennye knigi*, 1:265–66, 6–7 March 1636.

59. RGADA, f. 16, op. 1, d. 709, ll. 270b.–28, 16 May 1649.

60. Ibid., ll. 11–12, 16 May 1649.

61. RGADA, f. 281, op. 1, d. 268, 23 January 1632.

62. The challenges were summarized in the *gramota* to the convent in 1688, once again upholding the convent's right to the mill. The challenges were made in 1606/7, 1608/9, 1614/15, 1615/16, and 1632/33. RGADA, f. 281, op. 1, d. 317, 13 January 1688. Similarly, the Voskresenskii Khrista Church in Arzamas survived with the revenue from its mill in the village of Osinovka in Arzamas district, preventing its priest's attempt to receive more funding from the central government in 1657. Patriarch Nikon notified Archpriest Trofim that the mill provided sufficient revenue to support the church. RGADA, f. 281, op. 1, d. 296, 23 September 1657.

63. Ermolaev and Mustafina, *Dokumenty po istorii Kazanskogo kraia*, 107–9, no. 47, March 1632.

64. Ibid., 113–14, no. 51, no earlier than 1636.

65. As another example, Grigorii Trusov ran six mills between Kazan and Malmyzh and failed to pay the local *voevody* his yearly duties for several years. Rather than seize or shut down the mill, the Prikaz sent Trusov a reminder to start paying. Law Library of Congress, Russian Manuscript Scrolls Collection, I-3, 19 August 1641.

66. RGADA, f. 16, op. 1, d. 709, l. 140b., 16 May 1649.

67. Ermolaev and Mustafina, *Dokumenty po istorii Kazanskogo kraia*, 98, no. 42, 15 October 1622.

68. Ibid., 99–101, no. 43, 7 June 1623.

69. The merchant Iakov Ilantov syn Lukoshkov bought 320 puds of salt for 100 rubles from the Zilantov Uspenskii Monastery. RGADA, f. 1455, Gosudarstvennye i chastnye akty pomestno-votchinnykh arkhivov XVI–XIX vv., op. 5, d. 223, January 1665. Richard Hellie demonstrated in his study of the Russian economy that salt prices were seasonally variable.

Therefore, the increased price for salt sold in January of 1665 versus an average salt price over a year might only reflect that seasonal transition. Hellie, *Economy and Material Culture*, 157–60.

70. The original grant was made on 13 July 1606; the increase was granted on 3 August 1613. Ermolaev and Mustafina, *Dokumenty po istorii Kazanskogo kraia*, 60–62, no. 24.

71. Ibid., 92–95, no. 39, 11 March 1621.

72. For other studies of the regional salt trade, see N. V. Ustiugov, *Solevarennaia promyshlennost' soli kamskoi v XVII veke: K voprosy o genezise kapitalisticheskikh otnoshenii v Russkoi promyshlennosti* (Moscow, 1957); and Razdorskii, *Torgovliia Kurska*, 150–58.

73. RGADA, f. 281, op. 8, d. 11548, 21 March 1682.

74. This split of supervising responsibilities was relayed to Samara's *voevoda* in a *gramota*. RGADA, f. 281, op. 8, d. 11552, 23 January 1684.

75. For a discussion of the early negotiations, see Samuel H. Baron, "Ivan the Terrible, Giles Fletcher, and the Muscovite Merchantry: A Reconsideration," *Slavonic and East European Review* 56 (1978).

76. TNA, SP 91/1, Secretaries of State: State Papers Foreign, Russia, ff. 55r.–58r., February 1587. See also the quote that begins this chapter, which is a later restatement of these privileges.

77. TNA, PRO 22/60, English Royal Letters in the Soviet Central State Archive of Ancient Records, 1557–1655, no. 17, 30 May 1600.

78. TNA, SP 91/1, ff. 209r.–210r. [ca. 1605].

79. English difficulties in Moscow during the Time of Troubles are discussed in Geraldine M. Phipps, *Sir John Merrick, English Merchant—Diplomat in Seventeenth-Century Russia* (Newtonville, MA, 1983), 47–73. For a more optimistic assessment, see Maria Salomon Arel, "The Muscovy Company in the First Half of the Seventeenth Century: Trade and Position in the Russian State; A Reassessment" (PhD diss., Yale University, 1995).

80. This argument is summarized in J. T. Kotilaine, "Competing Claims: Russian Foreign Trade via Arkhangel'sk and the Eastern Baltic Ports in the Seventeenth Century," *Kritika* 4 (2003).

81. See Massa, *Short History of the Beginnings*.

82. The classic introduction to the topic is Niels Steensgaard, *Carracks, Caravans, and Companies: The Structural Crisis in the European-Asian Trade in the Early Seventeenth Century* (Odense, Denmark, 1973). For the Russian side, see M. F. Fekhner, *Torgovlia Russkogo gosudarstva so stranami vostoka v XVI veke* (Moscow, 1952); M. Iu. Iuldashev, *K istorii torgovykh sviazei Srednei Azii s Rossiei v XVI–XVII vv.* (Tashkent, 1964).

83. For a full picture of the competition for the silk trade, see Rudolph P. Matthee, *The Politics of Trade in Safavid Iran: Silk for Silver, 1600–1730* (New York, 1999), esp. 91–118.

84. See P. P. Bushev, *Istoriia posol'stv i diplomaticheskikh otnoshenii russkogo i iranskogo gosudarstv v 1586–1612 gg.* (Moscow, 1976), and P. P. Bushev, *Istoriia posol'stv i diplomaticheskikh otnoshenii russkogo i iranskogo gosudarstv v 1613–1621 gg.* (Moscow, 1987).

85. In addition to the sources in note 2, see also M. Polevktov, "The Ways of Communication between Russia and Georgia in the Sixteenth and Seventeenth Centuries," *Journal of Modern History* 2 (1930).

86. The records of the embassies are reproduced in N. I. Veselovskii, ed., *Pamiatniki diplomaticheskikh i torgovykh snoshenii Moskovskoi Rusi s Persiei*, vol. 3, *Tsarstvovanie Mikhaila Feodoricha* (St. Petersburg, 1898).

87. Fedot Afansev syn Kotov, "Of a Journey to the Kingdom of Persia, from Persia to the Land of Turkey and to India and to Hormuz where the Ships Come," in *Russian Travellers to India and Persia (1624–1798): Kotov, Yefremov, Danibegov*, trans. and ed. P. M. Kemp (Dehli, 1959). The Russian original is reprinted in *Khozhenie kuptsa Fedota Kotova v Persiiu* (Moscow, 1958).

88. See, for example, Antonova and Gol'berg, *Russko-Indiiskie otnosheniia*, 33–37, no. 11, 24 June 1637.

89. For a discussion of the Russian attempts in the Muslim south, see Matthew P. Romaniello, "'In friendship and love': Russian Travels to Muslim Lands in the Early Modern Era," *Historical Yearbook* 6 (2009).

90. Iakovlev, *Tamozhennye knigi*, 1:20, 4 October 1633, recorded his arrival from Siberia with pelts in Velikii Ustiug on his way to Vologda. Early the next year he arrived in Velikii Ustiug on his way to Iaroslavl' with Andrei Antipin and a shipment of silk. Ibid., 1:30, 2 January 1634. A year later, his arrival in Vologda with 150 rubles worth of silk was entered in its customs book. Volkov and Frantsuzova, *Tamozhennaia kniga goroda Vologda*, 420, 22 February 1635. In April 1635, Andreev arrived in Velikii Ustiug with several furs, and later that year sold 9 beaver pelts and 13 red fox for 30 rubles in town. Iakovlev, *Tamozhennye knigi*, 1:158, 8 April 1635; and 166, 9 October 1635. His final appearance in the customs books was in February 1636 when he sold 100 rubles worth of silk in Ustiug on his way from Iaroslavl'. Ibid., 1:177, 9 February 1636.

91. Antonova and Gol'berg, *Russko-Indiiskie otnosheniia*, 38–39, no. 12, no earlier than 23 August 1638.

92. TNA, PRO 22/60, no. 33, 1 February 1626.

93. TNA, PRO 22/60, no. 38, 27 April 1629. The tsar did give his permission, though the Iranian ambassador did not use this route to England due to his untimely death in Iran. TNA, PRO 22/60, no. 49, 5 January 1631.

94. Inna Lubimenko, "The Struggle of the Dutch with the English for the Russian Market in the Seventeenth Century," *Transactions of the Royal Historical Society*, series 4, no. 7 (1924); S. I. Arkhangel'skii, "Anglo-Gollandskaia torgovlia s Moskvoi v XVII v.," *Istoricheskii sbornik* 5 (1936); E. Kh. Veinroks, "Mezhdunarodnaia konkurentsiia v torgovle mezhdu Rossiei i Zapadnoi Evropoi: 1560–1640," in *Russkii Sever i Zapadnaia Evropa*, ed. Iu. N. Bespiatykh (St. Petersburg, 1999); S. P. Orlenko, *Vykhodtsy iz Zapadnoi Evropy v Rossii XVII veka: pravovoi status i real'noe polozhenie* (Moscow, 2004); Jan Willem Veluwenkamp, *Arkhangel'sk: Niderlandskie predprinimateli v rossii, 1550–1785*, trans. N. Mikaelian (Moscow,

2006). It is important to note, however, that the historiographic importance of the Anglo-Dutch rivalry should not overshadow other important Muscovite trading partners. Concerning grain exports, for example, the Swedish exported twice as much as the Dutch and English combined in the first quarter of the seventeenth century. P. P. Smirnov, "Novoe chelobit'e Moskovskikh torgovykh liudei o vysylke inozemtsev, 1627 goda," *Chteniia v istoricheskom obshchestve Nestora-letopistse* 23, no. 1 (1912).

95. Lubimenko, "The Struggle of the Dutch," 44–45.

96. The East Indies Company petitioned Charles I after the Dutch Treaty of 1619, asking for an English ambassador to Iran in order to equalize the Dutch advantage. TNA, CO 77/4, East Indies Original Correspondence, 1570–1856, ff. 135r.–136r., April 1629.

97. One of the first Dutch monopolies in Muscovy was for the export of tar, establishing the pattern for later Dutch monopolies in the seventeenth century. An English merchant in Moscow, Thomas Wyche, petitioned Charles I for redress against the Dutch tar monopoly. TNA, SP 91/2, f. 244r., 1633.

98. TNA, SP 91/3, pt. 1, ff. 117r.–117v., 6 December 1666.

99. In 1622, James I petitioned Mikhail Fedorovich for the release of Dr. John Scroop from service in Kazan. While Scroop was not a merchant, his presence in a city forbidden to the English displays the limitation of Muscovite prohibition. TNA, PRO 22/60, no. 28, 1622.

100. Maria Salomon Arel, "Making an Honest Ruble in the Russian North: Aspects of Muscovite Trade in the First Half of the Seventeenth Century," *Forschungen zur osteuropäischen Geschichte* 54 (1998).

101. See n.6 above.

102. In exile from England, the future King Charles II asked for the revocation of the tax-free status, to punish his rebellious subjects. TNA, PRO 22/60, no. 75, 16 September 1648.

103. *Polnoe sobranie zakonov Rossiiskoi Imperii* (hereafter cited as *PSZ*), series 1, 45 vols. (St. Petersburg, 1830), 1:651–65, no. 408, 22 April 1667. For a discussion of the Code, see E. V. Chistiakova, "Novotorgovnyi ustav 1667 goda," *Arkheograficheskii ezhegodnik za 1957 god* (Moscow, 1958), and Kotilaine, *Russia's Foreign Trade*, 220–25.

104. Lit. "*inozemtsy ili russkie liudi za more.*" Antonova and Gol'berg, *Russko-Indiiskie otnosheniia*, 174–79, no. 98, 28 July 1672.

105. For example, the English attempted to both pressure the tsar through the Muscovy Company and with direct appeals from the king to the tsar. TNA, SP 91/3, pt. 2, ff. 210r.–212v., "Instructions from the Right Woell. the Governor and fellowship of English Merchants for Discovery of New Trades, Usually called the Muscovia Company, unto John Hebdon Esq., London," 16 September 1676; and TNA, SP 91/3, pt. 2, ff. 217r./v., letter from Charles II to Feodor Aleksevich, 16 September 1676.

106. See *Knigi Moskovskoi bol'shoi tamozhni, 1693–1694 gg.: Novgorodskaia, Astrakhanskaia, Malorossiiskaia* (Moscow, 1961), 64–76.

107. RGADA, f. 16, op. 1, d. 709, ll. 100–101, 22 March 1677; and *PSZ*, vol. 1, 665–68, no. 409, 31 May 1667; 668–70, no. 410, 31 May 1667.

108. Several documents recording the transit of the Bukharan merchants through Nizhnii Novgorod are published in Arkhangel'skii and Privalova, *Nizhnii Novgorod v XVII veke*, 82–84, no. 46–48, 4 December 1633–11 March 1634. For the trade negotiations with Bukhara after 1552, see A. N. Samoilovich, ed., *Materialy po istorii Uzbekskoi, Tadkhikskoi i Turkmenskoi SSR*, pt. 1, *Torgovlia s Moskovskim gosudarstvom i mezhdunarodnoe polozhenie Srednei Azii v XVI–XVII vv.* (Leningrad, 1932).

109. The Armenians and Bukharans were both well-established diasporic mercantile communities in the early modern era, and Muscovy's use of them in this manner was not atypical. See R. W. Ferrier, "The Armenians and the East India Company in Persia in the Seventeenth and Early Eighteenth Centuries," *Economic History Review* 26 (1973); Michel Aghassian and Kéram Kévonian, "Armenian Trade in the Indian Ocean in the Seventeenth and Eighteenth Centuries," in *Asian Merchants and Businessmen in the Indian Ocean and the China Sea*, ed. Denys Lombard and Jean Aubin (New Delhi, 2000); and Audrey Burton, *The Bukharans: A Dynastic, Diplomatic and Commercial History, 1550–1702* (New York, 1997).

110. The Foreign Office instructed Hebdon to seek the restoration of the tax-free privileges as one of his highest priorities. TNA, SP 104/118, Secretaries of State: State Papers Foreign, Entry Books, ff. 17r.–19v., 30 September 1676.

111. TNA, SP 91/3, pt. 2, f. 222r., 4 December 1676.

112. The English ambassador to the Netherlands reported on the presence of an Armenian enclave in Holland as early as 1630, when the Armenians established their own churches in Schoonhoven and Leland. TNA, SP 84/142, State Paper Office: State Papers Foreign, Holland, ff. 120r.–122r., 2/12 October 1630. For a study of Dutch-Armenian relations later in the seventeenth century, see Kéram Kévonian, "Marchands Arméniens au XVIIe siècle: A propos d'un livre arménien publié à Amsterdam en 1699," *Cahiers du monde russe et soviétique* 16 (1975).

113. Though the northern European merchants had lost their travel rights through the Volga by 1649, both Armenian and Indian merchants were permitted to transport goods through the region as long as they had been residents of Moscow for "many years." Antonova and Gol'berg, *Russko-Indiiskie otnosheniia*, 152, no. 76, June 1665.

114. TNA, SP 104/119, f. 11v., 29 November 1681.

115. RGADA, f. 159, op. 2, d. 1361, 9 May 1675. Many of the ironworks in Muscovy were established by the Dutch, so this transaction is not unusual in that regard. Lubimenko, "The Struggle of the Dutch," 45–46.

116. RGADA, f. 159, Prikaznye dela novoi razborki, op. 2, Posol'skii prikaz, d. 328, 29 March 1677.

117. Antonova and Gol'berg, *Russko-Indiiskie otnosheniia*, 276–77, no. 172, 29 September 1677 and 8 October 1677. Petitions from Indian and Iranian merchants to the authorities in Astrakhan continued throughout the rest of the century. A combined group of Iranian and Indian merchants sought approval for to transport to Kazan an itemized caravan of goods. Ibid., 350, no. 244, 3 October 1690.

118. P. Martynov, *Seleniia Simbirskogo uezda (Materialy dliia istorii Simbirskogo dvoriantstvo i chastnogo zemlevladeniia v Simbirskom uezde)* (Simbirsk, 1903), 30–31, no. 30, 28 February 1669.

119. Similar petitions were produced from other cities, but without clear success for the petitioners. For example, when merchants in Saratov petitioned the Posol'skii Prikaz for access to local fishing waters, the Posol'skii Prikaz only turned the petition to the Prikaz Bol'shogo dvortsa for a decision. Since the Prikaz Kazanskogo dvortsa had ultimate authority for fishing rights in the region, the merchants would have had more success directly petitioning them. RGADA, f. 159, op. 2, d. 1161, September 1670.

120. RGADA, f. 16, op. 1, d. 709, ll. 69–71.

121. Ibid., ll. 71–76.

122. Ibid., ll. 92–99ob.

123. Antonova and Gol'berg, *Russko-Indiiskie otnosheniia*, 189–236, nos. 107–37, 1675–1716.

124. Ibid., 226, no. 134, no later than 22 February 1678.

125. Whitworth to the Foreign Office, TNA, SP 91/5, pt. 1, ff. 34r.–37v., 31 January 1707.

Chapter 4. Loyal Enemies

1 For the development of Kazan's land grant system, see Jaroslaw Pelenski, "State and Society in Muscovite Russia and the Mongol-Turkic System in the Sixteenth Century," *Forschungen zur osteuropäischen Geschichte* 27 (1980).

2. For a discussion of elite co-option in Europe, see Elliott, "A Europe of Composite Monarchies." For another Russian example, see Chantal Lemercier-Quelquejay, "Co-optation of the Elites of Kabarda and Daghestan in the Sixteenth Century," in *The North Caucasus Barrier: The Russian Advance towards the Muslim World*, ed. Marie Bennigsen Broxup (New York, 1992).

3. N. I. Zagoskin, *Materialy istoricheskie i iuridicheskie raiona byvshago Prikaza Kazanskogo dvortsa*, vol. 1, *Arkhiv Kniazia V. I. Baiusheva* (Kazan, 1882), 16–17, no. 15, 1640.

4. The continuity of Tatar families in the earliest land cadastre is discussed in R. E. F. Smith, *Peasant Farming in Muscovy* (Cambridge, 1977), 197–218.

5. István Vásáry, "The Tatar Ruling Houses in Russian Genealogical Sources," *Acta Orientalia Academiae Scientiarum Hungaricae* 61 (2008).

6. See the discussion of *mestnichestvo* in chaps. 1 and 2.

7. Janet Martin, *Medieval Russia, 980–1584* (Cambridge, 1995), esp. 271–72, 299–300. For a discussion of the extension of *pomest'e* in the sixteenth century, see S. V. Rozhdestvenskii, *Sluzhiloe zemlevladenie v Moskovskom gosudarstve XVI veka* (St. Petersburg, 1897).

8. Pelenski, "State and Society," 163–65.

9. For studies of the Tatars' military service outside of the region, see Janet Martin, "The *Novokshcheny* of Novgorod: Assimilation in the 16th Century," *Central Asian Survey* 9

(1990); J. Martin, "Multiethnicity in Muscovy: A Consideration of Christian and Muslim Tatars in the 1550s–1580s," *Journal of Early Modern History* 5 (2001); and J. Martin, "Tatars in the Muscovite Army during the Livonian War," in *The Military and Society in Russia, 1450–1917*, ed. Eric Lohr and Marshall Poe (Leiden, 2002).

10. J. Martin, "Muscovite Frontier Policy"; Rakhimzianov, *Kasimovskoe khantsvo.*

11. Ermolaev and Mustafina, *Dokumenty po istorii Kazanskogo kraia*, 95–97, no. 40, 13 April 1622.

12. Outside of this region, residence requirements did not become standard practice until 1649, when the Law Code (*Ulozhenie*) specified that all service Tatars in Muscovy reside on their lands. Hellie, *Ulozhenie*, 112, chap. 16, art. 45.

13. For a narrative, see Pavlov and Perrie, *Ivan the Terrible*, 107–203.

14. See R. G. Skrynnikov, *Tsartsvo terrora* (St. Petersburg, 1992); Zimin, *Oprichnina.*

15. Political prisoners also played a role in Siberia's settlement. See S. I. Rostislavovich's study of Poles and Lithuanians in the seventeenth century, *Sluzhilye "inozemtsy" v Sibiri XVII veka (Tomsk, Eniseisk, Krasnoiarsk)* (Novosibirsk, 2004).

16. The idea of "redemption through service" as part of Muscovite governing strategies has been discussed in the Siberian context. Maureen Perrie, "Outlawry and Redemption through Service: Ermak and the Volga Cossacks," in *Culture and Identity in Muscovy, 1359–1584*, ed. Ann Kleimola and Gail Lenhoff (Moscow, 1997).

17. Ermolaev and Mustafina, *Dokumenty po istorii Kazanskogo kraia*, 49–51, no. 16, 18 July 1595. Or see the case of the Tatar Ivan Nekhev, who received his grant in Alatyr' province for his decade of service. Russian State Archive of Ancient Acts, Moscow (hereafter cited as RGADA), f. 1455, Gosudarstvennye i chastnye akty pomestno-votchinnykh arkhivov, d. 185, 19 November 1631.

18. Ermolaev and Mustafina, *Dokumenty po istorii Kazanskogo kraia*, 72–74, no. 31, 13 April 1622.

19. Alishev, *Istoricheskie subdy narodov Srednego Povolzh'ia* , 191.

20. D. M. Makarov, *Samoderzhavie i khristianizatsiia narodov Povolzh'ia v vtoroi polovine XVI–XVII vv.* (Cheboksary, 1981); I. K. Zagidullin, "Kkristianizatsiia tatar Srednego Povolzh'ia vo vtoroi polovine XVI–XVII vv.," *Uchenye zapiski (Kazan')*, no. 1 (1997); F. G. Islaev, *Pravoslavnye missionery v Povolzh'e* (Kazan, 1999); Paul W. Werth, "Coercion and Conversion: Violence and Mass Baptism of the Volga Peoples, 1740–55," *Kritika* 4 (2003).

21. Ermolaev and Mustafina, *Dokumenty po istorii Kazanskogo kraia*, 51–52, no. 17, 11 April 1597; 56–57, no. 21, no earlier than September 1602; 58–59, no. 23, 18 November 1604; 74–75, no. 32, after 16 February 1616; 76–78, no. 33, 22 February 1616.

22. Ibid., 107–9, no. 47, March 1632; 113–14, no. 51, no earlier than 1636; 82, no. 36, 10 June 1620; 146–47, no. 66, no earlier than 1645.

23. Ibid., 99–101, no. 43, 7 June 1623; Evfimii Malov, comp., *Drevniia gramoty i raznye dokumenty (Materialy dlia istorii Kazanskoi eparkhii)* (Kazan, 1902), 8–9, 5 October 1633.

24. Ermolaev and Mustafina, *Dokumenty po istorii Kazanskogo kraia*, 109–11, no. 48, no earlier than 1633; Malov, *Drevniia gramoty i raznye dokumenty*, 10–11, 14 December 1638.

25. Ermolaev and Mustafina, *Dokumenty po istorii Kazanskogo kraia*, 136–37, no. 61, 20 April 1641; Malov, *Drevniia gramoty i raznye dokumenty*, 12–15, 16 July 1653.

26. Begishev was identified as a Chuvash in the earliest documents, though later records identify his family as "service Tatars." However, in the seventeenth century, Muscovite sources might label any Muslim as a "Tatar." Stepan Mel'nikov, ed., *Akty istoricheskie i iuridicheskie i drevniia tsarskiia gramoty Kazanskoi i drugikh sosedstvennykh gubernii* (Kazan, 1859), 8–9, no. 4, 26 June 1619; 11–12, no. 6, 1621; 13–14, no. 7, 9 July 1621.

27. Mel'nikov, *Akty istoricheskie i iuridicheskie*, 15–16, no. 9, 8 February 1624; 28–29, no. 15, 5 February 1636; 29–30, no. 16, after 16 February 1636.

28. The land was seized from Ivan and Kalin Esipov and awarded to Men'shov Andreianov on 26 June 1613. Ermolaev and Mustafina, *Dokumenty po istorii Kazanskogo kraia*, 66–67, no. 28.

29. Ibid., 67–70, no. 29, 10 August 1613; 112–13, no. 50, 9 July 1636.

30. The dowry is printed in Ermolaev and Mustafina, *Dokumenty po istorii Kazanskogo kraia*, 112–13, 9 July 1636; an example of the transactions between Andreianov and Brekhov is found in ibid., 132, no. 58, 25 July 1640.

31. RGADA, f. 1455, op. 3, d. 185, 19 November 1931.

32. The land had been first granted to his father in 1603. Malov, *Drevniia gramoty i raznye dokumenty*, 7–8, 11 January 1637. Other examples of Russian Orthodox servitors losing claims to Muslim lands can be found in Ermolaev and Mustafina, *Dokumenty po istorii Kazanskogo kraia*, 125–27, no. 55, 11 September 1638; 163–67, no. 76, 9 April 1650.

33. Ermolaev and Mustafina, *Dokumenty po istorii Kazanskogo kraia*, 53–54, no. 18, 18 June 1598.

34. Hellie, *Ulozhenie*, 111, chap. 16, art. 41.

35. Ibid., 112, chap. 16, art. 43. This law does signify a major change from earlier years, when land transactions between Russians and those groups were not uncommon. For example, a charter from 26 January 1632 records a land exchange by a Tatar from a Russian, with the Tatar receiving land in the countryside in exchange for his house in the city of Arzamas; another from 27 February 1633 records a land transaction between a Russian and a Mordvin, with the Mordvin receiving service lands in the countryside and the Russian receiving the rights to space with the market at the Troitsii-Sergeiv Monastery in Arzamas. RGADA, f. 281, d. 267; RGADA, f. 281, d. 276, respectively.

36. Hellie, *Ulozhenie*, 112, chap. 16, art. 43.

37. There has been no single study of Tatar-Russian marriages, though they were not uncommon, including several examples in this chapter's discussions of dowries.

38. Hellie, *Ulozhenie*, 112, chap. 16, art. 45. While many Tatar servitors did receive notices for failure to provide service, this not an uncommon phenomenon in Russia. Vasilii Elatin was reminded by the Prikaz Kazanskogo dvortsa that he owed them both taxes and service, which he had failed to provide the previous year. RGADA, f. 1209, op. 78, d. 2753, 16 April 1654. The Prikaz reminded Savin Fedorov syn Aukin and Petr Painravevich Nechaev in 1688 to fulfill their duties in Saransk district. RGADA, f. 1209, Pomestnyi Prikaz, op. 78,

d. 2749; Aukin's is l. 1, Nechaev's is l. 2. The Pomestnyi Prikaz reminded Boris Skaskev in Saransk on 20 May 1694 or his failure to fulfill his obligations. RGADA, f. 1209, op. 78, d. 2750.

39. This was not an innovation, but rather a longstanding tradition in East Slavic lands now confirmed in the Law Code. Hellie, *Ulozhenie*, 56, chap. 10, art. 161.

40. Ibid., 97–98, chap. 14, art. 3.

41. RGADA, f. 210, op. 21, d. 245, 22 June 1670. Earlier scholars argued single-district landholdings were a rare exception by 1700, but single-district landholdings as in Saransk correspond with Valerie Kivelson's study of provincial landholding. For a complete historiographic discussion as well as Kivelson's findings, see her *Autocracy in the Provinces: The Muscovite Gentry and Political Culture in the Seventeenth Century* (Stanford, CA, 1997), 84–92.

42. For a discussion of military reforms, see Esper, "Military Self-Sufficiency and Weapons Technology"; Marshall Poe, "The Consequences of Military Revolution in Russia: A Comparative Perspective," *Comparative Studies in Society and History* 38 (1996); Paul, "The Military Revolution in Russia"; Stevens, *Russia's Wars of Emergence*, esp. 187–216; Donald Ostrowski, "The Replacement of the Composite Bow by Firearms in the Muscovite Cavalry," *Kritika* 11 (2010).

43. RGADA, f. 210, op. 21, d. 228, l. 70b., 1668/69.

44. RGADA, f. 210, Razriadnyi prikaz, op. 21, d. 228, ll. 1–70b., 1669. For another comparison, see *Russkaia istoricheskaia biblioteka*, vol. 17 (St. Petersburg, 1898), esp. "Atemarskaia desiatnia 1669–70," cols. 131–426, which covers both Atemar and Saransk.

45. Bushkovitch, *Religion and Society*, 22–26.

46. The classic work on canonization is E. Golubinskii, *Istoriia kanonizatsii sviatykh v russkoi tserkvi* (Moscow, 1903), but recent works challenge this. See Bushkovitch, *Religion and Society*, 75–127; Eve Levin, "From Corpse to Cult in Early Modern Russia," in *Orthodox Russia: Belief and Practice Under the Tsars*, ed. Valerie A. Kivelson and Robert H. Greene (University Park, PA, 2003); and Eve Levin, "False Miracles and Unattested Dead Bodies: Investigations into Popular Cults in Early Modern Russia," in *Religion and the Early Modern State: Views from China, Russia, and the West*, ed. James D. Tracy and Marguerite Ragnow (New York, 2004).

47. While the early seventeenth-century manuscript version of the "Tale" used here has fourteen miracles, later printed versions included in Germogen's complete work contain sixteen. Three of the earlier fourteen miracles were not included in either of the printed versions. *Tvoreniia svateishago Germogena patriarkha Moskovskagoi vseia Rossii* (Moscow, 1912), 1–34.

48. SGU 1756, ff. 36v.–37r.

49. SGU 1756, ff. 28v.–29r.

50. SGU 1756, ff. 30r.–30v.

51. Moscow State University (hereafter MGU) General Slavic Fond, pt. 1, no. 50118, *Sbornik Kazanskikh zhitiakh*, ff. 158v.–159v.

52. MGU, no. 50118, ff. 148–149.

53. Ibid., ff. 144–145.

54. Ibid., ff. 138v.–139.

55. Ibid., ff. 139v.–140.

56. Ibid., ff. 166–169.

57. According to a nineteenth-century source, the Sergeiv Makar'evskii Zheltovodskii Monastery was established in 1435, though Makarii died on 25 July 1504. Denisov, *Pravoslavnye monastyri*, 560–61.

58. SGU 343, "Service and Life of Makarii, Abbot of Zheltovod and Unzha," early seventeenth century, ff. 1–38, courtesy of Eve Levin.

59. SGU 343, ff. 29v.–32.

60. SGU 343, ff. 37–38.

61. Marshall Poe, "What Did Russians Mean When They Called Themselves 'Slaves of the Tsar'?" *Slavic Review* 57 (1998).

62. Sergei Bogatyrev, *Sovereign and His Counselors*.

63. RGADA, f. 1455, op. 3, d. 251, 27 October 1646.

64. Ann Kleimola, "'In accordance with the canons of the Holy Apostles': Muscovite Dowries and Women's Property Rights," *Russian Review* 51 (1992); George G. Weickhardt, "Legal Rights of Women in Russia, 1100–1750," *Slavic Review* 55 (1996); Kivelson, *Autocracy in the Provinces*, 101–16. For widows' and daughters' legal rights, see Hellie, *Ulozhenie*, 109, chap. 16, arts. 30 and 31.

65. RGADA, f. 1209, op. 78, d. 13, no earlier than 1666, includes an account of all of the family's property and upholds the exclusive grant to Nikita, denying any land to his brothers, Ivan and Petr.

66. RGADA, f. 1455, op. 3, d. 393, 28 January 1667.

67. Kleimola, "'In accordance with the canons,'" 215, 226.

68. RGADA, f. 1209, op. 78, d. 2746.

69. RGADA, f. 1455, op. 3, d. 493, 22 June 1675.

70. For a discussion of military servitors' dowries, see Kivelson, *Autocracy in the Provinces*, 101–28.

71. RGADA, f. 1455, op. 3, d. 296, 6 July 1654; RGADA, f. 1455, op. 2, d. 6450, 18 March 1683.

72. RGADA, f. 1209, op. 78, d. 1474, 1671/72; f. 281, op. 1, d. 290, 1646/47; f. 1455, op. 3, d. 309, 9 March 1657.

73. Ermolaev and Mustafina, *Dokumenty po istorii Kazanskogo kraia*, 37, no. 4, no earlier than September 1567.

74. See, for example, ibid., 103–5, no. 45, 19 June 1626; 105–6, no. 46, 2 May 1627; 125–27, no. 55, 11 September 1638; and 130–32, no. 57, 20 July 1639.

75. Ibid., 98, no. 42, 1622.

76. RGADA, f. 1455, op. 3, d. 286, 13 February 1652.

77. Ermolaev and Mustafina, *Dokumenty po istorii Kazanskogo kraia*, 65, no. 27, no earlier than February 1613.

78. Ibid., 46, no. 12, 13 September 1585.

79. Ibid., 41, no. 7, 29 August 1583.

80. RGADA, f. 1209, op. 78, d. 98, [1613–45].

81. Ibid., d. 10, 2 June 1660.

82. Ibid., d. 4, no earlier than 1622/23.

83. RGADA, f. 1455, op. 2, d. 7118, 18 September 1677.

84. RGADA, f. 1209, op. 78, d. 176, March 1652.

85. RGADA, f. 1455, op. 3, d. 424, 31 August 1671.

86. RGADA, f. 281, op. 4, d. 6451, August 1616. At least one local resident attempted to claim the metropolitanate's new lands, leading to another declaration of the metropolitanate's ownership just two years later. RGADA, f. 281, op. 4, d. 6452, 10 May 1618.

87. RGADA, f. 281, op. 1, d. 261, 3 September 1628.

88. Ibid., d. 273.

89. Ermolaev and Mustafina, *Dokumenty po istorii Kazanskogo kraia*, 39–41, no. 6, 22 June 1583.

90. RGADA, f. 1455, op. 5, d. 859, 29 September 1669.

91. RGADA, f. 1209, op. 78, d. 147, ll. 2–4, 25 September 1676. Elagin and Petrov protested the loss of their family's land but were denied.

Chapter 5. Irregular Subjects

1. For the different agricultural methods employed in the sixteenth century, see R. Smith, *Peasant Farming in Muscovy*, 197–218.

2. Most of the *Sudebnik* of 1550 concerns the tsar's relationship with the boiars; very few groups are mentioned at all. G. G. Tel'berg, ed., *Sudebniki Velikago Ivan III i Tsaria Ivana IV* (Kharbin, 1926).

3. Khodarkovsky, "Four Degrees of Separation."

4. A. S. Morris, "The Medieval Emergence."

5. R. Smith, *Peasant Farming in Muscovy*, 197–218.

6. For an introduction, see Dewey, "Russia's Debt to the Mongols."

7. B. D. Grekov and V. I. Lebedev, eds., *Dokumenty i materialy po istorii mordovskoi ASSR* (Saransk, 1940), 1:235–48, no. 42, 1618–19.

8. Aiplatov and Ivanov, *Monastyrskaia kolonizatziia Mariiskogo Povolzh'ia*, 60–61, no. 6, 8 February 1641.

9. Zertsalov, *Materialy dlia istorii Sinbirska*, 49–71, 98–102.

10. I. M. Pokrovskii, "Bortnichestvo (pchelovodstvo)."

11. Grekov and Lebedev, *Dokumenty i materialy*, 1:233, no. 38, 1614–15.

12. Martynov, *Seleniia Simbirskogo uezda*, 127–28, 1625.

13. For the Tatar, see Law Library of Congress, Russian Manuscript Scrolls Collection, I-2, no earlier than 1639; for the Mordvins, see Russian State Archive of Ancient Acts, Moscow (hereafter cited as RGADA), f. 281, Gramoty kollegii ekonomii, op. 1, d. 289, 17 March 1642.

14. E. N. Sheikovskaia, *Gosudarstvo i krest'iane Rossii: Pomor'e v XVII veke* (Moscow, 1997).

15. Grekov and Lebedev, *Dokumenty i materialy*, 1:279–81, no. 52, 25 September 1629.

16. For a discussion of tax policy, see Kliuchevsky, *Kurs russkoi istorii* 3:213–36.

17. Episkop Nikaron, "Vladennyia gramaty Kazanskago Spasopreobrazhenskago Monastyria," 357.

18. Ibid., 361–62, 5 November 1595; 362–63, 29 January 1601.

19. Ermolaev and Mustafina, *Dokumenty po istorii Kazanskogo kraia*, 84–92, no. 38.

20. The monasteries were Kazan's Troitse-Sergeevskii and Zilantov Uspenskii, and Sviiazhsk's Bogoroditsii. I. Pokrovskii, "K istorii Kazanskikh monastyrei do 1764 goda," *Izvestiia obshchestva arkheologii, istorii i etnografii pri Imperatorskom Kazanskom universitete* 18 (1902). Pokrovskii's information is from the census of 1646 in Kazan province. Similar data does not exist for most of the region's monasteries, because of the inconsistent information kept in the census records.

21. Dubman, *Khoziaistvennoe osvoenie Srednego Povolzh'ia.*

22. Kuntsevich, "Gramoty Kazan'skogo Zilantova monastyria," 279–81.

23. RGADA, f. 281, op. 1, d. 293, 23 February 1648.

24. Ibid., op. 1, d. 303, 30 March 1679.

25. Romaniello, "Mission Delayed." For a different assessment, see Leonid Taimasov, "Mezhkonfessional'nye otnosheniia na nachal'nom etape khristianizatsii narodov Kazanskogo kraia (Vtoraia polovina XVI–XVII vv.)," *Forschungen zur osteuropäischen Geschichte* 63 (2004).

26. For example, Sviiazhsk's Troitse-Sergeevskii Monastery lost a village of Russian peasants in Sviiazhsk province to the governor of Kazan in 1669. RGADA, f. 1455, Gosu-darstvennye i chastnye akty pomestno-votchinnykh arkhivov XVI–XIX vv., op. 5, d. 859, 29 September 1669.

27. For example, in Siberia the relationship between the non-Russians and local monasteries appeared more adversarial. See L. P. Shorokhov, "Vozniknovennie monastyrkikh votchin v Vostochnoi Sibiri," in *Russkoe naselenie Pomor'ia Sibiri (period feodalizma)*, ed. V. I. Shunkov and A. P. Okladnikov (Moscow, 1973).

28. For an introduction to enserfment, see the classic works by Jerome Blum, *Lord and Peasant in Russia: From the Ninth to the Nineteenth Century* (Princeton, NJ, 1961); and Richard Hellie, *Enserfment and Military Change in Muscovy* (Chicago, 1971).

29. Alishev suggests that by the end of the sixteenth century, 71 percent of the land in Arzamas province was divided into *pomest'ia*, resulting in large numbers of Mordvins under direct Russian control. Alishev, *Istoricheskie subdy narodov Srednego Povolzh'ia*, 97.

30. Blum, *Lord and Peasant*, 256, 261; Hellie, *Enserfment and Military Change*, 132.

31. These petitions are reprinted in A. A. Novosel'skii, "Kollektivnye dvorianskie chelobitnye o syske beglykh krest'ian i kholopov vo vtoroi polovine XVII v.," in *Dvorianstvo i krepostnoi stroi Rossii XVII–XVIII vv.*, ed. N. I. Pavlenko (Moscow, 1975).

32. P. D. Vereshchagin, ed., *Proshloe nashego kraia 1648–1917* (Ul'ianovsk, 1968), 30, no. 11, 24 February 1630.

33. Ermolaev and Mustafina, *Dokumenty po istorii Kazanskogo kraia*, 51–52, no. 17, 11 April 1597; 56–57, no. 21, no earlier than September 1602, 58–59, 18 November 1604; 74–75, no. 32, after 16 February 1616; 76–78, no. 33, 22 February 1616.

34. For the Andreianovs, see Ermolaev and Mustafina, *Dokumenty po istorii Kazanskogo kraia*, 66–67, no. 28, 26 June 1613. For the Khoziashevs, see Ermolaev and Mustafina, *Dokumenty po istorii Kazanskogo kraia*, 99–101, no. 43, 7 June 1623; Malov, *Drevniia gramoty i raznye dokumenty*, 8–9, 5 October 1633.

35. Ermolaev and Mustafina, *Dokumenty po istorii Kazanskogo kraia*, 37, no. 4, no earlier than September 1567; 39–41, no. 6, 22 June 1583.

36. RGADA, f. 210, Razriadnyi prikaz, op. 21, d. 228, ll. 1–70b., 1669.

37. RGADA, f. 16, op.1, d. 709, ll. 3a ob.–3v., 16 April 1613.

38. Dmitriev, "Vosstanie iasachnykh liudei Srednego Povolzh'ia i Priural'ia 1615–1616 godov."

39. For an introduction to Muscovite resettlements, see Janet Martin, "Mobility, Forced Resettlement, and Regional Identity in Muscovy," in *Culture and Identity in Muscovy, 1359–1584*, ed. Ann Kleimola and Gail Lenhoff (Moscow, 1997).

40. A. V. Emmausskii argued that Muscovite persecution against the Mordvins began under Ivan III, but increased dramatically with the rise in Muscovy's Mordvin population after 1552. A. V. Emmausskii, "Iz istorii bor'by za zemliui krest'ian v Arzamasskom uezde v XVI–XVII vv.," *Trudy Kirovskogo nauchno-issledovatel'skogo instituta kraevedeniia* 7, no. 3 (1934).

41. A. Geraklitov, *Alatyrskaia Mordva po perepisiam 1624–1721 gg.* (Saransk, 1936), 15–24.

42. A. G. Brikner, "Chuma v Moskve v 1654 godu," *Istoricheskii vestnik: Istoriko-literaturnyi zhurnal* 16 (April 1884).

43. Peterson, *Istoricheskii ocherk Kerenskogo kraia*, 10. Similarly, Penza was established with a large non-Russian population in 1663. A. F. Dergachev et al., *Ocherki istorii Penzenskogo kraia*, 19–26.

44. RGADA, f. 1103, Arzamasskaia prikaznaia izba, op. 1, d. 24, January 1681. Other examples include RGADA, f. 281, op. 7, d. 10824, ll. 2–20b., no earlier than 1685; f. 281, op. 1, d. 277, ll. 6–9, 2 August 1686; ll. 1–5.5, 16 February 1688.

45. RGADA, f. 281, op. 7, d. 10824, ll. 1–10b., February 1683.

46. For an introduction to the agricultural production challenges of migration, see David Moon, "Peasant Migration and the Settlement of Russia's Frontiers, 1550–1897," *Historical Journal* 40 (1997).

47. RGADA, f. 281, op. 1, d. 277, ll. 36–37.5, 3 February 1693; ll. 32–34.5, 16 November 1693.

48. RGADA, f. 281, op. 1, d. 277, ll. 1–39, contains thirteen documents between 1633 and 1695, detailing the monastery's struggle to keep its Mordvin villages.

49. Mordvins Ivan and Anashno Leoniv, Sëmen Eogdanov, and Nevbrii and Mikhail Vetisko were listed among its new peasants. RGADA, f. 281, op. 1, d. 277, ll. 14.5–17, 1633/34.

50. RGADA, f. 281, op. 1, d. 277, ll. 9–11.5 to the tsar; ll. 11.5–14.5 to the *voevoda*, both on 5 January 1646.

51. RGADA, f. 281, op. 8, d. 11568, 11 September 1688.

52. For a comparative examination, see Will F. Ryan, "The Witchcraft Hysteria in Early Modern Europe: Was Russia an Exception?" *Slavonic and East European Review* 76 (1998).

53. N. Novombergskii, ed., *Koldovstvo v Moskovskoi Rusi XVII-go stoletiia (Materialy po istorii meditsiny v Rossii t. III ch. I)* (St. Petersburg, 1906), 14–25, no. 4.

54. N. Novombergskii, ed., *Vrachebnoe stroenie v do-Petrovskoi Rusi* (Tomsk, 1907), viii–xxvi, no. 5; N. Novombergskii, ed., *Materialy po istorii meditsiny v Rossii* (Tomsk, 1907), 4:172–73, no. 27.

55. Russell Zguta, "Witchcraft and Medicine in Pre-Petrine Russia," *Russian Review* 37 (1978); Eve Levin, "Healers and Witches in Early Modern Russia," in *Saluting Aron Gurevich: Essays in History, Literature and Related Disciplines*, ed. Yelena Matusevich and Alexandra Korros (Leiden, 2010). For other crimes associated with witchcraft, see Valerie A. Kivelson, "Patrolling the Boundaries: Witchcraft Accusations and Household Strife in Seventeenth-Century Muscovy," *Harvard Ukrainian Studies* 19 (1995); and Kivelson, "Political Sorcery in Sixteenth-Century Muscovy," in *Culture and Identity in Muscovy, 1359–1584*, ed. A. M. Kleimola and G. D. Lenhoff (Moscow, 1997).

56. Brian L. Davies, *State Power and Community in Early Modern Russia: The Case of Kozlov, 1635–1649* (Houndsmills, Basingstoke, Hampshire, 2004), esp. 75–116.

57. RGADA, f. 16, op.1, d. 709, ll. 10–11, 16 May 1649.

58. Donnelly, *Russian Conquest of Bashkiria*, 139–41.

59. RGADA, f. 16, op.1, d. 709, ll. 11–12, 16 May 1649.

60. Ibid., ll. 9–10, 16 May 1649.

61. Ibid., l. 10, 16 May 1649.

62. For more on hostage-taking, see Khodarkovsky, *Russia's Steppe Frontier*, 56–60.

63. RGADA, f. 16, op.1, d. 709, ll. 12–130b., 16 May 1649.

64. Brian Davies, "The Razin Rebellion at Tambov and Kozlov, 1670–1671," *Russian History* 34 (2007): 271.

65. Hellie, *Enserfment and Military Change*, 123–40.

66. Alishev, *Istoricheskie sudby narodov Srednego Povolzh'ia*, 96. By the end of the eighteenth century, only 32 percent of the peasantry in Kazan province were serfs, while the remainder were state peasants (albeit former monastic peasants or *iasachnye liudi*). Janet M. Hartley, *A Social History of the Russian Empire, 1650–1825* (London, 1999), 19.

67. Hellie, *Ulozhenie*, 85, chap. 11, art. 1. A discussion of the evolution of this policy can be found in Blum, *Lord and Peasant*, 261–66; and Hellie, *Enserfment and Military Change*, 141–45.

68. Kazan was one of the four regions specified in the *Ulozhenie*, along with Moscow, Novgorod, and Pskov. Hellie, *Ulozhenie*, 91, chap. 11, art. 20.

69. RGADA, f. 1209, op. 78, d. 126, 16 December 1626.

70. Ermolaev and Mustafina, *Dokumenty po istorii Kazanskogo kraia*, 137–38, no. 62, 9 March 1642.

71. There are many studies about runaway peasants in Volga Region, including I. D. Kuznetsov, *Ocherki po istorii Chuvashskogo krest'ianstva* (Cheboksary, 1957), 78–154; N. V. Razorekova, "Beglye krest'iane v pervoi chetverti XVII veka (Po materialam Alatyrskoi perepisnoi kantseliarii)," *Problemy istorii SSSR* 4 (1974); V. P. Pushkov and I. M. Promakhina, "Sem'ia v sisteme Russkogo krest'ianskogo khoziaistva (Po materialam syska beglykh krest'ian 60-x godov XVII v. v Alatyrskom i Arzamasskom uezdakh)," in *Sotsial'no-demograficheskie protsessy v Rossiiskoi derevne (XVI–nachalo XX v.)*, ed. I. D. Koval'chenko (Tallin, 1986), 1:26–34; E. L. Dubman, "Beglye krest'iane kak istochnik formirovaniia naseleniia krupnoi votchiny Simbirsko-Samarskogo Povolzh'ia v XVII–nachale XVIII vv.," in *Sotsial'no-ekonomicheskoe razvitie i klassovaia bor'ba na iuzhnom Urale i v Srednom Povolzh'e (Do revoliutsionnyi period)*, ed. I. G. Akmanov et al. (Ufa, 1988); V. V. Dolzhenkov, "Beglye krest'iane v Penzenskom krae v XVII veke," *Iz istorii oblasti: Ocherki kraevedov* I (1989).

72. RGADA, f. 1455, op. 1, d. 2296, l. 2. Unsuccessful with his first petition, Lunevskii petitioned again later that same year to ask the tsar for compensation for his lost peasants in the amount of 267 rubles, 8 *altyn*, and 2 *dengi*. Ibid., 1. 3.

73. The *voevoda* included the location of his peasant in both of his petitions to the tsar. RGADA, f. 1209, op. 78, d. 17, l. 1 and l. 2, both before 24 June 1669. The tsar replied to the petitions on 24 June 1669, but whether the peasant was returned or not is unknown, because the reply is torn. RGADA, f. 1209, op. 78, d. 17, l. 3.

74. RGADA, f. 1209, op. 78, d. 1885, 13 December 1661.

75. Ibid., d. 2752, ll. 1–2, 16 December 1666.

76. Specifically, the commissions arrived in Alatyr' in 1661/62, and 1662–69, Arzamas in 1661–63, Sviiazhsk in 1662, and Saransk and Simbirsk in 1661–63, and 1668. These commissions are discussed in A. P. Gudzinskaia, "Dokumenty sysknykh komissii vtoroi poloviny XVII v. kak istoricheskii istochnik," in *Arkheograficheskii ezhegodnik za 1967 god* (Moscow, 1969).

77. Dolzhenkov, "Beglye krest'iane," 31–36.

78. In 1678 the total peasant population (both serfs and *iasachnye liudi*) in Penza district was 10,500. Had the runaways remained, the population could have been as much as 11, 683. Ia. E. Vodarskii, *Naselenie Rossii v kontse XVII–nachale XVIII veka (Chislennost', soslovo-klassovyi sostav, razmeshchenie)* (Moscow, 1977), 110, 229.

79. In 1678 Arzamas and Alatyr' collectively had 26,442 households, producing a population of just more than 90,000. The results of the commissions are taken from Puskhov and Promakhina, "Sem'ia i sisteme," 27; the population statistics are from Vodarskii, *Naselenie Rossii*, 110, 221, 228.

80. Dolzhenkov, "Beglye krest'iane, 31–36.

81. Pushkov and Promakhina, "Sem'ia i sisteme," 27.

82. "State peasants" is a blanket term used to classify a variety of peasants who resided on state lands as opposed to hereditary estates or on the personal property of the tsar's family.

The process of creating state peasants as a legal category defined by paying the poll tax was accelerated by Peter the Great. See the brief discussions in Lindsey Hughes, *Russia in the Age of Peter the Great* (New Haven, CT, 1998), 160–72; Hartley, *Social History of the Russian Empire*, 19–23; and David Moon, *The Russian Peasantry 1600–1930: The World the Peasants Made* (London, 1999), 77–79.

83. Martynov, *Seleniia Simbirskogo uezda*, 184–85, 25 May 1664.

84. Vereshchagin, *Proshloe nashego kraia*, 23, no. 4, 6 August 1662; 23–24, no. 5, no earlier than 26 September 1663.

85. Grekov and Lebedev, *Dokumenty i materialy*, 1:320–21, no. 115, 1 March 1667.

86. *Akty iuridicheskie, ili sobranie form starinnago deloproizovodstva*, 211–14, no. 202, 23 June 1663 (Nizhnii Novgorod), 23 June 1663 (Koz'modem'iansk), and 20 June 1664 (Kurmysh).

87. Lit. "*inoverets, ili kreshchen, ili pravoslava khristian*." To ensure this policy, the Prikaz also notified the current governor of the change in policy. RGADA, f. 1103, Arzamasskaia prikaznaia izba, op. 1, d. 25a, 1682.

88. This officially began in 1764 with the secularization of Church lands. Hartley, *Social History of the Russian Empire*, 20–21; Moon, *Russian Peasantry*, 79.

Chapter 6. Subdued Rebels

1. Davies, *Warfare, State, and Society*, chap. 6.

2. Khodarkovsky, *Russia's Steppe Frontier*, chaps. 3–4.

3. The major primary published source is the comprehensive five-volume document collection, A. A. Novosel'skii, ed., *Krest'ianskaia voina pod predvoditel'stvom Stepana Razina: Sbornik dokumentov* (Moscow, 1955–1976).

4. For a traditional interpretation, see Avrich, *Russian Rebels*. For an examination of the urban revolts as a separate event, see James Gerard Hart, "The Urban and Rural Response to Stepan Razin's Rebellion in the Middle Volga Region of Muscovy, 1670–1671" (PhD diss., University of Virginia, 1981). For the revolt as a Cossack military action, see Boeck, *Imperial Boundaries*, 68–85.

5. The folk aspects are discussed most recently in Vladimir Solov'ev, *Anatomiia Russkogo bunta: Stepan Razin: Mify i real'nost'* (Moscow, 1994); and V. I. Buganov, *Razin i Razintsy* (Moscow, 1995).

6. For an excellent account of these events, see Boeck, *Imperial Boundaries*, 68–85.

7. The local *voevody* reported 5,000 men under arms; Soviet historiographical accounts have preferred larger numbers. For the former, see Vereshchagin, *Proshloe nashego kraia*, 51–52, no. 23, 28 August 1670; for the latter, see K. Naiakshin, *Ocherki istorii Kuibyshevskoi oblasti* (Kuibyshev, 1962), 45–49.

8. As discussed in chap. 5.

9. I. V. Stepanov, *Krest'ianskaia voina v Rossii v 1670–1671 gg.*, bk. 2, pt. 1, *Nachal'nyi period krest'ianskoi voiny* (Leningrad, 1672), 152.

10. I. V. Stepanov, "Bor'ba krest'iansko-kazatskogo povstansheskogo voiska Stepana Razina za Simbirsk," in *Problemy istorii feodal'noi Rossii: Sbornik statei k 60-letii v Prof. V. V. Mavrodina*, ed. A. L. Shapiro et al. (Leningrad, 1971).

11. As discussed in chap. 5.

12. See Geoffrey Parker, *Europe in Crisis, 1598–1648*, 2nd ed. (Oxford, 2001), 1–10.

13. Novosel'skii, *Krest'ianskaia voina*, vol. 2, pt. 1, 60–62, no. 48, 10 and 16 September 1670.

14. Ibid.

15. Ibid., 69–71, no. 58, 21 September 1670.

16. Ibid., 76–78, no. 66, 23 September 1670; 92–93, no. 79, between 30 September and 2 October 1670.

17. Ibid., 71–72, no. 60, 22 and 29 September 1670.

18. Ibid., 104–5, no. 88, 2 October 1670.

19. Ibid., 183–84, no. 155, between 21 October and 1 November 1670; 187–89, no. 159, no earlier than 22 October 1670; 424–27, no. 338, 17 December 1670.

20. Ibid., 220–21, no. 186, 30 October 1670; 248–51, no. 205, no earlier than 6 November 1670; 282–83, no. 234, no later than 17 November 1670.

21. Ibid., 91, no. 78, no later than 30 September 1670; 212, no. 177, 28 October 1670.

22. Ibid., 82–84, no. 70, 27 September 1670.

23. Ibid., 115–18, no. 100, 7 October 1670.

24. Ibid., 526–27, no. 407, earlier than 16 January 1671.

25. Ibid., 192–94, no. 162, 25 October 1670; Hart, "Urban and Rural Response," 113–28.

26. V. A. Osipov et al., eds., *Istoriia Saratovskaia kraia 1590–1917* (Saratov, 1983), 29–32, no. 12, 29 July 1667.

27. This includes V. I. Lebedev, *Krest'ianskaia voina pod predvoditel'stvom Stepana Razina* (Moscow, 1955); A. G. Mankov, ed., *Zapiski inostrantsev o vosstanii Stepana Razina* (Leningrad, 1968); A. Sakharov, *Stepan Razin (Khronika XVII veka)* (Moscow, 1973).

28. For a discussion of the limits of the Soviet interpretation, see Michael Khodarkovsky, "The Stepan Razin Uprising: Was It a 'Peasant War'?" *Jahrbücher für Geschichte Osteuropas* 42 (1994).

29. Russian State Archive of Ancient Acts, Moscow (hereafter cited as RGADA), f. 16, op. 1, d. 709, copy from 1720, 22 March 1677, ll. 38, 640b.–69.

30. RGADA, f. 16, op. 1, d. 709, ll. 49–51.

31. Ibid., ll. 51–52.

32. Ibid., ll. 770b.

33. *Polnoe sobranie zakonov Rossiiskoi Imperii* (hereafter cited as *PSZ*), ser. 1, 45 vols. (St. Petersburg, 1830), 2:488, no. 980, 1682; 2:914, no. 1688, 7 March 1688; 3:303–4, no. 1582, 22 April 1697.

34. Grekov and Lebedev, *Dokumety i materialy*, 2:14, no. 169, no earlier than 15 February 1676.

35. V. M. Terekhin, "Istoricheskie materialy v otnoshenii inorodtsev penzenskago kraia kontsa XVII st.," *Izvestiia obshchestva arkheologicheskii, istorii i etnografii pri Imperatorskom Kazanskom universitete* 14, no. 2 (1897).

36. RGADA, f. 1156, Saranskaia prikaznaia izba, op. 1, d. 9, ll. 7–9.

37. As discussed in chap. 4.

38. On 27 June 1680 the Prikaz notified the current *voevoda* of Saransk, Pavl Petrovich Iazykov, to expect Azter'ev's immediate arrival. RGADA, f. 1156, op. 1, d. 9, ll. 4–5.

39. RGADA, f. 1209, Pomestnyi prikaz, op. 78, d. 18, 1672/73.

40. RGADA, f. 1209, op. 78, d. 144, ll. 1–2, 1675/76.

41. For the revolt, see Law Library of Congress, Russian Manuscript Scrolls Collection, Scroll I-19, no earlier than June 1674. The Kalmyks later complained about late payment for their services in Simbirsk. RGADA, f. 159, Prikaznye dela novoi razborki, op. 2, Posol'skii prikaz, d. 1349, 15 June 1675.

42. Gudzinskaia, "Dokumenty sysknykh komissii vtoroi poloviny."

43. A similar examination of the land of the Novodevichii Convent along the banks of the Volga in 1705 also found peasants originating from outside the region, but all of those 796 peasant households began on the convent's own estates in the central provinces. Dubman, "Beglye krest'iane," 15–17.

44. RGADA, f. 1455, Gosudarstvennye i chastnye akty pomestno-votchinnykh arkhivov XVI–XIX vv., op. 3, d. 477, l. 2.

45. RGADA, f. 1209, op. 78, d. 958, 10 September 1680.

46. RGADA, f. 1455, op. 1, d. 140, 28 June 1685.

47. RGADA, f. 1455, op. 1, d. 144, l. 1.

48. RGADA, f. 1209, op. 78, d. 2269, l. 1, 1692/3.

49. RGADA, f. 1103, Arzamasskaia prikaznaia izba, op. 1, d. 12, l. 1, 3 May 1672.

50. All of these petitions and reports are contained in RGADA, f. 1455, op. 1, d. 941, ll. 2–10. On 25 May 1692, the Narmukov's petitioned the *voevoda* of Kazan to intervene with the Prikaz Kazanskogo dvortsa to force another investigation, l. 2. The Prikaz's notification of the presence of Aprov on the estate of the *voevoda* of Saransk follows on l. 5; ll. 9–10 contains the details of the compensation payments to be made by the Prikaz.

51. For the Muslim Tatar *mirza*s, see *PSZ*, 2:267, no. 823, 21 May 1680; *PSZ*, 2:312–13, no. 867, 16 May 1681; and *PSZ*, 2:315, no. 870, 24 May 1681.

52. Apollon Mozharovskii, "Po istorii prosveshcheniia Nizhegorodskoi mordvy," *Nizhegorodskiia eparkhial'nyia vedomosti* 16 (1890): 664–65.

53. *PSZ*, 2:467–68, 23 September 1682.

54. *PSZ*, 3:70–80, 22 August 1690.

55. Grekov and Lebedev, *Dokumenty i materialy*, 2:72, no. 208, 16 November 1687.

56. I. Peretrukhin, "Staroobriadtsy v Kniagininskom uezd, Nizhegorodskoi guber.," *Staroobriadets* 3 (1907); S. V. Sirotkin, "'Raskol'nich'ia prelest' v Arzamasskom uezde v 70-e gg. XVII v.," in *Staroobriadchestvo v Rossii (XVII–XX veka)*, ed. E. M. Iukhimenko (Moscow, 1999).

57. I. Peretrukhin, "Kazanskaia obshchina staroobriadetsev, priemliushchikh belokrinitskoe sviashchenstvo," *Staroobriadets* 1 (1907): 86. Georg Michels identified possible indications among isolated churchmen in Nizhnii Novgorod and Kazan in the 1660s. See his *At War with the Church: Religious Dissent in Seventeenth-Century Russia* (Stanford, CA, 1999), 101.

58. V. C. Rumiantseva, comp., *Narodnoe antitserkovnoe dvizhenie v Rossii XVII veka: Dokumenty Prikaza tainykh del o raskol'nikakh, 1665–1667 gg.* (Moscow, 1986), 61–62, 120–21, 143–46.

59. RGADA, f. 159, op. 3, Novgorodskii prikaz, d. 448, ll. 25–28, no later than 12 October 1675.

60. RGADA, f. 159, op. 3, d. 448, ll. 29–30, 13 October 1675. See also N. F. Filatov, ed., *Arzamas v XVII veke: Ocherki istorii; Dokumenty* (Arzamas, 2000), 73–75.

61. RGADA, f. 159, op. 3, d. 563, ll. 93–97, 12 May 1676.

62. For a discussion of all of the changes after 1649, see Pisar'kova, *Gosudarstvennoe upravlenie Rossii.*

63. RGADA, f. 159, op. 2, d. 1490, ll. 9–10.

64. The law was promulgated on 12 November 1680. S. I. Por'firev, "Kazanskii stol Razriadnyi prikaz," *Izvestiia obshchestva arkheologicheskii, istorii i etnografii pri Imperatorskom Kazanskom universitete* 28, no. 6 (1913).

65. See Carol B. Stevens, "Evaluating Peter's Army: The Impact of Internal Organization," in *The Military and Society in Russia, 1450–1917*, ed. Eric Lohr and Marshall Poe (Leiden, 2002); and Stevens, *Russia's Wars of Emergence, 1460–1730*, esp. chaps. 6 and 8.

66. RGADA, f. 1455, op. 1, d. 1330, 23 September 1690.

67. RGADA, f. 1209, op. 78, d. 36, 1687/88.

68. RGADA, f. 159, op. 2, d. 3852.

69. RGADA, f. 1209, op. 78, d. 39, l. 1, 1685/86; f. 1209, op. 78, d. 156, ll. 6–10, 1689/90; f. 1209, op. 78, d. 39, ll. 2–4, 1685/86.

70. Martynov, *Seleniia Simbirskogo uezda*, 168.

71. Bolkovskii petitioned the *voevoda* of Arzamas in 1690/91 without success. In 1692 he petitioned the tsar. RGADA, f. 210, Razriadnyi prikaz, op. 20, November 1692.

72. RGADA, f. 1209, op. 78, d. 2783. Ruzhevskii's letter is ll. 1–4; Khlopov's petition is l. 5.

73. RGADA, f. 1455, op. 3, d. 831.

74. Konstantin originally had inherited half of his uncle's land—they were split between him an one other cousin, Iakov. When Iakov died in 1686, his children rejected his lands, allowing Konstantin to inherit all of them. RGADA, f. 1455, op. 2, d. 6207.

75. Bogtachevskii's grandfather had been the original *pomeshchik*. Though his father had inherited the village from his grandfather, Bogtachevskii had left Simbirsk while his father was alive. The Prikaz Kazanskogo dvortsa had given the village to Voronko upon Bogtachevskii's father's death, on 2 July 1685. Martynov, *Seleniia Simbirskogo uezda*, 20 March 1686, 94–95.

76. RGADA, f. 159, op. 2, d. 1490, l. 13, 11 May 1676.

77. RGADA, f. 159, op. 2, d. 4356, after 1692.

78. RGADA, f. 159, op. 2, d. 3924, l. 1, 17 August 1689.

79. The National Archives, Kew, England, SP 104/118, Secretaries of State: State Papers Foreign, Entry Books, ff. 32r.–34v., 22 April 1682.

80. *PSZ*, 3:149–51, no. 1460, 10 January 1693.

81. RGADA, f. 1455, op. 1, d. 2294.

82. RGADA, f. 1156, op. 1, d. 6, 15 October 1685, ll. 1–3, is the original accusation; d. 1163, 1686, l. 4, is the *voevoda*'s petition; 18 August 1686, l. 5, is the final verdict.

83. *PSZ*, 2:784, no. 711, 19 December 1678.

84. RGADA, f. 281, Gramoty kollegii ekonomii, op. 1, d. 299, ll. 2–40b., 3 May 1672.

85. On 28 April 1677, the monastery petitioned the tsar claiming the peasants of Cherukha had asked to be returned to their possession. RGADA, f. 281, op. 1, d. 302. This produced a response from the *voevoda* to the villagers of Cherukha, informing the peasants any further petitions to return to the monastery would be rejected. RGADA, f. 281, op. 1, d. 303, 30 March 1679. The monastery received another rejection on 11 July 1683, when the *voevoda* of Arzamas informed them that claiming the village should remain in their possession because they converted the peasants was not valid. RGADA, f. 281, op. 1, d. 305. The monastery persisted at least until 13 January 1688, when the current *voevoda* notified them that they must stop petitioning. RGADA, f. 281, op. 1, d. 312.

86. RGADA, f. 281, op. 1, d. 310, 30 November 1686; and f. 281, op. 1, d. 319, 25 May 1694.

87. RGADA, f. 281, op. 7, d. 10826.

88. RGADA, f. 281, op. 8, d. 11557, 26 July 1686.

89. RGADA, f. 281, op. 1, d. 301, 10 May 1676.

90. RGADA, f. 281, op. 1, 313, 27 January 1688.

Afterword

1. Edward Said, *Orientalism* (New York, 1979). Said's framework has been challenged as a method of analysis for European views of the outside world; among others, see Mary Louise Pratt, *Imperial Eyes: Travel Writing and Transculturation* (New York, 1992); Maria Todorova, *Imagining the Balkans* (New York, 1997); and Muzaffar Alam and Sanjay Subrahmanyam, *Indo-Persian Travels in the Age of Discoveries, 1400–1800* (New York, 2007). For a discussion of European travelers' view of Muscovite Russia, see Marshall Poe, *"A People Born to Slavery": Russia in Early Modern European Ethnography, 1476–1748* (Ithaca, NY, 2001).

2. Larry Wolff, *Inventing Eastern Europe: The Map of Civilization in the Mind of the Enlightenment* (Stanford, 1994).

3. V. O. Kliuchevskii, *Sochineniia v deviati tomakh*, 9 vols. (Moscow, 1987), 1:50.

4. Wortman, *Scenarios of Power*, 43–83.

5. Daniel Schafer, "Building Nations and Building States: The Tatar-Bashkir Question in Revolutionary Russia, 1917–1920" (PhD diss., University of Michigan, 1995).

6. This continued into the post-Soviet era. See, for example, Alishev, *Ternistyi put' bor'by*.

7. See Ronald Grigor Suny, *The Revenge of the Past: Nationalism, Revolution, and the Collapse of the Soviet Union* (Stanford, CA, 1993); Rogers Brubaker, *Nationalism Reframed: Nationhood and the National Question in the New Europe* (New York, 1996), esp. chap. 2.

8. For the rise of Tatar nationalism and its independence movement, see Sergei Kondrashov, *Nationalism and the Drive for Sovereignty in Tatarstan, 1988–92* (New York, 2000).

9. "On Delimitation of Jurisdictional Subjects and Mutual Delegation of Powers between Bodies of Public Authority of the Russian Federation and Bodies of Public Authority of the Republic of Tatarstan," http://www.kcn.ru/tat_en/politics/dfa/inform/treaty.htm, accessed 25 May 2010.

10. R. M. Amirkanov, "Islam in Tatar National Ideology and Policy," in *The Christian-Muslim Frontier: Chaos, Clash or Dialogue?* ed. Jørgen S. Nielsen (London, 1998), 78.

11. Some of the tensions between Tatar nationalists and Tatarstan relate to the role of Islam in the republic. See E. O. Khabenskaia, *Tatary o Tatarskom* (Moscow, 2003). For a broader discussion of the situation, see Dmitry Gorenburg, *Minority Ethnic Mobilization in the Russian Federation* (New York, 2003).

12. "Treaty on Delimitation of Jurisdictional Subjects and Powers between Bodies of Public Authority of the Russian Federation and Bodies of Public Authority of the Republic of Tatarstan," http://www.tatar.ru/English/append2o.html, accessed 25 May 2010. For a discussion of the changing relationship, see Matthew Derrick, "Contested Autonomy: Tatarstan under Putin (2000–2004)," *Journal of Central Asian and Caucasian Studies* 4, no. 7 (2009).

13. See Katherine E. Graney, "Education Reform in Tatarstan and Bashkortostan: Sovereignty Projects in Post-Soviet Russia," *Europe-Asia Studies* 51 (1999); Aurora Alvarez Veinguer, "Building a Tatar Elite: Language and National Schooling in Kazan," *Ethnicities* 7 (2007).

14. U.S. Secretary of State Hillary Clinton visited Kazan to praise its cultural diversity during a diplomatic mission to Moscow in 2009. See Mark Landler, "In Moscow, Clinton Urges Russia to Open Its Political System," *New York Times*, 15 October 2009.

15. The folktale is "Kak Mariitsy pereshli na storony Moskvy." The story is featured on the official website of Kazan. See http://www.kzn.ru/page11236.htm, accessed 25 May 2010.

16. Torrey Clark, "Chuvashia Fetes 450-Year Union with Russia," *Moscow Times*, 25 June 2001.

17. Of course, these are not permanent identities, but rather very slow to reflect historical reality. For one example, see Durmuş Arik, "Islam among the Chuvashes and Its Role in the Change of Chuvash Ethnicity," *Journal of Muslim Minority Affairs* 27 (2007).

Bibliography

Archival Sources

Hilandar Research Library, Columbus, Ohio
>   Aronov Collection, no. 18, *Chronograph*, last quarter of the 17th century

Law Library of Congress, Washington, DC
>   Russian Manuscript Scrolls Collection

The National Archives (TNA), Kew, Richmond, Surrey, Great Britain
>   CO 77/4, East Indies Original Correspondence, 1570–1856
>   PRO 22/60, English Royal Letters in the Soviet Central State Archive of Ancient Records, 1557–1655
>   SP 84/142, State Paper Office: State Papers Foreign, Holland
>   SP 91/1–6, Secretaries of State: State Papers Foreign, Russia
>   SP 104/118–120, Secretaries of State: State Papers Foreign, Entry Books

Moscow State University (MGU), Moscow, Russia (Available on microfilm at the Hilandar Research Library, Columbus, Ohio)
>   General Slavic Fond, pt. 1, no. 50118, *Sbornik Kazanskikh zhitiakh*

Russian State Archive of Ancient Records (RGADA), Moscow, Russia
>   f. 16, Gosudarstvennyi arkhiv, r. XVI, Vnutrennee upravlenie, op. 1
>   f. 156, Istoricheskie i tseremonial'nye dela
>   f. 159, Prikaznye dela novoi razborki, op. 2, Posol'skii prikaz; and op. 3, Novgorodskii prikaz
>   f. 210, Razriadnyi prikaz, op. 20–21
>   f. 281, Gramoty kollegii ekonomii, op. 1, 4, 7–8
>   f. 1103, Arzamasskaia prikaznaia izba, op. 1
>   f. 1156, Saranskaia prikaznaia izba, op. 1
>   f. 1209, Pomestnyi prikaz, op. 78
>   f. 1455, Gosudarstvennye i chastnye akty pomestno-votchinnykh arkhivov XVI–XIX vv., op. 1–3, 5

Saratov State University Library (SGU), Saratov, Russia (Available on microfilm at the Hilandar Research Library, Columbus, Ohio)

343, "Service and Life of Makarii, Abbot of Zheltovod and Unzha," early seventeenth century

1073, *Sbornik*, 1630s–1650s

1756, "Tale of the Appearance of the Kazan Icon of the Mother of God with Service and Miracles," first half of seventeenth century

Primary Sources

Aiplatov, G. I., and A. G. Ivanov, eds. *Monastyrskaia kolonizatsiia Mariiskogo Povolzh'ia: Po materialam Spaso-Iunginskii monastyria Koz'modem'ianskogo uezda, 1625–1764 gg.* Ioshkar-Ola, 2000.

Akty istoricheskie, sobrannye i izdannye arkheograficheskoiu kommissieiu. 5 vols. St. Petersburg, 1841–43.

Akty iuridicheskie, ili sobranie form starinnago deloproizvozstva. St. Petersburg, 1838.

Akty Moskovoskago gosudarstva. Vol. 1, *Razriadnyi prikaz, Moskovskii stol', 1571–1631.* St. Petersburg, 1890.

Akty, sobrannye v bibliotekakh i arkhivakh Rossiiskoi Imperii Arkheograficheskoiu ekspeditsieiu. Vol. 1, *1294–1598.* St. Petersburg, 1836.

Antonova, K. A., and N. M. Gol'berg, eds. *Russko-Indiiskie otnosheniia v XVII v.: Sbornik dokumentov.* Moscow, 1958.

Arkhangel'skii, S. I., and N. I. Privalova, eds. *Nizhnii Novgorod v XVII veke: Sbornik dokumentov i materialov k istorii Nizhnogo Novgoroda i ego okrugi.* Gor'kii, 1961.

Arkhiv P. M. Stroeva. Vol. 1. Russkaia istoricheskaia biblioteka 32. Petrograd, 1915.

Arkhiv P. M. Stroeva. Vol. 2. Russkaia istoricheskaia biblioteka 35. Petrograd, 1917.

Berry, Lloyd E., and Robert O. Crummey, eds., *Rude and Barbarous Kingdom: Russia in the Accounts of Sixteenth-Century English Voyagers.* Madison, 1968.

Buganov, V. I. *Razriadnaia kniga, 1637/38.* Moscow, 1983.

Buganov, V. I., and L. F. Kuz'min, comps. *Razriadnye knigi, 1598–1638 gg.* Moscow, 1974.

Chronicle of the Carmelites in Persia and the Papal Mission of the XVIIth and XVIIIth Centuries. Vol. 1. London, 1939.

Collins, Samuel. *The Present State of Russia.* London, 1671.

Dmitriev, V. D., ed. "Tsarskie nakazy Kazanskim voevodam XVII veka." *Istoriia i kul'tura Chuvashskoi ASSR: Sbornik statei* 3 (1974): 284–419.

Dopolneniia k aktam istoricheskim, sobranniia i izdaniia Arkheograficheskoiu kommisseiu. 12 vols. St. Petersburg, 1846–72.

Emchenko, E. B. *Stoglav: Issledovaniia i tekst.* Moscow, 2000.

Ermolaev, I. P., and D. A. Mustafina, eds. *Dokumenty po istorii Kazanskogo kraia: Iz arkhivokhranilits Tatarskogo ASSR (vtoraia polovina XVI–seredina XVII): Teksty i comment.* Kazan, 1990.

Fennell, J. L. I., ed. and trans. *Prince A. M. Kurbsky's History of Ivan IV.* Cambridge, 1965.

Filatov, N. F., ed. *Arzamas v XVII veke: Ocherki istorii. Dokumenty.* Arzamas, 2000.

Fletcher, Giles. *Of the Russe Commonwealth.* London, 1591. Reprinted in *Rude and Barbarous Kingdom: Russia in the Accounts of Sixteenth-Century English Voyagers,* edited by Lloyd E. Berry and Robert O. Crummey, 109–246. Madison, 1968.

Gallatin, James. *A Great Peacemaker: The Diary of James Gallatin, Secretary to Albert Gallatin, 1813–1827.* New York, 1914.

Grekov, B. D., and V. I. Lebedev, eds. *Dokumenty i materialy po istorii mordovskoi ASSR.* 2 vols. Saransk, 1940.

Hakluyt, Richard. *The Principal Navigations, Voyages, Traffiques and Discoveries of the English Nation.* 12 vols. Glasgow, 1903–5.

Haxthausen, August von. *Studies on the Interior of Russia.* Edited by S. Frederick Starr. Translated by Eleanore L. M. Schmidt. Chicago, 1972.

Hellie, Richard, trans. and ed. *The Muscovite Law Code (Ulozhenie) of 1649.* The Laws of Russia I, Medieval Russia, vol. 3. Part 1, *Text and Translation.* Irvine, 1988.

Herberstein, Sigmund von. *Notes upon Russia.* Vol. 2. Translated by Richard Henry. London, 1852.

Iakovlev, A. I., ed. *Tamozhennye knigi Moskovskogo gosudarstva XVII veka.* 3 vols. Moscow, 1950–51.

———, ed. *Saranskaia tamozhennaia kniga za 1692 g.* Saransk, 1951.

Knigi Moskovskoi bol'shoi tamozhni, 1693–1694 gg.: Novgorodskaia, Astrakhanskaia, Malorossiiskaia. Moscow, 1961.

Kotoshikhin, G. K. *O Rossii v tsarstvovnanie Aleksei Mikhailovicha.* Moscow, 2000.

Kotov, Fedot Afansev syn. "Of a Journey to the Kingdom of Persia, from Persia to the Land of Turkey and to India and to Hormuz where the Ships Come." In *Russian Travellers to India and Persia (1624–1798): Kotov, Yefremov, Danibegov,* translated and edited by P. M. Kemp, 1–42. Dehli, 1959.

Kuntsevich, G. Z., comp. "Gramoty Kazanskogo Zilantova monastyria." *Izvestiia obshchestva arkheologii, istorii i etnografii pri Imperatorskom Kazanskom universitete* 17 (1901): 268–344.

Lashkov, F., ed. *Pamiatniki diplomaticheskikh snoshenii Krymskago khanstva s Moskovskim gosudarstvom v XVI i XVII vv.* Simferopol', 1891.

Lentin, A., ed. *Voltaire and Catherine the Great: Selected Correspondence.* Cambridge, 1974.

Malov, Evfimii, comp. *Drevniia gramoty i raznye dokumenty (Materialy dlia istorii Kazanskoi eparkhii).* Kazan, 1902.

Martynov, P. *Seleniia Simbirskogo uezda (Materialy dliia istorii Simbirskogo dvoriantstvo i chastnogo zemlevladeniia v Simbirskom uezde).* Simbirsk, 1903.

Massa, Isaac. *A Short History of the Beginnings and Origins of These Present Wars in Moscow under the Reign of Various Sovereigns down to the Year 1610.* Translated and edited by G. Edward Orchard. Toronto, 1982.

Mel'nikov, Stepan, ed. *Akty istoricheskie i iuridicheskie i drevniia tsarskiia gramoty Kazanskoi i drugikh sosedstvennykh gubernii.* Kazan, 1859.

Nikaron, Episkop, ed. "Vladennyia gramaty Kazanskago Spasopreobrazhenskago monastyria." *Izvestiia obshchestva arkheologii, istorii, i etnografii pri Imperatorskom Kazanskom universitete* 11 (1893): 338–68.

Novombergskii, N., ed. *Koldovstvo v Moskovskoi Rusi XVII-go stoletiia (Materialy po istorii meditsiny v Rossii t. III ch. I)*. St. Petersburg, 1906.

———. *Materialy po istorii meditsiny v Rossii*. Vol. 4. Tomsk, 1907.

———. *Vrachebnoe stroenie v do-Petrovskoi Rusi*. Tomsk, 1907.

Novosel'skii, A. A., ed. *Krest'ianskaia voina pod predvoditel'stvom Stepana Razina: Sbornik dokumentov*. 5 vols. Moscow, 1955–1976.

Olearius, Adam. *Travels of Olearius in Seventeenth-Century Russia*. Translated and edited by Samuel H. Baron. Stanford, 1967.

Osipov, V. A., et al., eds. *Istoriia Saratovskaia kraia 1590–1917*. Saratov, 1983.

Polnoe sobranie russkikh letopisei. 37 vols. St. Petersburg, 1862–1928.

Polnoe sobranie zakonov Rossiiskoi Imperii. Series 1, 45 vols. St. Petersburg, 1830.

Preobrazhenskii, I. D., ed. *Nakaz gosudaria, tsaria Mikhaila Fedorovicha, dannyi na upravelenie g. Kokshaiskom s uezdom, chuvashskimi i cheremisskimi volostiami*. Kostroma, 1913.

Rubinshtein, N. L., ed. *Istoriia Tatarii v materialakh i dokumentakh*. Moscow, 1937.

Rumiantseva, V. C., comp. *Narodnoe antitserkovnoe dvizhenie v Rossii XVII veka: Dokumenty Prikaza tainykh del o raskol'nikakh, 1665–1667 gg.* Moscow, 1986.

Russkaia istoricheskaia biblioteka, vol. 17 (Sbornyi). St. Petersburg, 1898.

Saint-Julien, Charles de. *Voyage pittoresque en Russie*. Paris, 1852.

Samoilovich, A. N., ed. *Materialy po istorii Uzbekskoi, Tadkhikskoi i Turkmenskoi SSR*, Chast' 1, *Torgovlia s Moskovskim gosudarstvom i mezhdunarodnoe polozhenie Srednei Azii v XVI–XVII vv.* Leningrad, 1932.

Sears, Robert. *An Illustrated Description of the Russian Empire*. New York, 1855.

Smirnov, P. P. "Novoe chelobit'e Moskovskikh torgovykh liudei o vysylke inozemtsev, 1627 goda." *Chteniia v istoricheskom obshchestve Nestora-letopistse* 23, no. 1 (1912): 3–32.

Staden, Heinrich von. *The Land and Government of Muscovy: A Sixteenth-Century Account*. Translated and edited by Thomas Esper. Stanford, 1967.

Tel'berg, G. G. ed. *Sudebniki Velikago Ivan III i Tsaria Ivana IV*. Kharbin, 1926.

Tolstoy, Leo. *Anna Karenina*. Moscow, 1878.

Tomsinskii, S. G., ed. *Materialy po istorii Tatarskoi ASSR: Pistsovye knigi goroda Kazani 1565–68 gg. i 1646 g.* Leningrad, 1932.

Tvoreniia svateishago Germogena patriarkha Moskovskagoi vseia Rossii. Moscow, 1912.

Uroff, Benjamin Phillip. "Grigorii Karpovich Kotoshikhin, On Russia in the Reign of Alexis Mikhailovich: An Annotated Translation." PhD diss., Columbia University, 1970.

Vereshchagin, P. D., ed. *Proshloe nashego kraia, 1648–1917*. Ul'ianovsk, 1968.

Veselovskii, N. I., ed. *Pamiatniki diplomaticheskikh i torgovykh snoshenii Moskovskoi Rusi s Persiei*. Vol. 3, *Tsarstvovanie Mikhaila Feodoricha*. St. Petersburg, 1898.

Volkov, M. Ia., and E. B. Frantsuzova, eds. *Tamozhennaia kniga goroda Vologdy, 1634–35 gg.* Moscow, 1983.

Wallace, Donald Mackenzie. *Russia*. London, 1886.

Weber, Friedrich Christian. *The Present State of Russia*. London, 1723.

Zagoskin, N. I. *Materialy istoricheskie i iuridicheskie raiona byvshago Prikaza Kazanskogo dvortsa*. Vol. 1, *Arkhiv Kniazia V. I. Baiusheva*. Kazan, 1882.

Zertsalov, A. N. *Materialy dlia istorii Sinbirska i ego uezda (Prokhodo-raskhodnaia kniga Sinbirskoi prikaznoi izby) 1665–1667 gg.* Simbirsk, 1896.

Secondary Sources

Aghassian, Michel, and Kéram Kévonian. "Armenian Trade in the Indian Ocean in the Seventeenth and Eighteenth Centuries." In *Asian Merchants and Businessmen in the Indian Ocean and the China Sea*, edited by Denys Lombard and Jean Aubin, 154–77. New Delhi, 2000.

Aiplatov, G. N. "'Cheremisskie voiny' vtoroi poloviny XVI v. v otechestvennoi istoriografii." In *Voprosy istorii narodov Povolzh'ia i Priural'ia*, edited by Iu. P. Smirnov, 70–79. Cheboksary, 1997.

Akaemov, N. F. "Gorod Kurmysh v XIV–XVIII vekakh." *Izvestiia obshchestva arkheologii, istorii i etnografii pri Kazanskom universitete* 11, no. 6 (1894): 511–15.

Akhmetov, A. *Agrarno-krest'ianskie otnosheniia i sotsial'no-politicheskoe razvitie simbirsko-ul'ianovskogo zavolzh'ia v XVII–XX vekakh*. Ul'ianovsk, 2004.

Alam, Muzaffar, and Sanjay Subrahmanyam. *Indo-Persian Travels in the Age of Discoveries, 1400–1800*. New York, 2007.

Alef, Gustave. "The Adoption of the Muscovite Two-Headed Eagle: A Discordant View." *Speculum* 41 (1966): 1–21.

Alishev, S. Kh. *Istoricheskie subdy narodov Srednego Povolzh'ia XVI–nachalo XIX v.* Moscow, 1990.

———. *Kazan' i Moskva: Mezhgosudarstvennye otnosheniia v XV–XVI vv.* Kazan, 1995.

———. *Ternistyi put' bor'by za svobodu: Sotsial'naia natsional'no-osvoditel'naia bor'ba Tatarskogo naroda; II polovina XVI–XIX vv.* Kazan, 1999.

Allsen, Thomas T. *Mongol Imperialism: The Policies of the Grand Qan Möngke in China, Russia, and the Islamic Lands, 1251–1259*. Berkeley, 1987.

Amirkhanov, R. M. "Islam in Tatar National Ideology and Policy." In *The Christian-Muslim Frontier: Chaos, Clash or Dialogue?*, edited by Jørgen S. Nielsen, 67–81. London, 1998.

Andreev, Aleksandr. *Stroganovy*. Moscow, 2000.

Andreianov, A. A. *Gorod Tsarevokokshaisk: Stranitsy istorii: Konets XVI–nachalo XVIII veka*. Ioshkar-Ola, 1991.

Anpilogov, G. N. "Polozhenie gorodskogo i sel'skogo naseleniia Kurskogo uezda nakanune vosstaniia 1648 g." *Vestnik Moskovskogo universiteta*, series 9, *Istoriia*, no. 5 (1972): 47–60.

Arel, Maria Salomon. "Making an Honest Ruble in the Russian North: Aspects of Muscovite

Trade in the First Half of the Seventeenth Century." *Forschungen zur osteuropäischen Geschichte* 54 (1998): 7–26.

———. "The Muscovy Company in the First Half of the Seventeenth Century: Trade and Position in the Russian State. A Reassessment." PhD diss., Yale University, 1995.

Arik, Durmuş. "Islam among the Chuvashes and Its Role in the Change of Chuvash Ethnicity." *Journal of Muslim Minority Affairs* 27 (2007): 37–54.

Arkhangel'skii, S. I. "Anglo-Gollandskaia torgovlia s Moskvoi v XVII v." *Istoricheskii sbornik* 5 (1936): 5–38.

Avrich, Paul. *Russian Rebels 1600–1800.* New York, 1972.

Azletskii, P., comp. *Opisanie Ioanno-Predtechenskogo muzhskogo monastyria v gorode Kazani.* Kazan, 1898.

Bakhtin, A. G. *XV–XVI veka v istorii Mariiskogo kraia.* Ioshkar-Ola, 1998.

Bakhtin, V. S. *Russkii lubok, XVII–XIX vv.* Moscow, 1962.

Baklanova, N. A. *Torgovo-promyshlennaia deiatel'nost' Kalmykovykh vo vtoroi polovine XVII v.: K istorii formirovaniia Russkoi burzhuazii.* Moscow, 1959.

Ball, J. N. *Merchants and Merchandise: The Expansion of Trade in Europe 1500–1630.* London: Croom Helm, 1977.

Balzaretti, Ross. "Cities, Emporia and Monasteries: Local Economies in the Po Valley, c. AD 700–875." In *Towns in Transition: Urban Evolution in Late Antiquity and the Early Middle Ages,* edited by N. Christie and S. T. Loseby, 213–34. Brookfield, 1996.

Barkey, Karen. *Empire of Difference: The Ottomans in Comparative Perspective.* Cambridge, 2008.

Baron, Samuel H. "The *Gosti* Revisted." In *Explorations in Muscovite History,* 1–21. Hampshire, 1991.

———. "Ivan the Terrible, Giles Fletcher, and the Muscovite Merchantry: A Reconsideration." *Slavonic and East European Review* 56 (1978): 563–85.

Barsov, Ioann. "Nikolaevskii devichii monastyr' v g. Cheboksarakh." *Izvestiia obshchestva arkheologii, istorii i etnografii pri Imperatorskom Kazanskom universitete* 14 (1898): 519–35.

Barsukov, Aleksandr, comp. *Spiski gorodovykh voevod i drugikh lits voevodskago upraveleniia Moskovskago gosudarstva XVII stoletiia.* St. Petersburg, 1902.

Bennigsen, Alexandre, and Chantal Lemercier-Quelquejay. "La poussée vers les mers chaudes et la barrière du Caucase: La rivalité Ottomano-Moscovite dans la seconde moitié du XVIe siècle." *Journal of Turkish Studies* 10 (1986): 15–46.

Benton, Laura. *A Search for Sovereignty: Law and Geography in European Empires, 1400–1900.* New York, 2010.

Bilz-Leonhardt, Marlies. "Deconstructing the Myth of the Tatar Yoke." *Central Asian Survey* 27 (2008): 33–43

Blum, Jerome. *Lord and Peasant in Russia: From the Ninth to the Nineteenth Century.* Princeton, NJ, 1961.

Boeck, Brian J. *Imperial Boundaries: Cossack Communities and Empire-Building in the Age of Peter the Great.* Cambridge, 2009.

Bogatyrev, Sergei. "Reinventing the Russian Monarchy in the 1550s: Ivan the Terrible, the Dynasty, and the Church." *Slavonic and East European Review* 85 (2007): 271–93.

———. *The Sovereign and His Counselors: Ritualized Consultations in Muscovite Political Culture, 1350s–1570s*. Helsinki, 2000.

Borin, Vasilii. *Sviatieishii Patriarkh Germogen i mesto ego zakliucheniia*. Moscow, 1913.

Braudel, Fernand. *The Mediterranean and the Mediterranean World in the Age of Philip II*. 2 vols. Translated by Siân Reynolds. Berkeley, 1995.

Breyfogle, Nicholas. "Enduring Imperium: Russia/Soviet Union/Eurasia as Multiethnic, Multiconfessional Space." *Ab Imperio*, no. 1 (2008): 75–126.

Brikner, A. G. "Chuma v Moskve v 1654 godu." *Istoricheskii vestnik: Istoriko-literaturnyi zhurnal* 16 (April 1884): 5–23.

Broadbridge, Anne F. *Kingship and Ideology in the Islamic and Mongol Worlds*. New York, 2008.

Brown, Peter B. "Bureaucratic Administration in Seventeenth-Century Russia." In *Modernizing Muscovy: Reform and Social Change in Seventeenth-Century Russia*, edited by Jarmo T. Kotilaine and Marshall Poe, 57–78. London, 2004.

———. "Muscovite Government Bureaus." *Russian History/Histoire Russe* 10 (1983): 269–330.

Brubaker, Rogers. *Nationalism Reframed: Nationhood and the National Question in the New Europe*. New York, 1996.

Buganov, V. I. *Razin i Razintsy*. Moscow, 1995.

Burton, Audrey. *The Bukharans: A Dynastic, Diplomatic and Commercial History, 1550–1702*. New York, 1997.

Bushev, P. P. *Istoriia posol'stv i diplomaticheskikh otnoshenii russkogo i iranskogo gosudarstv v 1586–1612 gg*. Moscow, 1976.

———. *Istoriia posol'stv i diplomaticheskikh otnoshenii russkogo i iranskogo gosudarstv v 1613–1621 gg*. Moscow, 1987.

Bushkovitch, Paul. "The Epiphany Ceremony of the Russian Court in the Sixteenth and Seventeenth Centuries." *Russian Review* 49 (1990): 1–17.

———. *The Merchants of Moscow 1580–1650*. New York, 1980.

———. "Princes Cherkasskii or Circassian Murzas: The Kabardians in the Russian Boyar Elite, 1560–1700." *Cahiers du monde russe* 45, nos. 1–2 (2004): 9–29.

———. *Religion and Society in Russia: The Sixteenth and Seventeenth Centuries*. New York, 1992.

Butler, Francis. *Enlightener of Rus': The Image of Vladimir Sviatoslavich across the Centuries*. Bloomington, IN, 2002.

Cherkashin, E. *Patriarkh Germogen: K 300 letiiu so dnia smerti 1612–1912*. Moscow, 1912.

Cherniavsky, Michael. "Khan or Basileus: An Aspect of Russian Medieval Political Theory." *Journal of the History of Ideas* 20 (1959): 459–76.

Chetyrkin, I. N., ed. *Istoriko-Statisticheskoe opisanie Arzamasskoi Alekseevskoi zhenskoi obshchiny*. Nizhnii Novgorod, 1887.

Chistiakova, E. V. "Novotorgovnyi ustav 1667 goda." In *Arkheograficheskii ezhegodnik za 1957 god*, 102–26. Moscow, 1958.

Croskey, Robert M. "The Diplomatic Forms of Ivan III's Relationship with the Crimean Khan." *Slavic Review* 43 (1984): 257–69.

Crummey, Robert O. *Aristocrats and Servitors: The Boyar Elite in Russia, 1613–1689.* Princeton, NJ, 1983.

———. "Court Spectacles in Seventeenth-Century Russia: Illusion and Reality." In *Essays in Honor of A. A. Zimin,* edited by Daniel Clark Waugh, 130–58. Columbus, OH, 1995.

———. *The Formation of Muscovy, 1304–1613.* London, 1987.

———. "Reflections on Mestnichestvo in the Seventeenth Century." *Forschungen zur osteuropäischen Geschichte* 27 (2000): 269–81.

d'Encausse, Hélène Carrère. "Les routes commerciales de l'Asie centrale et les tentatives de reconquête d'Astrakhan d'après les registres des 'Affaires importantes' des Archives ottomans." *Cahiers du monde russe et sovietique* 11 (1970): 391–422.

Dale, Stephen Frederic. *Indian Merchants and Eurasian Trade, 1600–1750.* New York, 1994.

Davies, Brian L. "The Razin Rebellion at Tambov and Kozlov, 1670–1671." *Russian History/ Histoire Russe* 34 (2007): 263–76.

———. *State Power and Community in Early Modern Russia: The Case of Kozlov, 1635–1649.* New York, 2004.

———. "The Town Governors of Ivan IV." *Russian History/Histoire Russe* 14 (1987): 77–143.

———. *Warfare, State, and Society on the Black Sea Steppe 1500–1700.* New York, 2007.

Demidova, N. F. *Sluzhiliia biurokratiia v Rossii XVII v. i ee rol' v formirovanii absolutizma.* Moscow, 1987.

Denisov, L. I. *Pravoslavnye monastyri Rossiiskoi imperii: Polnyi spisok.* Moscow, 1903.

Dergachev, A. F., et al., eds. *Ocherki istorii Penzenskogo kraia: S drevneishikh vremen do kontsa XIX veka.* Penza, 1973.

Derrick, Matthew. "Contested Autonomy: Tatarstan under Putin (2000–2004)." *Journal of Central Asian and Caucasian Studies* 4, no. 7 (2009): 45–74.

DeWeese, David. *Islamization and Native Religion in the Golden Horde: Baba Tükles and Conversion to Islam in Historical and Epic Tradition.* University Park, PA, 1994.

Dewey, Horace W. "The 1497 Sudebnik: Muscovite Russia's First National Law Code." *American Slavic and East European Review* 15 (1956): 325–38.

———. "The 1550 Sudebnik as an Instrument of Reform." In *Government in Reformation Europe,* edited by Henry J. Cohn, 284–309. New York, 1972.

———. "Russia's Debt to the Mongols in Suretyship and Collective Responsibility." *Comparative Studies in Society and History* 30 (1988): 249–70.

Dmitriev, V. D. *Chuvashiia v epokhu feodalizma (XVI–nachale XIX vv.).* Cheboksary, 1986.

———. "Uchastie naseleniia Chuvashii v bor'be protiv Pol'skoi i Shvedskoi interventsii v nachale XVII veka." *Voprosy drevnei i srednevekovoi istorii Chuvashii* 105 (1980): 70–108.

———. "Vosstanie iasachnykh liudei Srednego Povolzh'ia i Priural'ia 1615–1616 godov." *Voprosy drevnei i srednevekovoi istorii Chuvashii* 105 (1980): 109–19.

Dolzhenkov, V. V. "Beglye krest'iane v Penzenskom krae v XVII veke." *Iz istorii oblasti: Ocherki kraevedov* 1 (1989): 31–36.

Donnelly, Alton S. *The Russian Conquest of Bashkiria, 1552–1740*. New Haven, CT, 1968.

Dubman, E. L. "Beglye krest'iane kak istochnik formirovaniia naseleniia krupnoi votchiny Simbirsko-Samarskogo Povolzh'ia v XVII–nachale XVIII vv." In *Sotsial'no-ekonomicheskoe razvitie i klassovaia bor'ba na iuzhnom Urale i v Srednom Povolzh'e (Do revoliutsionnyi period)*, edited by I. G. Akmanov et al., 12–18. Ufa, 1988.

———. *Khoziaistvennoe osvoenie Srednego Povolzh'ia v XVII veke: Po materialam tserkovnoe-monastyrskikh vladenii*. Kuibyshev, 1991.

———. *Kniaz' Griogrii Zasekin (Khronika zhizhni i deiatel'nosti stroitelia volzhskikh gorodov)*. Samara, 1995.

Dunning, Chester S. L. *Russia's First Civil War: The Time of Troubles and the Founding of the Romanov Dynasty*. University Park, PA, 2001.

Dunning, Chester S. L., and Norman S. Smith. "Moving Beyond Absolutism: Was Early Modern Russia a 'Fiscal-Military' State?" *Russian History/Histoire Russe* 33 (2006): 19–43.

Elliott, J. H. "A Europe of Composite Monarchies." *Past and Present* 137, no. 1 (November 1992): 48–71.

Emmausskii, A. V. "Iz istorii bor'by za zemliui krest'ian v Arzamasskom uezde v XVI–XVII vv." *Trudy Kirovskogo nauchno-issledovatel'skogo instituta kraevedeniia* 7, no. 3 (1934): 7–8.

Ermolaev, I. P. "Gorod Kazan' no pistsovoi knige 1565–1568 godov." In *Stranitsy istorii goroda Kazani*, edited by M. A. Usanov, 3–15. Kazan, 1981.

———. *Srednee Povolzh'e vo vtoroi polovine XVI–XVII vv. (Upravlenie Kazanskim kraem)*. Kazan, 1982.

Ermolaeva, L. K. "Krupnoe kupechestvo Rossii v XVII–pervoi chetverti XVIII v. (po materialam astrakhanskoi torgovli)." *Istoricheskie zapiski* 114 (1986): 303–25.

Eskin, Iu. M. *Ocherki istorii mestnichestva v Rossii XVI–XVII vv.* Moscow, 2009.

Esper, Thomas. "Military Self-Sufficiency and Weapons Technology in Muscovite Russia." *Slavic Review* 28 (1969): 185–208.

Fekhner, M. F. *Torgovlia Russkogo gosudarstva so stranami vostoka v XVI veke*. Moscow, 1952.

Fennell, John. *A History of the Russian Church to 1448*. Harlow, Essex, 1995.

Ferrier, R. W. "The Armenians and the East India Company in Persia in the Seventeenth and Early Eighteenth Centuries." *Economic History Review* 26 (1973): 38–62.

Filjushkin, Alexander. *Ivan the Terrible: A Military History*. London, 2008.

Fisher, Alan. *The Crimean Tatars*. Stanford, CA, 1978.

———. "Muscovite-Ottoman Relations in the Sixteenth and Seventeenth Centuries." *Humaniora Islamica* 1 (1973): 207–17.

———. "The Ottoman Crimea in the Sixteenth Century." *Harvard Ukrainian Studies* 5 (1981): 135–70.

Flier, Michael S. "Breaking the Code: The Image of the Tsar in the Muscovite Palm Sunday Ritual." In *Medieval Russian Culture*, vol. 2, edited by Michael S. Flier and Daniel Rowland, 213–42. Berkeley, 1994.

———. "Filling in the Blanks: The Church of the Intercession and the Architectonics of Medieval Muscovite Ritual." *Harvard Ukrainian Studies* 19 (1995): 120–37.

———. "Golden Hall Iconography and the Makarian Influence." In *The New Muscovite Cultural History*, edited by Valerie Kivelson et al., 63–75. Bloomington, IN, 2009.

———. "The Iconography of Royal Ritual in Sixteenth-Century Muscovy." In *Byzantine Studies: Essays on the Slavic World and the Eleventh Century*, edited by Speros Vryonis and Henrik Birnbaum, 53–76. New Rochelle, NY, 1992.

Flier, Michael S., and Daniel Rowland. *Medieval Russian Culture*. Vol. 2. Berkeley, 1994.

Foucault, Michel. *Power/Knowledge*. Edited by Colin Gordon. New York, 1980.

Frank, Andre Gunder. *ReORIENT: Global Economy in the Asian Age*. Berkeley, CA, 1998.

Frost, Robert I. *The Northern Wars: War, State and Society in Northeastern Europe, 1558–1721*. Harlow, Essex, 2000.

Fuhrmann, Joseph T. *The Origins of Capitalism in Russia: Industry and Progress in the Sixteenth and Seventeenth Centuries*. Chicago, 1972.

Ganeev, R. G., M. V. Murzabulatov, and L. I. Nagaeva. *Narody Povolzh'ia i Priural'ia: Istoriko etnograficheskie ocherki*. Moscow, 1985.

Geertz, Clifford. "Centers, Kings, and Charisma: Reflections on the Symbolics of Power." In *Culture and Its Creators: Essays in Honor of Edward Shils*, edited by Joseph Ben-David and Terry Nichols Clark, 150–71. Chicago, 1977.

Gentes, Andrew A. *Exile to Siberia, 1590–1822*. Houndsmills, Basingstoke, Hampshire, 2008.

Geraklitov, A. A. *Alatyrskaia Mordva po perepisiam 1624–1721 gg.* Saransk, 1936.

———. "Spisok Saratovskikh i Tsaritsynskikh voevod XVII v." *Trudy Saratovskoi uchenoi arkhivnoi komissii* 30 (1913): 61–80.

Glete, Jan. *War and the State in Early Modern Europe: Spain, the Dutch Republic, and Sweden as Fiscal-Military States, 1500–1660*. New York, 2002.

Gluiantskii, N. F., ed. *Gradostroitel'stvo Moskovskogo gosudarstva XVI–XVII vekov*. Moscow, 1994.

Goldfrank, David. "*Muscovy and the Mongols*: What's What and What's Maybe." *Kritika* 1 (2000): 259–66.

Golikova, N. B. "Torgovlia krepostnymi bez zemli v 20-kh godakh XVIII v. (Po materialam krepostnykh knig gorodov Povolzh'ia)." *Istoricheskie zapiski* 90 (1972): 303–31.

Golubinskii, E. *Istoriia kanonizatsii sviatykh v russkoi tserkvi*. Moscow, 1903.

Gorenburg, Dmitry. *Minority Ethnic Mobilization in the Russian Federation*. New York, 2003.

Goto, Masanori. "Metamorphosis of Gods: A Historical Study on the Traditional Religion of the Chuvash." *Acta Slavica Iaponica* 24 (2007): 144–65.

Graney, Katherine E. "Education Reform in Tatarstan and Bashkortostan: Sovereignty Projects in Post-Soviet Russia." *Europe-Asia Studies* 51 (1999): 611–32.

Gudzinskaia, A. P. "Dokumenty sysknykh komissii vtoroi poloviny XVII v. kak istoricheskii istochnik." In *Arkheograficheskii ezhegodnik za 1967 god*, 107–18. Moscow, 1969.

Grimmelshausen, Johann Jakob Christoffel von. *Simplicissimus*. Translated by Mike Mitchell. Sawtry, Cambs, 1999.

Haidar, Mansura. *Medieval Central Asia: Polity, Economy, and Military Organization (Fourteenth to Sixteenth Centuries)*. New Delhi, 2004.

Halperin, Charles J. "Ivan IV and Chinggis Khan." *Jahrbücher für Geschichte Osteuropas* 51 (2003): 481–97.

———. "Muscovite Political Institutions in the 14th Century." *Kritika* 1 (2000): 237–57.

———. *Russia and the Golden Horde: The Mongol Impact on Medieval Russian History*. Bloomington, IN, 1987.

Hart, James Gerard. "The Urban and Rural Response to Stepan Razin's Rebellion in the Middle Volga Region of Muscovy, 1670–1671." PhD diss., University of Virginia, 1981.

Hartley, Janet M. *A Social History of the Russian Empire, 1650–1825*. London, 1999.

Hellie, Richard. "The Costs of Muscovite Military Defense and Expansion." In *The Military and Society in Russia, 1450–1917*, edited by Eric Lohr and Marshall Poe, 41–66. Leiden, 2002.

———. *The Economy and Material Culture of Russia, 1600–1725*. Chicago, 1999.

———. *Enserfment and Military Change in Muscovy*. Chicago, 1971.

Herrin, Judith. *Byzantium: The Surprising Life of a Medieval Empire*. Princeton, NJ, 2008.

Hughes, Lindsey. *Russia in the Age of Peter the Great*. New Haven, CT, 1998.

Iablokov, A. *Pervoklassnyi muzhskii Uspensko-Bogoroditskii monastyr v gorode Sviiazhske, Kazanskoi gubernii*. Kazan, 1907.

Iakubov, K. "Rossiia i Shvetsiia v pervoi polovine XVII vv., VI: 1647–1650 gg. Doneseniia koroleve Khristine i pis'ma k korolevskomu sekretariu shvedskogo rezidenta v Moskve Karla Pommereninga." *Chteniia v imperatorskom obshchestve istorii i drevnostei rossiskikh pri Moskovskom universitete* 1 (1898): 407–74.

Iskhakov, D. M. *Ot srednevekovykh tatar k tataram novogo vremeni*. Kazan, 1998.

———. *Tiurko-tatarskie gosudarstva XV–XVI vv.* Kazan, 2009.

Islaev, F. G. *Pravoslavnye missionery v Povolzh'e*. Kazan, 1999.

Israel, Jonathan. "England, Dutch, and the Struggle for Mastery of World Trade in the Age of the Glorious Revolution (1682–1702)." In *The World of William and Mary: Anglo-Dutch Perspectives on the Revolution of 1688–89*, edited by Dale Hoak and Mordechai Feingold, 75–86. Stanford, CA, 1996.

Iuldashev, M. Iu. *K istorii torgovykh sviazei Srednei Azii s Rossiei v XVI–XVII vv.* Tashkent, 1964.

Ivanov, Ananii. "Razvitie regiona Mariiskogo Povolzh'ia v sostave Rossiiskogo gosudarstva vo vtoroi polovine XVI–XVII vv." *Forschungen zur osteuropäischen Geschichte* 63 (2004): 349–54.

Ivanova, M. G., ed. *Finno-Ugry Povolzh'ia i Priural'ia v srednie veka*. Izhevsk, 1999.

Kappeler, Andreas. *The Russian Empire: A Multi-Ethnic History*. Harlow, Essex, 2001.

———. *Russlands erste Nationalitäten: Das Zarenreich und die Völker der Mittleren Wolga vom 16. bis 19. Jahrhundert*. Cologne, 1982.

Kappeler, Andreas, ed. *Die Geschichte Russlands im 16. und 17. Jahrhundert aus der Perspektive seiner Regionen*. Forschungen zur osteuropäischen Geschichte 63. Wiesbaden, 2004.

Kashtanov, S. M. "K istorii Volzhskogo torgovogo sudokhodstva vo vtoroi polovine XVI v." In *Voprosy istorii narodov Povolzh'ia i Priural'ia*, edited by Iu. P. Smirnov et al., 44–58. Cheboksary, 1997.

Kaufmann-Rochard, J. *Origines d'une bourgeoisie Russe (XVIe et XVIIe siècles)*. Paris, 1969.

Keenan, Edward. *Muscovy and Kazan' 1445–1552: A Study in Steppe Politics*. PhD diss., Harvard University, 1965.

Kerner, Robert. *The Urge to the Sea: The Role of Rivers, Portages, Ostrogs, Monasteries and Furs*. New York, 1942.

Kévonian, Kéram. "Marchands Arméniens au XVIIe siècle: A propos d'un livre arménien publié à Amsterdam en 1699." *Cahiers du monde russe et soviétique* 16 (1975): 199–244.

Khabenskaia, E. O. *Tatary o Tatarskom*. Moscow, 2003.

Khamidullin, Bulat. *Narody Kazanskogo Khanstva: Etnosotsiologicheskoe issledovanie*. Kazan, 2002.

Khlebnikov, A. V., et al., eds. *Istoriia Mariiskoi ASSR*. Vol. 1, *Sredneishikh vremen do Velikoi Oktiabr'skoi sotsialisticheskoi revoliutsii*. Ioshkar-Ola, 1986.

Khodarkovsky, Michael. "Four Degrees of Separation: Constructing Non-Christian Identities in Muscovy." In *Culture and Identity in Muscovy, 1359–1584*, edited by Ann Kleimola and Gail Lenhoff, 248–66. Moscow, 1997.

——. "Not by World Alone: Missionary Policies and Religious Conversion in Early Modern Russia." *Comparative Studies in Society and History* 38 (1996): 267–93.

——. *Russia's Steppe Frontier: The Making of a Colonial Empire, 1500–1800*. Bloomington, IN, 2004.

——. "The Stepan Razin Uprising: Was It a 'Peasant War'?" *Jahrbücher für Geschichte Osteuropas* 42 (1994): 1–19.

——. *Where Two Worlds Met: The Russian State and the Kalmyk Nomads, 1600–1771*. Ithaca, NY, 1992.

Kivelson, Valerie. *Autocracy in the Provinces: The Muscovite Gentry and Political Culture in the Seventeenth Century*. Stanford, CA, 1997.

——. *Cartographies of Tsardom: The Land and its Meanings in Seventeenth Century Russia*. Ithaca, NY, 2006.

——. "The Devil Stole His Mind: The Tsar and the 1648 Moscow Uprising." *American Historical Review* 98 (1993): 733–56.

——. "Merciful Father, Impersonal State: Russian Autocracy in Comparative Perspective." *Modern Asian Studies* 31 (1997): 635–63.

——. "Patrolling the Boundaries: Witchcraft Accusations and Household Strife in Seventeenth-Century Muscovy." *Harvard Ukrainian Studies* 19 (1995): 302–23.

——. "Political Sorcery in Sixteenth-Century Muscovy." In *Culture and Identity in Muscovy, 1359–1584*, edited by A. M. Kleimola and G. D. Lenhoff, 267–83. Moscow, 1997.

Kleimola, Ann. "'In accordance with the canons of the Holy Apostles': Muscovite Dowries and Women's Property Rights." *Russian Review* 51 (1992): 204–29.

———. "Status, Place, and Politics: The Rise of Mestnichestvo during the *Boiarskoe Pravlenie.*" *Forschungen zur osteuropäischen Geschichte* 27 (1980): 195–214.

Kliuchevskii, V. O. *Kurs russkoi istorii.* 5 vols. Reprint, Moscow, 1956.

———. *Sochineniia v deviati tomakh.* 9 vols. Moscow, 1987.

Kochekaev, B. A. *Nogaisko-Russkie otnosheniia v XV–XVIII vv.* Alma-Ata, 1988.

Koenigsberger, H. G. *Politicians and Virtuosi: Essays in Early Modern History.* London, 1986.

Kollmann, Jack Edward. *The Moscow* Stoglav *("Hundred Chapters") Church Council of 1554.* 2 vols. PhD diss., University of Michigan, 1978.

Kollmann, Nancy Shields. *By Honor Bound: State and Society in Early Modern Russia.* Ithaca, NY, 1999.

———. "Judicial Authority in the Criminal Law: Beloozero and Arzamas." *Forschungen zur osteuropäischen Geschichte* 63 (2004): 52–68.

———. "Pilgrimage, Procession and Symbolic Space in Sixteenth-Century Russian Politics." In *Medieval Russian Culture,* vol. 2, edited by Michael S. Flier and Daniel Rowland, 164–81. Berkeley, CA, 1994.

Kondrashov, Sergei. *Nationalism and the Drive for Sovereignty in Tatarstan, 1988–92.* New York, 2000.

Kopanev, A. I. and A. G. Man'kov, eds. *Vosstanie I. Bolotnikova: Dokumenty i materialy.* Moscow, 1959.

Korman, Sharon. *The Right of Conquest: The Acquisition of Territory by Force in International Law and Practice.* Oxford, 1996.

Korsakov, V. D., comp., "Spisok nachal'stuiushchikh lits v gorodakh tepereshnei Kazanskoi gubernii: S 1553 g. do obrazovaniia Kazanskoi gubernii v 1708 g." *Izvestiia obshchestva arkheologii, istorii i etnografii pri Imperatorskom Kazanskom universitet* 24 (1908): Prilozhenie, 1–18, 1–13.

Kortepeter, Carl M. "Ottoman Imperial Policy in the Black Sea Region in the Sixteenth Century." *Journal of the American Oriental Society* 86, no. 2 (1966): 86–113.

Kotilaine, Jarmo T. "Competing Claims: Russian Foreign Trade via Arkhangel'sk and the Eastern Baltic Ports in the Seventeenth Century." *Kritika* 4 (2003): 279–311.

———. "Mercantilism in Pre-Petrine Russia." In *Modernizing Muscovy: Reform and Social Change in Seventeenth-Century Russia,* edited by Jarmo T. Kotilaine and Marshall Poe, 143–73. London, 2004.

———. *Russia's Foreign Trade and Economic Expansion in the Seventeenth Century: Windows on the World.* Leiden, 2005.

Krasovskii, V. E., comp. *Kievo-Nikolaevskii byvshii Pokrovskii Ladinskii Todrovskii Novodevichii monastyr' Simbirskoi eparkhii (Istoriko-arkheologicheskoe opisanie).* Simbirsk, 1899.

Kurat, N. "The Turkish Expedition to Astrakhan in 1569, and the Problem of the Don-Volga Canal." *Slavonic and East European Review* 40 (1961): 7–23.

Kuznetsov, I. D. *Ocherki po istorii Chuvashskogo krest'ianstva.* Cheboksary, 1957.

Lebedev, V. I. *Krest'ianskaia voina pod predvoditel'stvom Stepana Razina.* Moscow, 1955.

Lefebvre, Henri. *The Production of Space.* Translated by Donald Nicholson-Smith. Malden, MA, 1991.

Lemercier-Quelquejay, Chantal. "Co-optation of the Elites of Kabarda and Daghestan in the Sixteenth Century." In *The North Caucasus Barrier: The Russian Advance towards the Muslim World*, edited by Marie Bennigsen Broxup, 18–44. New York, 1992.

———. "Les routes commerciales et militaires au Caucase du Nord aux XVIème et XVIIème siècles." *Central Asian Survey* 4 (1985): 1–19.

Levin, Eve. "False Miracles and Unattested Dead Bodies: Investigations into Popular Cults in Early Modern Russia." In *Religion and the Early Modern State: Views from China, Russia, and the West*, edited by James D. Tracy and Marguerite Ragnow, 253–83. New York, 2004.

———. "From Corpse to Cult in Early Modern Russia." In *Orthodox Russia: Belief and Practice Under the Tsars*, edited by Valerie A. Kivelson and Robert H. Greene, 81–103. University Park, PA, 2003.

———. "Healers and Witches in Early Modern Russia." In *Saluting Aron Gurevich: Essays in History, Literature and Related Disciplines*, edited by Yelena Matusevich and Alexandra Korros, 105–33. Leiden, 2010.

Lezina, E. P. *Goroda na territorii mordovii v XVI–XVII vv.* Saransk, 2002.

Lincoln, W. Bruce. *The Conquest of a Continent: Siberia and the Russians.* New York, 1994.

Liseitsev, D. B. *Prikaznaia sistema Moskovskogo gosudarstva v epokhu Smuty.* Tula, 2009.

Lubimenko, Inna. "The Struggle of the Dutch with the English for the Russian Market in the Seventeenth Century." *Transactions of the Royal Historical Society*, 4th ser., 7 (1924): 27–51.

Machiavelli, Niccoló. *The Prince.* Edited and translated by David Wootton. Indianapolis, 1995.

Madariaga, Isabel de. *Ivan the Terrible: First Tsar of Russia.* New Haven, CT, 2006.

Makarov, D. M. *Samoderzhavie i khristianizatsiia narodov Povolzh'ia v vtoroi polovine XVI–XVII vv.* Cheboksary, 1981.

Malov, E. A. *Kazanskii Bogoroditskii devich' monastyr': Istoriia i sovremennoe ego sostoianie.* Kazan, 1879.

Mankov, A. G., ed. *Zapiski inostrantsev o vosstanii Stepana Razina.* Leningrad, 1968.

Martin, Janet. *Medieval Russia, 980–1584.* Cambridge, 1995.

———. "Mobility, Forced Resettlement, and Regional Identity in Muscovy." In *Culture and Identity in Muscovy, 1359–1584*, edited by Ann Kleimola and Gail Lenhoff, 431–49. Moscow, 1997.

———. "Multiethnicity in Muscovy: A Consideration of Christian and Muslim Tatars in the 1550s–1580s." *Journal of Early Modern History* 5 (2001): 1–23.

———. "Muscovite Frontier Policy: The Case of the Khanate of Kasimov." *Russian History/Histoire Russe* 19 (1992): 169–79.

———. "Muscovite Travelling Merchants: The Trade with the Muslim East (15th and 16th Centuries)." *Central Asian Survey* 4 (1985): 21–38.

———. "The *Novokshcheny* of Novgorod: Assimilation in the 16th Century." *Central Asian Survey* 9 (1990): 13–38.

———. "Tatars in the Muscovite Army during the Livonian War." In *The Military and Society in Russia, 1450–1917*, edited by Eric Lohr and Marshall Poe, 366–87. Leiden, 2002.

Martin, Russell E. "Gifts for the Bride: Dowries, Diplomacy, and Marriage Politics in Muscovy." *Journal of Medieval and Early Modern Studies* 38 (2008): 119–45.

Matthee, Rudolph P. *The Politics of Trade in Safavid Iran: Silk for Silver, 1600–1730.* New York, 1999.

———. "Suspicion, Fear, and Admiration: Pre-Nineteenth Century Iranian Views of the English and the Russians." In *Iran and the Surrounding World: Interactions in Culture and Cultural Politics*, edited by Nikki R. Keddie and Rudi Matthee, 121–45. Seattle, 2002.

Maxwell, Mary Jane. "Afanasii Nikitin: An Orthodox Russian's Spiritual Voyage in the Dar al-Islam, 1468–1475." *Journal of World History* 17 (2006): 243–66.

Michels, Georg B. *At War with the Church: Religious Dissent in Seventeenth-Century Russia.* Stanford, CA, 1999.

———. "Rescuing the Orthodox: The Church Policies of Archbishop Afanasii of Kholmogory, 1682–1702." In *Of Religion and Empire: Missions, Conversion, and Tolerance in Tsarist Russia*, edited by Robert P. Geraci and Michael Khodarkovsky, 19–37. Ithaca, NY, 2001.

———. "Ruling Without Mercy: Seventeenth-Century Russian Bishops and Their Officials." *Kritika* 4 (2003): 515–42.

Miller, David B. "Creating Legitimacy: Ritual, Ideology, and Power in Sixteenth-Century Russia." *Russian History/Histoire Russe* 21 (1994): 289–315.

———. "The Cult of Saint Sergius of Radonezh and its Political Uses." *Slavic Review* 52 (1993): 680–99.

Mizis, Iu. A. *Zaselenie Tambovskogo kraia v XVII–XVIII vekakh.* Tambov, 1990.

Monod, Paul Kléber. *The Power of Kings: Monarchy and Religion in Europe, 1589–1715.* New Haven, CT, 1999.

Moon, David. "Peasant Migration and the Settlement of Russia's Frontiers, 1550–1897." *The Historical Journal* 40 (1997): 859–93.

———. *The Russian Peasantry 1600–1930: The World the Peasants Made.* London, 1999.

Morris, A. S. "The Medieval Emergence of the Volga-Oka Region." *Annals of the Association of American Geographers* 61 (1971): 697–710.

Mozharovskii, Apollon. "Izlozhenie khoda missionerskago dela po prosveshcheniiu khristianstvom kazanskikh inorodtsev s 1552 do 1867 god." In *Chteniia v imperatorskom obshchestve*, 1–237. Moscow, 1880.

———. "Po istorii prosveshcheniia Nizhegorodskoi mordvy." *Nizhegorodskiia eparkhial'nyia vedomosti* 16 (1890): 664–74.

Naiakshin, K. *Ocherki istorii Kuibyshevskoi oblasti.* Kuibyshev, 1962.

Nevostruev, K. comp. *Istoricheskoe opisanie byvshikh v gorode Samara muzheskogo Spaso-Preobrazhenskago i zhenskago Spasskogo monastyrei.* Moscow, 1867.

Nexon, Daniel H. *The Struggle for Power in Early Modern Europe: Religious Conflict, Dynastic Empires, and International Change.* Princeton, NJ, 2009.

Nogmanov, Aidar. *Tatary srednego Pololzh'ia i Priural'ia v rossiiskom zakonodatel'stve vtoroi poloviny XVI–XVIII vv.* Kazan, 2002.

Notariusa, Evgeniia Aleksovicha, ed., *Istoricheskoe opisanie Alatyrskago Kievo-Nikolaevskogo zhenskogo monastyria.* Alatyr', 1997.

Novikova, Olga. "Le couronnement d'Ivan IV: La conception de l'empire à l'Est de l'Europe." *Cahiers du monde russe* 46, no. 1/2 (2005): 219–32.

Novosel'skii, A. A. "Kollektivnye dvorianskie chelobitnye o syske beglykh krest'ian i kholopov vo vtoroi polovine XVII v." In *Dvorianstvo i krepostnoi stroi Rossii XVII–XVIII vv.,* edited by N. I. Pavlenko, 303–43. Moscow, 1975.

Nurminskii, S. "Vliianie monastyrei na raselenie narodnoe v Kazanskom krae." *Pravoslavnyi sobesiednik*i, no. 2 (1864): 1–30, 181–226.

Obolensky, Dmitri. "Russia's Byzantine Heritage." *Oxford Slavonic Papers* 1 (1950): 37–63.

Orlenko, S. P. *Vykhodtsy iz Zapadnoi Evropy v Rossii XVII veka: pravovoi status i real'noe polozhenie.* Moscow, 2004.

Ostrowski, Donald. "The Façade of Legitimacy: Exchange of Power and Authority in Early Modern Russia." *Comparative Studies in Society and History* 44 (2002): 534–63.

———. "The Mongol Origins of Muscovite Political Institutions." *Slavic Review* 46 (1987): 525–42.

———. "Muscovite Adaptation of Steppe Political Institutions: A Reply to Halperin's Objections." *Kritika* 1 (2000): 267–304.

———. *Muscovy and the Mongols: Cross-Cultural Influences on the Steppe Frontier, 1304–1589.* New York, 1998.

———. "The Replacement of the Composite Bow by Firearms in the Muscovite Cavalry." *Kritika* 11 (2010): 513–34.

Parker, Geoffrey. *Europe in Crisis, 1598–1648.* 2nd ed. Oxford, 2001.

———. *The Military Revolution: Military Innovation and the Rise of the West, 1500–1800.* Cambridge, 1996.

Paul, Michael C. "The Military Revolution in Russia, 1550–1682." *Journal of Military History* 68 (2004): 9–45.

Pavlov, Andrei, and Maureen Perrie. *Ivan the Terrible.* New York, 2003.

Pelenski, Jaroslaw. "The Incorporation of the Ukrainian Lands of Kievan Rus' into Crown Poland (1569)." In *The Contest for the Legacy of Kievan Rus',* 151–87. Boulder, CO, 1998.

———. *Russia and Kazan: Conquest and Imperial Ideology (1438–1560s).* The Hague, 1974.

———. "State and Society in Muscovite Russia and the Mongol-Turkic System in the Sixteenth Century." *Forschungen zur osteuropäischen Geschichte* 27 (1980): 156–67.

Peretrukhin, I. "Kazanskaia obshchina staroobriadetsev, priemliushchikh belokrinitskoe sviashchenstvo." *Staroobriadets* 1 (1907): 85–93.

———. "Staroobriadtsy v Kniagininskom uezd, Nizhegorodskoi guber." *Staroobriadets* 3 (1907): 323–31.

Perrie, Maureen. "Outlawry and Redemption through Service: Ermak and the Volga Cossacks." In *Culture and Identity in Muscovy, 1359–1584,* edited by Ann Kleimola and Gail Lenhoff, 530–42. Moscow, 1997.

————. *Pretenders and Popular Monarchism in Early Modern Russia: The False Tsars of the Time of Troubles.* Cambridge, 1995.

Peterson, G. P. *Istoricheskii ocherk Kerenskogo kraia.* Penza, 1882.

Phipps, Geraldine M. *Sir John Merrick, English Merchant—Diplomat in Seventeenth-Century Russia.* Newtonville, MA, 1983.

Pierling, P. *Iz smutnago vremeni: Stati i zametki.* St. Petersburg, 1902.

————. *La Russie et le Saint-Siège: Études diplomatiques.* Vol. 3. Paris, 1901.

Pisar'kova, L. F. *Gosudarstvennoe upravlenie Rossii s kontsa XVII do kontsa XVIII veka: Evolutsiia biurokraticheskoi sistemy.* Moscow, 2007.

Poe, Marshall. "The Consequences of Military Revolution in Russia: A Comparative Perspective." *Comparative Studies in Society and History* 38 (1996): 603–18.

————. *"A People Born to Slavery": Russia in Early Modern European Ethnography, 1476–1748.* Ithaca, NY, 2001.

————. *The Russian Elite in the Seventeenth Century.* Vol. 2, *A Quantitative Analysis of the 'Duma Ranks' 1613–1713.* Helsinki, 2004.

————. "What Did Russians Mean When They Called Themselves 'Slaves of the Tsar'?" *Slavic Review* 57 (1998): 585–608.

Poe, Marshall, with Ol'ga Kosheleva, Russell Martin, and Boris Mironov. *The Russian Elite in the Seventeenth Century.* Vol. 1, *The Consular and Ceremonial Ranks of the Russian "Sovereign's Court" 1613–1713.* Helsinki, 2004.

Pokrovskii, I. M. "Bortnichestvo (pchelovodstvo), kak odin iz vidov natural'nago khoziaistva i promysla bliz Kazani v XVI–XVII vv." *Izvestiia obshchestva arkheologii, istorii i etnografii pri Imperatorskom Kazanskom universitete* 17 (1901): 67–73.

————. "K istorii Kazanskikh monastyrei do 1764 goda." *Izvestiia obshchestva arkheologii, istorii i etnografii pri Imperatorskom Kazanskom universitet* 18 (1902): 16–22.

————. *K istorii pomestnogo i ekonomicheskom byta v Kazanskom krae v polovine XVII veka.* Kazan, 1909.

————. "K voprosy o naspedstvennom prave tserkovnykh uchrezhdenii, v chastnosti Kazanskago arkhiereiskago doma, v kontse XVII veka." *Izvestiia obshchestva arkheologii, istorii i etnografii pri Imperatorskom Kazanskom universitete* 18, nos. 1–3 (1902): 1–6.

Pokrovskii, N. N. *Tomsk 1648–1649 gg.: Voevodskaia vlast' i zemskie miry.* Novosibirsk, 1989.

Polevktov, M. "The Ways of Communication between Russia and Georgia in the Sixteenth and Seventeenth Centuries." *Journal of Modern History* 2 (1930): 367–77.

Pollock, Sean. "Empire by Invitation? Russian Empire-Building in the Caucasus in the Reign of Catherine II." PhD diss., Harvard University, 2006.

Pomeranz, Kenneth. *The Great Divergence: China, Europe, and the Making of the Modern World Economy.* Princeton, NJ, 2000.

Por'firev, S. I. "Kazanskii stol Razriadnyi prikaz." *Izvestiia obshchestva arkheologicheskii, istorii i etnografii pri Imperatorskom Kazanskom universitete* 28, no. 6 (1913): 535–53.

————. "Spiski voevod i d'iakov po Kazani i Sviiazhsku, sostavlennye v XVII stoletii." *Izvestiia obshchestva arkheologii, istorii i etnografii pri Imperatorskom Kazanskom universitete* 27 (1911): 61–74.

Pratt, Mary Louise. *Imperial Eyes: Travel Writing and Transculturation*. New York, 1992.

Pushkov, V. P. and I. M. Promakhina. "Sem'ia v sisteme Russkogo krest'ianskogo khoziaistva (Po materialam syska beglykh krest'ian 60-x godov XVII v. v Alatyrskom i Arzamasskom uezdakh)." In *Sotsial'no-demograficheskie protsessy v Rossiiskoi derevne (XVI–nachalo XX v.)*, no. 1, edited by I. D. Koval'chenko, 26–34. Tallin, 1986.

Rakhimzianov, Bulat. *Kasimovskoe khantsvo (1445–1552 gg.): Ocherki istorii*. Kazan, 2009.

Razdorskii, A. I. *Torgovliia Kurska v XVII veke (Po materialam tamozhennykh i obrochnykh knig goroda)*. St. Petersburg, 2001.

Razorekova, N. V. "Beglye krest'iane v pervoi chetverti XVII veka (Po materialam Alatyrskoi perepisnoi kantseliarii)." *Problemy istorii SSSR* 4 (1974): 113–31.

Romaniello, Matthew P. "Absolutism and Empire: Governance in the Early-Modern Russian Frontier." PhD diss., Ohio State University, 2003.

———. "Ethnicity as Social Rank: Governance, Law, and Empire in Muscovite Russia." *Nationalities Papers* 34 (2006): 447–69.

———. "'In friendship and love': Russian Travels to Muslim Lands in the Early Modern Era." *Historical Yearbook* 6 (2009): 111–22.

———. "Mission Delayed: The Russian Orthodox Church after the Conquest of Kazan'." *Church History* 76 (2007): 511–40.

———. "The Profit Motive: Regional Economic Development in Muscovy after the Conquest of Kazan'." *Journal of European Economic History* 33 (2004): 663–85.

Romashin, I. S. *Ocherki ekonomiki Simbirskoi gubernii XVII–XIX vv.* Ul'ianovsk, 1961.

Rostislavovich, S. I. *Sluzhilye "inozemtsy" v Sibiri XVII veka (Tomsk, Eniseisk, Krasnoiarsk)*. Novosibirsk, 2004.

Rowland, Daniel B. "Biblical Military Imagery in the Political Culture of Early Modern Russia: The Blessed Host of the Heavenly Tsar." In *Medieval Russian Culture*, vol. 2, edited by Michael S. Flier and Daniel Rowland, 182–217. Berkeley, 1994.

———. "Did Muscovite Literary Ideology Place Limits on the Power of the Tsar (1540s-1660s)?" *Russian Review* 49 (1990): 125–55.

———. "Moscow—The Third Rome or the New Israel?" *Russian Review* 55 (1996): 591–614.

———. "The Memory of St. Sergius in Sixteenth-Century Russia." In *The Trinity-Sergius Lavra in Russian History and Culture*, edited by Vladimir Tsurikov, 56–69. Jordanville, NY, 2005.

Rozhdestvenskii, S. V. *Sluzhiloe zemlevladenie v Moskovskom gosudarstve XVI veka*. St. Petersburg, 1897.

Rumiantseva, V. C. *Narodnoe antitserkovnoe dvizhenie v Rossii v XVII veke*. Moscow, 1986.

Ryan, Will F. "The Witchcraft Hysteria in Early Modern Europe: Was Russia an Exception?" *The Slavonic and East European Review* 76 (1998): 49–84.

Rywkin, Michael. "Russian Central Colonial Administration: From the *prikaz* of Kazan to the XIX Century, A Survey." In *Russian Colonial Expansion to 1917*, edited by Michael Rywkin, 8–15. London, 1988.

Said, Edward. *Orientalism*. New York, 1979.

Sakharov, A. *Stepan Razin (Khronika XVII veka)*. Moscow, 1973.

Schafer, Daniel. "Building Nations and Building States: The Tatar-Bashkir Question in Revolutionary Russia, 1917–1920." PhD diss., University of Michigan, 1995.

Schmähling, Angelika. *Hort der Frömmigkeit—Ort der Verwahrung: Russische Frauenklöster im 16.–18. Jahrhundert*. Stuttgart, 2009.

Scott, James C. *Seeing Like a State: How Certain Schemes to Improve the Human Condition Have Failed*. New Haven, CT, 1998.

Seed, Patricia. *Ceremonies of Possession in Europe's Conquest of the New World, 1492–1640*. Cambridge, 1995.

Senyk, Sophia. *Women's Monasteries in Ukraine and Belorussia to the Period of Suppressions*. Rome, 1983.

Shaw, D. J. B. "Southern Frontiers of Muscovy, 1550–1700." In *Studies in Russian Historical Geography*, edited by R. A. French and James Bater, 1:118–42. London, 1983.

Sheikovskaia, E. N. *Gosudarstvo i krest'iane Rossii: Pomor'e v XVII veke*. Moscow, 1997.

Shorokhov, L. P. "Vozniknovennie monastyrkikh votchin v Vostochnoi Sibiri." In *Russkoe naselenie Pomor'ia Sibiri (period feodalizma)*, edited by V. I. Shunkov and A. P. Okladnikov, 148–63. Moscow, 1973.

Sirotkin, S. V. "'Raskol'nich'ia prelest'' v Arzamasskom uezde v 70-e gg. XVII v." In *Staroobriadchestvo v Rossii (XVII–XX veka)*, edited by E. M. Iukhimenko, 261–68. Moscow, 1999.

Siroux, Maxine. "Les caravanserais routiers safavids." *Iranian Studies* 7 (1974): 348–75.

Skrynnikov, R. G. "Ermak's Siberian Expedition." *Russian History/Histoire Russe* 13 (1986): 1–39.

———. *Gosudarstvo i tserkov' na Rusi XIV–XVI vv*. Novosibirsk, 1991.

———. *Tsartsvo terrora*. St. Petersburg, 1992.

Smirnov, I. I. *Vosstanie Bolotnikova, 1606–1607*. Leningrad,1951.

Smirnov, Ivan. *Mordva: Istoriko-ethnograficheskii ocherk*. Saransk, 2002.

Smith, Dianne L. "Muscovite Logistics, 1462–1598." *Slavonic and East European Review* 71 (1993): 35–65.

Smith, R. E. F. *Peasant Farming in Muscovy*. Cambridge, 1977.

Soja, Edward W. *Postmodern Geographies: The Reassertion of Space in Critical Social Theory*. London, 1989.

Solov'ev, Vladimir. *Anatomiia Russkogo bunta: Stepan Razin: Mify i real'nost'*. Moscow, 1994.

Spruyt, Hendrik. *The Sovereign State and Its Competitors: An Analysis of Systems Change*. Princeton, NJ, 1994.

Squatriti, Paolo. "Digging Ditches in Early Medieval Europe." *Past and Present* 176, no. 1 (August 2002): 11–65.

Steensgaard, Niels. *Carracks, Caravans, and Companies: The Structural Crisis in the European-Asian Trade in the Early Seventeenth Century*. Odense, 1973.

Stepanov, I. V. "Bor'ba krest'iansko-kazatskogo povstansheskogo voiska Stepana Razina za Simbirsk." In *Problemy istorii feodal'noi Rossii: Sbornik statei k 60-letii v prof. V. V. Mavrodina*, edited by A. L. Shapiro et al., 174–85. Leningrad, 1971.

————. *Krest'ianskaia voina v Rossii v 1670–1671 gg.* Book 2, part 1, *Nachal'nyi period krest'ianskoi voiny.* Leningrad, 1966.

Stevens, Carol B. "Evaluating Peter's Army: The Impact of Internal Organization." In *The Military and Society in Russia, 1450–1917,* edited by Eric Lohr and Marshall Poe, 147–71. Leiden, 2002.

————. *Russia's Wars of Emergence, 1460–1730.* Harlow, 2007.

————. *Soldiers on the Steppe: Army Reform and Social Change in Early Modern Russia.* DeKalb, IL, 1995.

Sugonin, N. I. *Insar: Dokumental'no-istoricheskii ocherk o gorode i raione.* Saransk, 1975.

Sultanov, F. M. *Islam i Tatarskoe natsional'noe dvizhenie v Rossiiskom i mirovom musul'manskom kontekste: Istoriia i sovremennost'.* Kazan, 1999.

Sunderland, Willard. *Taming the Wild Field: Colonization and Empire on the Russian Steppe.* Ithaca, NY, 2004.

Suny, Ronald Grigor. *The Revenge of the Past: Nationalism, Revolution, and the Collapse of the Soviet Union.* Stanford, CA, 1993.

Superanskii, M. F. *Simbirsk i ego proshloe (1648–1898 gg.): Istoricheskii ocherk.* Simbirsk, 1898.

Taimasov, Leonid. "Mezhkonfessional'nye otnosheniia na nachal'nom etape khristianizatsii narodov Kazanskogo kraia (Vtoraia polovina XVI–XVII vv.)." *Forschungen zur osteuropäischen Geschichte* 63 (2004): 322–41.

Takács, Sarolta A. *The Construction of Authority in Ancient Rome and Byzantium: The Rhetoric of Empire.* New York, 2009.

Talbot, Alice-Mary. "Women's Space in Byzantine Monasteries." *Dumbarton Oaks Papers* 52 (1998): 113–27.

Tarlovskaia, V. R. *Torgovlia Rossii perioda pozdnego feodalizma (Torgovye krest'iane vo vtoroi polovine XVII–nachale XVIII v.).* Moscow, 1988.

Terekhin, V. M. "Istoricheskie materialy v otnoshenii inorodtsev penzenskago kraia kontsa XVII st." *Izvestiia obshchestva arkheologicheskii, istorii i etnografii pri Imperatorskom Kazanskom universitete* 14, no. 2 (1897): 195–202.

Thaden, Edward C. *Russia's Western Borderlands, 1710–1870.* Princeton, NJ, 1984.

Thomas, Marie A. "Muscovite Convents in the Seventeenth Century." *Russian History/Histoire Russe* 10 (1983): 230–42.

Tilly, Charles. *Coercion, Capital, and European States, AD 990–1992.* Rev. ed. Malden, MA, 1992.

Timoshina, A. A. "Raselenie gostei, chlenov gostinoi i sukonnoi soten v russkikh gorodakh XVII v." In *Torgovlia i predpreinimatel'stvo v feodal'noi Rossii,* edited by A. Iu. Karlov. Moscow, 1994, 117–51.

Todorova, Maria. *Imagining the Balkans.* New York, 1997.

Tokmakov, I. F., comp. *Istoriko-statisticheskoe i arkheologicheskoe opisanie Sviato-Troitskogo muzhskogo monastyria v gorode Alatyre, Simbirskogo gubernii.* Moscow, 1897.

Trepavlov, V. V. *Belyi Tsar': Obraz monarkha i predstavleniia o poddanstve u narodov Rossii XV–XVIII vv.* Moscow, 2007.

Troebst, Stefan. "Die Kaspi-Volga-Ostsee-Route in der handelskontrollpolitik Karls XI: Die Schwedischen Persien-missionen von Ludvig Fabritius 1679-1700." *Forschungen zur osteuropäischen Geschichte* 54 (1998): 127–204.

Ustiugov, N. V. *Solevarennaia promyshlennost' soli kamskoi v XVII veke: K voprosy o genezise kapitalisticheskikh otnoshenii v Russkoi promyshlennosti.* Moscow, 1957.

Vásáry, István. "The Tatar Ruling Houses in Russian Genealogical Sources." *Acta Orientalia Academiae Scientiarum Hungaricae* 61 (2008): 365–72.

Veinguer, Aurora Alvarez. "Building a Tatar Elite: Language and National Schooling in Kazan." *Ethnicities* 7 (2007): 186–207.

Veinroks, E. Kh. "Mezhdunarodnaia konkurentsiia v torgovle mezhdu Rossiei i Zapadnoi Evropoi: 1560–1640." In *Russkii Sever i Zapadnaia Evropa,* edited by Iu. N. Bespiatykh, 9–41. St. Petersburg, 1999.

Veluwenkamp, Jan Willem. *Arkhangel'sk: Niderlandskie predprinimateli v rossii, 1550–1785.* Trans. N. Mikaelian. Moscow, 2006.

Veretennikov, Makarii. *Moskovskii mitropolit Makarii i ego vremia.* Moscow, 1996.

Veselovskii, S. V. *D'iaki i pod'iachie XV–XVII vv.* Moscow, 1975.

Vladmirskii, A., ed. *Tserkovnyia drevnosti g. Kazani.* Kazan, 1887.

Vodarskii, Ia. E. *Naselenie Rossii v kontse XVII–nachale XVIII veka (Chislennost', soslovo-klassovyi sostav, razmeshchenie).* Moscow, 1977.

Voronin, I. D. *Saransk: Istoriko-dokumental'nye ocherki.* Saransk, 1961.

Ward, Kerry. *Networks of Empire: Forced Migrations in the Dutch East India Company.* Cambridge, 2009.

Washbrook, David. "India in the Early Modern World Economy: Modes of Production, Reproduction and Exchange." *Journal of Global History* 2 (2007): 87–111.

Weickhardt, George G. "Legal Rights of Women in Russia, 1100–1750." *Slavic Review* 55 (1996): 1–23.

Werth, Paul W. "Coercion and Conversion: Violence and Mass Baptism of the Volga Peoples, 1740–55." *Kritika* 4 (2003): 543–69.

Wieczynski, Joseph. *The Russian Frontier: The Impact of the Borderlands upon the Course of Early Russian History.* Charlottesville, VA, 1976.

Witzenrath, Christoph. *Cossacks and the Russian Empire, 1598–1725: Manipulation, Rebellion, and Expansion into Siberia.* London, 2007.

Wolff, Larry. *Inventing Eastern Europe: The Map of Civilization in the Mind of the Enlightenment.* Stanford, CA, 1994.

Wong, R. Bin. "The Search for European Differences and Domination in the Early Modern World: A View from Asia." *American Historical Review* 107 (2002): 447–69.

Wortman, Richard. *Scenarios of Power: Myth and Ceremony in Russian Monarchy.* Vol. 1. Princeton, NJ, 1995.

Zabelin, I. E. *Minin i Pozharskii: Priamye i krivye v Smutnoe vremia.* Moscow, 1999.

Zagidullin, I. K. "Kristianizatsiia tatar Srednego Povolzh'ia vo vtoroi polovine XVI–XVII vv." *Uchenye zapiski (Kazan)* no. 1 (1997): 109–65.

Zaitsev, I. V. *Astrakhanskoe khanstvo*. Moscow, 2004.

Zguta, Russell. "Witchcraft and Medicine in Pre-Petrine Russia." *Russian Review* 37 (1978): 438–48.

Zimin, A. A. *Oprichnina*. Moscow, 2001.

———. *Reformy Ivana Groznogo*. Moscow, 1960.

Zorin, A. N. *Gorozhane Srednego Povolzh'ia vo vtoroi polovine XVI-nachale XX v.: Istoriko-ethnograficheskii ocherk*. Kazan, 1992.

Index

Abbas I of Iran, 109

abbesses, 41, 80–81, 164. *See also* clergy; convents

abbots, 33, 76–78, 80, 81–82, 97, 98, 153–55, 157, 163, 165, 171, 194, 227n35, 235n38. *See also* clergy; monasteries

administration, 5, 8, 11, 13–15, 17–18, 23, 27, 36, 53, 57, 64, 67, 69, 72, 80, 85, 91, 94, 105–6, 140–41, 146–47, 152, 157–59, 163–64, 168, 175, 177, 178, 180–82, 187–90, 194, 195, 201, 204, 208, 214. *See also* bureaucracy; cameralism; cooperative competition; postal system; *prikazy*

Adrian, Patriarch of Moscow, 73, 75, 193. *See also* metropolitans; patriarchs

Agibalov, Artemii Ivanov syn, 142

Aginev, Teregul, 141

Agramakov, Aleksei, 133

agriculture, 8, 11, 20, 29, 72, 83, 89, 97, 103, 142, 146–51, 156, 158, 213. *See also* farming; lifestyles; slash-and-burn; three-field rotation

Alatyr', 17, 38, 40, 42, 47, 66–67, 75, 80–81, 91–92, 100, 122, 124, 126, 137, 139, 141–42, 152, 156, 160–61, 162, 165, 171–74, 180, 182, 184–88, 189–91, 198, 199. *See also* Kievo-Nikolaevskii Convent; Nikolaevskii Novodevichii Convent; Sviiato-Troitskii Monastery

Aleksei Mikhailovich (Tsar), 80, 85, 93, 203. *See also* tsars

Alenin, Ivan Alekseev syn, 138

Alferov family, 138

Amirkhanov, R. M., 210

Anastasiia Romanova, 25

Andreev, Prokopei, 107, 239n90

Andreianov family, 125–26, 138, 157, 224n28

Anikeev, Fedot, 98, 236n43

animism, 8, 12, 20, 27, 29, 37–38, 117, 127, 129, 134–35, 147–48, 154–55, 157, 160, 165, 169, 179, 193. *See also* confessional identity

Aprov family, 192

Aptekarskii Prikaz, 56. See also *prikazy*

Ara River, 101, 140

archbishops, 6, 32–34, 38, 45, 72–73, 75, 76, 98, 168, 224n91. *See also* clergy; German, Archbishop of Kazan; Gurii, Archbishop of Kazan

archimandrites, 76, 133, 171, 193, 194–95, 234n27. *See also* clergy; Varsonofii, Archimandrite of the Spaso-Preobrazhenskii Monastery

Aristov family, 192

Arkhangel'sk, 56, 97, 104, 108, 110, 111, 233n7

Armenian Company, 110–12

Armenian merchants, 111, 116, 241n109, 241n112. *See also* merchants

arms. *See* munitions

army, 5, 26–27, 29–30, 32, 34–35, 38, 49, 52, 54, 69, 75, 95, 105, 118, 120–31, 124, 128–29, 145–46, 149, 159, 170, 177, 184, 186, 190, 209. *See also* cavalry; enlistment; garrisons; infantry; mercenaries; militia; *strel'tsy*

Arsk, 67–68

Arzamas, 17, 38, 40, 44, 47–48, 56, 67, 68, 70, 75, 77, 81, 83, 91, 93, 96, 100, 109, 118–19, 124, 132, 143, 137, 139, 140–43, 144, 148, 152, 155,

businesses, 80–81, 93, 98, 100, 102–3, 105, 109–10, 112, 144, 204. *See also* industry; metallurgy; mills; mines; salt refineries; taverns

Buturlin, Akinfii, 184

Byzantine culture, 20–22, 23–25, 26–27. *See also* Orthodoxy

Byzantine Empire, 21–22, 26

caesar. *See* tsar

cameralism, 14–15, 63, 175, 217n22. *See also* administration; bureaucratization; centralization

cannons, 30, 71, 181, 186. *See also* munitions

canonization, 130. *See also* saints

captivity, 134, 196. *See also* hostage-taking

caravans, 92–93, 94, 103–4, 110, 114. *See also* merchants

Carmelites, 48–49. *See also* Catholicism

Caspian Sea, 37, 102, 106, 116, 181

Catholicism, 47, 75. *See also* Carmelites; confessional identity

Cat of Kazan, 211–12

Caucasus, 11, 106. *See also* Chechnia; Dagestan

cavalry, 27, 29–30, 71, 118, 120–24, 126, 128–30, 137, 145–46, 159, 190, 198–99. *See also* army; gentry; military servitors

Central Asia, 3, 106, 110, 209. *See also* Bukhara

centralization, 9, 13, 14, 22, 53–54, 56–57, 178, 208. *See also* bureaucratization; cameralism; modernization

Chaadaev, Ivan Ivanovich, 191–92

chancelleries. See *prikazy*

charisma, 6, 8, 21, 23, 26–27, 35–36, 54. *See also* Chingissid dynasty; Gediminid dynasty; legitimacy; rituals; Romanov dynasty; Rurikid dynasty; symbolism

Charles I of England, 107–8, 240nn96–97, 240n102

Cheboksary, 38, 40, 47–48, 67–68, 70, 75, 79–80, 91, 97, 100, 124, 160–61, 177. *See also* Nikolaevskii Devichii Convent

Chechnia, 211, 214. *See also* autonomous republics; Caucasus

Chelobitnyi Prikaz, 71. See also *prikazy*

Chemodanov, Ivan Ivanov syn, 171

Cheremisses. *See* Maris

Cherry, Francis, 104

China, 88, 104–5. *See also* Asia

Chingissid dynasty, 36, 65, 120, 123. *See also* charisma; genealogy; Mongol Empire

Chirikov, Aleksei Panteleevich, 77

Christianity. *See* Catholicism; Church Militant; Orthodoxy

churchmen, 16, 33, 75, 150. *See also* clergy

Church Militant, 32, 135. *See also* Orthodoxy

Church of the Intercession on the Moat (St. Basil's), 6, 7, 21, 35, 205, 213. *See also* Moscow

Chuvashes, 5, 12, 16, 29, 30, 37, 42, 51, 54, 59, 60, 79, 102, 125–27, 140, 147, 155, 156–59, 160–61, 166–68, 174, 175, 182, 185–86, 209, 211, 213

Chuvashia, 209, 211. *See also* autonomous republics

civil war. *See* Time of Troubles

clergy. *See* abbesses; abbots; archbishops; archimandrites; bishops; churchmen; hegumen; metropolitans; monks; nuns; officials; patriarchs

climate, 161. *See also* environment

Collins, Samuel, 87, 206, 209

colonists, 12, 164, 189–90. *See also* exiles

colonization, 83, 164. *See also* forced relocation; settlement

commodities. *See* fish; flax; furs; grain; hemp; honey; horses; pitch; salt; silk; specie; spices; tar; timber; wax

communication, 54, 60, 62, 180, 188. *See also* networks

Company of Filippo, 108. *See also* Dutch merchants

composite monarchies, 9–10, 24, 53. *See also* composite sovereignty; layered sovereignty

composite sovereignty, 8–11, 17–18, 207, 209, 213. *See also* composite monarchies

confessional identity, 11, 22, 23, 26, 119, 120, 154. *See also* animism; conversions; Islam; *novokreshchane*; Orthodoxy

conquests, 6, 21, 90, 121, 134; of Kazan, 5, 8, 10–12, 14, 19–20, 26–31, 35–36, 42, 45, 54, 102,

conquests (*continued*)
120–21; religious, 31–35, 40, 63, 145, 150. *See also* Church Militant; expansion; "Gathering of the Russian Lands"

Constantinople, 3, 21–22, 25, 31, 35

constitution, 210–11. *See also* law codes

convents. *See* Bogoroditskii Devichii Convent (Kazan); Kievo-Nikolaevskii Convent (Alatyr'); Nikolaevskii Devichii Convent (Cheboksary); Nikolaevskii Novodevichii Convent (Alatyr'); Novodevichii Alekseevskii Convent (Arzamas); Novodevichii Convent (Moscow); Spaso-Preobrazhenskii Convent (Arzamas); Spaso-Preobrazhenskii Convent (Simbirsk); Troitskii Fedorovskii Convent (Kazan); Vvedenskii Devichii Convent (Tikhvin)

conversion, 13, 20, 22, 32, 37, 44, 49, 63, 75, 77, 120, 123, 125–29, 130, 134, 136, 154, 155, 157, 167–69, 176, 193, 206, 213. *See also* assimilation; confessional identity; incentives; *novokreshchane*

converts. See *novokreshchane*

cooperative competition, 11–13, 15–16, 76, 82–86, 96, 120, 208. *See also* administration; bureaucracy

"copper riots," 178, 180. *See also* revolts

coronations, 22, 25. *See also* legitimacy; rituals

Cossacks, 5, 17, 48–49, 63, 178–81, 184, 185, 186, 189. *See also* Ermak; Stepan Razin

courts, 57, 59, 71, 95, 101, 127, 144, 192, 194, 201. *See also* judiciary

courtyards. *See* markets

Crimea. *See* Khanate of Crimea

Crimean Tatars, 54, 59, 159, 178. *See also* Khanate of Crimea

crimes, 51, 62, 77–78, 164, 178. *See also* bootlegging; bribery; domestic violence; murders; robbery; smuggling; witchcraft

customs office, 97. *See also* administration; officials; trade

Dagestan, 211. *See also* autonomous republics

Dashkov, Ivan Ivanovich, 113

daughters, 126, 133, 136–39, 144, 211. *See also* dowries; women

debt slavery, 61. *See also* slavery

defensive lines, 8, 10, 14, 17, 21, 38, 41–42, 44–45, 46, 47, 49, 63, 67, 79–80, 83, 85–86, 91, 93, 100, 115, 117, 121, 145, 159–62, 164, 179–80, 182, 185, 188, 203, 213. *See also* Arzamas Line; Belgorod Line; fortifications; Simbirsk Line

Dement'ev, Fëdor Maksimov syn, 139

demography, 162, 164, 172. *See also* population

demon-possession, 132, 133. *See also* illness

Derevii, Fëdor Prokof'ev syn, 138–39

d'iaki, 12, 51, 53, 57, 58–59, 64–66, 69–72, 76, 82–83, 184–85, 190, 198, 201, 227n20. *See also* bureaucracy; officials

discrimination, 16. *See also* confessional identity

disease, 188. *See also* illness; plague

distance, 9, 13, 14, 54, 55, 62, 66, 82–83, 91, 167, 179. *See also* networks

diversity, 9, 10–11, 14, 17, 20, 23, 54, 63, 119, 127–28, 136, 144, 148–49, 157, 175, 178–79, 205, 207, 211. *See also* confessional identity; ethnolinguistic identity

Dmitrii Ivanovich (Tsarevich), 46. *See also* False Dmitrii

Dolgorukov, Iurii, 186

Dolgorukov, Volodimir Timof'evich, 75, 99

domestic violence, 77, 134. *See also* crimes

Domozhirov, Petr Gavrilov syn, 198

Don Cossacks. *See* Cossacks

Dormition Cathedral, 35. *See also* Kremlin (Moscow)

dowries, 136–40, 143, 197, 198. *See also* daughters; marriages

Dubman, E. L., 153, 224n93

Dubrovskii, Aleksei Bogdanov syn, 137

Dulov, Savva Vasil'ev syn, 198

dumnye d'iaki, 65. *See also* elites

Dutch East India Company, 111

Dutch merchants, 48, 88–90, 95, 105–8, 110–12, 240n97. *See also* Company of Filippo; merchants

Dutch Republic, 15, 116, 241n112

honey, 87, 89, 98, 102, 146, 150, 151, 174–75, 236nn42–43. *See also* beekeeping; commodities

horse archers, 30. *See also* cavalry

horses, 60–61, 98, 99–100, 111, 119, 126. *See also* commodities

hostage-taking, 60, 167, 169, 188–89, 196. *See also* captivity; pacification

hunting, 20, 83, 146, 163. *See also* lifestyles

Iadrin, 46–47, 67–68, 124–25, 160–61, 174

Ianchurin, Bakrach, 123

Iaransk, 44

Iaroslavl', 23, 104, 107, 122, 239n90

iasachnye liudi, 16, 61, 147–48, 150–56, 158, 167, 169–70, 173–75. *See also* non-Russian peoples; peasantry

iasak, 150–51. *See also* taxation

Iazykov, Ivan Pavlov syn, 190

iconography, 26–27

icons, 34, 41, 73, 130. *See also* "Blessed Is the Host of the King of Heaven"; miracle cults; Mother of God Icon (Kazan); Russian Orthodox Church

identity. *See* confessional identity; ethnolinguistic identity

ideology, 11–12, 22, 36, 45, 145. *See also* charisma; legitimacy; rhetoric

illness, 133–34. *See also* demon-possession; disease; healing; medicine; plague

incentives, 95, 99, 145, 165, 193. *See also* colonization; conversion

incursions, 14, 28, 44, 45, 52, 121, 158. *See also* invasions; nomads

India. *See* Mughal India

Indian merchants, 107, 110, 113, 241n113, 241n117. *See also* merchants

industry, 112, 126. *See also* businesses; commodities

infantry, 128, 146, 159, 160, 165, 169, 181. *See also* army; garrisons

infrastructure, 5, 8, 45, 56, 89, 90, 93, 95, 113, 115, 126. *See also* fortifications; granaries; networks; trade routes

inheritance, 136, 137–39, 197, 199. *See also* estates; widows

inovertsy, 117, 135. *See also* animism; Catholicism; confessional identity; Islam

Inozemskii Prikaz, 71, 196, 200. *See also* mercenaries; *prikazy*

inozemtsy, 94, 127. *See also* foreigners

Insar, 68, 83, 85, 162

instructions. *See nakazy*

insurrection, 50, 66, 158, 159, 178, 180. *See also* revolts

integration, 6, 10, 36, 195, 205, 211. *See also* assimilation; conversion; geography

international trade. *See* global trade

interrogations, 51, 59, 158, 166, 169, 173–74. *See also* investigations

invasions, 17, 28, 33, 46, 52, 53, 172, 179–82, 202, 205, 209, 211. *See also* incursions

investigations, 16, 17, 59, 60, 62, 117, 130, 148–49, 158, 165–67, 169–74, 177, 179, 188, 189, 191–92, 201. *See also* interrogations; runaway peasant commissions

investments, 41, 49, 90–91, 93, 96, 102, 107. *See also* trade

Ioanno-Predtechenskii Monastery (Kazan), 40, 73, 76

Iosifo-Volokolamskii Monastery (Volokolamsk), 34

Iran. *See* Safavid Empire

Isheev, Aladiachek Bivaev syn, 151

Islam, 3, 6, 8, 16–17, 20, 22, 28–29, 31, 33, 35, 37–38, 63, 119–20, 130, 135, 136, 179, 213. *See also* confessional identity; Muslims

Issev, Efrem, 201

Isupov, Sëmen, 119

Itagasheva, Elena, 132

Iurii Danilovich (Grand Prince), 23

Iurii Vasil'evich (Prince), 33

Ivan III Vasil'evich (Tsar), 23–24, 25, 26. *See also* tsars

Ivan IV Vasil'evich (Tsar), 6, 14, 20, 24–26, 27–28, 32, 34, 35, 38, 41, 47, 54, 75, 88, 104, 117, 122, 156, 170, 211. *See also* conquest of Kazan; Livonian War; *Oprichnina*; tsars

James I of England, 104, 240n99

Jenkinson, Anthony, 36, 90

landlords, 16–17, 60, 147–48, 155–57, 167, 170–73, 190, 192, 195, 198; monastic, 153–54, 162–64, 167–68, 173–74, 176, 184, 187, 203. *See also* estates; gentry; monasteries

language. *See* ethnolinguistic identity

law codes. *See* constitution; legislation; New Commercial Code of 1667; *Sudebnik* of 1497; *Sudebnik* of 1550; *Ulozhenie* of 1649

layered sovereignty, 8–9. *See also* composite monarchy

legal system, 5, 9, 12, 24, 61–62, 77–80, 101, 127–29, 137, 143, 148–49, 150–53, 157–58, 169, 173–75, 197, 201–3. *See also* courts; judiciary

legislation, 12, 25, 46, 53, 112, 127–29, 136–44, 156, 167, 170, 180, 191–92, 199, 203. *See also* administration; governance; law codes; *nakazy*

legitimacy, 20, 23–24, 46–48, 49. *See also* charisma; ideology; "right by conquest"; rituals, symbolism

Leont'ev, Fëdor Isakovich, 106

Levashev family, 199

Levashov, Andrei Vasil'ev syn, 67

"Life of Gurii and Varsonofii," 33, 73–75, 132–35, 230n73. *See also* Gurii, Archbishop of Kazan; miracle cults; saints; Varsonofii, Archimandrite of the Spaso-Preobrazhenskii Monastery

lifestyles, 119, 149–50, 156, 161, 175. *See also* agriculture; beekeeping; fish; hunting; nomads; trapping

Lithuania *See* Poland-Lithuania

Lithuanians, 167

liturgy, 25, 34, 129. *See also* rituals; Russian Orthodox Church

Livonian War, 20, 46, 52–53, 104, 118, 147, 156

logistics, 30–31, 33. *See also* army; fortifications; munitions

London, 88, 108, 111, 200

Lunevskii, Vasilii Mikhalovich, 171, 251n72

Machiavelli, Niccoló, 19

Makar'evskii Zheltovodskii Monastery (Arzamas), 174, 186, 202

Makarii, Metropolitan of Moscow, 25–26, 32–34. *See also* metropolitans

Makarii Zheltovodskii, 134–35. *See also* saints

Makmametev family, 138

Malmyzh, 44, 124, 160, 237n65

Mari-El Republic, 221. *See also* autonomous republics

Maris, 5, 10, 12, 16, 29–30, 37, 42, 51, 54, 59, 60, 79, 102, 127, 146, 147, 150, 151–52, 156, 158–61, 166–68, 174, 175, 182, 185, 192, 205, 209, 211, 213

Markel, Metropolitan of Kazan, 75. *See also* metropolitans

markets, 61, 89, 93, 95–97, 98, 99, 105, 107, 110, 115. *See also* commodities; entrepôts, global trade; merchants; trade

marriages, 22, 77, 123, 126–27, 135, 137–39. *See also* wives

martyrs, 35, 75. *See also* Orthodoxy

Massa, Isaac, 48, 88, 105

Matfei, Metropolitan of Kazan, 75. *See also* metropolitans

Matveev, Boris, 190

medicine, 56, 165. *See also* disease; healing; illness; plague

Meil' River, 99

Melent'ev, Boris, 126

Meller, Peter, 112

mercantile system, 15, 109, 111–12, 217n22. *See also* commodities; monopolies; New Commercial Code of 1667; tariffs, trade

mercenaries, 26, 71, 95, 166–67, 191, 196, 205. *See also* army; foreigners

merchants, 29, 48, 56, 87–100, 102–16, 146, 174, 177, 181–82, 200. *See also* Armenian merchants; Bukharan merchants; caravans; Dutch merchants; English merchants; *gosti*; Indian merchants; Portuguese merchants; Swedish merchants

mestnichestvo, 25–26, 65–66, 68, 120–21, 123, 126, 129, 196–97, 204, 214. *See also* elites; hierarchy; precedence

metallurgy, 112. *See also* businesses

metropole, 8–9, 91, 173, 207, 209. *See also* geography; heartland

metropolitans, 12, 22, 26, 32, 41, 64, 73, 76, 100, 168, 193–94. *See also* Adrian, Patriarch of

metropolitans (*continued*)
    Moscow; clergy; Germogen, Metropolitan of Kazan; Kornilii, Metropolitan of Kazan; Makarii, Metropolitan of Moscow; Markel, Metropolitan of Kazan; Matfei, Metropolitan of Kazan
Meverall, Thomas, 200–201
Miakin, Konstantin, 199
Middle East, 89–90, 103, 107–8, 112, 114. *See also* Mughal India; Safavid Empire
migration, 42, 86, 138, 161, 174, 180, 182, 188–89, 203. *See also* colonization; forced relocations; nomads
Mikhail Fedorovich (Tsar), 47, 51, 54, 59, 61, 79–80, 105, 106, 107, 141, 152, 231n94, 240n99. *See also* tsars
military. *See* army; conquests; insurrections; invasions; munitions; Razriadnyi Prikaz; revolts; security; wars
military-service land. See *pomest'ia*
military servitors, 15, 17, 60–61, 101, 117–45, 148–49, 154–57, 162, 164–65, 167–68, 171, 173, 175, 181, 184, 190–93, 195–204. *See also* estates; gentry; landlords
militia, 11, 163. *See also* garrisons
mills, 80–81, 100–101, 125, 237n65. *See also* businesses
Miloslavskii, Ivan Bogdanovich, 181
mines, 112. *See also* businesses
Mingaev, Banda, 113
miracle cults. *See* icons; "Life of Gurii and Varsonofii"; saints; "Tale of the Appearance of the Kazan Icon"
*mirza*s, 29, 47, 51, 59, 69, 101, 120–21, 123, 125, 127, 141, 146, 160–61, 167, 184, 186, 201. *See also* elites; Tatars
Misail, Archbishop of Riazan, 168
modernization, 14, 175. *See also* bureaucratization; cameralism; centralization
monarchy, 19–20, 24. *See also* composite monarchy
monasteries. *See* Blagoveshchenskii Monastery (Viaz'ma); Bogoroditskii Monastery (Sviiazhsk); Ioanno-Predtechenskii Monastery (Kazan); Iosifo-Volokolamskii Monastery (Volokolamsk); Kazanskii

Bogoroditsii Monastery (Saransk); Makar'evskii Zheltovodskii Monastery (Arzamas); Novospasskii Monastery (Saratov); Pecherskii Monastery (Nizhnii Novgorod); Prechistii Bogoroditsii Monastery (Kazan); Savva-Storozhevskii Monastery (Kazan); Savvo-Storozhevskii Monastery (Simbirsk); Spaso-Iuginskii Monastery (Koz'modem'iansk); Spaso-Preobrazhenskii Monastery (Arzamas, Kazan, or Samara); Spasskii Monastery (Saransk); Sviiato-Troitskii Monastery (Alatyr'); Troitse-Sergeevskii Monastery (Arzamas, Kazan, Murom, Simbirsk, or Sviiazhsk); Voskresenskii Monastery (Atemar); Zilantov Uspenskii Monastery (Kazan)
monastic peasants, 147, 153–58, 173, 175, 190. *See also* peasantry
Monastyrskii Prikaz, 55, 164, 202. See also *prikazy*
Mongol Empire, 3, 20, 22–23, 26–27, 29. *See also* Chingissid dynasty; Qipchaq Khanate
monitoring, 15, 42, 56, 59–60, 63, 66, 92–93, 96, 100, 115, 151, 163, 166, 189, 193, 195, 198, 200. *See also* pacification; registration; surveillance
monopolies, 101, 107–8, 109–11, 112–13, 115, 240n97. *See also* commodities; mercantile system
Mordvins, 5, 10, 12, 16–17, 29–30, 37, 42, 78, 81, 83, 127, 140, 147–48, 150–52, 154–58, 160–70, 174–76, 178, 182, 184–85, 188–90, 193, 195, 203, 205, 209, 213
Morozov, Boris, 141–42
Morozov, Vasilii Petrovich, 77
Moscow. *See* Church of the Intercession on the Moat (St. Basil's); grand princes; heartland; Kremlin (Moscow); metropole; rituals; tsars
Mother of God Icon (Kazan), 41, 49, 73, 75, 79, 132, 230n75. *See also* icons; "Tale of the Appearance of the Kazan Icon"
Mother of God Icon (Smolensk), 41. *See also* icons
Mughal India, 88, 104–8, 110, 112, 114–15
Mukhanov, Aleksei Ivanov syn, 201

munitions. *See* cannons; gunpowder; logistics; muskets

murders, 31, 78, 188. *See also* crimes

Murzin, Dzhan, 69

Muscovy. *See* Russian Empire

Muscovy Company, 87, 104, 108–11. *See also* English merchants

muskets, 60, 128, 159, 166, 191. *See also* gunpowder; *strel'tsy*

Muslims. *See* Bashkirs; Chuvashes; Islam; Khanate of Crimea; *mirza*s; Ottoman Empire; Safavid Empire; Mughal India; Tatars

myrrh, 133

Myshchetskii, Ivan Danilov syn, 171

Nagovo, Andrei Aleksandrov syn, 67

nakazy, 51, 57–65, 83, 92, 94–95, 100, 113–14, 158, 161, 166–67, 180, 189, 225n1, 227n20, 228n37. *See also* governance; legislation

Narmukimov family, 192

national minorities, 209–10. *See also* ethnolinguistic identity; non-Russian populations

nations, 10, 36, 206, 211. *See also* national minorities; non-Russian populations

negotiations, 5, 12–13, 119, 136–39, 141, 143, 144, 177, 190; trade, 104–6, 108, 115. *See also* petitions; resistance

Nekhaev, Ivan, 126

networks, 5, 8–11, 13, 22, 94, 103, 207. *See also* communication; silk roads; trade routes

New Commercial Code of 1667, 15, 109–10, 112–14, 177, 200, 205. *See also* law codes; mercantile system

Nikolaevskii Devichii Convent (Cheboksary), 40, 79

Nikolaevskii Novodevichii Convent (Alatyr'), 81

Nizhnii Lomov, 83, 85, 124, 185, 229n60

Nizhnii Novgorod, 8, 29–30, 38, 48, 56, 82–83, 89, 91, 102, 137, 141–42, 151, 164–65, 171, 174, 186, 187, 192, 194, 198. *See also* Pecherskii Monastery

nobles, 87, 122. *See also* boiars; elites

Nogai Tatars, 10, 28, 37, 40, 41, 59, 60, 63, 83, 98, 99–100, 179. *See also* nomads; Tatars

nomads, 3, 10–11, 14, 20, 22, 28, 38, 40, 42, 44, 46, 52, 59–60, 63, 79, 85, 88, 91, 98, 99–100, 103, 115, 117–18, 147–49, 158–59, 163, 167, 179–82, 191, 195, 202, 206–7. *See also* Bashkirs; Cossacks; Kalmyks; lifestyles; Nogai Tatars

non-Russian peoples. *See* Bashkirs; Chuvashes; *inozemtsy*; Kalmyks; Maris; Mordvins; Tatars; Udmurts

Nordermann, Konrad Filipov syn, 112

Novgorod, 23, 32–33, 56, 89, 110, 111, 121

Novgorodskaia chetvert', 55–56, 164, 194. See also *prikazy*

Novodevichii Alekseevskii Convent (Arzamas), 75, 80

Novodevichii Convent (Moscow), 164, 254n43

novokreshchane, 37, 47, 101, 123, 125–30, 136, 140, 148, 155, 157, 160–61, 167–68, 171, 174, 193, 197, 202. *See also* confessional identity; conversion

Novospasskii Monastery (Saratov), 77, 99

nuns, 41, 79–81, 100, 133. *See also* clergy; convents

Nurkeev, Nurmamet, 123

obedience, 54, 119, 130, 132–35, 137, 144, 145. *See also* pacification

Obolensk, 122

occupations, 83, 98, 132, 147, 174. *See also* lifestyles

Odoevskii, Iakov Nikitich, 144

officials, 6, 11, 14–17, 45, 48–49, 52–53, 56–72, 93, 108, 128, 132, 150, 161–62, 180–81, 184–85, 187, 188, 192, 196, 204; customs, 56, 87–88, 94–95, 96, 110; Orthodox, 21, 41, 54, 72–82, 83, 132, 143, 153, 155, 176. *See also* administration; bailiffs; bureaucracy; clergy; *d'iaki*; *voevody*

okol'nichii, 65–66, 68, 192. *See also* elites

Old Believers, 193–94. *See also* Orthodoxy; schismatics

Olearius, Adam, 146, 177

Ol'gov, Nikita Fedorov syn, 140, 143, 157

Onanin, Gerasim, 154

Onuchin, Toma, 59

procession, 33–34, 38, 168, 222n65. *See also* Russian Orthodox Church

protectionism. *See* mercantile system

Pskov, 32–33, 56, 68, 110–11, 121

Pushkarskii Prikaz, 71. See also *prikazy*

Pushkin, Matvei Stepanov syn, 196

Putivl', 110

Qipchaq Khanate, 3, 22, 28. *See also* Mongol Empire

Ramodanovskii, Petr Grigor'evich, 198

Razin, Stepan, 5, 17, 179–82, 184–85, 187–88, 202, 209. *See also* Cossacks; revolts

Razriadnyi Prikaz, 55, 70–71, 123, 170–71, 196, 200. *See also* military; *prikazy*

rebellion. *See* revolts

Red Square, 21, 35. *See also* Moscow; Kremlin (Moscow)

redemption, 122, 243n16. *See also* exiles

refineries. *See* salt refineries

registration, 22–23. *See also* runaway peasant commissions; surveillance

Reitarskii Prikaz, 71. See also *prikazy*

relocations, 42, 148, 164, 191, 198. *See also* exiles; flight; forced relocations

republics. *See* autonomous republics

requisitions, 54, 64, 159. *See also* taxation

resistance, 5, 13–14, 21, 23, 35, 37, 42, 44–45, 47, 49, 63, 117, 147–48, 158, 189, 195, 210–11. *See also* flight; grievances; negotiations; petitions; revolts; runaway peasants

revolts, 5, 8, 13, 17, 20, 37–38, 42, 45–49, 52–54, 63, 66, 144, 147–49, 159–60, 166–69, 178, 195, 210; of 1648–49, 53, 60, 170, 178, 180; of 1670–71, 5, 13, 17, 148–49, 178–90, 193, 195, 202, 204, 209. *See also* "copper riots"; insurrection

rhetoric, 8, 18, 33, 35, 119–20, 137, 171, 179, 205. *See also* ideology

Riazan', 33, 121, 168, 172

"right by conquest," 5. *See also* legitimacy

rituals, 22, 25–27, 32, 34, 45, 165. *See also* charisma; coronations; legitimacy; Orthodoxy; symbolism

robbery, 78. *See also* crimes

Rolant, Elizarii, 56

Romadinovskii, Ivan, 142

Roman Empire, 21–22, 35

Romanov dynasty, 14, 47, 49–50, 52, 54, 72, 80, 88, 90, 105–7, 148. *See also* charisma; legitimacy; tsars

Rostov, 23, 33, 122, 132

Rostovskii, Petr Ivanovich, 143

runaway peasant commissions, 16–17, 148, 172–76, 184, 191–93, 204. *See also* administration; registration; surveillance

runaway peasants, 60, 156, 167, 170–72. *See also* flight; peasants; resistance

Rurikid dynasty, 22–23, 47, 65, 120. *See also* charisma; grand princes; legitimacy; tsars

Russian Empire. *See* administration; authority; conquests; expansion; Romanov dynasty; Rurikid dynasty; social categories

Russian Federation, 10, 209–11, 214

Russian Orthodox Church, 3, 6, 9, 11, 14–17, 20, 22–26, 31–33, 41, 52–53, 55, 63–64, 72–82, 93, 95, 96, 98, 103, 115, 119–20, 125, 129–30, 134–36, 144–45, 146–48, 151–55, 167–69, 176, 178–78, 184, 187, 193–95, 204, 207–8, 213. *See also* clergy; convents; icons; liturgy; miracle cults; monasteries; Old Believers; Orthodoxy; piety; pilgrimages; prayer; procession; saints; schism; sermons; shrines; Stoglav

Ruzhevskii, Mikhail, 199

Safavid Empire, 28, 37, 49, 90, 104–16, 179, 181

St. Basil's Cathedral. *See* Church of the Intercession on the Moat (St. Basil's)

St. George's Day, 25, 156. *See also* enserfment; Forbidden Years

saints. *See* canonization; Gurii, Archbishop of Kazan; Makarii Zheltovodskii; Russian Orthodox Church; Varsonofii, Archimandrite of the Spaso-Preobrazhenskii Monastery

Salamykov, Nedai, 57

salt, 89, 97–98, 102, 200, 234nn26–27, 237n69. *See also* commodities

salt refineries, 102, 194. *See also* businesses

Spaso-Preobrazhenskii Monastery (Arzamas), 93, 99, 154, 203

Spaso-Preobrazhenskii Monastery (Kazan), 34, 40–41, 76–77, 96, 98, 100, 125, 153

Spaso-Preobrazhenskii Monastery (Samara), 41, 191

Spasskii Monastery (Saransk), 27

specie, 97, 103–5, 107, 109. *See also* commodities

spices, 89–90, 107. *See also* commodities

Staden, Heinrich von, 177

Starodub, 122

state peasants, 173, 175–76, 250n66. *See also* peasantry

Stepan Razin Revolt. *See* revolts: of 1670–71

Stepennaia kniga, 35. *See also* legitimacy

steppe, 3, 9–11, 16–17, 20, 21–22, 27–28, 38, 42, 45–46, 83, 85, 88, 103, 117, 121, 135, 148–50, 159–60, 161–63, 167, 178–81, 188, 190–91, 195, 202. *See also* environment; geography; nomads

Stilenev, Fëdor, 197

Stoglav, 25. *See also* Russian Orthodox Church

Stol Kazanskogo dvortsa, 54–55. *See also* Prikaz Kazanskogo dvortsa

strel'tsy, 37, 60, 81, 85, 113, 133, 159–60, 165–66, 173, 177, 181, 184, 186, 189, 202. *See also* army; gunpowder; muskets

Sudebnik of 1497, 24–25, 149, 156. *See also* law codes

Sudebnik of 1550, 25, 149, 247n2. *See also* law codes

Sudnyi Prikaz, 201, 228n40. See also *prikazy*

Sura River, 42, 174

surveillance, 63–64, 69, 72, 113, 204. *See also* interrogations; investigations; monitoring; pacification

Suzdal, 33

Sviiaga River, 30, 141

Sviiato-Troitskii Monastery (Alatyr'), 40, 75

Sviiazhsk, 30, 32–34, 40, 47, 51, 59, 67–68, 70, 72, 75, 77–78, 98–99, 101–2, 124–25, 128, 140, 143–44, 151, 153, 157, 160–61, 171–72, 186, 193. *See also* Bogoroditskii Monastery; Troitse-Sergeevskii Monastery

Sweden, 27

Swedish merchants, 227n27, 240n94. *See also* merchants

Sychov, Fëdor, 190

symbolism, 13, 17, 21–23, 25–27, 31–33, 34–35, 40, 45, 49, 80, 147, 208, 213. *See also* charisma; legitimacy; rituals

Tagishchev, Mikhail Brevich, 202

"Tale of the Appearance of the Kazan Icon," 73, 132–35. *See also* Mother of God Icon (Kazan)

Tambov, 17, 168

tar, 89, 103, 108, 240n97. *See also* commodities

tariffs, 20, 52, 63, 72, 75, 94–95, 99, 104, 107, 109–10, 151, 200–201. *See also* customs; mercantile system; taxation

Tatars, 5, 10, 12, 14–56, 20, 29–32, 36–38, 42, 47–48, 51, 59–60, 69, 78, 83, 98, 101–2, 118–29, 130, 134–35, 36, 139, 141, 143, 145, 147, 151–59, 160–61, 166–68, 174–75, 177, 184, 186, 190, 193, 196–97, 200, 203, 205, 209–11, 213. *See also* Crimean Tatars; *mirza*s; Nogai Tatars

Tatarstan, 210–11. *See also* autonomous republics

taverns, 94, 101, 125, 140–41, 189. *See also* businesses

taxation, 12, 19–20, 22, 26, 52–53, 56, 58, 61–64, 70, 78, 81–82, 94–95, 97–99, 102, 104, 109, 111–16, 125, 136–37, 140, 142–44, 148, 150–54, 157–59, 163, 168, 171, 174–75, 195, 198–99, 202, 213, 235n36, 240n102, 241n110, 244n38. See also *iasak*; requisitions; tariffs

Telepov, Aleksandr, 185

Temnikov, 38, 40, 68, 70, 72, 85, 124, 160–62, 186, 189

Teregulov, Enbai, 151

Terent'ev, Nikita, 98, 236n44

Tetiushii, 38, 40, 67–68, 87, 91–92, 95, 124, 160–61, 184

Thirteen Years' War, 53, 178, 180–81

three-field rotation, 150. *See also* agriculture

timber, 36, 89, 103, 108. *See also* commodities

Time of Troubles, 20, 46–49, 52, 53, 66–67, 72, 88, 90, 105, 108, 124, 147

Timofeev family, 126

wax, 87, 89, 98, 150–51, 175, 234nn42–44. *See also* beekeeping; commodities

Weber, Friedrich Christian, 206, 209

White, John, 27, 109

Whitworth, Charles, 116

widows, 137. *See also* inheritance; wives; women

witchcraft, 47, 164–65, 167, 176, 178. *See also* crimes; healing

wives, 119, 132–37, 144, 170, 192, 194, 211. *See also* marriages; widows; women

women, 16, 79, 119, 130, 132–36, 164–65, 194, 204. *See also* daughters; nuns; widows; wives

Zakharov, Grigor Ivanov syn, 192

Zamanov, Mamatagei, 200

Zheliabuzhskii, Petr Grigor'ev syn, 72

Zherebtsovykh family, 141

Zheriskii, Ivan Rodinov syn, 198

Zhukov, Lov, 187

Zilantov Uspenskii Monastery (Kazan), 32–33, 40, 41, 77–79, 81, 94–95, 153–54, 224n91, 227n35, 234n26

Ziminiskii, Grigor Mikhailovich, 171

Ziushin, Danil, 67